THE ULTIMATE ENCYCLOPEDIA OF

BASKETBALL

THIS IS A CARLTON BOOK

Copyright © Carlton Books Limited 1996

This edition published by Carlton Books Limited in 1996

10 9 8 7 6 5 4 3 2 1

A CIP catalogue record for this book is available from the
British Library

ISBN 1 85868 151 0

Project Editor: Martin Corteel
Project art direction: Paul Messam
Production: Garry Lewis
Picture research: Sharon Hutton
Designer: Steve Wilson
Editorial assistant: David Ballheimer

Printed and Bound by Jarrold Book Printing, Norfolk, England

(OPPOSITE) HIGH-SCORING *Houston All-Star Clyde Drexler*
(NEXT PAGE) HIGH-SOARING *Chicago scoring machine Michael Jordan*

THE ULTIMATE ENCYCLOPEDIA OF
BASKETBALL

The definitive illustrated guide to the NBA

Ron Smith

CARLTON

CONTENTS

MASTER SCORER *Kareem Abdul-Jabbar*

POWER PACKED *Shaquille O'Neal*

INTRODUCTION

As the 1995–96 Chicago Bulls shredded any notions of parity with an unprecedented 72–10 regular-season run and their fourth NBA championship of the decade, the inevitable question was being asked: Was this Chicago team the best in professional basketball history?

The answer is simple: Yes and no. In the hearts, minds and fantasies of Bulls fans and most young NBA followers, an emphatic yes—and the numbers, although diminished by talent-depleted expansion rosters, certainly support their beliefs. But in the memories and opinions of older and more nostalgic fans, an equally emphatic no—feelings that can be defended with Hall of Fame fervor.

The truth probably falls somewhere between a simple yes or no. Would the Bulls beat the 1960s Celtics or the 1966–67 76ers in a head-to-head match? Probably so. Today's players are bigger, stronger, quicker and more athletic—qualities that probably would serve the Bulls well in such a matchup. But are the Bulls better within the context of the eras in which teams compete? Probably not. It's impossible to deny the greatness of a Boston franchise that won an astounding eight consecutive championships and a Wilt Chamberlain-led Philadelphia team that was good enough to win 68 regular-season games and interrupt the Celtics' title streak.

And what about the 1970–71 Bucks, the 1971–72 Lakers or the Pat Riley-coached Lakers that won five titles in the 1980s—a team that might have matched up well physically against the Bulls? It's all a matter of perspective.

And so is any book that provides fuel for such questions while offering insight into the intricacies and nuances that are part of the NBA experience. *The Ultimate Encyclopedia of Basketball* is an attempt to link the professional game's modest past with its flamboyant present—while exploring its exciting and lucrative future.

This painstaking task has been executed through the research and memories of someone who grew up watching Bill Russell, Elgin Baylor, Jerry West, Wilt Chamberlain, Oscar Robertson and many other players set basketball standards by which future generations would be judged. Someone who cringed with the passing of each era, revitalized with the blossoming of each new crop of stars and marveled at the NBA's perseverance and the incredible marketing and popularity boom that vaulted it into worldwide acclaim. And now it's time to admit: the Michael Jordans, Charles Barkleys, Karl Malones, David Robinsons and Shaquille O'Neals of today's game are every bit the athletic equals of their predecessors—and sometimes more.

The Ultimate Encyclopedia of Basketball offers plenty of perspective on every facet of the NBA, from its on-court champions and wondrous feats to its draft, business enterprises, storied arenas, rules and even its shrine—the basketball Hall of Fame. And while the book might not settle any arguments about "Best" teams or players, it certainly provides insight into the candidates and consideration for such lofty status. And, by the way, the Bulls were the best team in NBA history. And so were the Celtics; and the Bucks; and the Lakers ....

Ron Smith, St. Louis, July 1996

CELEBRITY FANS *Spike Lee (left) and Jack Nicholson (right) ponder the fate of their respective teams, the New York Knicks and Los Angeles Lakers*

THE HISTORY OF THE NBA

Nobody knows who made the first shot in basketball history, but it happened on a December day in 1891. One of 18 students who were trying out a new game invented by their Canadian-born professor claimed the honor by throwing a soccer ball into one of two peach baskets hanging from a gymnasium balcony railing at the Young Men's Christian Association Training School in Springfield, Mass.

SHOOTING FOR THE STARS

For Dr. James Naismith, "basket ball" was a simple matter of expediency. Forced to deal with testy students who were bored with the winter physical education routines of calisthenics and gymnastics, he decided to invent an indoor game that would give them a competitive outlet. Naismith, a future Presbyterian minister who played on the school's football team for legendary coach Amos Alonzo Stagg, envisioned a contest that would promote the subtler sporting arts of finesse, agility and teamwork over brute strength and power.

But when he nailed his two peach baskets to a 10-foot-high railing at opposite ends of the gym, assigned ball retrievers to stand on ladders near the baskets and divided his gym class into two nine-man squads, little did he suspect the almost instantaneous craze he would touch off in a sports-hungry society.

The basic elements of Naismith's game were not all that different from those that govern the basketball played today. But the early rules dictated a slow, plodding, almost stationary game that mirrored the rural, take-life-as-it-comes society it would entertain in the early stages of its existence. As society evolved, so did basketball—into the fast, high-tech, above-the-rim sport that has captured worldwide affection more than a century later.

Less than a month after "basket ball's" humble introduction, Naismith's rules were printed in the school newspaper and on February 12, 1892, two branches of the Springfield YMCA met for the first organized game—a 2–2 tie that was witnessed by a crowd of about 100. Naismith, sensing the enormity of his invention, began staging exhibitions and word of the new game spread like wildfire. By 1893, "basket ball" had become so popular that the Hartford, Conn., YMCA organized a five-team league that drew more than 10,000 spectators over one winter.

Almost overnight, the game spread its roots into high schools and colleges, where enamored students clamored for "basket ball" almost to the exclusion of all other sports and activities. Amateur teams and leagues began forming and regional rivalries developed. The game even transcended gender barriers, giving girls an outlet they could not enjoy through the all-male team sports of football and baseball.

The Professionals

Necessity was the mother of professional basketball. As more and more amateur teams began competing for time and space at the local YMCAs throughout the Northeast, other sports and activi-

A BASKET CASE *Dr. James Naismith had a peach of an idea when he developed the rules for "basket ball"*

League lasted until 1903 and spawned a series of other professional circuits that flourished briefly, mostly in the East. The early professional leagues were regional configurations and teams hired their players on a game-to-game basis and played their games in local armories and dance halls. A typical team might have two or three local players and several imported stars. This practice allowed the era's better players to sell their services to the highest bidder and even play for two or more teams at a time. It also led to fan confusion and displaced loyalties.

The professional game of the early 1900s more closely resembled a football scrimmage than a basketball contest. Players punished each other with hard body checks and anybody who dared leave his feet while shooting could count on being undercut. Offensive maneuvers were limited to two basic shots—the layup and a two-handed set or push. And layups were limited by a defensive strategy that placed a "standing guard" in the free-throw lane.

Another professional innovation was a cage that enclosed the court, keeping the ball in play and protecting the players from rowdy fans. While the cage did speed up the game, it also cut and bruised players who bounced off its wire and steel mesh sides as often as the ball.

"The ball was always in play in those cages, and only the brave went into the corners to get it," Joe Lapchick, an early professional star and long-time college and professional coach, told The Sporting News in 1963. "The boys stayed out while the men drove in. A fellow would come out of the corner of a wire cage striped like a zebra, after being sandwiched against the wire. All he would get out of it was a jump ball.

"Another difference in construction with the cages was the basket. With net cages, there were open hoops without backboards,

ties were being shortchanged. Complaints from long-time members forced YMCA officials to limit playing time.

On one such occasion in 1896, a team from Trenton, N.J., looked for an alternative rather than can-

cel its scheduled game. The solution was simple. The club rented the local armory, tacked up baskets and charged admission to cover expenses. The game attracted enough spectators to pay the rent and give each player

a $15 bonus. The game's professional roots were in place.

Buoyed by such spectator interest, the first known professional league was formed in 1898 by teams in the Philadelphia area. The National Basketball

which of course demanded precise shooting. With the chicken-wire setup, the basket was 6 to 10 inches from the backboard."

Many fans, denied courtside access to visiting players, would bring hairpins, nails and other sharp items to jab them through the wire. The cage remained popular in many professional cities through the 1920s.

Leagues weren't the only product of the early professional game. Barnstorming teams were put together and traveled from city to city, taking on all comers. Touring teams had the advantage of good players performing together over a long period. The Buffalo Germans, who compiled a 792–86 record from 1895 to 1929, were the best of the early barnstormers.

Moving Forward

As the nation plunged into the industrial revolution and the joys of big-city life, the recreational pursuits of Americans became more defined and their sports affections more lasting. Baseball already was the National Pastime and football was gaining appeal as the physical choice of the masses, but basketball was being played throughout the country and as far away as Europe and Australia.

By 1915, the game's evolution had passed infancy. Tailored basketballs had replaced soccer balls, backboards were required and baskets with wire or metal rims and open bottoms were being used. Five-man teams were standard, free-throw lines were 15 feet from the basket, players were allowed either four or five fouls before disqualification and field goals counted two points. But other rules kept the game in a relative dark age. A debate raged over dribbling—two hands, one hand or not at all. If allowed, should a player be permitted to shoot after dribbling? A more limiting rule required a center jump after every basket, giving teams with a tall leaper an advantage. That rule would not be changed until 1937, a decision

that would open up the game and set it on course toward prosperity.

That course was nudged forward ever so subtly in 1918, when a nation emerging from the depths of World War I got its first look at a talented and colorful barnstorming team that would have an impact on basketball's future. The team, which was formed by New York promoter Jim Furey, was called the Original Celtics because the owner of the New York Celtics, a team disbanded during the war, refused to relinquish rights to the name. With a lineup featuring Pete Barry, Ernie Reich, Joe Trippe, Eddie White, Mike Smolick, Swede Grimstead, Horse Haggerty and Dutch Dehnert, the Celtics became the dominant team of the East. Such subsequent additions as the 6-foot-5 Lapchick, Nat Holman, Chris Leonard, Johnny Beckman and Davey Banks extended that dominance to regions beyond.

The Celtics operated without a coach and were unlike any team fans had ever seen. The players, who were signed to exclusive season-long contracts, were innovative and dazzled spectators with their brilliant passing, ballhandling and shot-making. The Celtics pioneered the zone defense and the give-and-go passing play, using the center as the hub for their offense. They usually overmatched the independent teams they played.

When the American Basketball League opened play in 1925 as the first truly "national" professional circuit, the Celtics were conspicuously absent. That was fine with ABL organizers, who feared the Celtics might kill spectator interest with their dominance. But when the ABL completed its first season without any sustained signs of prosperity, ABL President Joe Carr and other officials did an about-face and decided they could not survive without the Celtics.

Getting the Celtics to join, however, was another matter. A simple invitation might not be enough, so the league's executive committee banned all ABL teams from playing the Celtics in exhibitions, thus cutting off their primary source of competition.

Facing the prospect of a weaker schedule and smaller crowds, the Celtics joined the ABL five games into the 1926–27 season and went on to claim consecutive titles—in dominating fashion.

With the Celtics in the fold, the ABL took major steps in the advancement of professional basketball. Exclusive player contracts were required and roster-jumping was outlawed. Standard-sized backboards were mandatory, two-handed dribbling was banned, caged courts were outlawed and other rules, which had varied from region to region and from the college game to the pros, were standardized to conform to the Amateur Athletic Union. The standardized rules, most notably the conformity of dribbling techniques, made it easier for college athletes to adjust to the professional game.

"The monkey dribble was a two-handed dribble and it could be started and stopped as often as desired," said Lapchick, referring to a rule that never gained widespread use at the college level. "The ball did not have to be

HOT SHOTS *Promoter Jim Furey (seated left) and his Original Celtics took professional basketball by storm*

CLOWN PRINCES *Talented players like Meadowlark Lemon (with ball) combined athletic skills and showmanship under the banner of the Harlem Globetrotters*

passed or shot after breaking the first dribble. The monkey dribble was a possession device."

And the product of a ball not fit for extensive dribbling.

"The ball might be any old thing," Lapchick said. "It started new as a leather cover of approximately round shape, with a bladder that was laced inside. The inflation tube often protruded. The ball might be used two or three years, with occasional aid from the shoemaker when a tear or scruffed spot developed. The ball got slick, it stretched out of shape and it inevitably got larger in size, reducing the chance of a basket."

The Cleveland Rosenblums, led by Honey Russell, captured the ABL's first championship. But the next two seasons belonged to the flashy Celtics, which rankled league officials. So when Furey was convicted of embezzlement and sent to prison after the 1927–28

season, ABL officials seized the opportunity and broke up the Celtics, dispatching their players to teams around the league.

The ABL lasted three more seasons, with the Rosenblums, bolstered by the addition of four Original Celtics, winning two more championships. But the once-ambitious circuit, which had stretched from New York to Chicago, fell on hard economic times after the great stock market crash of 1929 and disbanded in 1931, with the nation in the grips of the great Depression.

The next six years would belong to college basketball. The professional game was dominated once again by regional industrial leagues and barnstormers—gifted teams like the revived Original Celtics and all-black powerhouses like the New York Renaissance Five (the Rens) and the Harlem Globetrotters, who still perform their magic today in a less-com-

A Different Kind of Basketball

They have entertained millions of fans in hundreds of countries as the "Clown Princes of Basketball." They have performed for the Pope, penetrated the Iron Curtain and served as the subject of two motion pictures. The Harlem Globetrotters have, in every sense, conquered the world.

The Globetrotters were organized in 1927 by Chicago promoter Abe Saperstein as an all-black barnstorming team. They traveled through the rural midwest, booking games where they could and piling up victories against overmatched local teams. In order to assure return invitations, the Globetrotters began putting on a different kind of show,

turning basketball clowning into an artform that would carry them to international fame.

Players like Goose Tatum, dribbling wizard Marques Haynes and Meadowlark Lemon combined comedy with first-rate basketball skills and became hot attractions—so hot that Saperstein extended the team's travels from coast to coast and eventually fulfilled his goal: spreading the basketball message all around the world.

The Globetrotters' famous warmup routine, performed to the music of "Sweet Georgia Brown," is the signature for an act that has spread that message, loud and clear, beyond even Saperstein's wildest imagination

HANDY MAN *Hank Luisetti introduced the one-handed shot to the game*

stalling tactics. A three-second rule limited players from camping under the basket and the 1937 elimination of the center jump made the game less tedious and more competitive. Another 1937–38 innovation was the introduction of the one-handed shot by Stanford star Hank Luisetti during a game at Madison Square Garden.

"That was when fast, modern basketball began," Lapchick said, referring to Luisetti as well as the 10-second and center-jump rules. "The general concept of the game also changed. The Celtics and all other outstanding teams of the old times stressed a ball-holding game on the floor. The modern team still must control the ball, but the idea now is a sort of possession in the air, in the ability to capture rebounds, and that means height."

Former Celtics teammate and long-time City College of New York coach Nat Holman agreed. "That was the greatest thing that ever happened to basketball. Elimination of the center jump speeded up the game, made it more colorful for the spectator and helped us all."

Amazingly, when the National Basketball League began play in 1937 with 13 teams stretching from Buffalo and Pittsburgh in the East to Kankakee, Ill., and Oshkosh, Wis., in the Midwest, it failed to embrace the rules that had made the college game so popular. After arguing the merits of the center-jump rule in a league organizational meeting, it was decided to let the home team determine which way to play it. Uneven scheduling combined with non-uniform rules to make the NBL's first season difficult.

But the NBL, older and wiser, eliminated those problems before the 1938–39 season and thus pioneered a professional game that mirrored the blossoming college game. Finally operating under the same rules as the National Collegiate Athletic Association,

petitive manner. It wasn't until 1937 that pro basketball returned with serious major league designs and a rules change that would help make those designs a reality.

Try, Try Again

As the professional game remained in hibernation through the Depression years, college basketball flourished. Constructive rules changes made the college game cleaner, faster and more popular and promoter Ned Irish brought the sport into the spotlight by booking doubleheaders at New York's Madison Square Garden. His innovation was a financial bonanza and triggered similar promotional ventures throughout the East and Midwest.

Fans enthusiastically embraced a more streamlined game that now included a more functional, laceless ball, uniform baskets and backboards, two referees per game and a 10-second line that forced teams into their offensive frontcourts and minimized

LOOK OUT BELOW *NBL life was rough for Oshkosh's Eddie Riska (with ball) and Fort Wayne's Bobby McDermott (on back)*

the NBL began attracting graduating college stars familiar to fans on both a regional and national level.

With a streamlined field of eight teams and rules that encouraged faster play, the NBL began to flourish. But in 1941, just when the future began to look bright, progress was halted by the Japanese attack at Pearl Harbor, thrusting the United States into World War II. In 1942–43 and 1943–44, the NBL was operated as a four-team league and prospects did not improve until players began returning from war-time duty.

Two-handed set shot artist Bobby McDermott finished the 1944–45 season for the champion Fort Wayne Pistons with a 20.1-point scoring average and other stars were emerging. The Rochester Royals captured the 1945–46 championship with a backcourt featuring playmaker Bob Davies and Red Holzman.

Former DePaul University star George Mikan arrived in 1946, and he was the biggest force, literally, the basketball world had ever seen.

Mikan was a 6–10 giant who looked at the world through thick-rimmed glasses and cleared paths to the basket with nasty elbows. Mikan, who decided to stay in his hometown and signed with the NBL's Chicago Gears, missed the 1945–46 regular season and playoffs as he completed his college career, but he was eligible for the world professional tournament, an annual event open to all comers. The Gears reached the semifinals and Mikan served notice by scoring 100 points in five games, winning MVP honors.

But Mikan's presence would not be felt immediately in 1946–47. He sat out six weeks in a contract dispute before joining a team mired in fifth place. When the big man arrived, the Gears stormed to a playoff berth and powered their way to a championship with a three-games-to-one victory over Rochester.

CENTER OF ATTENTION *With George Mikan (99) in the middle, the Minneapolis Lakers celebrated a lot in the 1950s*

Just when it appeared the foundation for an NBL dynasty was in place, Maurice White, owner of the American Gear Company, changed the course of pro basketball. When White tried to form his own league around Mikan, the plan failed and his team collapsed. Mikan's rights were assigned to a first-year Minneapolis team and he combined with Jim Pollard to lead the Lakers to the 1947–48 NBL title.

Early Success, by George

Despite the fortuitous arrival of Mikan in 1946, the NBL still found itself on shaky ground. As Mikan was preparing for his first professional season, a new league arrived on the block complete with deep-pocketed owners, big-city arenas and a desire to promote a slicker game fed by the more-popular college players.

The Basketball Association of America, with Maurice Podoloff as president, was formed in 1946 with 11 teams—Boston, New York, Philadelphia, Providence, Toronto and Washington in the Eastern Division; Chicago, Cleveland, Detroit, Pittsburgh and St. Louis in the West. The league clearly boasted the bigger cities and better arenas, but the NBL still had the better players—a division that became clear over the BAA's first two seasons.

The Washington Capitols, coached by young Red Auerbach, grabbed regular-season honors with a 49–11 record, but Philadelphia, coached by Eddie Gottlieb and featuring jump-shooting Joe Fulks, won the first league championship. The Baltimore Bullets, a team imported from the American Basketball League when Detroit, Toronto,

Cleveland and Pittsburgh folded, won the second-year title.

But it wasn't until 1948 that the BAA was able to enhance its status. Right before the league's third season was to begin, officials made the stunning announcement that four teams—Fort Wayne, Minneapolis, Rochester and Indianapolis—were defecting from the NBL, giving the BAA a 12-team circuit and instant status as the best basketball money could buy. Four of the NBL's best teams were in the fold and, more importantly, its best player—Mikan.

Devastated by the defection, the NBL managed to piece together one more season while the Lakers were winning their first BAA championship. When the season ended, the NBL went out of business and six of its teams joined the BAA, creating a new 17-team

ROYALTY *Rochester's 1951 champions (from left) Red Holzman, Bobby Wanzer, Bob Davies, Arnie Johnson, Jack Coleman and Arnie Risen*

Gallatin, also came close. But Rochester's 1951 title was the only chink in the Lakers' six-year dynasty.

After the 1954 championship, Mikan stunned the league by announcing his retirement—at age 30. He had almost single-handedly given a struggling new league status while drawing excited fans to the game every time he played. He also had given the Lakers franchise a special place in professional basketball history.

Oh Shoot!

The 1950s dawned with a dark cloud hanging over the basketball world. Players for Manhattan College, City College of New York, New York University, Long Island University and other schools had been implicated in point-shaving scandals that rocked the college game and opened a door of opportunity for the NBA.

But that threshold would not be crossed without a serious restructuring of a professional game that was slow, conservative and filled with fouls and stalling tactics. NBA officials tried to address the dominance of Mikan in 1951 by widening the lane from 6 feet to 12, theoretically getting him away from the basket. But the change had little effect. That wasn't the case with two 1954 rules changes that pointed the NBA on the road to prosperity.

The most radical change was proposed by Syracuse owner Danny Biasone, who wanted a clock to put a time limit on ball

circuit. It was renamed the National Basketball Association.

But even without serious competition, the NBA struggled. Its new 17-team format was awkward and many of the inherited teams were based in small cities. After the 1949–50 season, six dropped out and a seventh folded in January 1951, leaving a more manageable 10 teams divided into two divisions with deeper and more talented rosters.

And despite such emerging stars as Max Zaslofsky, Dolph Schayes, Pollard, Ed Macauley, Slater Martin, Neil Johnston, Bob Cousy, Bill Sharman and Paul Arizin, the games often were rugged, foul-filled, plodding

yawners without much pace and little sustained excitement.

Much of the period was spent trying to beat the Lakers, who rode Mikan's broad shoulders to five championships in six seasons (1949–54), yielding only to Rochester in 1951. Mikan was the powerful centerpiece for a team that also featured forwards Pollard and Vern Mikkelsen and point guard Martin. Mikan was an offensive force who averaged 22.6 points per game over nine professional seasons, but he also was a ferocious rebounder and many other things.

"Big George reminds me of Babe Ruth," Knicks coach Lapchick said in 1953. "When the Babe was hitting home runs, everyone forgot he'd once been an exceptional pitcher. Everyone

also forgets that Mikan is the best feeder from out of the pivot that the game ever had. He whips in a bounce pass to cutting teammates that can't be stopped.

"He creates all situations. Cover him normally and he kills you with his scoring. Cover him abnormally, and he murders you with his passing. We've tried every known defense on him and nothing works."

Surprisingly, Mikan and the Lakers had to work for everything they won. They were challenged throughout the Mikan era by West Division-rival Rochester, which featured a talented lineup of center Arnie Risen, Holzman, Davies and Bobby Wanzer. Syracuse, with Schayes and Alex Hannum, and New York, coached by Lapchick and featuring Zaslofsky, Sweetwater Clifton and Harry

Up and Over The Color Barrier

When the Basketball Association of America became the NBA before the 1949–50 season, there were no blacks listed on any of the league's rosters.

Desegregation would begin in the spring of 1950, and with the professional game's first blacks would come hope for a whole new generation of Americans.

The first black to sign a professional contract was Nat (Sweetwater) Clifton, a 6–7 forward who would play eight seasons with New York and Detroit. Clifton, a former Harlem Globetrotter, signed with the Knicks for an estimated $10,000.

But the honor of breaking pro basketball's color barrier belonged to Earl Lloyd, who signed with the Washington Capitols and scored six points in his NBA debut—a day before Clifton and Boston's Chuck Cooper took the court for the first time. The 6–5 Cooper, the first black player drafted out of college, played six NBA seasons and the 6–6 Lloyd nine.

By 1958, every NBA team had at least one black player. The last to integrate was St. Louis, which acquired Sihugo Green from Rochester in the 1958 season.

possession. Biasone arrived at 24 seconds by dividing the number of seconds in a 48-minute game (2,880) by the average number of shots (120). Amazingly, his arbitrary formula has withstood the test of time.

The other rule limited the number of fouls any team could commit in a quarter. Anything over six would give the free-throw shooter three shots instead of two. The effects of the rules, the 24-second shot clock in particular, were felt immediately.

In the opening game of 1954, the Royals beat Boston, 98–95, and the eight teams produced a season average of 93.1 points per game. The 1954–55 Celtics became the first team to average 100 points and the other teams soon followed. The NBA game suddenly was faster, more fluid and exciting.

"It was the most important rules change in the last 50 years," former Boston coach and current President Red Auerbach said.

Auerbach's affection for the clock is understandable because it also fueled one of the great dynasties in sports history. With the running game as their trademark and the great Cousy to

BIG GUN *Bill Russell (6) brought defense and rebounding to Boston*

quarterback a devastating fast break, Auerbach's Celtics would win their first championship in 1957 and set the stage for an incredible 10 titles in 11 years from 1959–69.

The Dynasty of all Dynasties

Auerbach had his Celtics running and gunning in 1955–56, but a second-place Eastern Division finish was followed by a first-round playoff loss to Syracuse—the team's sixth consecutive early playoff failure. The Celtics, featuring the explosive backcourt of Cousy and Sharman, averaged 106 points per game but they gave up 105.3.

Auerbach knew that trend would continue unless he could beef up a frontcourt that was mobile offensively, but soft defensively and on the boards. When Auerbach discussed his problem with Bill Reinhart, his former coach at George Washington University, Reinhart provided a quick, concise answer—Bill Russell.

Auerbach, who did not enjoy the luxury of today's sophisticated scouting system, was only vaguely familiar with the name. He knew Russell played for the University of San Francisco and had led the Dons to the 1955 NCAA championship, but not much else. When Reinhart described Russell as a ferocious rebounder and defender with limited offensive skills, the decision was made: Auerbach would maneuver into position to get Russell in the 1956 draft.

In a series of moves that would impact the NBA for the next decade and a half, Auerbach grabbed Holy Cross sensation Tom Heinsohn with a territorial pick leading off the draft and then traded Ed Macauley and the rights to 1953 draftee Cliff Hagan to the St. Louis Hawks for their third selection—Russell. When Rochester picked Sihugo Green with the No. 2 selection, Auerbach had his man.

The only hitch was that Russell had committed to playing for the 1956 U.S. Olympic team and would not be available until December. But the Celtics were not exactly shorthanded, with beefy Jim Loscutoff manning the middle in Russell's absence, Heinsohn anchoring one forward position and Frank Ramsey, who was returning from military duty, at the other.

When Russell arrived, the pieces were in place for Boston's first championship. And the 6–9 center was everything Auerbach had hoped—and more. He was ferocious on the boards, intimidating defensively and intense beyond imagination. When the scowling Russell stepped onto the court, the entire Boston team took on another personality.

Told by Auerbach to concentrate on rebounding, triggering the Celtics' running game and

ANOTHER CHAMPIONSHIP *John Havlicek (17) and Coach Red Auerbach (with cigar) get a victory ride after Boston clinched its seventh straight title in 1965*

playing defense, Russell blossomed. So did his teammates, who were able to release quickly on the break and cheat defensively, knowing Russell was in the middle to cover up their mistakes. And cover up he did—with an above-the-rim shot-blocking presence that ushered in a new era of defensive basketball.

Offensively, Russell's contributions were limited to tip-ins and short jump hooks. But that didn't matter to Auerbach, who watched the Celtics defeat Bob Pettit and St. Louis in the 1957 NBA Finals, lose to the Hawks in a six-game Finals the next season and then roll off an incredible eight straight championships.

Over those eight seasons, the Celtics averaged 57.6 victories and won seven division crowns. They were extended to the seven-game limit in only three final series. As good as the Celtics were in the

regular season, they lifted their game in the playoffs to a different—and higher— level.

And they did it with an ever-changing cast of characters, courtesy of Auerbach's genius. Cousy arrived in 1950, Sharman in 1951, Ramsey in 1954, Russell and Heinsohn in 1956, Sam Jones in 1957, K.C. Jones in 1958, Tom Sanders in 1960, and John Havlicek and Don Nelson in 1962. From December 1956, the one constant was Russell.

"Russell is the greatest center who ever lived," said Auerbach in the midst of the title run. "The defense he plays is fantastic. He has a wonderful sense of timing. He may not be the greatest rebounder of all time, but he's the greatest in the clutch.

"No center in the history of basketball could run with this guy. George Mikan? He'd eat him up. Russell would drive Mikan crazy.

Bill would take him outside, give him the shot, then block it."

When Auerbach moved full-time into the Celtics' front office after the 1966 championship, he named Russell as his successor—the first black coach in the history of the NBA. Russell, performing double duty as a player and coach, watched the record-setting Philadelphia Warriors win the 1967 title but then took the aging Celtics to consecutive titles to close out the decade. When the big man retired after the 1968–69 season, the Boston dynasty came to an unofficial end.

Brute Force

While the 1959–60 Celtics were galloping to their second consecutive championship, another force was sending shock waves through the NBA. A 7–1 giant named Wilt Chamberlain arrived on the Philadelphia scene, and he began

ravaging the record books like a hurricane in a paper factory.

Chamberlain, an unstoppable offensive scorer and rebounder, tore through the league with an amazing 38.6-point rookie average. But that was just an appetizer. Chamberlain's offensive showcase was 1961–62 when he averaged a whopping 50.4 points and 25.7 rebounds while playing 3,882 minutes—of a possible 3,890. He also scored a record 100 points in a game against the Knicks.

Ironically, Chamberlain's second showcase season was 1966–67, when his scoring average dropped to 24.1. He was the centerpiece for a 76ers team (Billy Cunningham, Hal Greer, Chet Walker, Wali Jones) that produced a regular-season record 68 victories and ended the Celtics' championship run during an 11–4 postseason romp.

A CLASSIC BATTLE *Wilt Chamberlain (13) versus Bill Russell (6)*

Chamberlain, who helped the Lakers put together a phenomenal 33-game winning streak en route to a regular-season-record 69 victories. The Lakers needed only 15 postseason games to win their first title.

Such dramatics were played out amid a confrontational atmosphere. The NBA received its first serious challenge from a rival league when the upstart American Basketball Association, which seemed to drop out of nowhere, began play in 1967 without much of a product or any definitive game plan. With the tumultuous 1960s forming a perfect backdrop and George Mikan serving as the league's commissioner, 11 teams began operation on shoestring budgets from coast to coast.

At first, the NBA looked at its rival with understandable scorn. But what the ABA lacked in sub-stance, it made up for with creativity. Everybody laughed at the circuit's red-white-and-blue ball, but soon no respectable American playground was without one. The ABA also introduced the three-point shot and the slam-dunk contest, innovations that eventually would become NBA fixtures.

The ABA played nine seasons before small crowds and without a television contract. And it spent much of its existence fighting expensive courtroom battles and bidding against the NBA for top players. But before it died, the ABA made serious inroads in talent acquisition, primarily through its signing of underage college players—a tactic that incurred the wrath of the NCAA and NBA. Such players as Rick Barry, George McGinnis, George Gervin, Moses Malone, Artis Gilmore, Mel Daniels, Connie Hawkins, Spencer

The 1960s also introduced a bevy of new stars who would light up the NBA arenas. Names such as Elgin Baylor, Dave Bing, Jerry Lucas, Oscar Robertson, Nate Thurmond, Jerry West, Willis Reed and Wes Unseld would help the league rise to a new level of popularity.

Franchise shifts and expansion also brought the NBA to new, fertile markets. The Lakers moved to Los Angeles in 1960, the Warriors shifted to San Francisco in 1962 and the Nationals relocated to Philadelphia in 1963, changing their name to 76ers. By 1970, the NBA, under Commissioner Walter Kennedy, was operating as a 17-team circuit with its first solid franchise in Chicago (the Bulls) and clubs in Seattle, Portland, Milwaukee, Atlanta, Buffalo, San Diego, Phoenix, Baltimore and Cleveland.

A Changing of the Guard

The 1969–70 season marked a transition for the NBA. When center Reed, forward Bill Bradley and guard Walt Frazier led the New York Knicks to their first championship, they officially closed Boston's decade of domination. Eight different teams would claim titles in the new decade, giving credence to the league's claim of parity.

The 1969–70 season also introduced the game's next dominating center—a skinny 7–2 gazelle who would drop his sky hooks on helpless defenders for 20 record-setting seasons and lead his teams to six NBA titles. Kareem Abdul-Jabbar claimed his first championship ring in 1971 when, as Lew Alcindor, he led the three-year-old Milwaukee Bucks to 66 regular-season victories and a 12–2 playoff romp. But his greatest success would come in the 1980s, when he combined with Magic Johnson to lead the Los Angeles Lakers to five titles in nine seasons.

That domination was presaged by the Lakers' lone title of the 1970s—pre-Jabbar. The center for that team was an aging Wilt

THE EARLY YEARS *By any name, Kareem Abdul-Jabbar was a champion*

Haywood, Dan Issel and Julius Erving gave the league more than a passing respect.

The ABA also gave Erving, the flashy Dr. J, a forum for a theatrical playing style that eventually would influence the conservative NBA and elevate its game above the rim. Erving dazzled fans and fellow players with his spectacular dunks and aerial wizardry, the kind of showmanship the game badly needed.

When Erving was traded by financially strapped Virginia to the New York Nets in 1973, the wheels for an eventual ABA–NBA merger were set in motion. As the New York media and fans took note of the colorful Erving, so did new NBA Commissioner Larry O'Brien. On June 17, 1976, the ABA's New York, Indiana, San Antonio and Denver franchises merged with the NBA, increasing the field to 22 teams.

Bird and the Magic Man

As the NBA approached a new decade, officials were searching for answers. Television ratings, never outstanding, were on the decline and the league's top stars were viewed with indifference by would-be fans. The image problem was compounded by the sagging fortunes of teams in the NBA's leading markets: In 1978–79, New York and Boston had finished fourth and fifth, respectively, in the Atlantic Division, Chicago last in the Midwest and Los Angeles third in the Pacific.

In an effort to brighten up its game, NBA officials resurrected an ABA gimmick they once had chastised as cosmetic: the 3-point shot. It would be an instant success, a new weapon to open up offenses and add excitement in the final minutes. But two even more deadly weapons were discovered in the annual NBA draft.

When the Celtics selected 6–9 Indiana State forward Larry Bird and the Lakers went for 6–9 Michigan State point guard Earvin (Magic) Johnson, the league began a new era of pros-

perity. The two college stars had met in the recent NCAA Tournament finals, Michigan State, led by Johnson, winning the highest-rated basketball telecast in history. They were stars of the first magnitude, the kind of players a league could mold a marketing plan around.

Their contrasts were as important as their talents. Bird was a blue-collar worker from the farming community of French Lick, Ind. He represented the common man, earning everything he got with a determination more impressive than his physical abilities. Johnson was a slick-passing,

fast-talking city kid who could light up a court with his ever-present smile and flashy style. If Bird was a good fit for Boston and the East Coast, then Johnson was perfect for Los Angeles and the West Coast. Every time they played, fans flocked through the turnstiles.

SEEING STARS *The ABA got good mileage out of Indiana's George McGinnis (30) and New York's Rick Barry*

And they didn't disappoint. The Lakers, with Magic running the show and Jabbar dominating the middle, won five championships in the 1980s, beating Boston in the Finals two times. Boston, with Bird joining center Robert Parish and forward Kevin McHale, countered with three championships, beating Los Angeles in the 1984 Finals.

The Bird–Johnson magic vaulted the NBA to a new level of affection. Suddenly TV networks were interested, fans were flocking to games and more young stars were flashing their acrobatic talents. Michael Jordan arrived in 1984 to revive a sagging Chicago franchise and 7-foot Patrick Ewing arrived a year later to carry the Knicks back into the New York spotlight. They joined a growing cast of stars that gave the NBA its most attractive product in history: Hakeem Olajuwon, Isiah Thomas, Charles Barkley, Clyde Drexler, Karl Malone, Dominique Wilkins, David Robinson, John Stockton, James Worthy and many others.

And when David Stern took the reins in 1984 as the NBA's fourth commissioner, he built an ambitious marketing plan that would carry the league's message beyond American borders. By the end of the decade, NBA stars Bird, Johnson, Jordan and Barkley would rank among the most recognized athletes in the world and NBA merchandise would generate millions of dollars in previously untapped revenue. The former eight-team league would number 27 with rumors of even more expansion in the not-too-distant future.

The most fortuitous development of the mid-1980s was the arrival of Jordan, who combined an Erving-like style with an intensity and flair that won over a whole new legion of fans and attracted hungry television sponsors and promoters. Everything Erving did, Jordan did a little better while almost single-handedly turning basketball into an art form.

Jordan quickly established himself as the dominant player in the league en route to a record-tying seven straight scoring titles, three Most Valuable Player awards and three NBA championship rings. After carrying the Bulls to respectability with a weak supporting cast in the early years, he combined with Scottie Pippen, Horace Grant and John Paxson to give Chicago three consecutive championships in 1991, '92 and '93. And then, just like that, he retired at age 30, suggesting there were no more basketball worlds to conquer.

Beyond Michael

He was wrong. Shortly after Jordan's retirement, the NBA expanded to 29 teams, awarding franchises to the Canadian cities of Toronto and Vancouver. By the time the Raptors and Grizzlies began play in 1995–96, Jordan was back, having traded his long-shot baseball pursuits for another Bulls uniform.

Jordan was still king of the court, but he had to work hard to maintain that status. Like the fastest gun in the west, he was being tested every day by a whole new generation of skywalkers. Orlando giant Shaquille O'Neal was the new center of attention, both physically and commercially. But such coming attractions as Alonzo Mourning, Chris Webber, Shawn Kemp, Reggie Miller, Kenny Anderson, Grant Hill, Jamal Mashburn and Anfernee Hardaway were not far behind.

Everybody, it seemed, was performing Jordan-like exploits and professional basketball popularity was zooming toward the top of the charts. The 1995 NBA Finals meeting of centers O'Neal and Olajuwon was a promotional bonanza, even though Hakeem's Rockets swept Shaq's Magic in four games to claim their second straight championship.

And as the game heads for a new century and incredible financial success, many predict a future as the No. 1 sport of America—if not the world or beyond. Nothing, it seems, is out of reach for those who can fly.

COMING ATTRACTIONS *Larry Bird (middle) and Magic Johnson (behind Bird) met for the first time in the NCAA Tournament Finals in 1979*

The Kind of Team You Dream About

What the 1992 Barcelona Olympic basketball tournament lacked in suspense it made up for with glitter and hype. The United States easily captured the gold medal and it did so with passion, turning its mostly professional Dream Team loose on an overmatched world.

The Dream Team was, simply, the most sensational cast of basketball talent ever assembled on one team. Coach Chuck Daly's roster read like a Who's Who of NBA talent: Magic Johnson, Michael Jordan, Larry Bird, Charles Barkley, Patrick Ewing, David Robinson, Chris Mullin, Scottie Pippen, Clyde Drexler, John Stockton and Karl Malone. Duke star Christian Laettner represented the college ranks.

The Dream Team was a product of two developments:

The recent failures of U.S. amateur teams against world competition and the lifting of restrictions against the participation of NBA players in international games. When it was announced that NBA stars would be allowed to compete in the Olympics, players jumped at the chance.

And the world braced for the inevitable: an easy romp through the Olympic field by the best team in the history of sports. Sure enough, the Dream Team waded through the massive hype to take care of business.

The Dream Team won its games by an average margin of 44 points, defeating Lithuania, 127–76, in the medal round and Croatia, 117–85, in the gold-medal contest.

BASKETBALL ASSOCIATION OF AMERICA

The long, long road to stability

In the beginning there were Celtics, Knickerbockers and Warriors. But there also were Stags, Falcons, Huskies and Capitols. We can only surmise that fans of power basketball probably enjoyed watching the Ironmen and the Steamrollers. And that proponents of outside shooting might have supported the Bombers. Non-conformist fans most likely identified with the Rebels.

The 1946–47 Basketball Association of America was a colorful collection of professional wannabes, if not a bastion of franchise stability. But it also was the humble beginning for the National Basketball Association, a league that eventually would soar to great heights and prosperity.

The BAA was content to crawl in 1946–47 when it opened play with 11 teams, survived a shaky first season and then watched four franchises drop by the wayside. Four more of the original 11 would be gone by the end of the fifth season with only New York (Knickerbockers), Boston (Celtics) and Philadelphia (Warriors) able to bridge the long-term gap from the BAA to the NBA.

From the moment the Basketball Association of America was conceived, it stood a level above the 9-year-old National Basketball League in scope and viability. The NBL, which was born under the flag of corporate sponsorship, had been operating since the 1937–38 season in the midwest obscurity of small cities and dingy, makeshift arenas. The BAA had much bigger dreams and the means to make them come true.

All 11 of the original BAA franchise owners were members of the Arena Managers Association of America, an organization that controlled dates for the major arenas in the nation's biggest cities. All 11 owned an arena, were tied closely to hockey and were looking for events to provide extra revenue.

With 5-foot-2 Maurice Podoloff serving as its first president, the BAA opened with franchises in Boston, New York, Philadelphia, Chicago (Stags), Cleveland (Rebels), Detroit (Falcons), Pittsburgh (Ironmen), Providence (Steamrollers), St. Louis (Bombers) and Washington (Capitols). The 11th team took the BAA above and beyond national boundaries—the Toronto Huskies.

The Huskies, the Rebels, the Ironmen and the Falcons folded after one season, forcing Podoloff to scramble for reinforcements. Podoloff talked the Baltimore Bullets into making the jump from the American Basketball League, a minor East Coast circuit, giving the BAA a manageable eight-team configuration. Such was the talent level of the early BAA that the Bullets captured the league's second-year championship.

Such growing pains would be eased with one quick maneuver that fortified the BAA's status and sent the NBL tumbling toward oblivion before the 1948–49 season. Podoloff talked four NBL franchises—the Fort Wayne Pistons, Rochester Royals, Minneapolis Lakers and Indianapolis Jets—into jumping leagues, bringing with them such talent as Bob Davies, Arnie Risen, Jim Pollard and, most importantly, the greatest basketball drawing card in the nation— 6–10 giant George Mikan.

Indianapolis and Providence folded after the 1948–49 season, but the 1949 BAA/NBL merger into the NBA briefly expanded the league's roster to 17 members located in large and small cities from the East Coast as far west as Denver (the Nuggets). It took only one season to pare the field back to 11 with the loss of the Nuggets, the Anderson Packers, the Sheboygan Redskins and the Waterloo Hawks as well as two BAA originals—the St. Louis Bombers and Chicago Stags.

When the 1950–51 season opened, the ever-changing cast included BAA originals Boston, New York, Philadelphia and Washington; the former ABL Bullets; Minneapolis, Fort Wayne and Rochester, three of the four teams that made the 1948 NBL jump; the Syracuse Nationals and Tri-Cities Blackhawks, two NBL refugees; and the Indianapolis Olympians, a 1949–50 newcomer composed mostly of former University of Kentucky and 1948 Olympics stars.

The configuration would change again in January of '51 when the Capitols folded in midseason. And

THE PRESIDENT *Maurice Podoloff (center) was the NBA's little/big man*

Tri-Cities made history after the season when it performed the NBA's first franchise shift—from Moline, Ill., to the more populous Milwaukee market—and also shortened its nickname, from Blackhawks to Hawks.

When the Olympians ceased operations after the 1952–53 season and the Bullets followed suit after 1953–54, the NBA's franchise-juggling act came to a merciful end. Never again would a franchise go out of business because of financial or other difficulties. But the mid-1950s NBA was still many miles from stability—the miles its teams would log moving from one city to another.

When the NBA opened play as an eight-team circuit in 1954–55, only three cities could claim uninterrupted tenure from the BAA's first season and Philadelphia would soon lose that distinction. In the ensuing years, the alignment that now included Boston, Fort Wayne, Milwaukee, Minneapolis, Rochester, New York, Philadelphia and Syracuse would shift dramatically, in city identity if not in substance.

The Hawks started the relocation ball rolling by shifting to St. Louis after the 1954–55 campaign and other

SHOOTING STAR *Bob Davies (11) was a member of Rochester's Royal family*

moves followed quickly: Rochester to Cincinnati and Fort Wayne to Detroit after 1956–57; Minneapolis to Los Angeles after 1959–60; Philadelphia to San Francisco after 1961–62; and Syracuse to Philadelphia (as the 76ers) after 1962–63. Even the NBA's 1961 expansion to Chicago was short-circuited by the never-ending search for greener pastures. The Chicago Packers/Zephyrs packed their bags after two seasons and moved to Baltimore as the reincarnated Bullets.

The relocation bug continued to bite the league for two more decades (St. Louis to Atlanta, Cincinnati to Kansas City to Sacramento, San Francisco to Oakland—as Golden State—etc.), but another growth trend was more positive. When the Chicago Bulls were admitted to the league in 1966, the NBA stood at 10 teams and the time was right to expand its horizons. The San Diego Rockets (who moved to Houston after the 1970–71 season) and Seattle SuperSonics began play in 1967–68 and two more teams— the Phoenix Suns and Milwaukee Bucks—joined the circuit a year later. The 1970–71 arrival of the Portland Trail Blazers, the Cleveland Cavaliers and the Buffalo Braves (the future San Diego/Los Angeles Clippers) brought the league population to seventeen.

The 1974–75 addition of the New Orleans Jazz preceded by two years the arrival of four ABA teams—San Antonio, New York, Indiana and Denver. Dallas was admitted in 1980–81, setting the stage for the next wave of expansion to Charlotte and Miami (in 1988–89) and Minnesota and Orlando (1989–90). The Canadian markets of Vancouver and Toronto were added in 1995 and '96.

STAYING PUT *Jim Pollard was scoring points for the Lakers when they were still winning championships for Minneapolis*

AMERICAN BASKETBALL ASSOCIATION

It's as simple "as A-B-A"

HOT POTATO *Amigos and Muskies follow the bouncing red, white and blue ball in the ABA's first season*

When the NBA opened its doors to the San Antonio Spurs, New York Nets, Indiana Pacers and Denver Nuggets as part of a 1976 merger agreement, it brought down the curtain on the nine-year-old American Basketball Association and its game of musical franchises.

By the end of its run, the ABA had changed its once patriotic colors to a war-weary black and blue and basketball fans were left to piece together a franchise-shifting puzzle that put the early NBA to shame. In the beginning, there were 11 ABA teams; at the end there were six. The in-between was a blur of cities, near-empty arenas and team nicknames that scored high for originality if not endurance.

The ABA opened play with franchises in Anaheim, Denver, Indianapolis, Pittsburgh, Louisville, Minneapolis, New Orleans, Oakland, Houston, Dallas and the booming metropolis of Teaneck, N.J. The New Jersey Americans, in keeping with the spirit of the patriotic ABA, wore red, white and blue uniforms and played their games in an armory. The Denver Rockets, owned by the Rocket Truck Lines, were more interested in the long haul than an instant takeoff.

While the red, white and blue basketball, the innovation of Commissioner George Mikan, became the enduring symbol of the ABA, the colorful nicknames became its legacy. The Amigos (Anaheim), Chaparrals (Dallas), Oaks (Oakland), Pacers (Indiana), Mavericks (Houston), Colonels (Kentucky), Muskies (Minnesota), Buccaneers (New Orleans) and Pipers (Pittsburgh) gave the ABA a personality that changed faster than Jekyll and Hyde.

The Amigos, for instance, were Amigos for only one season. They spent their second and third seasons as the Los Angeles Stars and their fourth and fifth as the Utah Stars before folding 16 games into their sixth campaign. Their demise came less than two years after winning an ABA championship.

Likewise, two other franchises refused to let success force stability.

The Pipers claimed the ABA's first championship, moved to Minnesota for their second season and back to Pittsburgh for their third. In season No. 4, club officials, apparently bored again with life in Pittsburgh, changed the team name to "Condors" and struggled through two more seasons before folding. The Oakland Oaks won the ABA's second title, moved cross country to Washington the next season and relocated a few miles south to Virginia the next. From 1970 to the ABA's demise in 1976, the team played as the "Squires" in the Virginia cities of Norfolk, Hampton and Richmond.

And so life went in the unpredictable ABA. The Houston Mavericks transformed magically into the Carolina Cougars and later the St. Louis Spirits. The New Orleans Buccaneers relocated to Memphis after three seasons and tried on a series of nicknames: Pros, Tams and Sounds. The Dallas Chaparrals tried their luck for a season as the Texas Chaparrals before moving to San Antonio. And the Minnesota Muskies survived one season before relocating to Miami as the Floridians. Minnesota will go down in ABA annals as the city that welcomed and lost two different teams in consecutive seasons.

The ABA even had an expansion team—the San Diego Conquistadors, who began play in 1973 and competed for three seasons before becoming the "Sails." Another team, the Baltimore Claws (remnants of the defunct Memphis franchise), folded a few days before playing its first game.

When all was said and done, six franchises remained standing—Indiana, Denver, San Antonio, New York, Kentucky and St. Louis. Five of the six were originals and three competed the entire nine seasons in the same city—the Pacers, Rockets/Nuggets and Colonels.

Not surprisingly, the six final teams accounted for six of the nine ABA championships, proving, after all, there is something to be said for stability.

ON THE MOVE *Rick Barry was an Oak, a Capitol and a Net before returning to the NBA wars*

THE NBA TEAMS

In the spectacular world of reverse slam dunks, no-look passes and 3-point jump shots, the unspectacular bottom line can be found on the scoreboard. Individuals excite fans with their above-the-rim theatrics and showmanship but teams bring them back to arenas with their ability to outscore opponents and successfully achieve the common goal—victory.

The essence of sports is winning and losing, and winning most often is accomplished within the framework of a team. Success is determined by such mundane functions as fundamentals, rebounding, ball movement and defense.

Wilt Chamberlain always will be revered as the most spectacular offensive machine in NBA history, but while he was carving out his own special section of the record book, the Boston Celtics, dedicated to Coach Red Auerbach's principles of teamwork and defense, were claiming championship after championship. Many consider Oscar

Robertson to be the most complete player in basketball history, but a championship eluded him until he joined forces with a young Kareem Abdul-Jabbar at Milwaukee near the end of his career. And Michael Jordan, one of the game's ultimate offensive and defensive weapons, was a helpless superstar for an average Chicago team until Bulls management got him a championship-caliber supporting cast.

Chamberlain, Robertson, Jordan—any of the game's brightest stars—will tell you statistics are nice, but championship rings define the ultimate success of a career. And long-term team success

defines the ultimate goal of every franchise.

Team success like the Boston Celtics' 16 overall championships or the Lakers' 12 titles and 24 appearances in the NBA Finals. Like the 11 championship rings of Boston center Bill Russell, the prototypical team player. Like the Chicago Bulls, who already have carved out their historical niche as the team of the 1990s.

MAGIC TOUCH *The Lakers' vaunted "showtime" running attack of the 1980s was triggered and fueled by the effervescent Magic Johnson*

ATLANTA HAWKS

Somewhere in-between

If nothing else, the Hawks have been consistent. Only once have they ranked among the NBA's muscle men. Only occasionally have they ranked among its weaklings. Most of their St. Louis and Atlanta existence has been spent somewhere in between.

In the 40 seasons from 1955 through 1995, the Hawks finished within 10 games of .500 19 times, qualified for the playoffs 31 times and lost before reaching the NBA Finals 27 times. Only in one four-year span did they fail to reach the playoffs in consecutive seasons.

Not that the Hawks have been a bland, colorless franchise. From 1956 to '61, gifted forward Bob Pettit won a pair of scoring titles while leading the team to five consecutive Western Division titles and its only NBA championship—a six-game 1958 victory over the powerful Boston Celtics.

From 1966 to '74, Sweet Lou Hudson combined with Zelmo Beaty, Bill Bridges, Joe Caldwell and Pete Maravich over an eight-year run that produced two division titles and six second-place finishes.

And from 1985 to '89, high-flying Dominique Wilkins was the centerpiece for a Hawks team that recorded 50 or more victories in four consecutive seasons.

The Hawks trace their NBA roots back to 1949, when they joined the league as the Tri-Cities Blackhawks. The franchise, one of six survivors when the National Basketball League folded, spent six losing seasons in Moline, Ill., and Milwaukee before moving to St. Louis in 1955.

The 1954 arrival of Pettit was the franchise's first step forward. The Hawks joined the NBA elite in 1956 when Owner Ben Kerner

pulled off a draft-day trade that brought future Hall of Famers Ed Macauley and Cliff Hagan from Boston for a first-round draft pick. Pettit, Macauley and Hagan led the Hawks to four NBA Finals; the Celtics used their pick on center Bill Russell, who led them to 11 championships.

By 1965, Macauley was long gone, Pettit was ready to retire and Hagan was a year away. But new coach Richie Guerin was reloading his offensive arsenal around swingman Hudson, backcourt ace Lenny Wilkens, 6-foot-9 center Beaty and Bridges, a rebounding forward. Guerin's teams advanced to the Western Division finals four times in five seasons and that success carried through the franchise's 1968 move from St. Louis to Atlanta.

When Guerin left after the 1971–72 campaign, the Hawks fell on hard times. But they revived to win 50 games in 1979–80 and became a 1980s power under Mike Fratello. Wilkins provided the glitter and firepower for Fratello's Hawks, never averaging below 25.9 points from 1984 to 1994, when he was traded to the Clippers. Wilkins created excitement with his above-the-rim theatrics, which rivaled the shows being staged in other cities by Julius Erving and Michael Jordan.

The current-edition Hawks are in good hands. Lenny Wilkens took the coaching reins in 1993–94 and made history a year later when he passed Red Auerbach on the all-time victory list. Wilkens is trying to rebuild with a talent base that features free-agent center Dikembe Mutombo, guards Mookie Blaylock and Steve Smith and forwards Christian Laettner and Alan Henderson.

HARD DRIVE *Mookie Blaylock forms half of Atlanta's talented backcourt*

Facts and Figures

Conference/Division	*Eastern/Central Division*			
First Year in NBA	*1949–50*			
Arena (Capacity)	*The Omni (16,378)*			
Former Cities/Nicknames	*Tri-Cities Blackhawks, 1949–51,*			
	Milwaukee Hawks, 1951–55,			
	St. Louis Hawks, 1955–68			
NBA Finals Appearances	*1957, 1958, 1960, 1961*			
NBA Championships	*1958*			
Playing Record	G	W	L	Pct.
Regular Season	*3,714*	*1,884*	*1,830*	*.507*
Playoffs	*246*	*109*	*137*	*.443*

BOSTON CELTICS

The winning formula

Red Auerbach, Bill Russell, John Havlicek, Larry Bird. The names form an historical link of basketball generations. They fit together like "Abbott and Costello," "Peter, Paul and Mary," "NBA" and "championship" and "Boston" and "Celtics." Remove one and the chain is broken.

The common denominator, of course, is Auerbach, the coaching genius who fit together the pieces of the NBA's most storied franchise. He began his work in 1950, when he took over as coach of the 4-year-old Celtics, one of the BAA/NBA's original teams.

Auerbach's dream was to mold a team of rabbits that could run and gun its way past the more conservative teams of the era. He built a foundation by picking up guards Bob Cousy and Bill Sharman and forward Ed Macauley, perfect fits for his running blueprint.

But Auerbach's rabbits were being outmuscled by the league's better teams and it took a brilliant 1956 draft-day maneuver to provide the puzzle's biggest piece. Auerbach traded Macauley and the rights to Cliff Hagan, two future Hall of Famers, to St. Louis for Russell, the Hawks' first-round draft pick. He grabbed forward Tom Heinsohn with a territorial pick.

The beefed-up Celtics were on their way. With Russell rebounding, playing maniacal defense and triggering an explosive fast break from his center position, they raced to the 1957 NBA championship, the franchise's first, and ran off a record string of eight consecutive titles from 1959–66. It was the longest championship streak in team-sports history. Through the run, Auerbach sur-

Facts and Figures	
Conference/Division	Eastern/Atlantic Division
First Year in BAA/NBA	1946–47
Arena (Capacity)	FleetCenter (18,600)
Former Cities/Nicknames	None
NBA Finals Appearances	1957, 1958, 1959, 1960, 1961, 1962, 1963, 1964, 1965, 1966, 1968, 1969, 1974, 1976, 1981, 1984, 1985, 1986, 1987
NBA Championships	1957, 1959, 1960, 1961, 1962, 1963, 1964, 1965, 1966, 1968, 1969, 1974, 1976, 1981, 1984, 1986

Playing Record	G	W	L	Pct.
Regular Season	3,887	2,422	1,465	.623
Playoffs	461	272	189	.590

CELTIC PRIDE *Power forward Dino Radja (right) delivers points and rebounds*

rounded Russell with a steady stream of excellent supporting players: Cousy, Sharman, Sam Jones, Heinsohn, K.C. Jones, Tom Sanders, Havlicek and Don Nelson.

The end of the streak was only a temporary setback. Russell, who had taken over the coaching reins after the 1965–66 season, played two more years and collected two more championship rings, his 10th and 11th in 13 seasons. When he retired after the 1969 victory, the Celtics were forced to reload.

They did it quickly with Heinsohn as coach and Havlicek, the Celtics' former "Sixth Man," as the go-to star. Auerbach brought in center Dave Cowens, guards Jo Jo White and Charlie Scott, and rebounder Paul Silas, who combined with Havlicek to win five consecutive Atlantic Division titles and two more NBA championships from 1971–76. Again it was time to reload.

This time Auerbach did it with a first-round draft pick that he used to select Indiana State's Bird—after his junior season. The Celtics languished in the division basement in 1978–79 while Bird was playing his senior season, but the 6–9 forward would be worth the wait.

Auerbach complemented Bird with center Robert Parish, forward Kevin McHale and guards Dennis Johnson and Danny Ainge. Under Bill Fitch and K.C. Jones, the Celtics cruised through the 1980s, winning eight division titles and three more championships, bringing their record total to 16. When Bird was forced to retire in 1992 with a chronic back problem, the Celtics fell back into the pack.

The current-edition Celtics, under coach M.L. Carr, feature forwards Dino Radja and Rick Fox, guards Dee Brown, David Wesley and Dana Barros and 1996 No. 1 draft pick Antoine Walker. If that doesn't prove to be a winning combination, Carr might turn to the team's president for a word of advice.

His name is Red Auerbach.

CHARLOTTE HORNETS

Expanding horizons

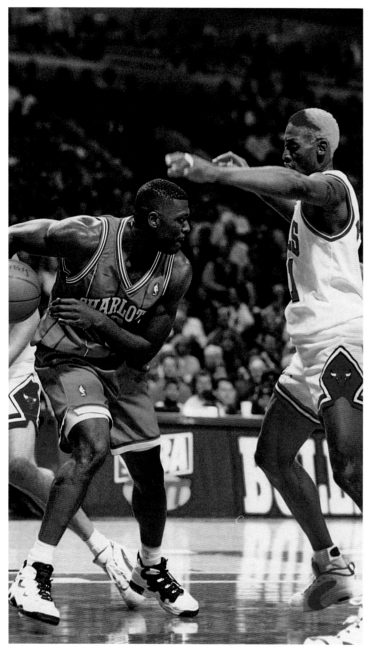

OUT PATTERN *Go-to forward Larry Johnson has taken his game to New York.*

The best prescription for NBA success: Draft or acquire a dominant big man, turn him loose in the paint and fit the rest of the puzzle around him. Charlotte officials followed that formula to the letter while molding the expansion Hornets, but a not-so-funny thing happened on their way to a championship.

Charlotte's ticket to success was Alonzo Mourning, who arrived out of Georgetown University as the second overall pick of the 1992 draft. Mourning, a 6-foot-10 leaper with a nice blend of offensive,

defensive and rebounding skills, was the perfect fit for a 4-year-old team aspiring to ascend into the league's upper echelon.

Mourning joined forces with 6–7 Larry Johnson in one of the league's most potent frontcourts and concluded his first season with 21-point and 10.3-rebound averages and 271 blocked shots. Not surprisingly, the Hornets improved from 31 to 44 victories, posted their first winning record and made their first trip to the playoffs. They capped a rewarding season by disposing of Boston in a first-round series before losing to the rugged New York Knicks.

The Hornets came back to post a 41–41 record in 1993–94 when Johnson missed 31 games with a bad back, but they shed their expansion cloak in 1994–95, winning a franchise-record 50 games. An inspiring regular season was followed by a playoff disaster as the Chicago Bulls, revitalized by the return of Michael Jordan, swatted the Hornets in a quick first-round series.

But that disappointment was nothing compared to the news that greeted fans as the team prepared for its eighth NBA campaign. Mourning and management were engaged in a bitter contract hassle that finally resulted in the big center turning down a $20-million deal and demanding a trade. Shortly before the season, he was sent to Miami for forward Glen

Rice, 7-foot center Matt Geiger and guard Khalid Reeves.

A midseason deal brought ball-handling wizard Kenny Anderson to Charlotte. The new-look Hornets were stronger on the perimeter, but softer and less intimidating in the paint. Not even the offseason acquisition of Lakers' center Vlade Divac could ease the pain. Such tribulations were but a distant dream for North Carolina fans in 1987 when the NBA announced that four cities would be granted expansion franchises: Charlotte and Miami would begin play in 1988–89; Orlando and Minnesota would begin a year later.

Charlotte had been considered a longshot, but the league was rewarded by devoted fans who filled the 24,042-seat Charlotte Coliseum game after game. Those fans were rewarded by a front office that drafted wisely, built patiently and marketed the Hornets into one of the league's most popular franchises.

That popularity will be tested in the immediate future. Two players from the team's 20-victory first season—5-3 point guard Muggsy Bogues and sixth man Dell Curry—remain with the team. But long-time power forward Larry Johnson and Anderson were traded after the 1995–96 season.

The spotlight now focuses on center Divac and forwards Anthony Mason and Brad Lohaus.

Facts and Figures

Conference/Division	*Eastern/Central Division*			
First Year in NBA	*1988–89*			
Arena (Capacity)	*Charlotte Coliseum (24,042)*			
Former Cities/Nicknames	*None*			
NBA Finals Appearances	*None*			
NBA Championships	*None*			
Playing Record	**G**	**W**	**L**	**Pct.**
Regular Season	*656*	*272*	*384*	*.415*
Playoffs	*13*	*5*	*8*	*.385*

CHICAGO BULLS

Up, up and away

History for Chicago fans begins in 1984, the season Michael Jordan was plucked out of the NBA draft with the third overall pick. That was the beginning of the rest of their basketball lives, the point where they could separate hope from futility.

Jordan brought excitement and acceptance to a city that had not always embraced the professional game. The Chicago Stags lasted four seasons as 1946 charter members of the Basketball Association of America. The Chicago Packers/Zephyrs joined the league in 1961 and lasted two seasons before moving to Baltimore.

The Bulls made their NBA debut as an expansion team in 1966 and began charting a course through the rough Chicago waters. The first four seasons were spent in search of .500; the next five provided false hope of great things to come.

The Bulls made their first serious foray into the NBA's upper stratosphere in 1970–71 when young coach Dick Motta guided them to a 51–31 record and a second-place finish in the Midwest Division. With forwards Chet Walker and Bob Love providing points, guard Norm Van Lier directing the offense and forward Jerry Sloan supplying defense, the Bulls won more than 50 games in four straight seasons and their first Midwest Division title. But four playoff appearances resulted in first-round failures and two others ended in the Western Conference finals.

Chicago's heart-breaking seven-game loss to Golden State in the 1975 conference finals signaled a fast fall to mediocrity. The next nine seasons would produce but two playoff appearances and a low position in the 1984 draft.

Jordan's early years were dazzling. In 1986–87, he earned the first of seven consecutive scoring titles. In 1987–88, he won the first of four MVPs. But try as he might, Jordan alone couldn't give the Bulls what everybody wanted most—playoff success.

Help finally arrived in 1987 when the Bulls acquired Scottie Pippen and drafted Horace Grant, two athletic front-court players, on the same day. In their first season with Jordan, the Bulls won 50 games and tied for second

TWO'S A CHARM *Scottie Pippen (33) is a perfect complement to Michael Jordan*

in the Central Division. Three years later, under second-year coach Phil Jackson, the Bulls won 61 times, cruised through the Eastern Conference playoffs and overpowered the Lakers in a five-game NBA Finals. The Bulls powered their way to a second straight championship in 1992 and became the third NBA team to pull off a three-peat a year later. Jordan capped the 1993 title by retiring to pursue a baseball career.

Life beyond Jordan was predictable. The Bulls sank in the standings and were headed toward an early playoff ouster in 1995 when Jordan, revitalized and

ready to play, came out of retirement for the final 17 games. He wasn't enough to get the Bulls past the second round, but the Jordan–Pippen reunion and Chicago's acquisition of rebounding master Dennis Rodman set the stage for an unprecedented 1995–96 season.

The new-look Bulls rolled to a record 72–10 regular-season mark, won 15 of 18 playoff games and posted their fourth championship in six years with a six-game NBA Finals romp past Seattle. In the process, they might have staked a claim to the title of "greatest team in NBA history."

Facts and Figures				
Conference/Division	Eastern/Central Division			
First Year in NBA	1966–67			
Arena (Capacity)	United Center (21,711)			
Former Cities/Nicknames	None			
NBA Finals Appearances	1991, 1992, 1993, 1996			
NBA Championships	1991, 1992, 1993, 1996			
Playing Record	G	W	L	Pct.
Regular Season	2,459	1,316	1,143	.535
Playoffs	213	117	96	.549

CLEVELAND CAVALIERS

The long and difficult road to respectability

When the NBA gave birth to the Cleveland Cavaliers in a three-team 1970 expansion, nobody could have imagined the pain and heartache that would track the unfortunate franchise through its first quarter century. But early omens should have put league officials and fans on red alert.

The Cavs opened their first season with 15 consecutive losses and dropped 34 of their first 36 games—the only two victories coming against Buffalo and Portland, their expansion mates. A final 15–67 record showed how thin their first-year roster really was.

Still, coach Bill Fitch saw reason for optimism. John Johnson had finished a solid rookie season with a 16.6-point average and the Cavs grabbed hot-shooting Notre Dame guard Austin Carr with the first pick of the 1971 draft. The second-year Cavs improved to 23 victories, the third-year Cavs won 32 and Fitch added a pair of muscular draft picks, 6-foot-9 Jim Brewer and 6–8 Campy Russell.

When 6–11 center Jim Chones arrived from the ABA in 1974 and veteran guard Dick Snyder was acquired in a trade, Fitch had the pieces in place for a championship run. And indeed the 1975–76 Cavaliers posted a franchise-record 49 victories, won chise-record 49 victories, won

their first Central Division title and made their playoff debut a successful one, advancing to the Eastern Conference Finals.

But just when everything appeared to be falling into place, misfortune began to dog the franchise. The 1976 playoff run was deflated when Chones suffered a broken ankle, making the Cavs easy prey for a veteran Boston team.

Never again would the Cavaliers win a division title. It would take 16 years before they would win another playoff series. The franchise would struggle through inept play in the late 1970s, near-disastrous misman-agement by owner Ted Stepien in the early 1980s and bad luck and injury problems in the 1990s. The wheeling and dealing Stepien so disfigured the 1981–82 Cavs that they sank back to expansion form with 15 victories.

When Stepien finally sold the franchise to George and Gordon Gund, the NBA had to guarantee the new owners four bonus first-round draft picks to help rebuild the team. With solid ownership in place, the Cavs began the slow climb back to respectability.

The breakthrough came in a lucrative 1986 draft that brought 7-foot center Brad Daugherty, shooting guard Ron Harper and

point guard Mark Price to Cleveland. That talented three-some soon was joined by 6–11 Hot Rod Williams and 6–10 Larry Nance in a lineup that Lakers guard Magic Johnson labeled the "Team of the '90s."

And indeed the young Cavs appeared to be headed in that direction under the steady hand of Lenny Wilkens, who arrived in 1986 and coached the team to 285 victories over a six-season stretch that included another trip to the

conference finals. But Cleveland's title dream was punctured by the Chicago Bulls, who dominated the Eastern Conference en route to three straight championships, and a career-threatening back injury that disabled Daugherty.

Mike Fratello replaced Wilkens in 1993 and Price was traded in 1995 as the Cavs began yet another rebuilding program around guards Terrell Brandon and Dan Majerle and forward Tyrone Hill.

DYNAMIC DUO *Cavs Coach Mike Fratello and point guard Terrell Brandon*

Facts and Figures

Conference/Division	*Eastern/Central Division*			
First Year in NBA	*1970–71*			
Arena (Capacity)	*Gund Arena (20,562)*			
Former Cities/Nicknames	*None*			
NBA Finals Appearances	*None*			
NBA Championships	*None*			
Playing Record	G	W	L	Pct.
Regular Season	*2,132*	*953*	*1,179*	*.447*
Playoffs	*73*	*27*	*46*	*.370*

DALLAS MAVERICKS

Back to the future

It wasn't much fun, but at least it was understandable. The new-born Mavericks, trying to take their first NBA steps under coach Dick Motta, stumbled, tottered and wheezed en route to a curtain-raising 15–67 record.

That was 1980–81 and management could take consolation in the belief that expansion teams are supposed to suffer; that the organization never again would experience such a low.

Now fast-forward to the 1990s as the older and supposedly wiser Mavs showed just how fickle NBA life can be. Under coaches Richie Adubato and Gar Heard, Dallas crashed to an 11–71 record in 1992–93. Under new coach Quinn Buckner in 1993–94, the Mavericks stumbled to a 13–69 mark. From January 1992 through April 1994, owner Donald Carter watched his Mavs compile an unbelievable 34–183 record.

But now it's the Dallas fans who can take consolation. For just as the Mavericks rose from the ashes in the years following their expansion debut, the 1990s Mavs appear capable of rising toward a new era of prosperity.

But not without a few growing pains. Building through the draft, the Mavericks have fashioned an exciting backcourt with Jim Jackson and Jason Kidd and two-thirds of a frontcourt with inside/out scorer Jamal Mashburn and rebounder Popeye Jones. The young team experienced a 36-victory revival in 1994–95, but sagged to 26 wins in a disappointing followup campaign.

Still, management remains convinced that big things are ahead if a big body can be plugged into the middle.

A major revival would not be unlike the dramatic rise Dallas executed in the 1980s. From their 15-victory debut, Motta's Mavericks jumped to 28 wins and improved in each of their first seven seasons. In 1983–84, they posted the franchise's first winning mark (43–39), finished second in the Midwest Division and won a first-round playoff series against Seattle.

The Mavericks were being rightly hailed as the model expansion franchise. Management had pulled all the right strings, building a solid foundation in a 1981 draft that produced guard Rolando Blackman and forwards Mark Aguirre and Jay Vincent. Guard Derek Harper was drafted in 1983 and forwards Sam Perkins and Detlef Schrempf in 1984 and '85.

When 7-foot-2 center James Donaldson was acquired in 1985 and rebounding ace Roy Tarpley was drafted in '86, the Mavericks appeared to have all the pieces for a championship run. They won 55 games and their first Midwest title in 1986–87 and followed with a 53-win campaign under new coach John MacLeod. The Mavs beat Houston and Denver in 1988 playoff series before losing a seven-game Western Conference Finals heart-breaker to the Lakers.

But just when it appeared the Mavs were on the brink, the bottom fell out. First Tarpley suffered a severe knee injury and a series of drug-related suspensions. Then Aguirre and Schrempf were traded and Donaldson suffered a knee injury.

As management groped for answers, the team's record slid, finally bottoming out from 1992 to '94. The answer, it turned out, could be found in their own history: the draft. The Mavericks also can find another answer there. They need to be patient and let a young team mature.

SLASHER *Jamal Mashburn can put points on the board quickly*

Facts and Figures

Conference/Division	Western/Midwest Division		
First Year in NBA	1980–81		
Arena (Capacity)	Reunion Arena (17,502)		
Former Cities/Nicknames	None		
NBA Finals Appearances	None		
NBA Championships	None		
Playing Record	G	W	L	Pct.
Regular Season	1,312	541	771	.412
Playoffs	48	21	27	.438

DENVER NUGGETS

A franchise on the run

If you measure franchise success by NBA Finals appearances and championships, the Denver Nuggets have been two-decade failures. But if you judge a franchise by its star-quality players, competitive teams, exciting style and fan appeal, the Nuggets have been NBA giants.

Consider: In their first 20 NBA seasons, the Nuggets led the league in scoring seven times and finished in the top four 12 times; they showcased high-flying and fast-scoring forwards David Thompson, Alex English and Dan Issel; they flashed and dashed their way to four Midwest Division titles; and they laid claim to one of the most stunning play-off upsets in league history.

The Nuggets came into existence in 1967 as the Denver Rockets, one of the 11 original franchises in the American Basketball Association. It quickly became apparent the Rockets would become one of the ABA's most stable teams, both on the court and off. They posted winning records in their first two seasons and stunned the basketball world in 1969 by signing NBA-ineligible Spencer Haywood, a high-scoring forward who had just finished his sophomore season at the University of Detroit.

Haywood would play only one season in Denver before bolting to the NBA, but the Rockets had clearly established a front-office tenacity. Denver's stock rose dramatically in the ABA's final two seasons when the Rockets/Nuggets —they changed their nickname in 1974—won 125 games, advanced to the league's final championship series (a loss to the New York Nets) and opened plush McNichols Arena, one of the best basketball facilities in the country.

It was no coincidence that the Nuggets were one of the four ABA teams invited to join the NBA in 1976. And it was no fluke that Denver raced to 50 victories and the Midwest Division title in its first season—the best finish ever for a new NBA entrant.

The Nuggets, coached by Larry Brown, were potent scorers with the high-flying and acrobatic Thompson, Issel and forward Bobby Jones. Denver lost to Portland in the Western Conference semifinals, but returned to claim a second division title in 1977–78 and advanced to the conference finals.

Brown departed in 1978 and Thompson's career faded shortly after. But a short lull was fol-

lowed by the 1981 arrival of coach Doug Moe, who gave the Nuggets a running start toward a new era of prosperity. Literally.

Moe preached run-and-shoot basketball with little regard for defense and the Nuggets spent most of the 1980s piling up gaudy statistics and moderate success. The top gun in Moe's arsenal was the 6–7 English, but Kiki Vandeweghe, Calvin Natt and Lafayette (Fat) Lever also provided significant firepower.

Moe left after the 1989–90 season and the Nuggets began assembling first-round draft picks: guards Jalen Rose and Mahmoud Abdul-Rauf, forwards LaPhonso Ellis and Antonio McDyess and 7–2 center Dikembe Mutombo. Abdul-Rauf and Rose were traded for veteran guards Mark Jackson and Ricky Pierce after the 1995–96 season.

The brightest moment of the 1990s occurred under Issel, who watched his eighth-seeded Nuggets pull off a stunning 1994 first-round playoff upset of No. 1-seeded Seattle, a 63-game winner. Issel left early in the 1994–95 season, handing over the reins to Bernie Bickerstaff.

SHORT STORY
The Nuggets will play smaller with the loss of center Dikembe Mutombo (right) to free agency.

Facts and Figures

Conference/Division	Western/Midwest Division			
First Year in ABA/NBA	1967–68/1976–77			
Arena (Capacity)	McNichols Sports Arena (17,171)			
Former Cities/Nicknames	Denver Rockets, 1967–74			
NBA Finals Appearances	None			
ABA/NBA Championships	None			
Playing Record	G	W	L	Pct.
ABA Regular Season	744	413	331	.555
NBA Regular Season	1,640	816	824	.498
ABA Playoffs	62	27	35	.435
NBA Playoffs	98	39	59	.398

DETROIT PISTONS

Blue-collar basketball and the "Bad Boys"

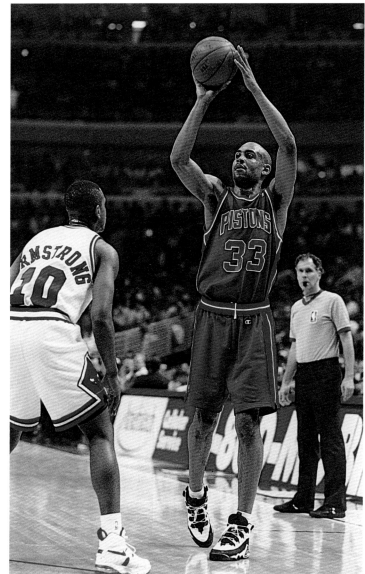

FIRING PISTON *Young Grant Hill is the centerpiece for Detroit's offense*

They were brought into the world by a blue-collar owner in a blue-collar city and given a blue-collar name. Fittingly, the Pistons have played blue-collar basketball through an existence that spans more than half a century.

It began in 1937 when Fred Zollner organized a team that he named after his Fort Wayne, Ind., factory that manufactured automobile pistons. The team barnstormed during its early years, played in the National Basketball League after World War II and then jumped to the Basketball Association of America (the pre-NBA) before the 1948–49 season.

The Pistons quickly discovered that life in a division dominated by Minneapolis (George Mikan) and Rochester (Arnie Risen, Bob Davies) would not be easy. For the first six seasons of its Fort Wayne existence, the team posted three winning records, never finished higher than third in the Western Division and won only seven of 21 playoff games.

But life after Mikan proved more rewarding. The Pistons, powered by forward George Yardley, guard Max Zaslofsky and bruising center Larry Foust, won three straight division titles and advanced to the 1955 and '56 NBA Finals.

But success would be fleeting. When Zollner fled Fort Wayne for more populous Detroit in 1957, the franchise began more than two decades of futility. For their first 13 Detroit seasons and 23 of their first 26, the Pistons failed to record a winning record.

Over that span, they won three playoff series and compiled a 23–36 postseason record.

There were a few bright spots. Such talented players as guard Gene Shue, forwards Bailey Howell, Dave DeBusschere and Terry Dischinger and center Walter Dukes passed through. And two of the franchise's all-time best players, smooth guard Dave Bing and 6–11 center Bob Lanier, lifted the Pistons' pulse during a 45-win 1970–71 season and a 52-win 1973–74 campaign.

But Detroit's first brush with success would not come until the 1983 arrival of coach Chuck Daly and it would be rooted in the old blue-collar ethics—hard work and defense. Daly inherited a team with one of the game's best point guards of all-time, Isiah Thomas, and a physical center, Bill Laimbeer. The rest of the puzzle was filled in through the draft and trades: center James Edwards, guard Joe Dumars, sixth man Vinnie Johnson and forwards Mark Aguirre, Dennis Rodman and John Salley.

By the late 1980s, the defensive-minded Pistons were playing with a bruising, no-holds-barred style that earned them a reputation as the game's "Bad Boys." Beginning in 1987–88, they bullied their way to three straight Central Division titles and NBA Finals. The Pistons lost in 1988 to Los Angeles, but they beat the Lakers in 1989 and Portland in 1990 to become the NBA's second repeat champions in more than two decades. In Daly's nine-year tenure, the

Pistons never won fewer than 46 games, never finished below third in the division and compiled a 71–42 postseason mark.

But after his 1992 departure, Detroit slipped to 40 victories and then consecutive seasons of 20 and 28 before re-entering the 1995–96 playoff picture under coach Doug Collins. Collins is trying to revive Daly's blue-collar work ethic and winning formula around multi-talented forward Grant Hill.

Facts and Figures

Conference/Division	Eastern/Central Division			
First Year in BAA/NBA	*1948–49*			
Arena (Capacity)	The Palace of Auburn Hills (21,454)			
Former Cities/Nicknames	Fort Wayne Pistons, 1948–57			
NBA Finals Appearances	1955, 1956, 1988, 1989, 1990			
NBA Championships	1989, 1990			
Playing Record	**G**	**W**	**L**	**Pct.**
Regular Season	3,776	1,783	1,993	.472
Playoffs	219	111	108	.507

GOLDEN STATE WARRIORS

California dreaming

Their NBA journey has passed through three cities and covered thousands of miles. It has produced championships, scoring titles and dominant personalities and performances. When the Warriors look back on a half century of basketball, it's easy to detect two unmistakable trends.

First, Warriors players have won a record 14 scoring titles—all in the franchise's first 22 seasons. Joe Fulks won two, Paul Arizin two, Neil Johnston three, Wilt Chamberlain six and Rick Barry one. No Warrior has won another for more than a quarter of a century.

Second, the Warriors have won three championships and played in three other NBA Finals—all in their first three decades. In their last two, they have never advanced beyond the second round of the playoffs and didn't even qualify for the postseason from 1977–86.

The Philadelphia Warriors, the creation of Eddie Gottlieb, were one of 11 charter 1946 franchises that began play in the Basketball Association of America, the league that evolved into the NBA. The team carved the first notch in the NBA's record book when it captured the new league's first championship.

But the Warriors would not win again until 1956, when the unstoppable inside-out combination of Johnston and Arizin combined to average 46.3 points per game. The franchise's final title, choreographed by the high-scoring Barry and coached by former guard Al Attles, was earned in 1975, 13 years after the Warriors made a coast-to-coast move from Philadelphia to San Francisco and four years after they became the "Golden State" Warriors with a move across the Bay to Oakland.

The 7-foot-1 Chamberlain rewrote the NBA record books during his five-plus seasons with the Warriors, but he couldn't get his team a championship. The man who averaged an incredible 50.4 points in his third NBA season did come close in 1964, but the Warriors lost a five-game NBA Finals series to Boston. It was Chamberlain's inability to carry San Francisco to the next level that prompted the Warriors to trade him to Philadelphia in 1965, turning over center duties to Nate Thurmond.

While the Warriors ranked among the NBA elite for their first three decades, the last two have been a different story. When they lost in the second round of the 1977 playoffs, that signaled the beginning of a bleak nine-year period in which they managed only two winning records and failed to generate momentum with a changing cast that included big men Robert Parish, Joe Barry Carroll and Ralph Sampson and long-range bombers Purvis Short and World B. Free. Prospects remained grim until Don Nelson took the coaching reins in 1988.

Nelson crafted his revival around 6–7 forward Chris Mullin, adding guards Mitch Richmond, Tim Hardaway and Latrell Sprewell and 6–10 forward Chris Webber. The Warriors vaulted to 55 victories in 1991–92 and 50 two years later, but Nelson's foundation was ripped apart when he feuded with Webber and traded the big man to Washington. It was an unpopular move that cost him his job early in 1995.

Richmond and Hardaway also have departed and new coach Rick Adelman is trying to rebuild around 6–10 forward Joe Smith, a potential franchise player, and newcomers Jerome Kersey and B.J. Armstrong.

POINT MAKER *High-scoring Latrell Sprewell (15) rules Golden State's perimeter*

Facts and Figures

Conference/Division	*Western/Pacific Division*
First Year in BAA/NBA	*1946–47*
Arena (Capacity)	*Oakland Coliseum Arena (15,025)*
Former Cities/Nicknames	*Philadelphia Warriors, 1946–62; San Francisco Warriors, 1962–71*
NBA Finals Appearances	*1947, 1948, 1956, 1964, 1967, 1975*
NBA Championships	*1947, 1956, 1975*

Playing Record	G	W	L	Pct.
Regular Season	*3,882*	*1,878*	*2,004*	*.484*
Playoffs	*214*	*99*	*115*	*.463*

HOUSTON ROCKETS

A dream come true

When the San Diego Rockets joined the NBA in 1967 as an expansion team, everybody anticipated a difficult road to respectability. But respectability, it turned out, would be much easier attained than a championship ring.

Respectability, in fact, would come in the 1968 draft with the selection of 6-foot-9 scoring machine Elvin Hayes. With the rookie Hayes averaging 28.4 points and 17.1 rebounds, the Rockets jumped from a 15-victory debut season to 37 and even qualified for the 1969 playoffs.

But the championship dream would not be realized for more than a quarter of a century. In 1993–94, 7-foot center Hakeem Olajuwon, appropriately nicknamed "The Dream," carried Houston's Rockets to the first of consecutive titles under the direction of coach Rudy Tomjanovich, a former star forward in the Hayes era.

Hayes was merely the first forward step on the Rockets' evolutionary trail. He led the team to a franchise-best 40 victories in 1970–71, but he was traded to Baltimore a year later after feuding with coach Tex Winter. Ironically, Hayes, a college star at the University of Houston, was dealt away one season after the Rockets had moved to Houston because of sagging attendance in San Diego.

Hayes' departure was even more unfortunate because the Rockets had added two outstanding prospects in the 1970 draft. The 6–8, 220-pound Tomjanovich joined Hayes at one forward slot and Calvin Murphy began his career as one of the best off-guards in NBA history.

The Rockets' fortunes did not improve dramatically until 1976, when guard John Lucas was drafted in the first round and 21-year-old center Moses Malone arrived after two ABA seasons. The Rockets won their first Central Division title in 1976–77 and advanced to the Eastern Conference Finals before losing to Philadelphia. In 1980–81, Murphy and Malone took Houston a step further. The Rockets advanced all the way to the NBA Finals, where they lost to Boston.

Malone departed after a quick 1982 playoff loss and so did the Rockets' momentum. But it didn't take long to reload. Operating on the notion that bigger is better, the Rockets drafted 7–4 Ralph Sampson in 1983 and Olajuwon in '84. The "Twin Towers" and hard-nosed forward Rodney McCray carried Houston to the 1985–86 Midwest Division title and another visit to the NBA Finals, but again the Rockets lost to the Celtics.

It wasn't until the team was handed to Tomjanovich in 1991 that the final puzzle began taking shape. As the Chicago Bulls and Michael Jordan were rolling to three consecutive championships, Olajuwon was maturing into a powerful NBA force. With a new supporting cast that included point guard Kenny Smith and forwards Otis Thorpe and Vernon Maxwell, the 1993–94 Rockets rolled to their second straight Midwest title, cruised through the playoffs and defeated the Knicks in a seven-game Finals.

In 1994–95, off-guard Clyde Drexler, sixth man Sam Cassell and forwards Robert Horry and Mario Elie stepped up to support Olajuwon in the successful pursuit of a second straight title—an NBA Finals sweep of Orlando.

Houston's dream, at long last, had become reality.

PLAY IT AGAIN, SAM *Sam Cassell provides a consistent spark off Houston's bench*

Facts and Figures

Conference/Division	Western/Midwest Division		
First Year in NBA	1967–68		
Arena (Capacity)	The Summit (16,611)		
Former Cities/Nicknames	San Diego Rockets, 1967–71		
NBA Finals Appearances	1981, 1986, 1994, 1995		
NBA Championships	1994, 1995		
Playing Record	**G**	**W**	**L**	**Pct.**
Regular Season	2,378	1,168	1,210	.491
Playoffs	174	88	86	.506

INDIANA PACERS

A little NBA fish swims with the sharks

RISING FORTUNES *Rik Smits has taken his place among the NBA's best big men*

For nine seasons, the Indiana Pacers were the biggest fish in the ABA pond. Over the next 17, they became microscopic tadpoles in the NBA ocean. Now, at last, they seem to have the coach (Larry Brown), the star presence (Reggie Miller, Rik Smits) and the tenacity to swim among the league's sharks.

The Pacers' basketball journey has been colorful and difficult. Born in 1967 as a charter member of the ABA, the team stepped into a basketball-crazy Indiana market that had enjoyed only two brief associations with the professional game—the Jets (1948–49) and the Olympians (1949–53). The Pacers won over skeptics by assembling a team that dominated the league from 1970 to '73 and produced some of its brightest stars.

The cornerstone of the early Pacers was 6-foot-9 center Mel Daniels, a bulldog rebounder and scorer. Fiery coach Bob (Slick) Leonard filled in the pieces around Daniels—forward Roger Brown, guards Billy Keller and Freddie Lewis—and the 1969–70 Pacers stormed to 59 victories, their second consecutive Eastern Division title and the first of three ABA championships.

The mix became even more potent in 1971 when Indianapolis signed Indiana University undergraduate George McGinnis. When the 6–8 McGinnis joined Brown and Daniels in an explosive frontcourt, the 1972 and '73 Pacers became the ABA's first back-to-back champions.

But the remainder of the Pacers' ABA tenure would be spent cutting costs in a desperate battle against red ink. By the time the ABA–NBA merger was forged, only McGinnis remained and even he would be gone before the franchise played its first NBA game. The Pacers, New York Nets, San Antonio Spurs and Denver Nuggets were accepted into the NBA in 1976—but not without a stiff price. The cash-short Pacers were required to pay a $3.2-million entry fee, forfeit television rights for four years and sit out the 1976 college draft. To stay afloat, they had to deal valuable future draft picks for journeyman players and entered the league with a soft, depleted roster.

Recovery from that shaky NBA debut would be painful. Over the next 17 years, the franchise was hindered by shaky ownership, unwise draft choices, bad trades and the inability to produce star-quality players. In the 17 seasons from 1976–77 through 1992–93, the team never won more than 44 games, missed the playoffs 11 times and won only four post-season games.

Playmaking guard Don Buse, high-scoring Billy Knight and power forward Clark Kellogg were the brightest stars in an ever-changing cast that included centers Herb Williams and Steve Stipanovich and forwards Detlef Schrempf and Wayman Tisdale. From 1989, Jack Ramsay's final season, through 1993, the Pacers employed five coaches before settling on Brown.

With Miller firing in points from the perimeter and Smits, 6–11 Dale Davis and 6–10 Derrick McKey providing inside muscle, Brown's Pacers piled up 47 victories in 1993–94, won 52 each of the next two years and captured their first Central Division title in 1994–95. Two of those seasons ended with heart-breaking seventh-game losses in the Eastern Conference finals.

But they also ended with hope for a brighter future.

Facts and Figures				
Conference/Division	Eastern/Central Division			
First Year in ABA/NBA	1967–68/1976–77			
Arena (Capacity)	Market Square Arena (16,530)			
Former Cities/Nicknames	None			
NBA Finals Appearances	None			
ABA/NBA Championships	1970, 1972, 1973 (all ABA)			
Playing Record	G	W	L	Pct.
ABA Regular Season	744	427	317	.574
NBA Regular Season	1,640	737	903	.449
ABA Playoffs	119	69	50	.580
NBA Playoffs	59	26	36	.441

LOS ANGELES CLIPPERS

Sailing against the wind

It hasn't been pretty. It hasn't even been close. For more than a quarter century, the Clippers have been giving new meanings to the word "futility". Among some of the more embarassing statistics, the Clippers have managed five winning seasons while stumbling through one 12- and three 17-victory campaigns and qualified for postseason play five times, but only twice since 1976.

The Clippers have won less than 38 percent of their games and no division titles, so maybe it is not quite so surprising that they have employed 18 coaches and made five in-season changes.

It certainly has not helped the franchise that they have played in three cities including Los Angeles, where the Clippers are overshadowed by the high-profile Lakers. The highlight—or lowlight maybe—came in a bizarre 1978 deal, when team owner John Y. Brown traded his Braves for Irv Levin's Boston Celtics.

The Clippers began their NBA life in 1970 in Buffalo as part of a three-team expansion that also included Portland and Cleveland. The Braves should have realized something was wrong when the team was sold one day before its first-ever game.

The first glimmer of hope arrived in 1972 when new coach Jack Ramsay grabbed high-scoring Bob McAdoo with the second overall pick of the draft and surrounded his 6-foot-9 center with guards Randy Smith and Ernie DiGregorio and forwards Jim McMillian and Garfield Heard. McAdoo won three consecutive scoring titles and the Braves earned three consecutive playoff berths, advancing to the second round in 1976.

But that glimmer flickered into darkness after the 1976 playoffs when Ramsay departed for Portland and McAdoo was inexplicably traded to the Knicks in an unpopular deal that foreshadowed the bleakest and most futile 15-year period for any team in NBA history.

Over those 15 seasons, the Clippers managed only one winning record and one campaign with more than 36 victories. It would not qualify for postseason play. After the 1977–78 campaign, when the owners traded franchises, the Braves were relocated to San Diego—Levin's base—as the Clippers and six years later they were shifted to Los Angeles. A lot of offense (World B. Free, Tom Chambers, Terry Cummings, Freeman Williams, Bill Walton) passed through the franchise, but little defense—and even fewer victories.

Relief finally appeared at the end of the 1991–92 season when Larry Brown took the coaching reins and quickly returned the team to respectability. Brown's Clippers, featuring guard Ron Harper and forwards Danny Manning and Ken Norman, finished 45–37 and 41–41 in his two seasons, although they did make quick playoff exits on both occasions. With the Lakers in a rebuilding mode, the Clippers were at last out of their illustrious neighbors' shadow. But the franchise quickly returned to its sad, familiar ways.

Brown left for Indiana after the 1993 playoffs and was followed in quick order by Harper (free agent), Manning (traded) and Norman (free agent). The 1994–95 Clippers, under new coach Bill Fitch, sank back to 17 victories before fighting through injury problems to post 29 in the following season.

Fitch's hopes centered around the improvement of such youngsters as guard Brent Barry, forwards Loy Vaught and Rodney Rogers and 7-foot, 290-pound center Stanley Roberts, who overcame numerous injuries in 1995–96.

BIG LOAD *Forward Loy Vaught is the Clippers' model of consistency*

Facts and Figures

Conference/Division	*Western/Pacific Division*	
First Year in NBA	*1970–71*	
Arena (Capacity)	*L.A. Memorial Sports Arena (16,005)*	
Former Cities/Nicknames	*Buffalo Braves, 1970–78,*	
	San Diego Clippers, 1978–84	
NBA Finals Appearances	*None*	
NBA Championships	*None*	

Playing Record	G	W	L	Pct.
Regular Season	2,132	778	1,354	.365
Playoffs	32	13	19	.406

LOS ANGELES LAKERS

The best in the west

They ruled the NBA through the first half of the 1950s, served as bridesmaids during the '60s, made a cameo appearance in the '70s and performed basketball Magic in the '80s. The Lakers might not be the game's most storied franchise, but they're close.

Franchise success is defined by the Boston Celtics, owners of 16 NBA championships, 19 conference titles, 24 division titles and the highest winning percentage in league history. But consider: The Lakers have won 11 championships, 24 conference titles and 25 division titles while winning more than 60 percent of their games. They have failed to reach the playoffs four times.

The Lakers' amazing consistency has been the product of three distinct eras: the George Mikan years with John Kundla as coach (1948–54); the Elgin Baylor-Jerry West period with Fred Schaus (1960–73), and the Magic Johnson-Kareem Abdul-Jabbar run with Pat Riley (1980–91).

The Lakers were based in Minneapolis when they abandoned the National Basketball League in favor of the two-year-old Basketball Association of America in 1948. Mikan, a bruising 6-foot-10, 245-pounder, redefined how the center position should be played, scoring and rebounding almost at will against smaller opponents. With Mikan winning four consecutive scoring titles and getting support from Jim Pollard, Vern Mikkelsen and playmaker Slater Martin, the Lakers rolled to four division titles and five championships in six years.

Mikan retired after the 1954 championship and the next push started with the 1958 draft selection of Baylor, a classy 6–5 forward. When Baylor, Mr. Inside, was joined in 1960 by guard Jerry West, Mr. Outside, the Lakers were primed for another run.

The Baylor-West show opened on the West Coast, where the Lakers moved after the 1959–60 season. From '62 to 1970, the Lakers won e division titles and reached the NBA Finals seven times. But without a center to compete against Bill Russell or Willis Reed, they lost six series to the powerful Celtics and one to the Knicks.

Baylor, plagued by knee problems, made only a cameo appearance for a 1972 Lakers team that finally broke through. With an aging Wilt Chamberlain playing center and West sharing backcourt duties with high-scoring Gail Goodrich, the 1971–72 Lakers piled up an incredible 33-game winning streak en route to an NBA-record 69 victories and bulled their way through a 12–3 playoff run.

The framework for the next run was built around 7–2 center Abdul-Jabbar, a 1975 acquisition from Milwaukee, and 6–9 point guard Magic Johnson, a 1979 draft pick. With Riley pulling the strings and Abdul-Jabbar and Johnson getting support from James Worthy, Byron Scott, Michael Cooper and Jamaal Wilkes, the Lakers won the 1980 championship and added four more before the decade closed. They also lost three times in the Finals.

Abdul-Jabbar retired after the 1988–89 season as the game's all-time leading scorer and Johnson retired in 1991 when he tested positive for HIV, the virus that causes AIDS.

But after watching the Lakers struggle through four difficult seasons, Johnson returned midway through 1995–96 as a 36-year-old power forward, helped the team post 53 victories, and promptly retired again. With Johnson's official departure, the Lakers embarked on a new era of prosperity with the free-agent signing of Orlando center, Shaquille O'Neal.

CENTER CUT *Vlade Divac (12) has taken his improving pivot skills to Charlotte.*

Facts and Figures

Conference/Division	*Western/Pacific Division*
First Year in BAA/NBA	*1948–49*
Arena (Capacity)	*The Great Western Forum (17,505)*
Former Cities/Nicknames	*Minneapolis Lakers, 1948–60*
NBA Finals Appearances	*1949, 1950, 1952, 1953, 1954, 1959, 1962, 1963, 1965, 1966, 1968, 1969, 1970, 1972, 1973, 1980, 1982, 1983, 1984 1985, 1987, 1988, 1989, 1991*
NBA Championships	*1949, 1950, 1952, 1953, 1954, 1972, 1980, 1982, 1985, 1987, 1988*

Playing Record	G	W	L	Pct.
Regular Season	*3,777*	*2,292*	*1,485*	*.607*
Playoffs	*507*	*301*	*206*	*.594*

MIAMI HEAT
Growing pains and gains

In the fragile early years of every expansion franchise, there comes a moment of truth—that point where opportunity knocks, the door to success opens and management is faced with a difficult decision. To pay or not to pay, that is the question.

The Miami Heat faced their moment of truth in 1995—twice. First they gave the New York Knicks a precious 1996 No. 1 draft pick to let Pat Riley out of the final year of his contract. Then they settled the Charlotte Hornets' $20-million feud with center Alonzo Mourning by trading three players for the 6-foot-10 star.

And just like that, Miami began heating up the NBA's Atlantic Division. Mourning, a first-class shot-blocker who possesses many of the same qualities Riley showcased with New York center Patrick Ewing, was the perfect addition for the new coach's defensive-minded philosophy.

Mourning quickly became the centerpiece for Riley's puzzle and the coach added pieces as the 1995–96 season progressed— guards Tim Hardaway, Sasha Danilovic and Rex Chapman and forward Chris Gatling. Riley's creation was good enough to claim the final playoff berth without any starters from the team that had produced the Heat's first winning

record (42–40) two years earlier.

The sudden makeover was shocking for Miami fans who had watched management build the team sensibly and patiently through the draft. Center Rony Seikaly and forward Grant Long, a pair of 1988 picks, were starters during the Heat's 15-victory expansion season (1988–89) and their 42-victory 1993–94 campaign. Long-range bomber Glen Rice was drafted in 1989 and guard Steve Smith in 1991.

The Heat's early stability was the product of a solid ownership group pieced together by former NBA player and coach Billy Cunningham. The group was awarded a franchise in April 1987 as part of a four-team expansion that also included Charlotte, Minnesota and Orlando. The Heat and Hornets began play in 1988–89, the Timberwolves and Magic a year later.

The Heat took their first NBA steps on wobbly legs under coach Ron Rothstein. They won 15 games in their debut season, 18 the next year and 24 in year three. Rothstein was replaced by Kevin Loughery in 1991–92 and the young team, which featured Seikaly, Rice, Smith and Long as well as Willie Burton and Brian Shaw, showed signs of life. The Heat jumped to 38 wins and

BIG ADDITION *Alonzo Mourning gives the Heat size and hope*

became the first of the four expansion teams to qualify for a playoff berth—a quick sweep by Chicago. The 1993–94 winner was a cause for celebration.

But everything unraveled in 1994–95. Just before the season opened, Miami shipped Seikaly to Golden State for Billy Owens and followed quickly by dealing Long

and Smith to Atlanta for Kevin Willis. Rice and 7-footer Matt Geiger were part of the 1995 package that brought Mourning.

The 1994 shuffle rekindled memories of early growing pains and the Heat struggled through a 32–50 season. Riley inherited that memory and the authority and resources to make it go away.

Facts and Figures

Conference/Division	Eastern/Atlantic Division			
First Year in NBA	1988–89			
Arena (Capacity)	Miami Arena (15,200)			
Former Cities/Nicknames	None			
NBA Finals Appearances	None			
NBA Championships	None			
Playing Record	G	W	L	Pct.
Regular Season	656	247	409	.377
Playoffs	11	2	9	.182

MILWAUKEE BUCKS

The flip of a coin

One year they were expansion babies, inexperienced and naïve in the ways of the NBA. The next year they were title-contending giants, confident and capable of mixing it up with the game's elite. All it took to transform the Milwaukee Bucks from a caterpillar into a butterfly was the flip of a coin and a stroke of luck that instantly changed the NBA's balance of power and the future course of two franchises.

The Bucks had struggled to a 27–55 first-year record, the worst in the Eastern Division. The Phoenix Suns, Milwaukee's expansion mates, had finished 16–66, the worst mark in the Western Division. A coin flip would determine the first pick of the 1969 draft and the prize would be 7-foot-2 UCLA center Lew Alcindor.

When the Suns made the wrong call, the Bucks moved into the NBA stratosphere. Alcindor, who later would change his name to Kareem Abdul-Jabbar, averaged 28.8 points and 14.5 rebounds in his rookie season and Milwaukee won 56 games, more than double its victory total of 1968–69.

The Bucks, suddenly thrust into the championship picture, quickly surrounded their big man with veteran talent. Venerable Oscar Robertson, still looking for

his first NBA title, was brought in to run the show and he was joined in a talented backcourt by Jon McGlocklin and Lucius Allen. Abdul-Jabbar was flanked in the frontcourt by Greg Smith and rebounding ace Bob Dandridge.

The 1970–71 season was no contest. Abdul-Jabbar won the first of consecutive scoring titles en route to league MVP honors and Milwaukee rolled to 66 victories. In a 12–2 postseason, the 3-year-old Bucks brushed past San Francisco, Los Angeles and Baltimore for their first NBA championship.

Although Milwaukee continued to dominate the Midwest Division with 192 victories over the next three seasons, there would be no more titles. Abdul-Jabbar carried them to the 1974 NBA Finals—a seven-game loss to the Boston Celtics—but the Bucks cleaned house after an injury-plagued 1974–75 campaign and Abdul-Jabbar was sent to Los Angeles for four young players.

The rebuilding program began paying dividends in 1979–80, when Don Nelson coached his young team to the first of seven consecutive Midwest and Central Division titles. From 1980–81 through 1986–87, Milwaukee victory totals ranged from 50 to 60 and the Bucks advanced deep

BIG DOG *Glenn Robinson is half of Milwaukee's 1–2 forward punch*

into the playoffs every season from 1983 to '87.

But a strong team built around such players as Quinn Buckner, Junior Bridgeman, Bob Lanier, Terry Cummings, Sidney Moncrief and Marques Johnson could not get past Eastern Conference powers Boston and Philadelphia and the Bucks never reached the NBA Finals.

The end of the decade was filled with 40-plus-win seasons

under coach Del Harris, but the 1990s began with another rebuilding program that is finally showing results.

The current-edition Bucks are young and strong at forward with Glenn Robinson and Vin Baker. Shawn Respert and Sherman Douglas are solid in the backcourt, but championship hopes will not be entertained until the Bucks can find a big body to plug into the middle.

Facts and Figures

Conference/Division	Eastern/Central Division			
First Year in NBA	1968–69			
Arena (Capacity)	Bradley Center (18,633)			
Former Cities/Nicknames	None			
NBA Finals Appearances	1971, 1974			
NBA Championships	1971			
Playing Record	G	W	L	Pct.
Regular Season	2,296	1,271	1,025	.554
Playoffs	169	85	84	.503

MINNESOTA TIMBERWOLVES

Out of the wilderness

In the politically correct world of the NBA, it's fair to call the Minnesota Timberwolves offensively-challenged. Or defensively-challenged. Or, to cover the full spectrum of their early existence, basketball-challenged.

Suffice it to say that the Timberwolves have been handicapped while their expansion brethren—Miami, Charlotte and Orlando—are showing an upward mobility beyond their years. Minnesota's growing pains have been induced by a combination of impatience, bad judgment and a lack of team chemistry, both on the court and off.

When the Timberwolves made their debut in 1989–90, they were greeted by a highly excited Minneapolis contingent that envisioned a rekindling of past glories. Four decades earlier, in the fledgling years of the League, the Minneapolis Lakers, featuring super center George Mikan, had begun an impressive run that produced five NBA championships in six seasons.

It seemed only fitting that Mikan, who had retired before the Lakers made their 1960 move to Los Angeles, was part of a task force that helped bring professional basketball back to the Twin Cities. And it appeared to be a good omen when the first-year 'Wolves, playing under the disciplined, defensive-minded umbrella of coach Bill Musselman, won 22 games—more than any of the other expansion beginners.

Musselman's second-edition team produced 29 victories and more encouragement, but as fans filled the new Target Center and embraced their young team with fanatic enthusiasm, an unsteady foundation began to crumble. First management decided to fire Musselman, who was accused of sacrificing development for immediate results. Then it hired untested Jimmy Rodgers, whose up-tempo style was not a good fit for the plodding Timberwolves.

It turned out to be a disastrous choice. Minnesota sagged to 15 victories in 1991–92 and Rodgers departed 29 games into the next season, a 63-defeat nightmare. Rodgers' successor, Sidney Lowe, did not fare any better as the Timberwolves suffered through a record four consecutive 60-loss seasons and became the doormat of the Midwest Division.

But losing does have an upside, which has given Minnesota fans reason for optimism. Early stars such as Pooh Richardson and Tony Campbell are gone, as are 7-foot draft flops Felton Spencer and Luc Longley and 6–11 former Duke star Christian Laettner. High-scoring guard Isaiah Rider, a fifth overall 1993 draft pick who is temperamental and hard on team chemistry, also is capable of helping the 'Wolves find their way out of the wilderness.

Donyell Marshall, the 1994 first-rounder, was traded to Golden State for Tom Gugliotta, a hard-working power forward, and the 'Wolves showed their commitment to patience and player development with their 1995 draft selection of 6–11 Kevin Garnett, who bypassed college and stepped into the professional wars right out of high school. Garnett improved steadily in his rookie season under coaches Bill Blair and Flip Saunders.

The 26 victories the Wolves' achieved in 1995–96 was their second-best season mark. But to illustrate just how low the team sank in its first seven seasons, consider this: The Timberwolves could go 82–0 each of the next three years and still be below .500.

QUICK STUDY *Kevin Garnett made a big jump from high school to the NBA*

Facts and Figures

Conference/Division	*Western/Midwest Division*			
First Year in NBA	*1989–90*			
Arena (Capacity)	*Target Center (19,006)*			
Former Cities/Nicknames	*None*			
NBA Finals Appearances	*None*			
NBA Championships	*None*			
Playing Record	G	W	L	Pct.
Regular Season	*574*	*152*	*422*	*.265*
Playoffs	*0*	*0*	*0*	*—*

NEW JERSEY NETS

A long and winding road

NET MINDING *Jayson Williams (55) does his best work in the trenches*

and advanced to the ABA Finals before losing to Indiana.

When a federal judge shocked the Nets by ordering Barry to take his 31.5-point average back to the NBA after the 1972 playoffs, Boe simply reloaded. He brought in Kevin Loughery as coach, acquired young forward Julius Erving from the Squires and signed a pair of talented draft picks in Larry Kenon and John Williamson. The 1973–74 Nets bolted to a 55–29 regular-season record, stormed to a 12–2 playoff mark and captured the first of two ABA championships in three years. The second would come in 1976, the ABA's final campaign.

The championship success and the excitement generated by the acrobatic Dr. J secured the Nets' inclusion in the 1976 ABA-NBA merger. But the financial responsibilities that accompanied the jump secured a long, grueling existence in the lower reaches of the Atlantic Division standings. In order to pay the bills, Boe was forced to sell Erving's contract to the Philadelphia 76ers, dooming his club to a long dry spell.

Over their first 16 NBA seasons, the Nets would post but four winning records (1981–82 through 1984–85) and win six playoff games. Five of the post-season wins came in 1984 when

coach Stan Albeck led the Nets in their only advance past the opening round. That team had balance with Otis Birdsong and Micheal Ray Richardson at guard, Albert King and Buck Williams at forward and Darryl Dawkins at center.

The early years were not a total disaster. The Nets moved back to New Jersey in 1977, spent four seasons playing at the Rutgers Athletic Center and finally moved into the plush new Meadowlands Arena, their current home. But on-court hope did not arrive until 1992 when Chuck Daly took over as coach.

Daly brought Nets fans their first winning record in seven seasons with a lineup that featured 6–10 Derrick Coleman, hot-shooting Drazen Petrovic and point guard Kenny Anderson. But Petrovic's tragic death in a 1993 automobile accident was a major setback, as was Daly's 1994 departure after his second straight winning season.

The Nets began another rebuilding project by trading Anderson and Coleman, an unsettling clubhouse influence. Skinny 7–6 center Shawn Bradley arrived in the Coleman trade and joined Kendall Gill and Jayson Williams as the keys to a brighter future.

During its three nomadic decades, the team has played home games in six arenas, represented two states in two leagues and sported two nicknames. Its wandering path through New York City and New Jersey has been mirrored by its aimless journey through the NBA standings.

The team was born into the erratic world of the American Basketball Association in 1967 as the New Jersey Americans and played a patriotic first season in colorful red, white and blue uniforms at a dingy armory in its

home base of Teaneck, N.J.

The Americans moved to Long Island's Commack Arena and adopted a new name (New York Nets) before their second season, but a blueprint for success would not be drawn until 1970 when Roy Boe bought the team, brought in very popular Lou Carnesecca as coach and acquired high-scoring Rick Barry from the Virginia Squires. The Nets, now playing in Island Garden Arena and armed with their first superstar attraction, qualified for the 1972 playoffs with a 44–40 record

Facts and Figures

Conference/Division	*Eastern/Atlantic Division*		
First Year in ABA/NBA	*1967–68/1976–77*		
Arena (Capacity)	*Meadowlands Arena (20,029)*		
Former Cities/Nicknames	*New Jersey Americans, 1967–68,*		
	New York Nets, 1968–77		
NBA Finals Appearances	*None*		
ABA/NBA Championships	*1974, 1976 (both ABA)*		
Playing Record	**G**	**W**	**L**	**Pct.**
ABA Regular Season	*744*	*374*	*370*	*.503*
NBA Regular Season	*1,640*	*660*	*980*	*.402*
ABA Playoffs	*69*	*37*	*32*	*.536*
NBA Playoffs	*36*	*9*	*27*	*.250*

NEW YORK KNICKS

A dedication to defense

The Knicks began play as a BAA/NBA original in 1946, but New York fans prefer to ignore the first 23 seasons. It all started, they'll tell you, in 1970, when one of the most perfectly sculpted teams in league history rose to the top of the basketball world.

The middle of that team was dominated by 6-foot-10 Willis Reed, an intelligent, hard-working center who had arrived as a second-round 1964 draft pick. The perimeters were manned by Bill Bradley, who later became a U.S. Senator, and sharp-shooting Dave DeBusschere, who also doubled as a major league baseball pitcher. The frontcourt was manned by reliable Dick Barnett and classy Walt Frazier, one of the game's greatest defensive guards.

In retrospect, the 1969–70 Knicks might have been a team of destiny. Boston's Bill Russell had retired after the 1969 playoffs, officially ending the Celtics' 13-year dynasty, and New York was positioned perfectly for a run at its first NBA championship. With coach Red Holzman espousing the principles of patience, discipline and defense, the Knicks rolled to 60 victories, captured their first Eastern Division title in 16 years and advanced to the NBA Finals, where they defeated the Lakers in seven games.

The Knicks

LONG SHOT *Guard John Starks does his best work from beyond the 3-point line*

returned to the top of the Eastern Division in 1970–71 and advanced to the NBA Finals in 1972 and again in '73. With fast-shooting guard Earl Monroe now in the mix, the 1973 Knicks earned their second title with a five-game victory over the Lakers.

That four-year, two-title run provided Madison Square Garden with a touch of magic that had been missing through the franchise's formative years. Small and fast, the early Knicks had contended for supremacy in the Eastern Conference under coach Joe Lapchick and even reached the NBA Finals three times, but they were no match for the bigger Rochester and Minneapolis teams. After that moderate success, the Knicks went 11 seasons (1955–56 to 1965–66) without winning a playoff game.

The 1970s success was followed by another lull marked by inconsistency and constant

change. The Knicks tried their luck with such players as Bob McAdoo, Campy Russell, Bill Cartwright and Ray Williams, but it wasn't until the 1985 draft yielded 7-foot Georgetown center Patrick Ewing that the team began to regain momentum.

Serious title thoughts returned to the Garden in 1991 when Pat Riley arrived to mold a winner around the intimidating Ewing. Riley surrounded Ewing with physical players such as Charles Oakley, John Starks, Charles Smith and Derek Harper, giving the Knicks a fierce defensive presence that bullied opponents and made high-scoring games obsolete. The Knicks became the most unpopular team in the NBA, but they laughed all the way to three straight Atlantic Division titles and a four-year average of 56 victories.

But defense and intimidation could only carry the Knicks so far. When a disillusioned Riley left after the 1995 playoffs, all he had to show for his New York tenure was one trip to the NBA Finals—a 1994 loss to Houston.

Don Nelson was hired to revitalize an aging roster, but Nelson feuded with Ewing and left midway through a turbulent 1995–96 season. A rebuilding plan was unveiled with the acquisitions of Allan Houston, Chris Childs and Larry Johnson.

Facts and Figures

Conference/Division	*Eastern/Atlantic Division*			
First Year in BAA/NBA	*1946–47*			
Arena (Capacity)	*Madison Square Garden (19,763)*			
Former Cities/Nicknames	*None*			
NBA Finals Appearances	*1951, 1952, 1953, 1970, 1972, 1973, 1994*			
NBA Championships	*1970, 1973*			
Playing Record	*G*	*W*	*L*	*Pct.*
Regular Season	*3,883*	*1,979*	*1,904*	*.510*
Playoffs	*289*	*146*	*143*	*.505*

ORLANDO MAGIC

A Magical mystery tour

Do you believe in Magic? Orlando basketball fans do, and with good reason. They're still trying to figure out the sleight of hand General Manager Pat Williams used to turn a tottering expansion team into an NBA powerhouse.

The transformation began in 1992 when Orlando, coming off a 21-victory season, struck gold in the Draft Lottery—a drawing to determine order of selection in the annual college draft. The stakes were high, with the lucky winner gaining rights to 7-foot-1, 300-pound Louisiana State center Shaquille O'Neal.

With the drawing weighted heavily toward the league's weaker teams, it was not a major surprise that the Magic became instant winners of the Shaquille sweepstakes; Orlando possessed the second to worst record in the NBA in the 1991–92 season. But what transpired just one year later sent shock waves through the NBA.

Orlando rose to a 41–41 record and barely missed qualifying for the 1993 playoffs, despite its 20-game improvement in the victory column. The Magic did, however, qualify again for the draft sweepstakes—this time with a 1-in-66 chance of landing the No. 1 pick. Amazingly, they won the lottery and selected 6–10 Michigan star Chris Webber as a prelude to a draft-day trade that would plot a quick course to the NBA Finals.

Many Magic fans drooled at the thought of a front line with O'Neal and Webber, but Williams had other ideas. Looking for a swing player with Michael Jordan-type abilities, he shipped Webber to Golden State for Anfernee Hardaway, the Warriors' first-round pick, and three future No. 1 selections.

Those who questioned the judgment of Williams quickly changed their minds. The young and talented Magic, with O'Neal controlling the middle, Hardaway scoring from everywhere on the court and Nick Anderson and Dennis Scott providing long-range scoring punch, powered their way to 50 victories in 1993–94 and a second-place finish in the Atlantic Division. A first-round playoff loss to Indiana only whetted a young team's growing appetite.

Williams added another big piece to the puzzle in 1994 by signing Horace Grant, a powerful rebounder for the 1991, '92 and '93 Chicago championship teams. The 1994–95 Magic rolled to 57 victories, captured their first division title and defeated Boston, Chicago and Indiana en route to an NBA Finals date against Houston. But the Rockets pulled off a stunning four-game sweep and a 60-victory 1995–96 effort was followed by a conference-finals loss to Chicago and the shocking departure of O'Neal to Los Angeles with the biggest free-agent contract in history.

Such possibilities seemed remote in 1989, when the Magic began play with Minnesota in the final phase of a four-team expansion. The Magic, led by such veterans as Reggie Theus and Terry Catledge, struggled to an 18–64 first-year record.

The following year showed much improvement with 31 victories, but the Magic stepped back—a 21-win season—as youngsters like Anderson and Scott learned the NBA game. Then came O'Neal, a franchise-turning center, and Hardaway. And the inevitable roller-coaster ride of a young and exciting franchise.

HE'S EVERYWHERE *Anfernee Hardaway is blessed with the Magic touch*

Facts and Figures

Conference/Division	Eastern/Atlantic Division		
First Year in NBA	1989–90		
Arena (Capacity)	Orlando Arena (16,010)		
Former Cities/Nicknames	None		
NBA Finals Appearances	1995		
NBA Championships	None		
Playing Record	G	W	L	Pct.
Regular Season	574	278	296	.484
Playoffs	36	18	18	.500

PHILADELPHIA 76ERS

Playing in the shadows

YOUNG GUN *Acrobatic Jerry Stackhouse offers hope for a quick 76ers turnaround*

heads with the powerful Minneapolis Lakers and Rochester Royals. The Nationals, who were built around high-scoring forward Dolph Schayes, lost to the Lakers in the 1950 and '54 Finals before rising up to claim their only title in 1955, the year after Minneapolis center George Mikan retired.

When the team relocated to Philadelphia in 1963, a year after the Warriors had moved from Philadelphia to San Francisco, winning became a matter of trying to keep up with the Joneses, and the Russells, and the rest of the powerful Celtics who were in the midst of an incredible championship run—11 titles in 13 seasons.

The 76ers rose up to win three straight Eastern Division titles and copped the 1967 championship under Alex Hannum with one of the most powerful lineups ever assembled. The 1966–67 team featured Wilt Chamberlain at center, Billy Cunningham, Chet Walker and Luke Jackson at forward, and Wali Jones and Hal Greer at guard.

The 76ers' championship ended Boston's run of eight straight titles, but the Celtics returned to the throne in 1967–68 despite Philadelphia's 62-victory campaign. Amazingly, the 76ers would gradually sink to 30 victories in 1971–72 and nine one year

later—the lowest win total in NBA history.

But just as quickly as they had faded, the 76ers rose back into prominence. The next glory period began in 1976 with the arrival of Julius (Dr. J) Erving and ended in 1985 with the departure of Cunningham as coach. In between, the 76ers won four Atlantic Division titles, topped 50 victories in nine of 10 seasons, reached the NBA Finals four times and won the franchise's third and final championship—a 1983 sweep of the Lakers. The title puzzle was completed with the insertion of center Moses Malone into a lineup with the fantastic Dr. J, Andrew Toney, Maurice Cheeks and Bobby Jones.

The post-championship era began with the arrival of Charles Barkley, a fiery power forward who kept the 76ers competitive for eight seasons with his rebounding and scoring. But Barkley didn't get much help and his 1992 trade to Phoenix signaled the beginning of a serious rebuilding program.

Top draft selections Clarence Weatherspoon and Jerry Stackhouse, a Michael Jordan clone, combine with 1995 acquisition Derrick Coleman to give the 76ers a strong nucleus and revived hope for a quick return to the NBA's upper stratosphere.

As one of three NBA franchises with more than 2,000 regular-season victories, the 76ers have been surprisingly inefficient. The Celtics and Lakers, the other 2,000-plus winners, have combined for 27 championships and 43 NBA Finals appearances. The 76ers have won three titles in eight Finals.

That's not to say the 76ers don't rank among the league's model franchises. Since making their debut in 1949–50 as the

Syracuse Nationals, the Nats/76ers have posted 31 winning records, qualified for postseason action 37 times and reached the 50-victory plateau on 15 occasions, including one stretch of seven straight seasons. The 1966–67 76ers compiled an amazing 68–13 record— the third-best mark in NBA history.

But too often the team's success has been lost in the shadow of other teams' accomplishments. Much of the Nationals' 14-year Syracuse stay was spent bumping

Facts and Figures

Conference/Division	*Eastern/Atlantic Division*		
First Year in NBA	*1949–50*		
Arena (Capacity)	*CoreStates Center (21,000)*		
Former Cities/Nicknames	*Syracuse Nationals, 1949–63*		
NBA Finals Appearances	*1950, 1954, 1955, 1967, 1977, 1980, 1982, 1983*		
NBA Championships	*1955, 1967, 1983*		
Playing Record	**G**	**W**	**L**	**Pct.**
Regular Season	*3,712*	*2,035*	*1,677*	*.548*
Playoffs	*328*	*175*	*153*	*.534*

PHOENIX SUNS

Suns rise in the west

When the Suns selected 6-foot-10 Florida center Neal Walk with their first pick of the 1969 draft, they set an unspectacular course that would lead them toward the higher elevations of the NBA.

Walk turned into a serviceable player who would average 12.6 points and 7.7 rebounds over an eight-year career and the Suns gradually turned into one of the game's most consistent franchises.

But, still, it's tempting to look back and wonder what might have been—if, for instance, the Suns had won the annual coin flip to determine rights to the first overall pick in 1969.

Phoenix had finished its expansion season of 1968–69 in the Western Division basement; their expansion cousins, the Milwaukee Bucks had finished in the same position in the East. The coin-flip winner would walk away with draft rights to 7–2 UCLA center Lew Alcindor, a franchise-turning big man.

With Alcindor, the Bucks became champions in their third NBA season. Without him, the

and 6–7 Truck Robinson the muscle. Again the Suns came up short in the middle.

And during a four-year rebuilding period in which Phoenix did not win a playoff game, the Suns reloaded their guard and forward positions but failed to find the big man who could take them to the next level.

From 1988–89, under coach Cotton Fitzsimmons, Phoenix began a seven-year run of 50-plus victory seasons. Guard Kevin Johnson and forwards Eddie Johnson and Tom Chambers keyed the early charge, but it wasn't until the 1992 arrivals of Westphal as coach and Charles

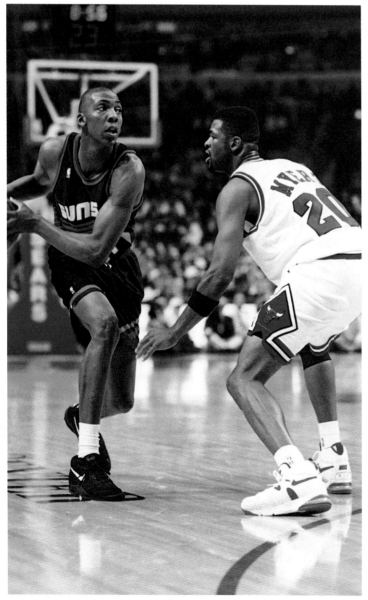

SUN SHINE *Wesley Person is a key member of the Suns' talented guard corps*

Facts and Figures

Conference/Division	Western/Pacific Division			
First Year in NBA	1968–69			
Arena (Capacity)	America West Arena (19,023)			
Former Cities/Nicknames	None			
NBA Finals Appearances	1976, 1993			
NBA Championships	None			
Playing Record	G	W	L	Pct.
Regular Season	2,296	1,246	1,050	.543
Playoffs	176	87	89	.494

Suns became consistent contenders who always seemed to be a big man away from a championship. The absence of a dominating center became a recurring theme.

In the early 1970s, Alcindor would have been a perfect fit for a team that featured Connie Hawkins, Dick Van Arsdale, Charlie Scott and Paul Silas. In 1975–76, a Suns team coached by John MacLeod won a modest 42 games but upended Seattle and Golden State in playoff series and advanced to the NBA Finals, where it lost in six games to Boston. That Suns team featured Paul Westphal, Alvan Adams, Van Arsdale and Curtis Perry with unspectacular Garfield Heard at center.

From 1977 to 1983, the Suns averaged more than 51 victories but failed to get past the Western Conference finals. Westphal, Adams and Walter Davis provided the firepower, 6–10 Larry Nance

Barkley as top gun that the Suns could return to the NBA Finals.

Barkley, a 6–6 power forward, led guards Johnson and Danny Ainge, swingman Dan Majerle and frontcourt players Cedric Ceballos and Oliver Miller through a franchise-record 62-victory season that was followed by an inspired 1993 playoff drive. But the Suns, soft in the middle, were thwarted by the Chicago Bulls.

The Suns appeared primed for another drive in 1994–95, but the season fell apart when newcomer Danny Manning suffered a season-ending knee injury and Barkley battled career-threatening back and knee problems.

Westphal was fired during a mediocre 1995–96 season and Fitzsimmons returned to direct a rebuilding project that had a nice backcourt foundation with Wesley Person, Elliot Perry and Michael Finley.

PORTLAND TRAIL BLAZERS

Fairy tale season is a magical memory

Bill Walton. Maurice Lucas. Lionel Hollins. Dave Twardzik. Bobby Gross. Larry Steele. The names are frozen in the memory of Portland fans who watched their 1976–77 Trail Blazers live out a fairy tale. For one glorious NBA season, Cinderella wore glass sneakers.

The script opened in 1970 when Portland began play with the Buffalo Braves and Cleveland Cavaliers as part of a three-team expansion. And true to expansion form, the Trail Blazers spent their first six seasons looking for a .500 season, a playoff berth and a coach with a plan.

Jack Ramsay had more than a plan when he arrived in 1976 as the 6-year-old franchise's fifth coach. He had a magic wand. He also had the 6-foot-11 Walton, who finally was healthy after two injury-plagued seasons. Walton, the former UCLA center, was ready to take his place in the middle of a Portland lineup that included Lucas, a frontcourt enforcer acquired by Ramsay, and Hollins, a talented guard.

With a healthy Walton scoring, rebounding and swatting away shots, the Blazers jumped from 37 to 49 victories and a second-place Pacific Division finish. Their first playoff appearance produced surprising first and second-round victories over Chicago and Denver. But the best was yet to come.

Portland swept the powerful Lakers and Kareem Abdul-Jabbar in the Western Conference finals and completed its shocking championship run by winning four consecutive games from Philadelphia after the Julius Erving-led 76ers had won the first two games of the NBA Finals. The fairy tale was complete.

Over the next two decades, Portland would make two more trips to the NBA Finals—and lose both times. The Blazers used the momentum of their 1977 success to build one of the NBA's most competitive franchises, but they never could match it.

The 1977–78 Blazers picked right up where they had left off, posting a franchise-record 58 victories. But Walton suffered a foot injury late in the season and hobbled through a quick playoff exit. The big redhead sat out the entire 1978–79 season and signed with San Diego a year later. Without Walton, the Blazers remained competitive, but seldom escaped the first playoff round.

It was during Ramsay's tenure that the Blazers made their best and worst decisions. The 1983 draft brought acrobatic guard Clyde Drexler, who would become one of the league's flashiest performers. In the 1984 draft, Portland selected 7–1 center Sam Bowie, passing up such future stars as Michael Jordan and Charles Barkley.

The Blazers stepped back into the spotlight in 1989–90 under Rick Adelman. A lineup featuring Drexler, master rebounder Buck Williams, forward Jerome Kersey and point guard Terry Porter posted consecutive seasons of 59, 63, 57 and 51 victories, won two division titles and made two more visits to the NBA Finals. One resulted in a five-game 1990 loss to Detroit, the other a six-game 1992 loss to Chicago.

Adelman departed after the 1994 playoffs and Drexler was traded early in 1995, putting new coach P.J. Carlesimo in a rebuilding mode. Carlesimo is trying to write a new fairy tale around such fresh characters as guard Kenny Anderson, forwards Rasheed Wallace and Clifford Robinson and 7–3 center Arvydas Sabonis.

SPECIAL DELIVERY *Guard Rod Strickland was traded in an offseason reshuffling*

Facts and Figures

Conference/Division	*Western/Pacific Division*			
First Year in NBA	*1970–71*			
Arena (Capacity)	*Rose Garden (21,500)*			
Former Cities/Nicknames	*None*			
NBA Finals Appearances	*1977, 1990, 1992*			
NBA Championships	*1977*			
Playing Record	G	W	L	Pct.
Regular Season	*2,132*	*1,129*	*1,003*	*.530*
Playoffs	*144*	*69*	*75*	*.479*

SACRAMENTO KINGS

A tale of five cities

They've logged more miles, lost more games and frustrated more fans than any team in NBA history. They've been "Royals", they've been "Kings" and they've been disappointments in five "home" cities on a long westward journey that took them south in the standings.

And the very things this itinerant franchise has been seeking—respect and success—are what it left behind when it moved from Rochester, N.Y., its first NBA home, to Cincinnati in 1957.

As the Rochester Royals, one of four National Basketball League franchises that jumped to the Basketball Association of America in 1948, Les Harrison's team had the tools to compete for a championship—center Arnie Risen and outstanding guards Bob Davies and Bobby Wanzer. But it didn't have big George Mikan, a barrier that would prove difficult to cross.

In three of the Royals' first four BAA/NBA seasons, they beat or tied Minneapolis for the division's best record. But that regular-season success translated into only one championship (1951) as Mikan and the Lakers captured five in six years.

After six consecutive winning seasons under Harrison, the Royals struggled through three losing campaigns and began looking elsewhere for relief. That "elsewhere" in 1957 turned out to be Cincinnati, which offered a larger population base, a more spacious arena and, most importantly, the opportunity to land University of Cincinnati all-everything guard Oscar Robertson with a territorial draft pick three years down the road.

The wait would be difficult, but worthwhile. After three disastrous seasons (33, 19 and 19 victories), the 6-foot-5 Robertson arrived with a 30.5-point rookie performance. Not surprisingly, the Royals jumped 14 games in the win column. In the Big O's second season, he averaged an incredible triple-double—30.8 points, 12.5 rebounds and 11.4 assists.

The Robertson era lived up to its billing for individual achievement, but fell short of team success. Despite surrounding Robertson with outstanding center Jerry Lucas and forwards Jack Twyman and Wayne Embry, the Royals managed only one big season—a 55–25 campaign that was short-circuited by powerful Boston in the 1964 Eastern Division finals.

Lucas was traded at the beginning of the 1969–70 season and Robertson was dealt a few months later, signaling the end of the Cincinnati era. Attendance dropped with the departure of the franchise's biggest stars and the journey west resumed in 1972.

For the next three seasons, the franchise operated as the Kansas City/Omaha Kings, splitting home games between the two midwestern cities. In 1975, the "Omaha" was dropped, but the losing continued. Despite such fine players as center Sam Lacey, guards Nate (Tiny) Archibald, Phil Ford and Reggie Theus and forward Scott Wedman, the Kings managed only four winning records and five post-season appearances in 13 years.

While the team has not found great success in Sacramento, it has found support. Even though the Kings did not give the city a winning record or a playoff victory in its first decade, fans continued to fill the 17,317-seat Arco Arena for every game. Their patience was rewarded by the 1995–96 team that qualified for postseason play and posted one victory over heavily favored Seattle.

Coach Garry St. Jean has built a young, competitive team around guards Mitch Richmond and Tyus Edney, forwards Walt Williams and Michael Smith and center Olden Polynice.

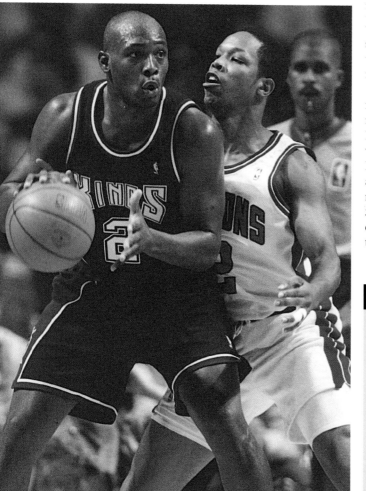

KING MITCH *Richmond is the fastest gun in Sacramento*

Facts and Figures

Conference/Division	*Western/Pacific Division*		
First Year in BAA/NBA	*1948–49*		
Arena (Capacity)	*ARCO Arena (17,317)*		
Former Cities/Nicknames	*Rochester Royals, 1948–57,*		
	Cincinnati Royals, 1957–72,		
	Kansas City-Omaha Kings, 1972–75,		
	Kansas City Kings, 1975–85		
NBA Finals Appearances	*1951*		
NBA Championships	*1951*		
Playing Record	**G**	**W**	**L**	**Pct.**
Regular Season	*3,777*	*1,731*	*2,046*	*.458*
Playoffs	*118*	*46*	*72*	*.390*

SAN ANTONIO SPURS
"Iceman" and "The Admiral": A tale of two eras

The San Antonio Spurs have never won a league championship or advanced to the NBA Finals. Before 1995, they had never even won two playoff series in the same season. When the postseason rolls around, they have been known to drop to the bottom of the playoff pool like a wet blanket.

But, oh the regular season! That's the time to watch basketball in San Antonio. Exciting. Fast. Lots of points. Lots of victories. Fun. "Iceman" and "The Admiral".

If NBA success was measured by regular-season results, the Spurs would rank among the game's most prestigious franchises. Since moving to the NBA in 1976, after nine unspectacular seasons in the ABA, the Spurs have won eight Central and Midwest Division titles, finished second four times and posted 47 or more victories 11 times.

And they've done it with flair. They led the league in scoring three of their first four NBA seasons and ranked anywhere from first to third for eight consecutive years. The Spurs, dating back to their ABA days as the Dallas and Texas Chaparrals, always have been able to put points on the board—from anywhere on the court.

From 1976, the year the Chaparrals moved to San Antonio, through 1985, many of those points came from 6–7 scoring machine George Gervin, alias "Iceman". Gervin, who liked to attack the basket with his silky, mesmerizing moves and beat his defender with a never-ending assortment of shots, won four scoring titles with averages ranging from 27.2 to 33.1 while helping the Spurs win five division titles.

Gervin was the centerpiece for an ever-changing cast that included such names as Larry Kenon, Billy Paultz, Ron Brewer, Mike Mitchell and Alvin Robertson. But never did he play with a dominating big man, which probably explains why the 1976–85 Spurs could do no better than three trips to the Western Conference finals.

Four years after Gervin's departure, San Antonio finally got that big man. The Spurs, coming off a 28-win season, grabbed 7–1 Navy center David Robinson with the first overall pick of the 1987 draft and then struggled through two more difficult seasons while Robinson completed his military commitment. The wait was worthwhile.

The Admiral arrived in 1989 and Larry Brown's Spurs stormed to 56 victories (35 more than the previous season) and a Midwest Division title. With able help from Terry Cummings, J.R. Reid, Willie Anderson, Dennis Rodman, Sean Elliott and Avery Johnson, the Spurs averaged more than 54 wins over the next six seasons and claimed three more Midwest titles.

The capper was a 62-victory cruise in 1994–95 under new Coach Bob Hill. With Rodman averaging 16.8 rebounds, the mobile Robinson was free to play more creatively. He averaged 27.6 points, 10.8 rebounds and claimed league MVP honors. San Antonio defeated Denver and the Los Angeles Lakers in the playoffs, but lost to Houston in a six-game Western Conference finals.

The volatile Rodman was gone in 1995–96, but the Spurs still raced to 59 victories and another division title—an effort that ended with another disappointing playoff loss, this one coming in the second round to Utah.

Facts and Figures

Conference/Division	Western/Midwest Division			
First Year in ABA/NBA	1967–68/1976–77			
Arena (Capacity)	Alamodome (20,662)			
Former Cities/Nicknames	Dallas Chaparrals, 1967–70, 1971–73,			
	Texas Chaparrals, 1970–71			
NBA Finals Appearances	None			
NBA Championships	None			
Playing Record	G	W	L	Pct.
ABA Regular Season	744	378	366	.508
NBA Regular Season	1,640	914	726	.557
ABA Playoffs	49	17	32	.347
NBA Playoffs	119	52	67	.437

MR. ROBINSON
David is Goliath as the center of attention in San Antonio's offense

SEATTLE SUPERSONICS

Teetering on the edge

They came out of nowhere to claim professional basketball's biggest prize, then quietly slipped back into middle-of-the-pack mediocrity. Now, more than a decade and a half later, the Seattle SuperSonics are standing again on the very brink of an NBA championship.

If history repeats itself, the Sonics will claim the 1997 top prize after falling two victories short in a 1996 NBA Finals loss to the high-powered Chicago Bulls. That's the way it worked in 1978 and '79, when the Sonics exploded into prominence without warning, earning consecutive NBA Finals appearances and their first championship. But nothing in the team's three-decade history has come without the element of surprise. When the team appeared headed for a championship in 1993–94 after posting a 63–19 record, it was humbled by Denver in the biggest opening-round playoff upset in league history.

Nothing in the Sonics' first 10 seasons prepared anybody for the shock of 1977–78. Born with the San Diego Rockets in 1967–68 as part of a two-team expansion, the Sonics struggled through their first seven seasons without quali-

fying for the playoffs and posted three winning records in their first 10. Five coaches tried their luck over that span, including former Boston great Bill Russell.

But it wasn't until Lenny Wilkens replaced Bob Hopkins after 22 games in 1977 that the team began to take shape. Wilkens, a former guard who had served as a player-coach for three of Seattle's early seasons, guided the team through a 42–18 stretch run that resulted in a 47–35 record and third-place finish in the Pacific Division.

With a frontcourt that included Jack Sikma and Marvin Webster and a guard rotation of Gus Williams, Dennis Johnson and "Downtown" Freddie Brown, the surprising Sonics shocked powerful Los Angeles, Portland and Denver in the early playoff rounds and fell just short of a championship in a seven-game NBA Finals loss to Washington.

There was no element of surprise in 1978–79 when the Sonics won 52 games, claimed their first division title and advanced again to the NBA Finals, where they beat the Bullets in five games. The franchise had its first championship in its 12th NBA season.

Wilkens coaxed a 56-win record out of the Sonics in 1979–80, but just as quickly as they had arisen from the dead, they slipped back into the pack. Players like Tom Chambers, Dale

FEARLESS IN SEATTLE *Shawn Kemp is a driving force for the Sonics*

Ellis and Xavier McDaniel sparkled in the 1980s, but the team did not make any more championship noise until George Karl arrived in 1991–92. And this time, expected to win, the Sonics stumbled badly.

Karl pieced together a fast-paced team that played furious defense and won 55 regular-season games in 1992–93. Guards Ricky Pierce and Gary Payton, forwards Shawn Kemp, Derrick McKey and Eddie Johnson and center Sam Perkins keyed a post-season effort that won two play-

off series and extended Phoenix to Game 7 of the Western Conference finals.

When offseason trades brought in forward Detlef Schrempf and guard Kendall Gill, the Sonics appeared primed for a championship run. But consecutive 63 and 57-victory seasons were followed by shocking first-round upset losses to Denver and Los Angeles. There was nothing shocking about 1995–96 as Seattle posted 64 victories and won three playoff series before losing to the Bulls.

Facts and Figures

Conference/Division	Western/Pacific Division			
First Year in NBA	1967–68			
Arena (Capacity)	Key Arena at Seattle Center (17,100)			
Former Cities/Nicknames	None			
NBA Finals Appearances	1978, 1979, 1996			
NBA Championships	1979			
Playing Record	G	W	L	Pct.
Regular Season	2,378	1,253	1,125	.527
Playoffs	174	87	87	.500

TORONTO RAPTORS
Oh Canada! Border Warfare, NBA-Style

HOT PROSPECTS *Guard Damon Stoudamire points the way for the rookie Raptors*

handling wizard sculpted in Thomas' basketball-playing image, completed his first NBA campaign as the league's outstanding rookie. He averaged 19 points and 9.3 assists per game, captured the hearts of the formerly skeptical Toronto fans with his exciting play and provided the hope and foundation for a bright future.

Stoudamire was the centerpiece for a first-year team that exceeded expectations and won 21 games, six more than expansion mate Vancouver and more than three of the four expansion teams (Miami, Charlotte, Orlando and Minnesota) did when they began play in the 1988–89 and 1989–90 seasons. The Raptors' roster had been stocked with reputed problem players made available by existing teams in the expansion draft, waiver-wire pickups and draft picks. Critics said the Raptors were short on size, long on immaturity and destined for a painful opening act.

But that was not the case. Stoudamire got help in the middle from burly Oliver Miller, a 6–9 center who had a history of weight problems. Miller averaged 12.9 points and 7.4 rebounds and rookie coach Brendan Malone got encouraging performances from 6–11 forward Sharone Wright and guard Doug Christie, two mid-

season pickups, and small forward Tracy Murray, a strong outside shooter. Leadership was supplied by veteran shooting guard Alvin Robertson.

But the real measure of Toronto's first-year success was provided by the same fans who had booed Thomas and Stoudamire on draft day 1995. The rookie team averaged 23,178 at the spacious SkyDome (the third-best figure in the league) and the Raptors challenged the Maple Leafs as the hottest ticket in a hockey-obsessed town.

That's exactly the kind of response the NBA had hoped for when Toronto was awarded a franchise in November 1993 as part of a two-team Canadian expansion. It marked the first location of an NBA team outside the United States since 1946–47, the league's inaugural season as the Basketball Association of America. The Toronto Huskies were members of that first circuit, but they folded after playing one season.

The one glitch in Toronto's debut was detected the day after the 1995–96 season ended. The 54-year-old Malone was replaced by 35-year-old assistant Darrell Walker. It gave the fledgling Raptors a younger presence on the bench.

Isiah Thomas, who always made the right decisions as a 13-year point guard for the Detroit Pistons, had to doubt his first big player move as part owner and rookie general manager of the expansion Toronto Raptors. Momentarily, at least.

When NBA Commissioner David Stern announced to the record draft crowd of 21,268 at Toronto's SkyDome that the hometown Raptors had selected 5-foot-10 Arizona point guard Damon Stoudamire with the seventh overall pick, boos cascaded through the arena like a swarm of hockey players through the crease. It quickly became clear that NBA life north of the border would not be a layup.

But less than a year later, Isiah Thomas the front-office guru was already looking every bit as sharp as Isiah Thomas the playmaker. Stoudamire, a fast-shooting, ball-

Facts and Figures

Conference/Division	*Eastern/Central Division*			
First Year in NBA	*1995–96*			
Arena (Capacity)	*SkyDome (23,178)*			
Former Cities/Nicknames	*None*			
NBA Finals Appearances	*None*			
NBA Championships	*None*			
Playing Record	G	W	L	Pct.
Regular Season	82	21	61	.256
Playoffs	0	0	0	—

UTAH JAZZ

A different kind of jazz

Before it had a nickname, before it even had a coach, the expansion New Orleans team had a superstar. When Pistol Pete Maravich arrived as the foundation for the NBA's 18th franchise in 1974, he provided an instant following, if not a long-range blueprint for success.

The flamboyant Maravich, one of the greatest ballhandling magicians ever to put on a uniform, had been a collegiate scoring machine at Louisiana State University and promised New Orleans fans excitement, if not victories. But he did not come cheaply.

To acquire Maravich from Atlanta, the team had to surrender two players and four draft picks—two No. 1s and 2s. Maravich indeed brought an entertaining, swashbuckling style to New Orleans, but without draft picks, management could never provide him with help. Pistol Pete won one NBA scoring title in five New Orleans seasons, but the team point guard John Stockton in 1984 and 6-9 Karl Malone, a.k.a. The Mailman, in 1985. Only a judgment error kept the Jazz from becoming a dominant team: Wilkins was traded to Atlanta for John Drew and Freeman Williams, a pair of aging guards.

After four unproductive seasons in Utah, the Jazz suddenly blossomed into playoff contenders. The transformation took place in 1983–84 under Frank Layden, who guided Utah to the franchise's first Midwest Division

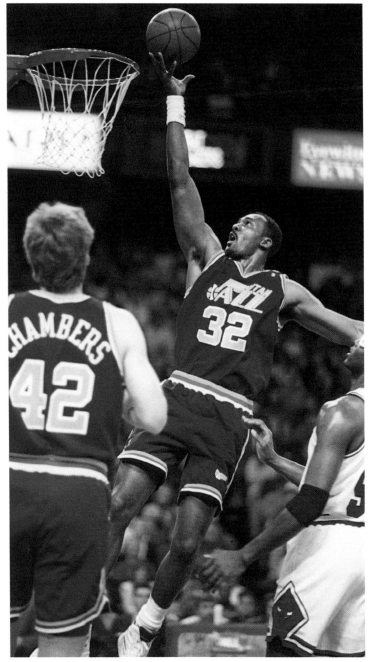

THE MAILMAN *Powerful Karl Malone delivers for Utah*

Facts and Figures

Conference/Division	Western/Midwest Division			
First Year in NBA	1974–75			
Arena (Capacity)	Delta Center (19,911)			
Former Cities/Nicknames	New Orleans Jazz (1974–79)			
NBA Finals Appearances	None			
NBA Championships	None			
Playing Record	G	W	L	Pct.
Regular Season	1,804	917	887	.508
Playoffs	100	45	55	.450

never won more than 39 games and was doomed to failure.

With Maravich in the lineup, management settled on a nickname that would reflect the spirited nature of the city and its famed French Quarter. But, ironically, when new ownership bought the team and relocated it to Salt Lake City in 1979, a city that was politically, religiously and socially conservative inherited a team and nickname that was none of those things.

But life in Utah agreed with the Jazz, a team that had gone through three coaches in its inaugural season and four in five years. The new ownership quickly began overhauling the roster, trading for high-scoring forward Adrian Dantley and letting a disgruntled Maravich buy out his contract.

From 1980 through 1985, the Jazz stocked their roster with a succession of outstanding draft picks. Guard Darrell Griffith arrived in 1980, forward Dominique Wilkins in 1982, 6-foot-11 Thurl Bailey in 1983, title and first playoff berth after nine misses.

The Jazz would not miss again, either under Layden or Jerry Sloan, his successor. Dantley and Griffith provided the firepower for a few years. Then Malone and Stockton developed into one of the best inside-outside combinations ever to play. Malone was devastating around the basket and Stockton, the greatest assist and steal man in NBA history, got him the ball.

With a supporting cast that included Bailey, 7-4 shot-blocker Mark Eaton and eventually guard Jeff Hornacek, the Jazz blossomed under Sloan, topping 50 victories in seven of his first eight years. They reached the Western Conference finals in 1992, '94 and '96, but couldn't take that next major step.

With Malone, Stockton and Hornacek in the lineup, that "next step" could come at any time. The maturity of small forward Chris Morris could make that step a little easier.

VANCOUVER GRIZZLIES

Bearing Down in the Great Northwest

BIG COUNTRY *Bryant Reeves made a sizeable impact in his rookie season*

to be founded on solid ground. The holes on their roster are obvious and the talent from top to bottom is precariously thin, but they do still have some reasons for optimism.

Such as burly 7-foot center Bryant Reeves, who averaged 13.1 points and 7.4 rebounds while showing a steady improvement throughout his rookie season. "Big Country," the 1995 draft's sixth overall pick and Vancouver's first-ever draft choice, more than lived up to the expectations of rookie coach Brian Winters.

Encouragement also was provided by point guard Greg Anthony, shooting guard Blue Edwards and rookie forward Ashraf Amaya. Anthony and Edwards were expansion-draft pickups, as was guard Byron Scott, who gave the Grizzlies a veteran presence. Adding to the optimism was a 1996 draft in which Vancouver owned three of the first 40 picks and Jackson's promise to look long and hard at top players on the free-agent market.

The Vancouver franchise was awarded in April 1994, more than five months after expansion mate Toronto had broken the long NBA border barrier. The Toronto Huskies had played for one season (1946–47) as charter

members of the Basketball Association of America, but no other franchise had existed outside the United States for almost five decades until the Raptors were born. The Vancouver market was viewed as enthusiastic and fertile, qualities that were confirmed in the Grizzlies' first season.

But nothing came easy in the team's formative process. After preparing more than a year for the expansion and college drafts, the Grizzlies made their choices and then had to endure an owners' lockout that kept them from even contacting their new players. The two expansion teams also were hobbled by an $18-million salary cap—about three-quarters of what the other teams had to work with—and they were not allowed a lottery No. 1 pick until 1999. So goes life in the expansion world.

But, everything considered, things could be worse. The Grizzlies head into their uncertain future with patient fans, a 7-foot center who should only get better and the front-office backing to buy free-agent players and time for the evolutionary process to work naturally.

That's a lot more than many long-existing franchises have to work with.

They suffered through a 23-game losing streak, the second longest in the history of the NBA, and another of 19 games. They won only 15 times, tying Dallas and Miami for the fewest victories by a first-year expansion team. At times they looked totally overmatched and out of synch. At others they appeared lost in the shadows of their NBA brethren. But through it all, Vancouver players, team officials and fans refused to let themselves get discouraged.

"Some of the rules of expansion lend themselves to a slow growth process," said General Manager Stu Jackson.

With a solid season-ticket base of more than 13,500 at the 20,004-seat General Motors Place and patient fans who seem understanding and willing to let the franchise take a natural expansion course, the Grizzlies appear

Facts and Figures				
Conference/Division	*Western/Midwest Division*			
First Year in NBA	*1995–96*			
Arena (Capacity)	*General Motors Place (20,004)*			
Former Cities/Nicknames	*None*			
NBA Finals Appearances	*None*			
NBA Championships	*None*			
Playing Record	G	W	L	Pct.
Regular Season	82	15	67	.183
Playoffs	0	0	0	—

WASHINGTON BULLETS

Shooting for the stars

DOUBLE TROUBLE *Washington's Chris Webber (left) and Juwan Howard*

When the team made its debut in 1961 as the NBA's first expansion franchise, nobody realized the road it would travel in search of an identity. From the aromatic stockyards of Chicago to the more traditional venues of Baltimore and Washington D.C., the Bullets' NBA journey has been both bumpy and exciting.

The team entered the NBA as the Chicago Packers and played its games in the Chicago Amphitheater, which was located next to the stockyards. Perhaps believing that a little west wind might dissipate the smell of hogs, cattle and the team's shoddy play, management changed the nickname from "Packers" to "Zephyrs" for its second season.

But not even the outstanding rookie play of center Walt Bellamy in 1961–62 or the arrival of forward Terry Dischinger in 1962–63 could sell Chicago fans on NBA life and the need for a new arena. So team owners packed up their franchise and moved it to the more friendly confines of Baltimore. Playing their third season with their third nickname, the "Bullets" topped the 30-victory mark for the first time and began building for a promising future.

That future began to take shape in 1967 with three important developments: the arrival of coach Gene Shue, the drafting of guard Earl (The Pearl) Monroe and a switch to the Eastern Division. When the Bullets grabbed a 6-foot-7, 245-pound wide body named Wes Unseld in 1968, they positioned themselves for the most glorious decade in franchise history.

With Monroe and Kevin Loughery in the backcourt and Gus Johnson, Jack Marin and Unseld up front, the 1968–69 Bullets rolled to their first winning record (57–25), their first division championship and a playoff appearance that ended in a first-round sweep. But that was merely an appetizer.

Over the next 10 seasons, the Bullets would win six more division titles, finish second three times and make four appearances in the NBA Finals. They also would win the franchise's lone championship—a 1978 Finals victory over Seattle. That team was coached by Dick Motta and still featured the rugged Unseld in the middle. It also included high-scoring Elvin Hayes, rebounding ace Bob Dandridge, Mitch Kupchak and guards Kevin Grevey and Phil Chenier. When the Sonics avenged that loss with a five-game 1979 Finals victory over the Bullets, the team's era of prominence came to an end.

The Bullets, who had moved to Washington in 1973 and spent one season as the "Capital Bullets" before adopting their current name, self-destructed in the 1980s, beginning with the retirement of Unseld and the 1981 trade of the aging Hayes. Over the next 16 seasons, the Bullets managed only three winning records under Gene Shue, Loughery, Unseld and current coach Jim Lynam.

But that long period of desolation could end quickly. Under the up-tempo Lynam, the Bullets have assembled a young and talented frontcourt featuring 6–10 Chris Webber, 6–9 Juwan Howard and 7–7 center Gheorghe Muresan. An offseason trade for Portland's Rod Strickland gave Lynam the top-notch point guard he needs to go with shooting guard Calbert Cheaney.

Facts and Figures

Conference/Division	*Eastern/Atlantic Division*		
First Year in NBA	*1961–62*		
Arena (Capacity)	*USAir Arena (18,756)*		
Former Cities/Nicknames	*Chicago Packers, 1961–62,*		
	Chicago Zephyrs, 1962–63,		
	Baltimore Bullets, 1963–73,		
	Capital Bullets, 1973–74		
NBA Finals Appearances	*1971, 1975, 1978, 1979*		
NBA Championships	*1978*		
Playing Record	**G**	**W**	**L**	**Pct.**
Regular Season	*2,859*	*1,334*	*1,525*	*.467*
Playoffs	*163*	*69*	*94*	*.423*

NBA Statistics

All-time regular season records

Atlanta Hawks	W	L	Pct.
Home	1,133	594	.656
Road	624	1,073	.368
Neutral	127	163	.438
Overall	1,884	1,830	.507

Boston Celtics	W	L	Pct.
Home	1,309	447	.745
Road	911	930	.495
Neutral	202	88	.697
Overall	2,422	1,465	.623

Charlotte Hornets	W	L	Pct.
Home	168	160	.512
Road	104	224	.317
Neutral	0	0	.000
Overall	272	384	.415

Chicago Bulls	W	L	Pct.
Home	791	417	.655
Road	494	693	.416
Neutral	31	33	.484
Overall	1,316	1,143	.535

Cleveland Cavaliers	W	L	Pct.
Home	623	443	.584
Road	324	731	.307
Neutral	6	5	.545
Overall	953	1,179	.447

Dallas Mavericks	W	L	Pct.
Home	336	320	.512
Road	205	451	.313
Neutral	0	0	.000
Overall	541	771	.412

Denver Nuggets	W	L	Pct.
Home	561	259	.684
Road	255	565	.311
Neutral	0	0	.000
Overall	816	824	.498

Detroit Pistons	W	L	Pct.
Home	1,065	684	.609
Road	574	1,127	.337
Neutral	144	182	.442
Overall	1,783	1,993	.472

Golden State Warriors	W	L	Pct.
Home	1,088	681	.615
Road	625	1,193	.344
Neutral	165	130	.559
Overall	1,878	2,004	.484

Houston Rockets	W	L	Pct.
Home	736	429	.632
Road	407	749	.352
Neutral	25	32	.439
Overall	1,168	1,210	.491

Indiana Pacers	W	L	Pct.
Home	495	325	.604
Road	242	578	.295
Neutral	0	0	.000
Overall	737	903	.449

Los Angeles Clippers	W	L	Pct.
Home	520	532	.494
Road	248	804	.236
Neutral	10	18	.357
Overall	778	1,354	.365

Los Angeles Lakers	W	L	Pct.
Home	1,299	458	.739
Road	854	906	.485
Neutral	139	121	.535
Overall	2,292	1,485	.607

Miami Heat	W	L	Pct.
Home	165	162	.505
Road	82	247	.249
Neutral	0	0	.000
Overall	247	409	.377

Milwaukee Bucks	W	L	Pct.
Home	764	358	.681
Road	483	652	.426
Neutral	24	15	.615
Overall	1,271	1,025	.554

Minnesota Timberwolves	W	L	Pct.
Home	101	186	.352
Road	51	236	.178
Neutral	0	0	.000
Overall	152	422	.265

New Jersey Nets	W	L	Pct.
Home	433	387	.528
Road	227	593	.277
Neutral	0	0	.000
Overall	660	980	.402

New York Knicks	W	L	Pct..
Home	1,130	677	.625
Road	719	1,093	.397
Neutral	130	133	.494
Overall	1,979	1,904	.510

Orlando Magic	W	L	Pct.
Home	183	104	.638
Road	95	192	.331
Neutral	0	0	.000
Overall	278	296	.484

Philadelphia 76ers	W	L	Pct.
Home	1,171	526	.690
Road	703	1,018	.408
Neutral	161	133	.548
Overall	2,035	1,677	.548

Phoenix Suns	W	L	Pct.
Home	803	337	.704
Road	434	695	.384
Neutral	9	18	.333
Overall	1,246	1,050	.543

Portland Trail Blazers	W	L	Pct.
Home	740	323	.696
Road	387	668	.367
Neutral	2	12	.143
Overall	1,129	1,003	.530

Sacramento Kings	W	L	Pct.
Home	1,057	676	.610
Road	525	1,228	.299
Neutral	149	142	.512
Overall	1,731	2,046	.458

San Antonio Spurs	W	L	Pct.
Home	581	239	.709
Road	333	487	.406
Neutral	0	0	.000
Overall	914	726	.557

Seattle SuperSonics	W	L	Pct.
Home	791	373	.680
Road	444	721	.381
Neutral	18	31	.367
Overall	1,253	1,125	.527

Toronto Raptors	W	L	Pct.
Home	15	26	.366
Road	6	35	.146
Neutral	0	0	.000
Overall	21	61	.256

Utah Jazz	W	L	Pct.
Home	612	290	.678
Road	305	597	.338
Neutral	0	0	.000
Overall	917	887	.508

Vancouver Grizzlies	W	L	Pct.
Home	10	31	.244
Road	5	36	.122
Neutral	0	0	.000
Overall	15	67	.183

Washington Bullets	W	L	Pct.
Home	822	543	.602
Road	455	888	.339
Neutral	57	94	.377
Overall	1,334	1,525	.467

Divisional, Conference and NBA Titles

Team	Div. Titles	Conf. Champ.	NBA Champ.
Atlanta Hawks	10	4	1
Boston Celtics	24	19	16
Charlotte Hornets	0	0	0
Chicago Bulls	5	4	4
Cleveland Cavaliers	1	0	0
Dallas Mavericks	1	0	0
Denver Nuggets	4	0	0
Detroit Pistons	6	5	2
Golden State Warriors	7	6	3
Houston Rockets	4	4	2
Indiana Pacers	1	0	0
Los Angeles Clippers	0	0	0
Los Angeles Lakers	25	24	11
Miami Heat	0	0	0
Milwaukee Bucks	12	2	1
Minnesota Timberwolves	0	0	0
New Jersey Nets	0	0	0
New York Knicks	8	7	2
Orlando Magic	2	1	0
Philadelphia 76ers	11	8	3
Phoenix Suns	3	2	0
Portland Trail Blazers	3	3	1
Sacramento Kings	4	1	1
San Antonio Spurs	9	0	0
Seattle SuperSonics	3	3	1
Toronto Raptors	0	0	0
Utah Jazz	3	0	0
Vancouver Grizzlies	0	0	0
Washington Bullets	7	4	1

LEGENDS OF THE NBA

KAREEM ABDUL-JABBAR
The Sky Is the Limit

CHARLES BARKLEY
The Round Mound of Rebound

RICK BARRY
A Golden Warrior

ELGIN BAYLOR
The Lakers' Mr. Inside

LARRY BIRD
The Birdman of Boston

WILT CHAMBERLAIN
The Offensive Machine

BOB COUSY
The Razzle-Dazzle Man

JULIUS ERVING
Dr. J

PATRICK EWING
New York's Middle Man

WALT FRAZIER
The Knicks' Clyde

JOHN HAVLICEK
Keep on Running

MAGIC JOHNSON
Weaving a Magic Spell

MICHAEL JORDAN
His Royal Highness

MOSES MALONE
Finding the Promised Land

GEORGE MIKAN
The First Big Man

HAKEEM OLAJUWON
The Dream Lives On

BOB PETTIT
Soaring With the Hawks

OSCAR ROBERTSON
The Big O

BILL RUSSELL
Celtics' Cornerstone

JERRY WEST
The Lakers' Mr. Outside

Like thieves in the night, they sneak into our consciousness, steal our hearts and slip away all too soon, leaving only memories of their wondrous feats. They leave traces of their basketball brilliance scattered throughout the NBA record book and they provide a stronger foundation upon which a whole new generation can build.

Nothing illuminates a sport more dramatically than its brightest stars and the NBA's have come in many shapes, sizes and forms. Wilt Chamberlain electrified fans with his size, strength and offensive skills; Bob Cousy dazzled them with his ballhandling wizardry. Bill Russell was a devastating rebounder and shot-blocker; Jerry West was a long-range shooting machine. Oscar Robertson could do all of the above, as could Magic Johnson, the tallest point guard in league history.

And they lit up NBA arenas with their charisma and their style as well as their athletic skills. Who will forget the above-the-rim theatrics of Julius Erving and Michael Jordan? Or the championship presence of John Havlicek, Larry Bird and Kareem Abdul-Jabbar? And what serious fan can help but appreciate the defensive brilliance of Walt Frazier or the power and domination of big man George Mikan?

Winning teams and championships are at the heart of professional basketball, but star power is its soul. It's the stuff legends are made of.

DOUBLE DREAM *Olympic gold medalists Michael Jordan (left), Magic Johnson*

56

ABDUL-JABBAR

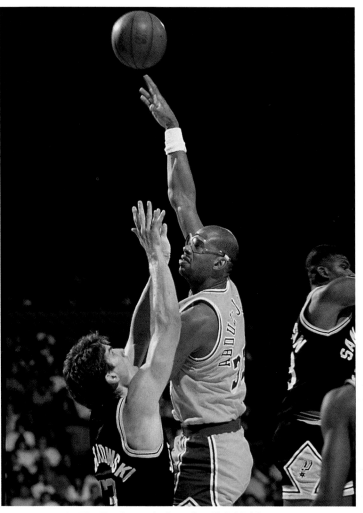

OVER THE TOP *The Sky Hook was the limit for Abdul-Jabbar*

Career Highlights

1969 Closed out college career after leading UCLA to three NCAA championships; selected by Bucks with first overall pick of draft.
1970 Made first of record 18 appearances in All-Star Game; named Rookie of the Year.
1971 Led Bucks to NBA championship; named regular-season MVP for first of six times; named NBA Finals MVP.
1974 Led Bucks to NBA Finals and earned third MVP award.
1975 Traded to Lakers as part of blockbuster six-player deal.
1980 Helped Lakers win NBA championship, the first of five they would win in the decade; named to NBA 35th Anniversary All-Time Team.
1984 Scored career point 31,420 to break Wilt Chamberlain's all-time record.
1989 Retired after record 20 seasons.
1995 Elected to the Naismith Memorial Hall of Fame.

> **❝ If there's been anyone any better, he'd have to be a heck of an athlete. ❞**

Bob Lanier, former Milwaukee and Detroit center.

He entered the NBA in 1969 as Lew Alcindor and left it 20 years later as Kareem Abdul-Jabbar. Over the course of 20 record seasons, he piled up more games (1,560), more minutes (57,446), more points (38,387) and more blocked shots (3,189) than any player in history.

While it's difficult to proclaim the 7-foot-2 Abdul-Jabbar as the best center in history, it's not a stretch to call him the most durable and consistent.

Three things set Abdul-Jabbar apart from previous big men: his agility around the basket, a dedication that allowed him to play until age 42 and, of course, the "sky hook."

Abdul-Jabbar fought his first NBA battles in 1969–70 for the Milwaukee Bucks. He had led UCLA to an unprecedented three consecutive national championships and he arrived amid predictions of Wilt Chamberlain-like offensive numbers.

He did nothing to discourage such talk in his first four Milwaukee seasons. Unveiling his unstoppable sky hook, Abdul-Jabbar averaged 28.8 points and 14.5 rebounds en route to 1970 Rookie of the Year honors and followed that with two scoring titles. He also led the 3-year-old Bucks to a 1971 championship.

But when the Bucks complied with Abdul-Jabbar's trade request in 1975 and sent him to the Lakers, critics were pointing to a scoring average that had dipped into the mid-20s and a playing style that relied on finesse. He never won a scoring title with the Lakers, but the team won five championships, all after Magic Johnson arrived in 1979. With Johnson running the show and Abdul-Jabbar playing his consistent all-around game, the Lakers became the scourge of the 1980s.

"I always appreciated his talents," said Bob Lanier, a Hall of Fame center for Detroit and Milwaukee. "The perfection of that one shot enabled him to endure time"

Abdul-Jabbar would get the ball on either side of the paint, back his defender toward the basket, pivot and extend either of his long arms to deliver a hook that seldom missed.

When Abdul-Jabbar retired in 1989, he might have been the most honored athlete in NBA history: six MVP awards; 10 first-team All-NBA selections; five selections to the All-Defensive first team; two playoff MVPs. And, of course, those six precious championship rings.

He's brash, arrogant, cocky, outspoken and controversial. But whenever Charles Barkley speaks, people listen.

On the court, he speaks to the NBA's big men with a dominating game that belies his 6-foot-6 (some claim he's only 6–4) height. What he lacks in height, he makes up for with a solid 250-pound girth that he uses to clear away defenders and a quick leaping ability that he uses to pull down rebounds and score points. But his greatest asset is a fierce determination to succeed.

"Hey, all I want to do is win," says Barkley. "Anybody who doesn't like that can just get out of the way."

From the time Barkley was drafted by Philadelphia in 1984, it was apparent he liked to win. He had done so at Auburn before leaving after his junior season. And he would do so with the 76ers, adding muscle to a lineup that included Julius Erving and Moses Malone. The 76ers won 58 games in Barkley's rookie season and 54 in 1985–86, when the youngster averaged 20 points and 12.8 rebounds.

Free to express his basketball talents, Barkley began muscling with the big boys and running with the little guys, demonstrating a surprising shooting range from the paint to the 3-point line. His all-around talent was impressive: In 1986–87, Barkley became the shortest rebounding champion in NBA history; in 1992–93, he led the league with six triple-doubles.

With the departure of Malone in 1986 and Erving in '87, the 76ers became Barkley's team. He earned All-NBA first-team honors four straight seasons and performed his duties with a fervent emotion that made fans, and opponents, take note.

"He can do anything he wants to on a floor," said Mychal Thompson, a former Portland and Los Angeles forward. "When he gets the ball, he's as close to unstoppable as any player I've seen."

Chuck Daly, a former Cleveland, Detroit and New Jersey coach, agreed. "He's one of a handful of players who can go out and win a game by himself," he said.

That's almost what Sir Charles had to do in Philadelphia. Not blessed with a lot of help after Erving's departure, Barkley kept the 76ers respectable but couldn't get them deep into the playoffs. In 1992, he was traded to Phoenix and he tuned up for his new beginning by playing for the U.S. Dream Team in the Barcelona Olympics.

Barkley enjoyed his best professional season in 1992–93 when he averaged 25.6 points and 12.2 rebounds en route to league MVP honors. But he fell short of his biggest goal, a championship, when the Suns advanced to the NBA Finals and lost a six-game series to Chicago.

After entertaining thoughts of retirement because of back problems, Barkley returned in 1994 and '95 to chase his elusive dream. But the Suns, beset by injuries, sank in the standings and Barkley's title hopes did likewise. He was forced to take consolation with his 1996 selection to Dream Team III.

Statistics

BORN: Feb. 20, 1963, Leeds, Ala.;
HEIGHT: 6–6   **WEIGHT:** 252
COLLEGE: Auburn (left after junior season)
PRO TEAMS:
Philadelphia 76ers, 1984–92; Phoenix Suns, 1992–present
NBA CAREER AVERAGES:
23.3 ppg; 11.6 rpg; 3.9 apg
NBA PLAYOFF AVERAGES:
24.4 ppg; 13.3 rpg; 4.1 apg

Career Highlights

1984 Gave up final year of college eligibility and was selected by 76ers with fifth overall pick of draft.
1987 Became shortest player to lead league in rebounding, averaging 14.6; selected to first All-Star Game.
1988 Earned first of four consecutive All-NBA first-team selections with 28.3-point and 11.9-rebound averages.
1991 Grabbed 22 rebounds and earned All-Star Game MVP honors.
1992 Traded to Suns for three players; played for U.S. on gold medal-winning Dream Team at Barcelona Olympic Games.
1993 Finished season with league-leading six triple-doubles; led Suns to NBA Finals, where they lost six-game battle to Bulls; named regular-season MVP.
1994 Scored career-high 56 points in first-round playoff game against Golden State.
1996 Played for Dream Team III in the Atlanta Olympic Games

❝ I want to win an NBA championship. Not a day goes by that I don't think about it. I will get it someday, or I'll die trying. ❞

Charles Barkley

ROUND MOUND *Barkley's physical shortcomings are an NBA illusion*

BARRY

Statistics

BORN: March 28, 1944, at Elizabeth, N.J.
HEIGHT: 6–7   **WEIGHT:** 220
COLLEGE: Miami (Fla.)
PRO TEAMS:
San Francisco/Golden State Warriors, 1965–67, 1972–78; Oakland Oaks/ Washington Capitols (ABA), 1968–70; New York Nets (ABA), 1970–72; Houston Rockets, 1978–80
NBA CAREER AVERAGES:
23.2 ppg; 6.5 rpg; 5.1 apg
NBA PLAYOFF AVERAGES:
24.8 ppg; 5.6 rpg; 4.6 apg

Career Highlights

1965 Closed college career by leading nation with a 37.4-point average; picked by Warriors in first round of NBA draft.
1966 Averaged 25.7 points and 10.6 rebounds while earning Rookie of the Year honors.
1967 Named MVP in All-Star Game; won scoring title with 35.6 average; led Warriors to NBA Finals; signed as free agent with ABA's Oaks; sat out 1967–68 season under court order.
1969 Captured ABA scoring title with 34-point average and led Oaks to ABA championship.
1970 Traded by Capitols to Nets.
1972 Returned to NBA's Warriors; earned first free-throw percentage title.
1975 Led Warriors to championship; named NBA Finals MVP; led league with 2.85 steals per game; earned fourth of five All-NBA first-team citations.
1978 Signed with Rockets as free agent.
1980 Retired with ABA/NBA combined point total of 25,279.
1986 Elected to Hall of Fame.

DRIVE TIME *Slashing past defenders was a Rick Barry specialty*

It was no coincidence that Rick Barry looked familiar to NBA opponents when he took his first dribbles toward Rookie of the Year honors with the San Francisco Warriors in 1965–66.

"Barry is a young Elgin Baylor," said Boston defensive ace Tom (Satch) Sanders at the time. "Rick gives you that quick little fake and then he's gone."

"I'm no Baylor," responded Barry, a 6-foot-7 forward, "but I'd like to be. Most of the moves I've got I copied from Elgin. I've been studying Baylor's floor game for a long time. But my shots are my own. I've always been able to shoot."

Nobody could dispute that claim. Barry shot his way to a collegiate national scoring title (37.4 points per game) as a senior at the University of Miami. After his Rookie of the Year campaign, he led the NBA with a 35.6-point average and combined with 6–11 center Nate Thurmond to lead the Warriors to the 1967 NBA Finals, where they lost to Wilt Chamberlain and the Philadelphia 76ers.

The intense and outspoken Barry was on his way to stardom, the toast of San Francisco. But with greatness at his fingertips, Barry made a controversial decision that would tarnish his Golden Boy image. He agreed to a free-agent contract with the rival ABA's Oakland Oaks, touching off a long and bitter legal tussle that would not be forgotten for years.

Barry was forced to the sideline in 1967–68, while the NBA and ABA were haggling in court. But he returned to action with a vengeance in 1968–69, leading the ABA with a 34-point average

and propelling the Oaks to the ABA championship.

From that point on, Barry became a self-described basketball gypsy. The next three ABA seasons would take him to Washington, New York and back to the NBA, via court order. When he rejoined the renamed Golden State Warriors for 1972–73, he was greeted by unsympathetic fans who perceived him as a traitor and criticized the emotional playing style they had once found endearing.

Not only could Barry create shots and instant points in the long-admired Baylor style, he was one of the game's best passing forwards, a clutch rebounder and a quick defender who led the league one season in steals. He was unmatched as a free-throw shooter, using his throwback underhand style to hit an NBA-record 90 percent of his career tosses.

Barry's best NBA season came in 1974–75, when he averaged 30.6 points and 6.2 assists while leading an overachieving Golden State team to its only West Coast championship. When the Warriors swept heavily-favored Washington in the Finals, he was named MVP.

Barry retired in 1980 after two seasons with Houston. Over 14 years, he carried a 24.8 professional scoring average and the distinction of being the only player to lead both the NBA and ABA in scoring. He also was a five-time All-NBA first-team selection and a six-time free-throw percentage champion.

❝ There is no doubt Rick's on-court demeanor hurt his image. But, boy, he sure could play. ❞

Butch Beard, former Warriors teammate.

BAYLOR

Statistics

BORN: Sept. 16, 1934, Washington, D.C.
HEIGHT: 6–5   **WEIGHT:** 225
COLLEGE: The College of Idaho; Seattle
PRO TEAM:
Minneapolis/Los Angeles Lakers 1958–72
NBA CAREER AVERAGES:
27.4 ppg; 13.5 rpg; 4.3 apg
NBA PLAYOFF AVERAGES:
27.0 ppg; 12.9 rpg; 4.0 apg

Career Highlights

1958 Led Seattle to finals of NCAA Tournament, where it lost to Kentucky; selected first overall by Lakers in NBA draft.
1959 Named All-Star Game co-MVP; set NBA single-game scoring record with 64 points against Boston; led Lakers to first of eight NBA Finals appearances (all losses) in 12 years; named Rookie of the Year; became All-NBA first-team selection for first of 10 times.
1960 Scored NBA-record 71 points against New York.
1962 Averaged 38.3 points for season, second only to Chamberlain's 50.4 mark of same season; scored NBA Finals-record 61 points in game against Boston.
1972 Played only nine games because of knee problems and watched Lakers capture first NBA championship; retired with 23,149 career points and 11,463 rebounds.
1976 Elected to Naismith Memorial Hall of Fame.
1980 Named to NBA 35th Anniversary All-Time Team.

❝ Sometimes you think he's got to eat the ball, but he's still hanging up there in the air, shooting or passing. ❞

John Kundla, former Minneapolis Lakers coach.

HANGING LOOSE *The acrobatic Baylor used every trick to deliver his creative shots*

All he needed was a tiny hole, a defensive crack that most players would not even notice. Suddenly, before anybody realized what was happening, Elgin Baylor would slice through, make an impossible cut to the basket and deliver two points.

Or Baylor would use his burly 6-foot-5 frame to back a helpless defender into the paint, turn and hang in the air until an opening developed for his deadly jump shot. Or he would simply post up the defender and fire a turn-around jumper; or a pinpoint pass to an open teammate. Whatever Baylor needed, he would simply dip into his bag of offensive tricks.

"He just floats," marveled John Kundla, Baylor's coach when he joined the Minneapolis Lakers in 1958. "For a man who weighs 225 pounds, I've never seen that kind of timing. The man amazes me."

Baylor, who spent his entire 14-year career with the Lakers, amazed more than Kundla. He averaged 24.9 points and 15 rebounds en route to Rookie of the Year honors in 1958–59 and increased his totals dramatically over his first four seasons, posting eye-popping totals of 38.3 points, 18.6 rebounds and 4.6 assists in 1961–62. And when he got into the scoring groove, he was virtually unstoppable.

He broke the NBA single-game record when he scored 64 points against Boston in 1959 and lifted the mark to 71 a year later against New York. In a 1962 NBA Finals game against the Celtics, Baylor poured in a record 61.

After leading the University of Seattle to the NCAA Tournament final in 1958, Baylor was selected first overall by the Lakers in the draft. He immediately lifted the sagging Minneapolis franchise back to respectability and when the team moved to Los Angeles in 1960, he was joined by hot-shooting guard Jerry West.

The Baylor/West tandem became synonymous with Lakers basketball and soon Los Angeles was a serious title contender. But the road to an NBA championship traveled through Boston in the 1960s and the Celtics proved more than the Lakers could handle. Eight times Baylor/West teams reached the NBA Finals and eight times they lost, seven to the Celtics. The closest Baylor came to a championship was 1972, a career-ending season in which he played only nine games, none in the playoffs, while the Lakers won their first title since moving to Los Angeles.

By that time, Baylor was only a shell of his former self, a victim of knee problems that plagued him consistently from the early 1960s until the end of his career. He finished with 27.4-point and 13.5-rebound averages, Hall of Fame numbers in anybody's book.

Statistics

BORN: Dec. 7, 1956, West Baden, Ind.
HEIGHT: 6–9   **WEIGHT:** 220
COLLEGE: Indiana State
PRO TEAM:
Boston Celtics, 1979–92
NBA CAREER AVERAGES:
24.3 ppg; 10.0 rpg; 6.3 apg
NBA PLAYOFF AVERAGES:
23.8 ppg; 10.3 rpg; 6.5 apg

When NBA scouts took their first look at Larry Bird, they had to wonder what all the commotion was about. The Indiana State star could not jump well, his footspeed was average and his quickness was suspect. But, still, there was something intriguing about the 6-foot-9 forward.

Maybe it was his 30.3 collegiate scoring average, much of it amassed off a deadly outside jump shot. Maybe it was his uncanny ability to get the ball to the open man, often with blind passes that had no business threading their way through the crowded lane. Or maybe it was the success of the Bird-powered Sycamores, who were on their way to an NCAA Tournament finals berth opposite Magic Johnson and Michigan State.

Boston President Red Auerbach saw plenty he liked and grabbed Bird after his junior season with the sixth pick of the 1978 draft. The struggling Celtics had to wait an entire season, but the payoff was big.

"You know if you're open, you'll get the ball," marveled center Dave Cowens, who watched rookie Bird carry the Celtics from a 29-victory disaster to 61 in 1979–80. And his Rookie of the Year performance also included 21.3 points and 10.4 rebounds per game. In his second season, Bird combined with center Robert Parish and forward Cedric Maxwell to carry the Celtics all the way to an NBA championship.

That was the first of three that Bird and the Celtics would win in the 1980s. Before his career was derailed by back problems that would force a premature retirement, Bird also would earn three MVP awards, nine consecutive first-team All-NBA selections, three All-Defensive Team nods and two citations as the outstanding player of the NBA Finals.

"The ultimate beauty of the kid is that he'll do anything—absolutely anything—to win," Auerbach gushed early in Bird's career.

And that, perhaps, is the quality that stands out more than any other. His lightning reflexes, his pinpoint passes, his incredible instincts and his sixth-sense feel for the court all combined to lift his teammates to a different level. Bird was always there at crunch time, but he could not have won championships without overachieving teammates.

And he couldn't have done it without the most consistent jump shot ever launched by an NBA forward. He finished his career with a 24.3 average, almost 2,000 of his 21,791 points coming on 3-point jumpers. If Bird wasn't the best all-around player to grace the NBA arenas, he was close.

His skill level was matched by his basketball charisma. The combination of Bird and Magic was a marketing bonanza for the NBA and they carried the league to a new level of popularity in the 1980s.

Bird was forced to the sideline by back problems after the 1991–92 season and made one more appearance in uniform—as a member of the 1992 U.S. Olympic Dream Team. His departure from basketball was noted with respect by Auerbach.

"I've done a lot of soul-searching," he said. "I've decided, quite frankly, that he's the greatest player ever to put on a uniform."

Career Highlights

1978 Selected by Celtics as sixth overall pick of NBA draft after junior season of college.
1979 Led Indiana State to NCAA Tournament final, where Sycamores lost to Magic Johnson and Michigan State; finished college career with 30.3-point average.
1980 Finished first season with 21.3 scoring average and earned Rookie of the Year honors; earned first of nine consecutive All-NBA first-team selections.
1981 Helped Celtics win first NBA championship since 1974.
1982 Scored 19 points and captured NBA All-Star Game MVP honors.
1984 Led Celtics to NBA championship and earned NBA Finals MVP; won first of three consecutive regular-season MVP awards.
1985 Scored career-high 60 points in game against Atlanta.
1986 Helped Celtics win third championship of decade with six-game Finals victory over Houston.
1992 Retired because of chronic back problem; finished with career total of 21,791 points; member of gold medal-winning U.S. Dream Team at Barcelona Olympic Games.

❝ Bird is the best passer I've ever seen. In fact he's so good, he makes his teammates look good.❞

Bob Cousy, former Boston great.

BIRD OF PREY *Larry Legend, the Celtics' driving force*

By the time Wilt Chamberlain brought his 7-foot-1, 275-pound body to the NBA wars in 1959, fans and players were comfortable with the idea of dominating centers. George Mikan, the first center to dominate with offense, had retired five years earlier and Bill Russell, a defensive and rebounding terror, already had led Boston to two championships. How could Chamberlain, coming off a season with the Harlem Globetrotters, compete with that?

What the basketball world witnessed in 1959–60 was the unveiling of the greatest offensive machine the game would ever produce. Not only was "Wilt the Stilt" big and amazingly strong, he could run the court like a gazelle, had the stamina of a mule and the quickness and determination to score and rebound almost at will.

His rookie numbers for the Philadelphia Warriors were 37.6 points and 27 rebounds per game. Only two players had topped 2,000 points in a season; Chamberlain scored 2,707. Only Russell had previously topped 1,500 rebounds; Chamberlain grabbed 1,941. And he was just getting started.

Chamberlain averaged 38.4 points and 27.2 rebounds per game in 1960–61 to set the stage for the greatest offensive season in history. In 1961–62, he put his fadeaway jumper into full gear and averaged an incredible 50.4 points and 25.7 rebounds, exploding for a record 100 points in a game against New York.

Through his first seven NBA seasons, Chamberlain's scoring average never dipped below 33.5. But the Warriors never won a championship. Despite his record-shattering exploits and tremendous drawing power, he became a much-maligned superstar, a scoring machine who couldn't take a

team to the highest level. He bristled at the suggestion.

"It's human nature," said Chamberlain, a four-time MVP. "No one roots for Goliath."

Ironically, Chamberlain's first taste of success came in 1967, after a campaign in which he averaged a career-low 24.1 points. In his second season after the transplanted San Francisco Warriors had traded him back to Philadelphia, he helped the 76ers end Boston's bid for a ninth consecutive championship. His only other title came in 1972 with the Los Angeles Lakers.

The biggest controversy, one that still rages on, pits Wilt against Russell, the offensive genius versus the defensive enforcer. Russell often gets the nod because of the Celtics' 11 championships.

But not everyone agrees. "To me, he's one in history," former Utah coach Frank Layden said. "One Babe Ruth. One Willie Mays. One Wilt."

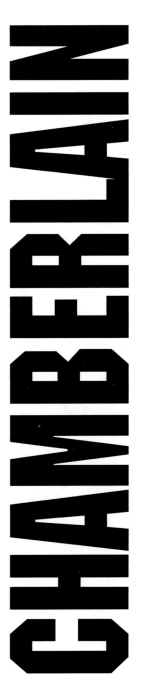

Statistics

BORN: Aug. 21, 1936, Philadelphia
HEIGHT: 7–1 **WEIGHT:** 275
COLLEGE: Kansas (three seasons)
PRO TEAMS:
Philadelphia/San Francisco Warriors, 1959–65; Philadelphia 76ers, 1965–68; Los Angeles Lakers, 1968–73
NBA CAREER AVERAGES:
30.1 ppg; 29.9 rpg; 4.4 apg
NBA PLAYOFF AVERAGES:
22.5 ppg; 24.5 rpg; 4.2 apg

Career Highlights

1959 Drafted by Warriors as territorial pick in first round.
1960 Set single-game record with 55 rebounds against Boston; completed season with record 37.6-point scoring and 27-rebound averages; named Rookie of the Year; earned first of four regular-season MVPs; earned first of seven All-NBA first-team selections.
1961 Finished season with record 2,149 rebounds and 3,033 points.
1962 Had 100-point game against Knicks; scored record 4,029 points, averaging season-record 50.4 points.
1967 Led 76ers to NBA championship.
1968 Led league with 702 assists.
1972 Earned NBA All-Defensive Team; led Lakers to NBA championship.
1973 Retired with 31,419 points and 23,924 rebounds.
1978 Elected to Naismith Memorial Hall of Fame.
1980 Named to NBA 35th Anniversary All-Time Team.

POWER SOURCE *Chamberlain reached out and the 76ers became 1967 champions*

❝ If you or I went to the gym alone, it would take us a half hour to make enough for 100 points.❞

Frank McGuire, Warriors coach, after Chamberlain's 100-point game.

COUSY

Statistics

BORN: Aug. 9, 1928, New York
HEIGHT: 6–1   **WEIGHT:** 175
COLLEGE: Holy Cross
PRO TEAMS:
Boston Celtics, 1950–63; Cincinnati
Royals, 1969–70
NBA CAREER AVERAGES:
18.4 ppg; 5.2 rpg; 7.5 apg
NBA PLAYOFF AVERAGES:
18.5 ppg; 5.0 rpg; 8.6 apg

Career Highlights

1950 Selected in first round of NBA
draft by Tri-Cities Blackhawks and traded
to Chicago Stags; NBA rights drawn out
of hat by Boston in dispersal of
Chicago franchise.
1952 Earned first of 10 consecutive
All-NBA first-team citations.
1953 Earned first of eight consecutive
assist titles with average of 7.7 per
game; scored playoff-record 50 points
in Boston's four-overtime first-round
victory over Syracuse.
1954 Scored 20 points and earned
first of two All-Star Game MVPs.
1957 Played on first of six NBA championship teams; named NBA regular-
season MVP.
1963 Retired with career totals of
16,960 points and 6,955 assists.
1969 Made brief seven-game *comeback* attempt after taking over as coach
of Cincinnati Royals, a job he held four-
plus seasons.
1970 Elected to Naismith Memorial
Hall of Fame; named to NBA 25th
Anniversary All-Time Team.
1980 Named to NBA 35th
Anniversary All-Time Team.

THE MAGICIAN *Bob Cousy was a ballhandling wizard, whether in traffic or the open court*

For 13 confounding seasons, Bob Cousy flitted and floated through the National Basketball Association like a horse fly in a stable. Frustrated opponents swatted, waved and thrashed at no-look passes, behind-the-back dribbles and other seemingly magical ball-handling feats that set up teammates for easy baskets time after time.

Cousy was the "Houdini of the Hardwood," a 6-foot-1 New Yorker who arrived on the NBA scene in 1950 after four outstanding seasons at Holy Cross. He brought with him a sleight-of-hand artistry that would lift the concept of playmaking guard to a new level. Now you see it, now you don't. The Cooz was a magician with a jump shot.

"The first game we played together, he bounced a pass off my head," said Bill Sharman, Cousy's Boston Celtics back-court mate from 1951 to '61. "It was a continual adjustment, a continual amazement."

In retrospect, Cousy was a forerunner to the razzle-dazzle basketball that has been played by such worthy successors as Pete Maravich, Magic Johnson and John Stockton. But in the 1950s, when professional basketball was still in its learning stage, he must have seemed like something from another planet.

"I used to stay awake all night thinking about him before I had to play him," said former Minneapolis Lakers guard Slater Martin.

When Cousy emerged from Holy Cross, he was selected by Tri-Cities in the first round of the draft and traded to Chicago. When the Stags folded before the 1950–51 season, the team's players were dispersed and Cousy's name was drawn out of a hat by disappointed Boston Coach Red Auerbach, who was hoping to get Max Zaslofsky or Andy Phillip.

Auerbach's bad luck was Boston's salvation. Cousy was the perfect fit for the running game Auerbach wanted to install at Boston Garden. In his rookie season, Cousy averaged 15.6 points and 4.9 assists as the Celtics improved from 22 victories to 39. In his third season, Cousy averaged 19.8 points and began a string of eight consecutive seasons as the league's assist leader.

But more importantly, he fueled a Celtics fast-break offense that would carry the franchise to six championships before his retirement in 1963. The first title came in 1957, when Cousy earned MVP honors. The Celtics went on to win championships every year from 1959–63.

When Cousy retired, he owned career regular-season averages of 18.4 points and 7.5 assists and playoff marks of 18.5 and 8.6. He had played in the All-Star Game every one of his 13 seasons. But his outstanding career still was defined by the championships and the hocus-pocus he used to constantly amaze fans as well as opponents and teammates.

❝You know, he looks one way, feints a second and passes a third. He bounced quite a few off my head before I adjusted.❞

Bill Sharman, former Celtics teammate.

He flew through the air with the greatest of ease and if Julius (Dr. J) Erving wasn't the best player in basketball history, he at least was its most eloquent.

At first glance, there was nothing unusual about Erving, a 6-foot-7 forward with thin, muscular legs and huge hands. But as soon as the clock began ticking, a spectacular transformation took place. He would glide around the court, palming the ball like a tiny grapefruit. He would soar above the crowd like a rim-seeking missile and drop the ball through from one of several impossible angles. He would drive the lane, hang in the air and either pass or shoot while mere mortal defenders returned to earth.

In an era where players left their feet only to shoot or defend, Dr. J wrote a special prescription for fan-pleasing showmanship.

"I'm a Pisces. I have a wild imagination and I've always been one to experiment," Erving explained. "I dunk the ball a lot of different ways because I know dunking excites people."

Dr. J signed with the American Basketball Association after his junior season at Massachusetts. The struggling ABA badly needed a star and Erving needed room to operate. Unshackled from the conservative college game, Dr. J unleashed a spectacular air show that left fans, coaches and players gasping.

In five ABA seasons with the Virginia Squires and New York Nets, Erving did everything imaginable to win fans and games. He scored (28.7 points per game), rebounded (12.1) and passed (4.8 assists). He also earned three ABA MVPs and carried the Nets to a pair of championships. When the ABA folded after the 1975–76 season and the Nets were admitted to the NBA for a hefty fee, Erving's contract was sold to the Philadelphia 76ers.

It was love at first sight, both in Philadelphia and around the NBA. "The things he does when he's airborne will never be done again," marveled former Portland Coach Jack Ramsay. "He takes off at the top of the circle, goes into the air and there are about six things that can happen."

Over the next 11 seasons, Erving transformed professional basketball from ground zero to an above-the-rim experience. Fans loved it and so did officials and coaches, who began unshackling other showmen. The stage was set for such future high-wire acts as Dominique Wilkins and Michael Jordan.

Erving led the 76ers to four NBA Finals and a 1983 championship. He finished his career in 1987 with a combined ABA/NBA total of 30,026 points, which ranks No. 3 on the all-time list.

But the legend of Dr. J was built on style, not numbers. Former ABA and NBA star Dan Issel watched Erving operate for 14 seasons. "If the NBA fans could have seen Julius in his ABA years," he said, "they would have thought he was the greatest player who ever put on basketball shoes."

Statistics

BORN: Feb. 22, 1950, Roosevelt, N.Y.
HEIGHT: 6–7   **WEIGHT:** 210
COLLEGE: Massachusetts (left after junior season)
PRO TEAMS:
Virginia Squires (ABA), 1971–73; New York Nets (ABA), 1973–76; Philadelphia 76ers (NBA) 1976–87
NBA CAREER AVERAGES:
22.0 ppg; 6.7 rpg; 3.9 apg
NBA PLAYOFF AVERAGES:
21.9 ppg; 7.0 rpg; 4.2 apg

Career Highlights

1971 Signed as free agent with ABA's Squires.
1972 Earned first of four ABA All-Star first-team citations.
1973 Won first of three ABA scoring titles with 31.9 average; traded to New York Nets.
1974 Led Nets to first of two ABA championships, capturing playoff MVP honors; claimed first of three consecutive ABA regular-season MVPs.
1976 Completed ABA career with 28.7-point and 12.1-rebound averages; sold by Nets to NBA's 76ers.
1977 Made first of 11 appearances in NBA All-Star Game, scoring 30 points and earning MVP honors; led 76ers to first of four NBA Finals appearances in seven years.
1978 Earned first of five All-NBA first-team citations.
1980 Named to NBA 35th Anniversary All-Time Team.
1981 Named NBA's regular-season MVP.
1983 Led 76ers to first NBA championship since 1967.
1987 Retired with combined ABA/NBA point total of 30,026.
1993 Elected to Naismith Memorial Hall of Fame.

> **❝I used to watch games on TV and I'd dream up fantastic moves and then go out on the court and try them.❞**
>
> *Julius Erving*

DOCTOR'S ORDER *Julius Erving spent most of his time above the ABA and NBA rims*

EWING

Away from the court, Patrick Ewing is a gentle giant: soft spoken, unassuming, quick to flash a reassuring smile. But when he puts on a jersey, Dr. Patrick turns to Mr. Hyde.

He scowls, he bumps and grinds, he powers his way to the basket and he physically dominates anybody who dares penetrate "his paint." There is nothing artistic about Ewing. He is a menacing 7-foot, 240-pounder who usually gets his way.

It was like that when he played for Georgetown University and led the Hoyas to a national championship and two more Final Four appearances. And it was like that in 1984, when he helped the U.S. win an Olympic gold medal at

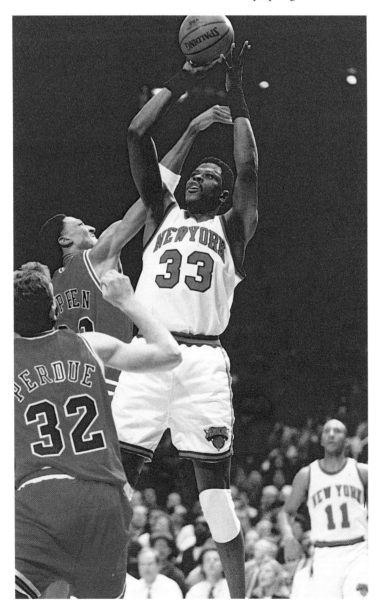

Los Angeles. When the Knicks grabbed him with the first overall pick of the 1985 draft, they thought they had the centerpiece for a championship-filled future.

It wouldn't be that easy. Ewing averaged 20 points and nine rebounds in 1985–86 en route to Rookie of the Year honors, but he also missed 32 games and the Knicks finished last in the Atlantic Division. Ewing, in fact, would not pay dividends until 1989–90, his fifth NBA season, when he blossomed both physically and mentally, averaging 28.6 points and 10.9 rebounds while blocking 327 shots.

But the Knicks would not blossom until two years later, when Pat Riley took over as coach and began molding a team around his big center. Soon, the Knicks would reflect the qualities of Ewing—methodical on offense, menacing on defense and physically intimidating. New York opponents drove the lane at their own risk and scores of Knicks games seldom reached triple figures.

Riley's game plan was a triumphant success but a public relations nightmare. Ewing was dominating in the half-court game and the Knicks became instant title contenders, but the physical battering they handed opponents cast them in the role of villains. Ewing was unfairly labeled a thug and the team's defensive style was criticized as a throwback to the boring basketball of yesteryear.

"I played with Chamberlain and coached Kareem," Riley said, "and never, ever did they get criticism like Patrick does. I think he's taken for granted. My heart goes out to him. He handles it better than anybody. "

❝ I've always said I thought he was the best center in the league. ❞

Pat Riley, former New York Knicks coach.

Statistics

BORN: Aug. 5, 1962, Kingston, Jamaica
HEIGHT: 7–0 **WEIGHT:** 240
COLLEGE: Georgetown
PRO TEAMS:
New York Knicks, 1985–present
NBA CAREER AVERAGES:
23.7 ppg; 10.4 rpg; 2.2 apg
NBA PLAYOFF AVERAGES:
22.5 ppg; 10.9 rpg; 2.4 apg

Career Highlights

1985 Led Hoyas to third NCAA Tournament final in four seasons; selected by Knicks with first overall pick of NBA draft.
1986 Finished injury-marred rookie season with 20-point and 9-rebound averages; named Rookie of the Year.
1989 Enjoyed first career 40–20 game (44 points, 24 rebounds) in contest at Golden State.
1990 Exploded for career-high 51 points in game against Boston; scored playoff career high of 45 in game against Detroit; finished regular season with career-high 28.6 scoring average; named to All-NBA first team.
1992 Played for U.S. Dream Team at Barcelona Olympic Games.
1993 Played in seventh All-Star Game and scored 15 points, including game-tying basket with 8 seconds left in regulation and six in overtime.
1994 Blocked NBA Finals-record 30 shots as Knicks lost to Rockets.

Love 'em or hate 'em, Riley's Knicks had to be dealt with. As Ewing and the rest of the team ignored the criticism and stubbornly stuck to the game plan, New York reeled off consecutive seasons of 51, 60, 57 and 55 victories. But twice they lost to the title-bound Chicago Bulls in preliminary playoff rounds and in 1993–94 they advanced to the NBA Finals, only to lose to Houston.

The seven-game loss was especially tough for the aging Ewing, who offered this postscript on his career: "When people talk about me, all I want them to say is, 'He's a winner.'"

Few would argue that point.

BRUTE FORCE *Patrick Ewing's power is demonstrated by his hard work and dedication*

Walt Frazier was never difficult to recognize. At work, he wore shorts and a jersey with a large No. 10 imprinted below a lettered "New York" insignia. Away from work, he wore eye-catching clothes that made him stand out, even on the streets of the Big Apple.

"I guess I inherited my fondness for clothes from my father," Frazier once said. His nickname, Clyde, came from a former teammate who said Frazier reminded him of the slick-dressing lead character in the movie *Bonnie and Clyde*.

The bottom line on Frazier was simple: Anything he did, he did it with style. Especially his play for the New York Knicks and Cleveland Cavaliers over a 13-year Hall of Fame career that ended in 1980.

"Walt Frazier was unquestionably one of the great guards of his era," said Boston Celtics President and former coach Red Auerbach.

When you think of Frazier, you think about the great Knicks teams of the early 1970s. Frazier, Dick Barnett and Earl Monroe in the guard rotation. Willis Reed at center. Dave DeBusschere and Bill Bradley at the forwards. Reed provided the muscle and Bradley, DeBusschere and Barnett supplied steady scoring and defense. But it was Frazier, the quarterback, who provided the spark.

When the Knicks needed points, there was Frazier, going to the basket with either hand or launching a jump shot off a teammate's screen. When they needed a big defensive play, there was Frazier, poking the ball free with lightning-quick hands and dribbling the length of the court for a basket. He could make a pass, smother an opposing scorer or do whatever else was necessary to ensure victory. Frazier was the ultimate do-everything player.

"My specialty was trying to turn games around by intercepting a pass or poking the ball away from opponents as they dribbled," said Frazier. "Nothing would shatter a team's morale faster than a steal. Stealing the ball and making a pass that led to a basket were the part of basketball I loved most."

With "Mr. Cool" pulling the strings and Reed providing the muscle, the Knicks won 60 regular-season games in 1969–70 and advanced to the NBA Finals, where they defeated Los Angeles in seven games. Three years later, with Monroe and forward/center Jerry Lucas now in the mix, they repeated that scenario with a five-game Finals romp past the Lakers.

Those two championships were the pinnacle of a career that ranks Frazier among the game's great stars. He was a seven-time All-Star Game selection and the classic's 1975 MVP; he was an All-NBA first team selection four times and a member of the league's All-Defensive first team seven consecutive years; he averaged more than 20 points in six regular seasons and averaged 20.7 points, 7.2 rebounds and 6.4 assists in eight postseasons.

But beyond the numbers, Clyde will be remembered for the style and grace he brought to basketball, both on the court and off. And in New York basketball lore, for the two championships he helped bring to a hungry city.

> **❝ Walt Frazier was a premier player because he understood that basketball is a team game and he used his abilities within a team context. ❞**
>
> *Red Auerbach, Boston Celtics President.*

THE RIGHT GUARD *The classy Frazier led the Knicks to two championships*

Statistics

BORN: March 29, 1945, Atlanta, Ga.
HEIGHT: 6–4   **WEIGHT:** 205
COLLEGE: Southern Illinois
PRO TEAMS:
New York Knicks, 1967–77;
Cleveland Cavaliers, 1977–80
NBA CAREER AVERAGES:
18.9 ppg; 5.9 rpg; 6.1 apg
NBA PLAYOFF AVERAGES:
20.7 ppg; 7.2 rpg; 6.4 apg

Career Highlights

1967 Selected by Knicks with fifth overall pick of NBA draft.
1969 Earned first of seven consecutive berths on NBA All-Defensive first team.
1970 Earned first of four All-NBA first-team citations; played in first of seven All-Star Games; quarterbacked Knicks to franchise's first NBA championship.
1973 Posted playoff averages of 21.9 points and 7.3 rebounds in Knicks' run to a second NBA title.
1975 Scored 30 points and earned All-Star Game MVP award.
1977 Acquired by Cavaliers in free-agent compensation deal.
1980 Retired with 15,581 career points.
1986 Elected to Hall of Fame.

John Havlicek was like the Energizer Bunny: He just kept running, and running, and running. And when he finally stopped after 16 seasons, he looked back at a trail of exhausted defenders, admiring fans and NBA championships.

"I think John's a freak of nature," said Kevin Loughery, one of many former NBA players who experienced the frustration of trying to guard Havlicek. "He's constant movement. You have to chase him until you're tripping over your tongue."

Havlicek, a 6-foot-5 forward who played on Ohio State's 1960 NCAA championship team, was not blessed with Oscar Robertson-like skills, but he did offer a nice blend of speed, quickness and determination. What separated him from the pack, however, was his legendary endurance.

Havlicek was a master at moving without the ball, shaking defenders and taking quick passes for layups and short jumpers. He was a perfect fit for the fast-break Celtics and he defended with tenacity, stealing passes and fearlessly diving for loose balls. "Hondo" was the ultimate team player.

"I'll tell you what was special about John Havlicek," said former Boston coach Red Auerbach. "He didn't have a lot to say and he never made waves, but he was someone we could always count on. He got the job done. Period."

Auerbach selected Havlicek in the first round of the 1962 draft. But the Celtics had won four consecutive NBA titles and there was no room in the talent-laden starting lineup for a rookie.

So Auerbach evaluated his draft pick, noted his exceptional stamina and envisioned a supporting role that would thrust Havlicek into prominence. The youngster became Boston's "Sixth Man," a super substitute who could play either guard or forward and recharge the offense at key moments. It was a perfect fit.

Havlicek averaged 14.3 points as a rookie and 19.9 in his second season. While Bill Russell, Sam Jones, Tom Heinsohn and other Boston stars drew headlines, Havlicek also rebounded, passed and sparked the team with his defensive play. He turned his role into an artform and the Celtics rolled to six more championships in Havlicek's first seven seasons.

But everything would change in 1969–70. Russell and Sam Jones retired after the 1969 championship and the Celtics dynasty crumbled fast. First-year coach Heinsohn needed an anchor for the foundering ship and he turned to Havlicek, who responded by leading the team in scoring (24.2 points per game), rebounding (7.8) and assists (6.8). He came back the next season to average 28.9 points and 45.4 minutes per game.

Over the next five seasons, Havlicek led the rebuilt Celtics to five consecutive Atlantic Division championships and two more NBA titles, bringing his career total to eight. He won NBA Finals MVP honors in 1974 against

ON THE MOVE *Havlicek never stopped running in 16 NBA seasons*

Statistics

BORN: April 8, 1940, Martins Ferry, O.
HEIGHT: 6–5 **WEIGHT:** 205
COLLEGE: Ohio State
PRO TEAM:
Boston Celtics, 1962–78
NBA CAREER AVERAGES:
20.8 ppg; 6.3 rpg; 4.8 apg
NBA PLAYOFF AVERAGES:
22.0 ppg; 6.9 rpg; 4.8 apg

Career Highlights

1960 Helped Ohio State win NCAA championship; helped Buckeyes reach NCAA finals in junior and senior seasons.
1962 Selected by Celtics in first round of NBA draft.
1963 Served as celebrated "Sixth Man" as Celtics won fifth of eight consecutive championships.
1966 Made first of 13 appearances in All-Star Game, scoring 18 points.
1971 Earned first of four consecutive All-NBA first-team citations while averaging career-high 28.9 points.
1972 Earned first of five consecutive All-Defensive team berths.
1974 Led Celtics to first post-Bill Russell championship and earned NBA Finals MVP.
1976 Played on eighth NBA championship team at age 36.
1978 Retired after 16 seasons with 26,395 points and 8,007 rebounds.
1980 Named to NBA 35th Anniversary All-Time Team.
1983 Elected to Naismith Memorial Hall of Fame.

Milwaukee.

Over the second phase of Havlicek's career, he was named to the All-NBA first team four times and to the All-Defensive Team five times.

❝If I was playing an imaginary pickup game among all the players I had ever seen, John Havlicek would be my first choice.❞

Bill Russell, former Boston teammate.

From the beginning, Earvin (Magic) Johnson was a basketball paradox. He handled the ball, passed it and shot it like a point guard. He ran the offense and controlled the flow of a game like a point guard. But at 6-foot-9, 225 pounds, he had the body of a power forward.

When Johnson burst into the NBA in 1979 with his infectious smile and creative genius, he helped push the stodgy game onto a new course of prosperity.

Johnson was indeed Magic. As a college sophomore, he vaulted into prominence with his scintillating play in Michigan State's 1979 NCAA Tournament championship game victory over Larry Bird and Indiana State. Then, in what should have been his junior season, he dazzled NBA fans and opponents with his shocking array of talents.

"He's a point guard-center," said Richie Adubato, former Dallas coach. "He rebounds like a center, he can shoot outside and you know he can post up your 6-foot-whatever guard."

In Johnson's first season in Los Angeles, he averaged 18 points, 7.7 rebounds and 7.3 assists but lost out in Rookie of the Year voting to Bird, who was providing a similar brand of excitement in Boston. But Magic had the last laugh. The Lakers advanced to the 1980 NBA Finals and, with center Kareem Abdul-Jabbar injured and unable to play in Game 6, Johnson moved to center and scored 42 points in a championship-clinching victory over Philadelphia. He was named NBA Finals MVP, the first of three he would receive in the 1980s.

That was a tough act to follow. But over the next dozen years, Magic upgraded his game with a continuous flow of no-look passes, creative drives and clutch performances that earned him three MVP awards and nine All-NBA first-team citations. He became the game's most prolific assist man, averaging in double figures nine straight seasons, and his career averages of 19.7 points and 7.3 rebounds could have been higher.

With Abdul-Jabbar and James Worthy providing the muscle and Johnson running the show, the Lakers reached the Finals eight times in the decade and won five championships.

But Johnson's most lasting contribution won't appear in the record books. The simultaneous arrival of Magic and Bird and their battles in a championship context triggered a popularity explosion that carried the game to global heights.

Johnson retired after the 1990–91 season when he tested HIV-positive. But he reappeared in 1992 as a member of the Dream Team and rejoined the Lakers midway through the 1995–96 season as a 36-year-old power forward. His return was dynamic but brief. He retired again after the Lakers lost in the first round of the playoffs.

Career Highlights

1979 Led Michigan State to the NCAA championship with a finals victory over Indiana State; declared for NBA draft after sophomore season and was selected first overall by Lakers.

1980 Capped rookie season by scoring 42 points in championship-clinching victory over 76ers in NBA Finals; named Finals MVP.

1981 Led NBA with 3.43 steals per game.

1982 Earned second NBA Finals MVP award as Lakers captured second championship of decade; led league with 2.67 steal average.

1983 Earned first of five assist titles with 10.5 average; earned first of nine straight All-NBA first-team citations.

1987 Earned first of three regular-season MVP awards; helped Lakers win fourth of five championships in decade.

1991 Set NBA's all-time career assist record with 9,921; announced retirement after testing HIV-positive; left game with five NBA championships, three MVPs and 17,239 points.

1992 Played for U.S. Dream Team in Barcelona Olympic Games; came out of retirement to compete in NBA All-Star Game, scoring 25 points and winning MVP honors.

1996 Came out of retirement and helped Lakers to 53-win season

EN GARDE *Johnson was the trigger man for the Lakers' "Showtime" offense*

Statistics

BORN: Aug. 14, 1959, Lansing, Mich.
HEIGHT: 6–9 **WEIGHT:** 225
COLLEGE: Michigan State (left after sophomore season)
PRO TEAMS:
Los Angeles Lakers, 1979–92, 1995–96
NBA CAREER AVERAGES:
19.5 ppg; 7.2 rpg; 11.2 apg
NBA PLAYOFF AVERAGES:
19.5 ppg; 7.7 rpg; 12.4 apg

❝ He refuses to let his team lose at the end of the game. He can beat you with the pass, shot, offensive rebound or defensive rebound. ❞

Richie Adubato, former Dallas coach.

Statistics

BORN: Feb. 17, 1963, Brooklyn, N.Y.
HEIGHT: 6–6   **WEIGHT:** 198
COLLEGE: North Carolina (three years)
PRO TEAM:
Chicago Bulls, 1984–93, 1995–present
NBA CAREER AVERAGES:
32.0 ppg; 6.4 rpg; 5.7 apg
NBA PLAYOFF AVERAGES:
33.9 ppg; 6.4 rpg; 6.2 apg

Career Highlights

1982 Hit 20-foot shot that gave North Carolina NCAA Tournament finals victory.
1984 Selected third overall by Bulls in NBA draft; co-captain of gold medal-winning Olympic team.
1985 Named NBA Rookie of the Year.
1986 Scored NBA playoff-record 63 in double-overtime victory at Boston.
1987 Selected All-NBA first team for first of seven straight seasons; won first of seven straight scoring titles (37.1 ppg).
1988 Won first of four regular-season MVP awards; named Defensive Player of the Year.
1991 Led Bulls to first NBA championship; named Finals MVP for first of record three straight years.
1992 Helped U.S. Dream Team win gold at Barcelona Olympic Games.
1993 Averaged NBA Finals-record 41 points as Bulls won third straight NBA championship.
1996 Won fourth NBA Finals MVP; led Bulls to fourth 1990s championship.

The legend of Michael Jordan started in 1982 with a 20-foot jump shot that decided a national championship. Over the next decade, it grew into a marketing missile that rose majestically over the NBA.

From the moment Jordan, a North Carolina freshman guard, connected on his NCAA Tournament-winning jumper against Georgetown, he was primed for greatness. He would fulfill his destiny above the rims of Chicago Stadium and the United Center, dazzling fans with his amazing grace and extraordinary athleticism, leaving opponents and coaches gasping for defensive answers and superlatives.

"Everybody knows he's going to get the ball, but you don't know what he's going to do with it," said former Los Angeles Lakers star Michael Cooper, one of the best defensive guards in NBA history.

Former Indiana Pacers Coach Dick Versace expressed a common sentiment when he called Jordan "a visitor from another planet."

Jordan's career numbers and honors lend credence to Versace's out-of-this-world description: a record-tying seven consecutive NBA scoring championships; four Most Valuable Player awards; 1984–85 Rookie of the Year; 1987–88 Defensive Player of the Year; a four-time NBA Finals MVP; a three-time leader in steals; a member of the 1992 U.S. Olympic Dream Team.

But Jordan's crowning achievement came when he led the long-struggling Bulls to the top of the NBA mountain. It was a dream come true. Jordan's early years had been filled with scoring titles, 40 and 50-point games and individual glory, but it wasn't until the arrival of Scottie Pippen, Horace Grant and John Paxson that the Bulls reached championship form. With Jordan fueling the charge, they became only the third NBA team to win three straight titles, defeating the Lakers, Portland and Phoenix from 1991–93.

Having established his credentials as an outstanding team player as well as the game's ultimate individual, a 30-year-old Jordan shocked the world in 1993 by announcing his retirement, saying he had no more basketball worlds to conquer. But after almost two years of pursuing a second-sport career in baseball, he changed his mind, returning to his exalted position on the NBA throne. Jordan rejoined the Bulls for the final 17 games of 1994–95, and, one year later, everything was back to normal in Chicago. The Jordan-led Bulls of 1995–96 posted an unprecedented 72–10 regular season record and claimed their fourth championship of the decade.

Jordan finished that record-setting campaign with a 32.0 career scoring average, the highest in league history. Most of those points have been produced off gliding, graceful jumps, hanging, double-clutching moves and in-your-face, either-hand slam dunks. His unprecedented popularity is a product of charisma and showmanship.

Whereas Magic Johnson and Larry Bird had ushered the NBA into a new era of prosperity in the early 1980s, Jordan helped lift the league to heights of popularity never before enjoyed. His name transcends conventional marketing strategies and carries worldwide renown.

> **❝ As soon as he touches the ball, it electrifies the intensity in you. ❞**
>
> *Michael Cooper, former Los Angeles Lakers guard.*

AIR BALL *Michael Jordan and the Bulls have been flying high since his return*

From the moment he put on his first professional uniform, at the tender age of 19, Moses Malone began searching for the basketball Promised Land. He wandered for more than 20 years through an ABA/NBA maze of teams, gathering the rebounds, points and awards he will use to carve out his niche in the Hall of Fame.

Malone's resume is very impressive. He ranks third on the NBA's all-time list for points scored (27,409), third in games played (1,329), fifth in rebounds (16,212), first in offensive rebounds (6,731) and first in free throws made (8,531). And these numbers do not include two ABA seasons.

Malone won six rebounding titles and was a three-time regular-season MVP, a 12-time All-Star, a four-time All-NBA first-team selection and an NBA Finals MVP. He carried an average Houston team to the NBA Finals and was the centerpiece for the Philadelphia 76ers team that won the 1983 NBA championship.

Not bad for a talented 6-foot-10 center who spent much of his career feeling unwanted.

Malone vaulted into prominence at age 19 when he gave in to big-money temptation and bypassed college, turning professional after his high school career in Petersburg, Va. He was young, inexperienced and naïve when he began banging bodies as a member of the ABA's Utah Stars.

Malone averaged 18.8 points and 14.6 rebounds in that first season, but his numbers slipped in 1975–76 when his contract was sold to the much weaker St. Louis Spirits and he discovered the realities of ABA life. When the ABA folded in 1976, he was picked up by Portland. Malone was then traded to Buffalo and Houston—before the next season had even started.

By 1978–79, the stern-faced, no-nonsense Moses, now stronger and quicker, was taking his place as one of the game's top centers. He won the first of six rebounding titles in seven seasons with a 17.6 average, scored 24.8 points per game and earned his first MVP.

He was ferocious on the offensive boards, turning teammates' misses into quick points.

From 1980 to 1983, Malone was the most dominant force in the game. He powered the Rockets to the 1981 NBA Finals, earned his second MVP award in 1982 and combined with Julius Erving to lead the 76ers to the 1983 NBA championship. He capped his championship season by winning both the NBA regular-season and Finals MVP citations.

Malone's Philadelphia stay lasted four seasons before he began a nomadic journey around the NBA, making stops at Washington, Atlanta, Milwaukee and—finally—San Antonio. He finally called it a career in 1995, after 21 professional seasons, with a combined ABA/NBA career points total of 29,580.

Statistics

BORN: March 23, 1955, Petersburg, Va.
HEIGHT: 6–10   **WEIGHT:** 255
COLLEGE: None
PRO TEAMS:
Utah Stars (ABA) 1974–75, St. Louis Spirits (ABA) 1975–76; Houston Rockets 1976–82; Philadelphia 76ers 1982–86, 1993–95; Washington Bullets 1986–88; Atlanta Hawks 1988–91; Milwaukee Bucks 1991–93; San Antonio Spurs 1994–95.
NBA CAREER AVERAGES:
20.6 ppg; 12.2 rpg; 1.4 apg
NBA PLAYOFF AVERAGES:
22.1 ppg; 13.8 rpg; 1.4 apg

Career Highlights

1974 Signed with ABA's Utah Stars after senior year of high school.
1975 Averaged 18.8 points and 14.6 rebounds as a 19-year-old ABA rookie.
1979 Recorded career game high 37 rebounds; NBA-record 587 offensive rebounds; earned first of three regular-season MVP awards (averaging 24.8 points and 17.6 rebounds).
1981 Won second NBA rebounding title (14.8); led Rockets to NBA Finals.
1982 Career-best 53-point game against Clippers; averaged career-high 31.1 points and earned second MVP.
1983 Led 76ers to NBA championship and earned Finals MVP award; won second straight regular-season MVP.
1985 Earned fourth All-NBA first-team citation.
1987 Scored 27 points in 10th All-Star Game appearance.
1995 Appeared in 17 games for Spurs, completing 21st pro season.

❝Everybody gave him no chance, but that changed in about two weeks, after he had dunked on everybody's head. He was one of the best rebounders I'd ever seen.❞

Maurice Lucas, former ABA and NBA star.

MASTER REBOUNDER *Malone was head and shoulders above the NBA crowd*

H e stood 6-foot-10, weighed 245 pounds and looked at the world through thick-rimmed glasses. Hulking George Mikan was a professor in basketball shorts and his classrooms were the big-city arenas around the NBA. He wrote a book on center-position play, held daily clinics on power basketball and taught a new league how to survive.

Mikan's short NBA tenure revolutionized pro basketball. His stature as the game's first dominating big man set the league on course to prosperity. When he joined the 2-year-old Basketball Association of America in 1948, he brought with him a deadly hook shot and the national atten- tion and media exposure the league needed to build a solid foundation.

"He was the Babe Ruth of bas- ketball," former Knicks coach Joe Lapchick liked to say. Other coaches saw it differently. "Monster," Rochester's Les Harrison said. "He's nothing but a monster."

That's the image Mikan brought to a game previously dom- inated by slick ballhandling and finesse. He was bigger and stronger than the centers he played against and he used his bulk to great advantage, backing his defender into the lane and extend- ing an elbow as protection for a deadly hook shot. The elbows also were lethal weapons in pursuit of a rebound or loose ball.

Mikan, a three-time All- American and two-time national scoring champion at DePaul, spurned the BAA for the more established National Basketball League when he turned pro amid much fanfare in 1946. But two years later, he became BAA property when his Minneapolis Lakers and three other NBL teams switched leagues.

Everywhere Mikan played, he drew big crowds and bigger head- lines. And he didn't disappoint. In an era when 20-point scoring averages were seldom seen, the Lakers' big man averaged a whopping 28.3 in 1948–49 and led Minneapolis to the first of five championships in six seasons. But Mikan was more than an offen- sive machine. He was an out- standing rebounder and an adept passer from the post.

Mikan, who won six straight professional scoring titles, also was blessed with a strong sup- porting cast. Forwards Jim Pollard and Vern Mikkelsen and guard Slater Martin ranked among the best players in the league. But the key to the Minneapolis dynasty, which included three straight champi- onships from 1952–54, was the immovable force in the middle.

Mikan, who survived double- and triple-teams as well as legisla- tion (the lane was widened; the three-second violation) aimed at slowing him down, still managed to average 22.6 points over a nine-year professional career. He retired in 1954 at age 30, made a brief comeback a year later and finally settled into a law career.

Statistics

BORN: June 18, 1924, Joliet, Ill.
HEIGHT: 6–10 **WEIGHT:** 245
COLLEGE: DePaul
PRO TEAMS:
Chicago Gears (NBL), 1946–47;
Minneapolis Lakers (NBL/NBA), 1947–56
NBA CAREER AVERAGES:
23.1 ppg; 13.4 rpg; 2.8 apg
NBA PLAYOFF AVERAGES:
24.0 ppg; 13.9 rpg; 2.2 apg

Career Highlights

1945 Led nation with a 23.3 average and DePaul to NIT championship.
1946 Earned third straight All-America citation; signed with NBL's Gears.
1947 Rights awarded to Lakers when Gears franchise disbanded.
1949 Won first of four consecutive scoring titles with 28.3-point average; led Lakers to first of five championships they would win in six years; earned first of six all-league first-team citations.
1953 Scored 22 points and earned All-Star Game MVP.
1956 Retired with record 11,764 career points.
1959 Elected to Naismith Memorial Hall of Fame.
1967 Named Commissioner of newly formed ABA.
1970 Named to NBA 25th Anniversary All-Time Team.
1980 Named to NBA 35th Anniversary All-Time Team.

❝He never quit on that floor and I shall always take my hat off to George Mikan as the basketball player who ranked above all the others.❞

Larry Foust, former Fort Wayne Pistons star.

INCREDIBLE HULK *The powerful Mikan carried the early NBA on his shoulders*

If you play him loose, he fakes one way, turns the other and hits a deadly fadeaway jump shot. Play him tight and he spins like lightning toward the basket for a dunk or jump hook. Double-team him and he finds the open man with a quick pass.

Oscar Robertson? Elgin Baylor? Larry Bird? Amazingly, this combination of power, finesse and quickness belongs to 7-foot, 255-pound Hakeem Olajuwon—the NBA's reigning center of attention.

As a total package, Olajuwon might be the best pivotman ever. Bill Russell was a master of defense, rebounding and shot-blocking; Wilt Chamberlain was an offensive machine; and Kareem Abdul-Jabbar brought finesse and durability. Olajuwon can do all of those things—and more. It's not unusual to see him block a shot at one end of the court and race to the other to finish a fast break.

"In terms of raw athletic ability, Hakeem is the best I have ever seen," said Magic Johnson.

The athletic ability has always been obvious, but Olajuwon's rise is the result of hard work and dedication. Amazingly, the man who led the Houston Rockets to consecutive championships in 1994 and '95, didn't even touch a basketball until age 15 and his early sports activity was limited to playing goalkeeper for a soccer team in his hometown of Lagos, Nigeria.

When Olajuwon, known then as Akeem, accepted a scholarship at the University of Houston in 1980, he was a 190-pound weakling with great leaping ability and little knowledge of the game. Cougars Coach Guy Lewis took one look and put him to work.

"It took him awhile to become a player," Lewis said. "He could run and jump, but that's about all the basketball skills he had. We worked him before the team got there and after the team left, but he had a desire for it."

Olajuwon bulked up and never stopped working. As a college player he was part of Houston's "Phi Slama Jama" fraternity and made three visits to the NCAA Tournament's Final Four. But he was primarily a shot-blocker and dunking machine who was still learning the fundamental skills.

Even with his on-the-job training, Olajuwon was good enough to average 20.6 points and 11.9 rebounds as a 1984–85 rookie while blocking 220 shots. A year later, he combined with fellow 7-footer Ralph Sampson to lead the Rockets to the NBA Finals, where they lost to Boston in six games.

As Olajuwon's basketball knowledge has increased, so have his numbers. His all-around domination can best be illustrated by the variety of his awards: regular-season and NBA Finals MVPs; Defensive Player of the Year; All-NBA first-team; rebounding and shot-blocking titles. He also is one of three NBA players to perform a single-game quadruple-double.

Career Highlights

1984 Helped Houston reach Final Four for third straight season and championship game for second; Cougars lost each year.
1984 Selected by Rockets with first overall pick of NBA draft.
1985 Averaged 20.6 points and 11.9 rebounds and finished second to Michael Jordan in Rookie of the Year voting.
1987 Earned first of three straight All-NBA first-team berths; made first of five appearances on NBA All-Defensive first team.
1988 Scored 21 points in fourth All-Star Game appearance.
1990 Recorded third quadruple-double in NBA history: 18 points, 16 rebounds, 11 blocks, 10 assists; exploded for career-high 52 points in game against Denver.
1993 Led league in blocked shots (4.17 per game) for third time in four seasons.
1994 Led Rockets to NBA championship, earning NBA Finals MVP honors; named regular-season MVP.
1995 Played in 10th All-Star Game; earned second straight NBA Finals MVP as Rockets repeated as champions.
1996 Played for Dream Team III in Atlanta Olympic Games

ROCKET MAN *The do-everything Olajuwon is living a Houston dream*

Statistics

BORN: Jan. 21, 1963, Lagos, Nigeria
HEIGHT: 7–0   **WEIGHT:** 255
COLLEGE: Houston
PRO TEAM:
Houston Rockets, 1984–present
NBA CAREER AVERAGES:
24.3 ppg; 12.3 rpg; 2.7 apg
NBA PLAYOFF AVERAGES:
27.8 ppg; 11.7 rpg; 3.4 apg

❝ I've come to understand why Hakeem is called 'The Dream.' We all dream of playing the way he plays.❞

Scott Brooks, former Houston teammate.

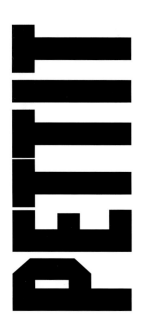

PETTIT

Statistics

BORN: Dec. 12, 1932, Baton Rouge, La.
HEIGHT: 6–9   **WEIGHT:** 215
COLLEGE: Louisiana State
PRO TEAM:
Milwaukee/St. Louis Hawks, 1954–65
NBA CAREER AVERAGES:
26.4 ppg; 16.2 rpg; 3.0 apg
NBA PLAYOFF AVERAGES:
25.5 ppg; 14.8 rpg; 2.7 apg

Career Highlights

1954 Finished college career with 27.4-point average and two All-America citations; selected by Hawks with second overall pick of NBA draft.
1955 Averaged 20.4 points in first season and earned Rookie of the Year award; earned first of 10 consecutive All-NBA first-team citations.
1956 Won first of two scoring titles with 25.7-point average; earned first of two regular-season MVP awards.
1957 Averaged 29.8 points in playoffs and led Hawks to first of four NBA Finals appearances in five years.
1958 Scored 50 points against Boston in Game 6 of NBA Finals, securing Hawks' first NBA championship.
1962 Scored 25 points and grabbed 27 rebounds to earn fourth All-Star Game MVP award.
1964 Scored 19,204th point to break NBA career scoring record; became league's first 20,000-point scorer.
1965 Retired with playoff career record for points (2,240).
1970 Elected to Naismith Memorial Hall of Fame; named to NBA 25th Anniversary All-Time Team.
1980 Named to NBA 35th Anniversary All-Time Team.

The Naismith Memorial Basketball Hall of Fame is full of former stars who crafted outstanding careers around natural athletic abilities. Bob Pettit is not one of them.

Pettit's Hall of Fame career was crafted without the superior athleticism he was forced to compete against. From his junior year at Baton Rouge (La.) High School (1948–49) to his final season (1964–65) with the St. Louis Hawks, Pettit captured fans and headlines with a winning combination of hard work, drive and determination.

"There's not a greater competitor in sports today than Bob Pettit," marveled Boston center Bill Russell, an intense workaholic himself. "He made second effort a part of the sports vocabulary."

Pettit needed every ounce of effort he could muster. After failing to make the Baton Rouge varsity team as a sophomore, he combined a conditioning and coordination program with hours of practice and turned himself into a high school star. Armed with a 6-foot-9 body, a deadly push shot and the understanding that hard work makes up for physical deficiencies, Pettit accepted a scholarship to Louisiana State University, where he earned All-America honors his junior and senior seasons.

When the Milwaukee Hawks made Pettit the second pick of the 1954 NBA draft, they were getting a highly motivated slasher who had a special knack for scoring points and chasing down rebounds from his forward position. Opponents quickly learned that the determined Pettit would never give them a moment's rest. "The only way to stop him is not to let him have the ball," said Lakers Coach Fred Schaus. "But he ruins that strategy by going and getting it himself."

Nobody ever accused Pettit of being artistic. But nobody ever figured out how to stop him, either. He averaged 20.4 points and 13.8 rebounds in 1954–55 en route to Rookie of the Year hon-

SCORING MACHINE *Bob Pettit soared with the Hawks for 12 NBA seasons*

ors. And those were the lowest marks of his 11-year professional career.

He was an All-Star every season, a two-time MVP and a two-time scoring champion. He also led the Hawks to five division titles while forging a 26.4-point regular-season average and a 25.5 playoff mark. He became the first NBA player to reach 20,000 career points.

But the greatest testimony to Pettit's career was his almost-legendary status in St. Louis, where the Hawks moved after his rookie season. In 1956–57, the Hawks, featuring Pettit, Ed Macauley and Cliff Hagan, reached the NBA Finals, where they lost to the Celtics in a seventh-game, double-overtime thriller.

The Hawks won the Western Division title in 1957–58 and again advanced to the Finals, this time handing the Celtics a six-game defeat. Pettit carried them to a 110–109 title-clinching victory with one of the greatest performances in playoff history: 50 points, including 19 of his team's last 21. It would be the only title in the Hawks' history.

> **❝There may have been greater players, but none with greater desire and dedication. Bob Pettit was the pro's pro, the owner's dream.❞**
>
> *Ben Kerner, Hawks owner.*

Statistics

BORN: Nov. 24, 1938, Charlotte, Tenn.
HEIGHT: 6–5 **WEIGHT:** 220
COLLEGE: Cincinnati
PRO TEAMS:
Cincinnati Royals, 1960–70;
Milwaukee Bucks, 1970–74
NBA CAREER AVERAGES:
25.7 ppg; 7.5 rpg; 9.5 apg
NBA PLAYOFF AVERAGES:
22.2 ppg; 6.7 rpg; 8.9 apg

Career Highlights

1955 Led Crispus Attucks to first of consecutive Indiana State High School championships.
1958 Became first sophomore to lead nation in scoring, averaging 35.1 points for the University of Cincinnati.
1960 Closed out college career with three straight national scoring championships, a career-record 2,973 points and two Final Four appearances; selected by Royals as territorial pick in NBA draft; helped U.S. win gold medal in Rome Olympic Games.
1961 Played in first of 12 consecutive All-Star Games, earning MVP honors; finished first season with 30.5 average and named NBA Rookie of the Year; earned All-NBA first-team selection for first of nine consecutive years.
1962 Became first player in league history to average triple-double: 30.8 ppg, 12.5 rpg, 11.4 apg.
1964 Earned regular-season MVP with 31.4 ppg, 9.9 rpg, 11.0 apg; claimed third of eight career assist titles.
1970 Traded to Bucks after 10 seasons in Cincinnati.
1971 Combined with Kareem Abdul-Jabbar to lead Bucks to first NBA championship.
1974 Retired with 26,710 career points and 9,887 assists.
1979 Elected to Naismith Memorial Hall of Fame.
1980 Selected to NBA 35th Anniversary All-Time Team.

❝Oscar Robertson was probably the best guard who ever played the game of basketball. ❞

Kevin Loughery, longtime former opponent.

From his junior year of high school, through his 14th and final professional season, Oscar Robertson was a national celebrity. Nobody had ever seen the combination of skills and size that Robertson brought to a basketball court and he used them like an athletic surgeon carving out his Hall of Fame career.

He was a 6-foot-5 package of amazing grace. Robertson could bang with the big boys, nail 20-foot jump shots from anywhere on the court, handle the ball like a Globetrotter and deliver dazzling, pinpoint passes to disbelieving teammates. He was Bob Cousy with size and when coaches began using him as a big guard, he presented all kinds of matchup problems.

"There may be better shooters than Oscar," said Ed Jucker, Robertson's coach at the University of Cincinnati. "But for the total game—shooting, rebounding, passing, handling the ball and, yes, defense—he's the greatest."

Basketball life started for the "Big O" in 1954 when word filtered out of Indianapolis that a new kind of prodigy was performing magic for Crispus Attucks High School. When the school won consecutive Indiana State championships, Robertson became the target of one of the most intense recruiting campaigns in college basketball history.

At Cincinnati, Robertson lived up to his reputation—and more. In his first varsity season, he led the nation with a 35.1-point average and went on to win two more scoring championships. Robertson finished his college career with a record 33.8 scoring average and an impressive .535 field-goal percentage while leading the Bearcats to a 79–8 record.

But the best was yet to come. Robertson, who would redefine the concept of guard play with his fluid style and size, was perfect for the professional game. He was drafted by Cincinnati in 1960 as a territorial pick, stepped into the Royals' starting lineup and earned Rookie of the Year honors with averages of 30.5 points, 10.1 rebounds and 9.7 assists per game. In his second season, Robertson averaged an unprecedented triple-double—30.8 points, 12.5 rebounds and 11.4 assists. Nobody could dominate a game in so many ways and few could do damage both inside and out.

"Oscar simply dominated the game," said Kevin Loughery, who played against Robertson for 10 seasons.

While Robertson's career statistics read like a Who's Who resume—a 25.7 scoring average, eight league assist titles, 7.5 rebounds per game, 12 All-Star Game appearances and one MVP award—one criticism dogged him during his playing days. Through 10 Cincinnati seasons, Robertson could not lead the talent-deficient Royals anywhere near a championship. But in 1970, he was traded to Milwaukee and combined with young center Kareem Abdul-Jabbar to lead the Bucks to 66 regular-season victories and the franchise's first NBA title.

The resume was complete. And Robertson retired three years later at age 36.

OSCAR WINNER *The Big O ended his career on a high note in Milwaukee*

RUSSELL

He arrived in Boston with two NCAA Tournament championships and an Olympic gold medal. Over the next 13 seasons, he would add 11 championship rings as the centerpiece for the best team in NBA history. No player in any sport can come close to matching Bill Russell's incredible winning legacy.

The 6-foot-10 Russell vaulted into national prominence in 1955 and '56 when he dominated the middle for a San Francisco team that captured consecutive NCAA titles and won 55 straight games. He was an athletically gifted leaper who rebounded and played defense with a fiery intensity that compensated for limited offensive ability. But many questioned whether a low-scoring center could survive in the demanding professional game.

Not Auerbach. The Boston coach already had plenty of scorers; what he needed was a rebounder who could trigger the fast break and provide solid defense in the middle. He envisioned Russell getting the rebound and whipping the outlet pass to Bob Cousy or Bill Sharman, who would perform their magic on the break.

It didn't take long for Russell to justify Auerbach's faith. After leading the United States to a gold medal at the 1956 Olympic Games, Russell joined the Celtics in December and stepped right into the lineup. Auerbach gave him one instruction: "Forget about scoring and get me the ball."

Russell averaged 19.6 rebounds in his rookie season and played an intimidating defense never before seen in the NBA. If an opponent missed a shot, Russell was there to grab the rebound and ignite the break. If a teammate made a defensive mistake, Russell was there to cover up. He turned the blocked shot into an art form, often using it like an outlet pass. With Russell smothering the middle, the Celtics rolled to their first championship in 1957.

Over the next 12 seasons, Russell would average a modest 15.1 points and a not-so-modest 22.5 rebounds. He would earn five MVP citations, play in the All-Star Game 12 times and set defensive standards beyond even Auerbach's wildest dreams. But his biggest contribution would be as the ultimate team player, the one constant in the 13-year Boston dynasty that produced eight straight titles and 11 overall.

"Russell put aside personal glory for the good of the team," Auerbach said. "Russell is the greatest center who ever lived."

Auerbach made that assessment despite the overpowering presence of Wilt Chamberlain. Auerbach thought so highly of Russell that he chose him as his coaching successor in 1966. The first black coach in team sports history, Russell led the Celtics to two more titles in three years.

HOOKED ON WINNING *Bill Russell was always at the top of his game*

Statistics

BORN: Feb. 12, 1934, at Monroe, La.
HEIGHT: 6–10   **WEIGHT:** 220
COLLEGE: San Francisco
PRO TEAM: Boston Celtics, 1956–69
CAREER AVERAGES:
15.1 ppg; 22.5 rpg; 4.3 apg
PLAYOFF AVERAGES:
16.2 ppg; 24.9 rpg; 4.7 apg

Career Highlights

1956 Led San Francisco to second consecutive NCAA Tournament championship and school's 55th straight victory; led U.S. to gold medal in Melbourne Olympics; selected by Hawks with third overall pick of draft; traded to Celtics.
1957 Grabbed record 32 rebounds in one half against Philadelphia; won first of five rebounding titles (19.6 average); led Celtics to first NBA championship.
1958 Earned first of 12 All-Star Game selections and first of five regular-season MVP awards.
1959 Averaged 16.7 points and 23 rebounds as Celtics won second NBA championship and first of record eight straight; averaged NBA Finals record 29.5 rebounds in series against Lakers.
1960 Set NBA record with 51 rebounds in game against Syracuse.
1966 Named player/coach of Celtics, becoming first black coach in a major team sport.
1968 Coached and powered Celtics to 10th NBA title in 12 years.
1969 Retired as player and coach after guiding Celtics to second straight title and 11th in 13 seasons.
1970 Named to NBA 25th Anniversary All-Time Team.
1973 Began four-year stint as coach/general manager of Seattle SuperSonics.
1974 Elected to Naismith Memorial Hall of Fame.
1980 Declared greatest player in history by Professional Basketball Writers Association of America; named to NBA 35th Anniversary All-Time Team.

❝Bill has great pride. He is proud of his team and proud of his own personal skills. He doesn't know what it means to play on a loser.❞

Red Auerbach, Boston Celtics President and former coach.

Jerry West came out of the mountains of West Virginia to the glitz and glitter of Los Angeles, armed with a deadly jump shot, quick hands and an indomitable will to succeed. He used those weapons to carve out a Hall of Fame career in a real-life Hollywood script, complete with a frustrating obstacle and a happy ending.

West was not your average, everyday, hillbilly basketball player when he was selected by the Minneapolis Lakers with the second overall pick of the 1960 draft. A 6-foot-2 shooting guard for West Virginia, he was well known for his MVP performance in the 1959 NCAA Tournament and his gold-medal-winning effort for the 1960 U.S. Olympic team. He would join the Lakers for the 1960–61 season, their first on the West Coast.

West, adjusting to the professional game, started off slowly, averaging 17.6 points, 7.7 rebounds and 4.2 assists. Teaming with Elgin Baylor, he had to restrain his free-lancing game and operate strictly out of the backcourt, providing a Mr. Outside to Baylor's Mr. Inside.

By his second season, West was more comfortable with the role. His average jumped to 30.8 and he collected 7.9 rebounds and 5.4 assists per game. The dynamic Baylor-West combination carried the Lakers to the NBA Finals, where they dropped a seventh-game overtime heartbreaker to Boston. Baylor and West combined for averages of 70.1 points and 24.5 rebounds in the 1962 postseason.

That on-court rapport would continue throughout the 1960s, and so would their frustrating chase of a championship. Seven times the Lakers would reach the Finals from 1962–70, and seven times they would lose. Six of those losses were to the powerful Celtics.

But as Baylor battled ever-worsening knee problems, more of the responsibility fell on West's shoulders—a role he welcomed. By mid-career, the scrappy West was known throughout the NBA as "Mr. Clutch" and one of the game's most well-rounded performers.

"West is the complete basketball player," said Fred Schaus, his coach at West Virginia and for seven seasons in Los Angeles. "He does everything well. He scores points, he rebounds, he plays defense, he sets up the plays. He's a poised leader."

If West had a weakness, it was that he expected to hit every shot, make every pass and win every game. When he didn't, his temper could get in the way.

West made the All-Star team every season of a 14-year career that ended in 1974 and was a four-time member of the NBA All-Defensive first team. He was especially good in the playoffs, where he carried a 29.1-point career mark. In 1965, West exploded for a 40.6-point average.

The happy ending? West averaged 25.8 points for the 1971–72 Lakers, who finally broke the playoff ice and captured the franchise's first Los Angeles championship with a five-game NBA Finals victory over the New York Knicks.

MR. CLUTCH *Jerry West made his mark as the Lakers' go-to guard*

> **❝He was a perfectionist. He'd actually be surprised that he would miss an open jump shot.❞**
>
> *Fred Schaus, former Lakers coach.*

Statistics

BORN: May 28, 1938, at Cheylan, W.Va.
HEIGHT: 6–2   **WEIGHT:** 185
COLLEGE: West Virginia
PRO TEAM: L. A. Lakers, 1960–74
CAREER AVERAGES:
27.0 ppg; 5.8 rpg; 6.7 apg
PLAYOFF AVERAGES:
29.1 ppg; 5.6 rpg; 6.3 apg

Career Highlights

1959 Led West Virginia to NCAA Tournament finals, where the Mountaineers lost to California, 71–70; earned MVP honors.
1960 Selected by Lakers with second overall pick of NBA draft; joined forces with Oscar Robertson to lead U.S. to gold medal in Rome Olympic Games.
1961 Played in first of 14 NBA All-Star Games.
1962 Set record for NBA guard when he scored 63 points in game against Knicks; finished second pro season with a 30.8-point average and earned first of 10 All-NBA first- team citations; made first of nine NBA Finals appearances for Lakers.
1965 Finished playoffs averaging 40.6 points per game.
1969 Named NBA Finals MVP, even though Lakers lost to Celtics.
1970 Earned first of four straight All-Defensive team selections.
1972 Named All-Star Game MVP; helped Lakers win first Los Angeles championship.
1974 Retired with 25,192 career points.
1976 Began three-year stint as coach of Lakers.
1979 Elected to Naismith Memorial Hall of Fame.
1980 Named to NBA 35th Anniversary All-Time Team.
1982 Became Lakers general manager, job he still holds today.

THE GREAT PLAYERS

THE NBA'S BRIGHTEST STARS WILL SHINE EVERY NIGHT

They soar. They fly. They dart. They hang. They slam. And they score from every possible angle, position and contortion. Their elegant feats are the product of athleticism and skill, but their greatness is measured by such qualities as desire, determination, poise and durability.

It has always been that way, from the early days of pass-and-shoot basketball through the evolution of the game into the aerial circus we know today. The great player comes in many shapes and sizes and is easily identified. He is the one who makes the clutch shot, threads the perfect pass, plays chest-to-chest defense and controls the pace of a game, night after night, season after season, bringing fans back for more.

There's no tried-and-true formula for greatness. Skill-limited players have forged outstanding careers out of the one or two areas of the game they have mastered. Multi-dimensional players have succeeded without ever having mastered a single skill. Some thrive because of their leadership abilities and others dominate because of their intensity and a

fierce blue-collar work ethic. Players with limited athletic ability often rank among the game's all-time greats; others with every athletic skill imaginable sometimes cannot overcome the lofty expectations predicted of them.

The following biographies profile two groups of players: those who retired after long careers that set them on a special plane above their peers; and current players who are completing outstanding careers or beginning NBA life with the extraordinary promise of greatness and success. Some of the can't-miss current players will miss and other unheralded performers will take their place.

But, most importantly, the revolving door to NBA greatness will continue to whirl, a dizzying motion that has not stopped since the league's birth in 1946.

KAREEM ABDUL-JABBAR
See Legends of the NBA *page 58*

ALVAN ADAMS
Born: 7–19–54, at Lawrence, Kan.
Position: Forward/center.
Team: Suns, 1975–88.

Adams was an underrated and undersized big man who gave the Phoenix Suns 13 solid NBA seasons. At 6–9 and 220 pounds, Adams was overmatched physically by many centers and was forced to operate in the high post. He did it well, forging a reputation

as one of the league's best passing big men while still banging the boards, running the floor and averaging in double figures. The intelligent Adams, who left the University of Oklahoma as a hardship draft pick in 1975, enjoyed a Rookie of the Year debut, averaging 19.0 points, 9.1 rebounds and 5.6 assists while leading the Suns to the NBA Finals. Over his 13 professional seasons, Adams' totals remained amazingly consistent as he changed gears and switched effectively between center and both forward positions. Adams, who played in one All-Star Game, ended his career in 1989 with 13,910 points (14.1 per game), 6,937 rebounds (7.0) and 4,012 assists (4.1).

DR. DETROIT *Isiah Thomas (right) pointed the way to a pair of championships*

MARK AGUIRRE

Born: 12–10–59, at Chicago, Ill.
Position: Forward.
Teams: Mavericks, 1981–89, Pistons, 1989–93, Clippers, 1993–94.

Aguirre was a multi-talented enigma who posted big numbers and frustrated coaches for 13 NBA seasons. The former DePaul star, the first overall pick of the 1981 draft, formed a love-hate relationship with Dallas coaches Dick Motta and John MacLeod for seven-plus seasons before being traded to Detroit in 1989. He proved to be a perfect role player for a Pistons team that posted back-to-back NBA championships (1989 and '90). The always showy, sometimes moody Aguirre was an explosive small forward. At 6–6, he could burn defenders with a feathery-soft jump shot from long range, he could pull up for the 10-foot power jumper and he could use his burly 235 pounds to slant across the middle or power to the basket. He also was an adept rebounder and passer who averaged better than 20 points for six straight seasons. The three-time All-Star finished his career in 1994 with 18,458 points (20.0) and 4,578 rebounds (5.0).

DANNY AINGE

Born: 3–17–59, at Eugene, Ore.
Position: Guard.
Teams: Celtics, 1981–89, Kings, 1989–90, Trail Blazers, 1990–92, Suns, 1992–95.

Ainge was a versatile shooting guard who helped the Boston Celtics win two championships and two other teams reach the NBA Finals. Ainge, a former Brigham Young University star who played four seasons of professional baseball, was an outstanding athlete who could drill timely jumpers from 3-point range and play a scrambling, physical defense that frustrated opponents and forced them into temperamental mistakes. He was especially adept at applying pressure to the ball and dropping back to

help out when it went to the middle. Ainge began his career in 1981 on the Celtics bench and was a role player for the 1984 champions. He worked his way into the starting lineup by 1985–86, when he averaged 10.7 points and 5.1 assists for another title team. The one-time All-Star later helped Portland and Phoenix reach the NBA Finals before retiring in 1995 with 11,964 points (11.5), including 1,002 from 3-point range.

KENNY ANDERSON

Born: 10–9–70, at Queens, N.Y.
Position: Guard.
Teams: Nets, 1991–96, Hornets, 1996; Trail Blazers, 1996–present.

The multi-talented Anderson is a ball-handling magician. He has the quickness and dribbling ability to take the ball anywhere he wants and either deliver it to the basket or an open teammate. The 6–1 Anderson was selected by New Jersey with the second overall pick of the 1991 draft after his sophomore season at Georgia Tech. Playing in his own backyard, he started slowly before jumping to the top of his position with averages of 18.8 points and 9.6 assists in a 1993–94 All-Star season. But he was plagued the next year by a lingering wrist injury and accusations that he was dominating the ball and taking bad shots. Anderson was traded to Charlotte in early 1996 and signed with Portland after the season, getting a fresh start with the rebuilding Blazers. The slender Anderson, more of a penetrator and scorer than a playmaker, has trouble fighting through defensive picks to utilize his great quickness and athleticism.

TINY DOUBLES *Archibald (left) was a prolific scorer and assist man for 13 seasons*

NATE (TINY) ARCHIBALD

Born: 9-2-48, at New York, N.Y.
Position: Guard.
Teams: Royals/Kings, 1970–76, Nets, 1976–77, Celtics, 1978–83, Bucks, 1983–84.

Archibald, a lightning-quick point guard out of the University of Texas-El Paso, showcased his triple-threat skills over a 13-year career that produced 16,481 points (18.8), 6,476 assists (7.4), three All-NBA first-team citations and six All-Star Game selections. The 6–1 Archibald was an outstanding passer and long-range shooter, but he was virtually unstoppable when penetrating the middle, either scoring, dishing off for an easy shot or drawing a foul (he led the league in free throws made three times). "Tiny" enjoyed his most impressive season for Kansas City-Omaha in 1972–73, when he won scoring (34.0) and assist (11.4) titles, becoming the first NBA player to lead the league in those two categories in the same season. With Archibald serving as their floor general, the Boston Celtics led the league in victories three consecutive seasons (1980–82) and won an NBA championship in 1981. He was elected to the Hall of Fame in 1991.

PAUL ARIZIN

Born: 4-9-28, at Philadelphia, Pa.
Position: Guard/forward.
Team: Warriors, 1950–52, 1954–62.

The 6–4 Arizin was a self-made star who didn't play competitive basketball until his sophomore season at Villanova. Two years later, in 1950, he led the nation with a 25.3 scoring average and was named College Player of the Year. Arizin's scoring prowess served him nicely during a 10-season NBA career that produced 16,266 points, a 22.8-point average, three All-NBA first-team citations and 10 All-Star Game invitations. Arizin, who lost two seasons to military service, was known for his picture-perfect jump shot and ability to carry a team. With Arizin and center Neil

Johnston forming a classic inside-outside combination in 1956, Philadelphia won an NBA championship. A year later, Arizin won the second of two scoring titles with a 25.6-point average. "Pitchin'" Paul retired in 1962 and was named to the NBA 25th Anniversary All-Time Team in 1970. He was elected to the Hall of Fame in 1977.

VIN BAKER

Born: 11–23–71, at Lake Wales, Fla.
Position: Forward/center.
Team: Bucks, 1993–present.

Baker came out of nowhere in 1993, to claim a spot among the game's top power forwards. That "nowhere" was the tiny college of Hartford where he still attracted enough attention to merit an eighth overall draft pick by the Milwaukee Bucks. The 6–11 Baker has blossomed quickly, establishing the paint as his personal playground where he outquicks opponents with a variety of spin moves and slide dribbles. Defenders have discovered the hard way that Baker is a warrior who punishes the offensive and defensive boards, goes hard to the basket and sacrifices his body on defense. He's also durable, a 40-minute player who led the league in minutes in his second season. The athletic Baker averaged 17.7 points and 10.3 rebounds in 1994–95 and the scoring average climbed to 21.1 in 1995–96. The two-time All-Star has the tools and work ethic to reach superstar status.

CHARLES BARKLEY

See Legends of the NBA *page 59*

RICK BARRY

See Legends of the NBA *page 60*

THE BUCK STOPS HERE *Young Milwaukee star Vin Baker has outstanding physical tools—and a work ethic to match*

ELGIN BAYLOR

See Legends of the NBA *page 61*

WALT BELLAMY

Born: 7–24–39, at New Bern, N.C.
Position: Center.
Teams: Packers/Zephyrs/Bullets, 1961–65, Knicks, 1965–68, Pistons, 1968–70, Hawks, 1970–74, Jazz, 1974–75.

Bellamy was an agile 6–11 center who provided serious competition for such contemporaries as Wilt Chamberlain, Bill Russell and a young Kareem Abdul-Jabbar. His Hall of Fame career spanned 14 seasons with five teams and produced 20,941 points (20.1 per game) and 14,241 rebounds (13.7), and his .516 field goal percentage ranked third all-time when he retired in 1975. The Chicago Packers grabbed the former Indiana University star with the first overall pick of the 1961 draft and he rewarded them immediately with averages of 31.6 points and 19 rebounds en route to Rookie of the Year honors. He averaged well over 20 points for the next four seasons and his rebounding average dipped below double digits only once in his first 12 years. Despite toiling in the massive shadows of Chamberlain and Russell, the steady and consistent Bellamy played in four All-Star Games, but he never hooked up with a championship team. He was elected to the Hall of Fame in 1993.

DAVE BING

Born: 11–24–43, at Washington, D.C.
Position: Guard.
Teams: Pistons, 1966–75, Bullets, 1975–77, Celtics, 1977–78.

Bing turned his graceful, fluid offensive skills into a Hall of Fame career that ended after 12 seasons and 18,327 points (20.3). The former Syracuse University star was an NBA Rookie of the Year (1967), a seven-time All-Star Game performer, a two-time All-NBA first-team selection and a one-time scoring champion (27.1 ppg in 1967–68). He joined the Pistons as the second overall draft pick in 1966 and became a classy playmaker for a weak Detroit team. The 6–3 Bing averaged 20 points as a rookie—the first of seven 20-point seasons—and claimed his scoring title in a breakthrough second campaign. But he would not play for a team with a winning record until 1970–71, and he would never fulfill his dream of a championship. Bing finished his career with two seasons in Washington and one in Boston. He was elected to the Hall of Fame in 1989.

LARRY BIRD

See Legends of the NBA *page 62*

ROLANDO BLACKMAN

Born: 2–26–59, at Panama City, Panama.
Position: Guard.
Teams: Mavericks, 1981–92, Knicks, 1992–94.

Blackman, who created defensive mismatches as a 6–6 guard, made good use of that advantage over an outstanding 13-year NBA career. The smooth Blackman, a 1981 draft pick out of Kansas State University, joined a second-year Dallas franchise and helped lead the Mavericks to respectability. From 1983–84 through 1991–92, the consistent Blackman averaged between 18.3 and 22.4

points, 2.7 and 3.8 assists and 3.2 and 4.6 rebounds per game. Blackman was equally deadly when penetrating the lane, posting up a shorter opponent or launching a jump shot from beyond the 3-point line. And he had the quickness to defend opposing point guards. Blackman, a four-time All-Star, teamed with Derek Harper for nine seasons in a first-rate backcourt that helped the Mavericks claim a Midwest Division title and a berth in the 1988 Western Conference finals. Blackman spent his final two seasons with the Knicks before retiring in 1994 with 17,623 career points (18.0 per game) and 2,981 assists (3.0).

EYES OF A HAWK
Guard Mookie Blaylock gives Atlanta fans a nice combination of offense, defense and durability

MOOKIE BLAYLOCK

Born: 3–20–67, at Garland, Tex.
Position: Guard.
Teams: Nets, 1989–92, Hawks, 1992–present.

The 6–1 Blaylock is a push-and-pass point guard who rates among the better defensive stoppers in the game. The former University of Oklahoma star is most highly regarded for his quick hands and a ball-hawking defensive style that has produced more then 200 steals in a season four times and two NBA All-Defensive first-team selections. But he's also a capable outside shooter, a fine passer who usually ranks among the league's assist leaders and a durable instigator of the fast break. Blaylock was taken by New Jersey in 1989 with the 12th overall pick of the NBA Draft and settled quickly into the Nets' rotation. But he was traded to Atlanta in 1992 and really blossomed a year later under new Hawks Coach Lenny Wilkens. The only knock against Blaylock, a 1994 All-Star, is his streaky outside shooting. When he's hot, look out. When he's not, he continues to fire, as evidenced by his 623 3-point attempts in 1995–96 (.371 success rate).

RON BOONE

Born: 9–6–46, at Oklahoma City, Okla.
Position: Guard.
Teams: Dallas Chaparrals (ABA), 1968–71, Utah Stars (ABA), 1971–75, St. Louis Spirits (ABA), 1975–76, Kings, 1976–78, Lakers, 1978–79, Jazz, 1979–81.

Boone was a durable all-around shooting guard who set a professional record by playing in 1,041 consecutive games, 135 more than NBA record-holder Randy Smith. The compact 6–2 former Idaho State University star played 660 of them in eight ABA seasons, compiling 12,153 points and an 18.4 average as the league's No. 3 all-time scorer. A member of Utah's 1971 ABA championship team, Boone was a physical player with powerful legs and the ability to mix it up with the big boys, but he also possessed a dangerous 20-foot jump shot. Boone, a 1975 ABA All-Star first-teamer, played in Dallas, Utah and St. Louis before signing with the Kansas City Kings after the ABA/NBA merger. He averaged 22.2 points as a 30-year-old NBA rookie and went on to finish his career with the Lakers and Jazz, never missing a game. Boone retired in 1981 with a combined ABA/NBA total of 17,437 points (16.8 per game).

BILL BRADLEY

Born: 7-28-43, at Crystal City, Mo.
Position: Forward.
Team: Knicks, 1967–77.

Bradley's story begins with his decision to spurn more than 70 scholarship offers and pay his own way to Princeton, where he became one of the most celebrated players in college basketball history as well as a Rhodes Scholar. "Dollar Bill" turned the Ivy League into his personal showcase, scoring 2,503 points and averaging 30.2 over his dazzling career. Before joining the Knicks in 1967, the 6–5 Bradley captained the U.S. to the 1964 Olympic gold medal and completed his Rhodes Scholar studies at Oxford in England. Bradley, a thinking-man's player and one of the game's best outside shooters, fit right into a New York Hall of Fame mix—Willis Reed, Dave DeBusschere, Earl Monroe, Walt Frazier—that produced NBA championships in 1970 and '73. He retired in 1977 with a 12.4-point average, but his contributions

IN THE KNICK OF TIME *New York's Bill Bradley was the ultimate team player*

were measured by intangibles that don't show up on statistical charts. Bradley, who went on to another career as a U.S. Senator from New Jersey, was elected to the Hall of Fame in 1982.

FRANK BRIAN

Born: 5-1-23, at Zachary, La.
Position: Guard.
Teams: Anderson Packers, 1949–50, Blackhawks, 1950–51, Pistons, 1951–56.

Brian was an intense, fast-shooting guard who could score from anywhere on the court. The 6–1 "Flash," whose career at Louisiana State University was interrupted by three years of military service in World War II, was signed by the Anderson Packers of the National Basketball League in 1947 and helped them win the 1949 championship. When the Packers folded after one season in the newly formed NBA, Brian played one year for Tri-Cities before finding a permanent home with the Fort

Wayne Pistons. Brian, who released the ball from a two-handed set with arms extended above his head, was known for his shifty drives to the basket, where he dipped into his sizeable bag of shots. He averaged double figures in each of his first four NBA seasons and helped the Pistons reach the NBA Finals in 1955 and '56, retiring after the five-game loss to Philadelphia. Brian was a 1949 All-NBL first-team selection and a two-time NBA All-Star.

BILL BRIDGES

Born: 4-4-39, at Hobbs, N.M.
Position: Forward.
Teams: Hawks, 1962–71, 76ers, 1971–72, Lakers, 1972–74, Warriors, 1975.

Bridges was the basketball equivalent of a football lineman: battling in the trenches, delivering and receiving elbows, getting little recognition. He was an outstanding rebounder, a tenacious defensive stopper and a battler under

the basket. Bridges made his NBA debut in 1962–63 for the St. Louis Hawks after spending a season and a half with Kansas City in the short-lived American Basketball League. The 6–6 former University of Kansas star started slowly, averaging 5.3 and 8.5 rebounds off the bench for a team that featured Hall of Famers Bob Pettit and Cliff Hagan. But over the next nine seasons, Bridges never dipped below double figures in either points or rebounds while taking on all of the Hawks' biggest defensive assignments. When he retired in 1975, after short stints with the 76ers, Lakers and Warriors, Bridges had pulled down 11,054 rebounds (11.9), scored 11,012 points (11.9) and played in three All-Star Games.

BILL CARTWRIGHT

Born: 7-30-57, at Lodi, Calif.
Position: Center.
Teams: Knicks, 1979–88, Bulls, 1988–94, SuperSonics, 1994–95.

Cartwright was a reliable if unspectacular 7–1 center who played 16 NBA seasons in New York, Chicago and Seattle, helping the Bulls capture consecutive championships in 1991, '92 and '93. The former University of San Francisco star was a combination of power and finesse. If a game called for a physical effort, Cartwright could power his 245 pounds to the basket. If finesse was required, he could pile up points with an accurate turn-around jumper. Cartwright carried more of a scoring load with the Knicks, twice averaging better than 20 points. But he played more of a supporting role for the Bulls, who had plenty of firepower with Michael Jordan and Scottie Pippen. Cartwright, a 1980 All-Star who sat out the 1984–85 and

SIXER FIXER *Point man Maurice Cheeks led the 76ers to a 1983 championship*

1985–86 seasons with a stress fracture in his foot, retired in 1995 with 12,713 points (13.2) and 6,102 rebounds (6.3).

AL CERVI

Born: 2-12-17, at Buffalo, N.Y.
Position: Guard.
Teams: Buffalo Bisons (NBL), 1937–38, Royals (NBL), 1945–48, Nationals (NBL/NBA), 1948–53.

Cervi was a scrappy, hustling two-way guard in the professional game's formative years. He began his career with the National Basketball League's Buffalo Bisons in 1937, advancing to the hardcourts from the sandlots of his Buffalo youth. Cervi's career was interrupted by a long stint in the military during World War II, but he joined the NBL's Rochester Royals in 1945 and played three seasons before moving to Syracuse as player-coach. When the Nationals moved to the NBA in 1949–50, Cervi led them to the NBA Finals. The 5-11 Cervi, an explosive one-on-one performer and an outstanding defender, was considered a master of the three-point play. But more than anything, he was a fiery leader who brought out the best in his teammates and players. After Cervi's 1953 retirement, he went on to coach the Nationals/76ers to 366 victories and the 1955 NBA championship. Cervi was elected to the Hall of Fame in 1984.

WILT CHAMBERLAIN

See Legends of the NBA *page 63*

MAURICE CHEEKS

Born: 9-8-56, at Chicago, Ill.
Position: Guard.
Teams: 76ers, 1978–89, Spurs, 1989–90, Knicks, 1990–91, Hawks, 1991–92, Nets, 1992–93.

Cheeks, the quiet point guard, was a coach's dream. He wasn't a big scorer, he didn't run up prolific assist numbers and he didn't dazzle fans with fancy ballhandling or passes. But the 6-1 Cheeks was one of the best floor generals of the 1980s. He seldom made turnovers or mistakes, he always got the ball to the right people in the right situations and when defenses sagged on Julius Erving or Moses Malone, he was a dangerous outside shooter. Not surprisingly, Cheeks also was one of the league's best defensive guards— a four-time All-Defensive first-team selection. The former West Texas State star arrived in Philadelphia in 1978 and guided the star-studded 76ers team to seven consecutive seasons of 50-plus wins, three NBA Finals and the 1983 championship. After brief stints in San Antonio, New York, Atlanta and New Jersey, Cheeks retired in 1993 with 15-year totals of 12,195 points (11.1 per game), 7,392 assists (6.7) and 2,310 steals.

DERRICK COLEMAN

Born: 6-21-67, at Mobile, Ala.
Position: Forward.
Teams: Nets, 1990–95, 76ers, 1995–present.

Talent-wise, Coleman is a gifted power forward who should be carving out a Hall of Fame career. Psychologically, the Syracuse University product is a 6-10 problem child who might never advance beyond predictions of stardom. There's nothing Coleman can't accomplish on the court. He's athletic, he can score with his lefthanded jumper inside or out, he can pass, he can handle the ball and he can block shots. He's a potential triple-double in every game. But in five-plus seasons with the Nets and one partial season in Philadelphia, Coleman has been a constant disruption, setting himself above team rules, begging out of games because of minor injuries and simply going through the motions sometimes when he does play. Still, the 1991 Rookie of the Year and 1994 All-Star has averaged better than 20 points and 10 rebounds three times. The bottom line: Coleman can be as good—or bad—as he wants to be.

MICHAEL COOPER

Born: 4-15-56, at Los Angeles, Calif.
Position: Guard/forward.
Team: Lakers, 1978–90.

Cooper, a 6-7 swingman with great quickness and leaping ability, was the defensive genius behind the Los Angeles Lakers' five championships of the 1980s. The lean, 170-pound hardbody was a classic stopper who never backed down from anybody. He could defend the quickest point guard or the 280-pound power forward. While teammates Kareem Abdul-Jabbar, Magic Johnson and James Worthy were taking care of offensive business, Cooper was coming off the bench to work in the trenches and provide inspirational leadership. But the five-time NBA All-Defensive first-team selection could provide other kinds of inspiration as well. Cooper was a good passer and he could nail the 3-pointer with his one-handed set shot. And the Lakers used him on an alley-oop slam that never failed to bring

PHILADELPHIA FREEDOM *Fiery Billy Cunningham (32), a jumping-jack forward, was a key member of the Philadelphia 76ers' powerful 1967 championship team*

down the rafters. Cooper, the NBA's 1986–87 Defensive Player of the Year, finished his career in 1990 after 12 Los Angeles seasons and 168 career playoff games.

LARRY COSTELLO

Born: 7-2-31, at Minoa, N.Y.
Position: Guard.
Teams: Warriors, 1954–57, Nationals/76ers, 1957–68.

Before beginning his successful coaching career, Costello toiled for 13 seasons as a fast-moving point guard for the Philadelphia Warriors and Syracuse Nationals. Costello knew only one speed: fast, and his style was intense, emotional and relentless. The 6–1 Costello, one of the last practitioners of the two-handed set shot, was at his best in a fast-break

offense where he could use his speed to blow past helpless defenders and create scoring opportunities. He was a defensive gambler, using his speed to make up for mistakes. Costello, who was picked on the second round of the 1954 draft out of Niagara University, began his career with the Warriors but enjoyed his best years in Syracuse and Philadelphia, where the Nationals moved in 1963. He was a member of the 76ers' powerful 1967 NBA championship team. Costello, a six-time All-Star, retired in 1968 with 8,622 points (12.2 per game) and 3,215 assists (4.6). Three years later, he coached the Milwaukee Bucks to their first championship.

BOB COUSY

See Legends of the NBA *page 64*

DAVE COWENS

Born: 10-25-48, at Newport, Ky.
Position: Center.
Teams: Celtics, 1970–80, Bucks, 1982–83.

The 6–9 Cowens, a mobile, under-sized center, played with an all-out intensity and aggressive style that helped the Celtics win two NBA championships. The former Florida State star disproved the theory that a center had to play with his back to the basket. Cowens roamed the perimeter sinking soft lefthanded jumpers, used his superior quickness on drives to the basket and played with a passion that gave him the edge over bigger opponents. He won co-Rookie of the Year honors in 1970–71 and a Most Valuable Player award in 1973. Cowens, a

seven-time All-Star Game performer, combined with John Havlicek and Jo Jo White on the Celtics' 1974 and '76 title teams. He served one season (1978–79) as player-coach and finished his career with 13,516 points (17.6) and 10,444 rebounds (13.6). Cowens, who was named to coach the Charlotte Hornets after the 1995–96 deason, was elected to the Hall of Fame in 1991.

BILLY CUNNINGHAM

Born: 6-3-43, at Brooklyn, N.Y.
Position: Forward.
Teams: 76ers, 1965–72, 1974–76, Carolina Cougars (ABA), 1972–74.

Cunningham, a.k.a. "the Kangaroo Kid," was known for his leaping ability and the fiery intensity he brought to the game. A lefthanded slasher out of the University of North Carolina, Cunningham vaulted into NBA prominence with a take-no-prisoners style that won the hearts of Philadelphia fans and earned him a prominent place on one of the greatest teams ever assembled. The 1967 76ers, featuring the 6–7 Cunningham, Wilt Chamberlain, Hal Greer and Chet Walker, stormed to 68 victories and ended the Celtics' eight-year championship reign. Cunningham, who also spent two seasons and won an MVP award in the ABA, scored 16,310 professional points and grabbed 7,981 rebounds in an 11-season career that included three All-NBA first-team selections and four NBA All-Star Game appearances. He later coached the 76ers to 454 victories (averaging 57 wins per season) and another championship. Cunningham was elected to the Hall of Fame in 1986.

LOUIE DAMPIER

Born: 11–20–44, at Indianapolis, Ind.
Position: Guard.
Teams: Kentucky Colonels (ABA), 1967–76, Spurs, 1976–79.

Dampier was a hustling, clever, straight-shooting point guard who spent most of his career with the Kentucky Colonels in the ABA. The 6-foot Dampier was living proof that a hard-working little man could thrive in the lofty world of professional basketball. He made a science out of the ABA's 3-point shot, connecting on 794, and he scored more points (13,726), handed out more assists (4,044) and played in more games (728) than any player in the league's nine-year existence. The impressive thing about Dampier was his ability to adjust to his sup-

porting players. In his first three seasons, the former University of Kentucky star averaged better than 20 points per game. When 7–2 Artis Gilmore and high-scoring Dan Issel arrived, he became more of a passer and floor general. Dampier helped the Colonels win the 1975 ABA championship and spent his final three seasons with San Antonio after the 1976 merger. He finished with combined ABA/NBA totals of 15,279 points and 4,687 assists.

BOB DANDRIDGE

Born: 11–15–47, at Richmond, Va.
Position: Forward.
Teams: Bucks, 1969–77, 1981–82, Bullets, 1977–81.

The hard-working Dandridge was an outstanding do-everything small forward who helped two teams win NBA championships. A slender 6–6, 195-pounder, he was the perfect supporting actor for young Lew Alcindor when the Milwaukee Bucks captured the 1971 title and for Washington big men Elvin Hayes and Wes Unseld when the Bullets won in 1978. He was an accomplished shooter, rebounder, passer and defender—a player who could read the game and do whatever his team might need to win. Most of Dandridge's best work was performed in the trenches—and in the locker room. Dandridge spent his first eight seasons in Milwaukee, averaging better than 18 points and six rebounds seven times. He played for two Washington teams that reached the NBA Finals before closing his career with a 1981–82 return engagement in Milwaukee. The four-time All-Star scored 15,530 points (18.5 per game), grabbed 5,715 rebounds (6.8) and handed out 2,846 assists (3.4).

MEL DANIELS

Born: 7–20–44, at Detroit, Mich.
Position: Center.
Teams: Minnesota Muskies (ABA), 1967–68, Indiana Pacers (ABA), 1968–74, Memphis Sounds (ABA), 1974–75, New York Nets (NBA), 1976–77.

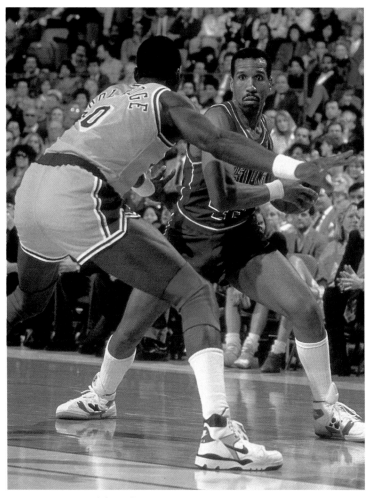

HAVE GUN, WILL TRAVEL *Adrian Dantley was a scoring machine over 15 seasons*

Daniels was a two-time ABA Most Valuable Player and a key figure on Indiana's 1970, '72 and '73 ABA championship teams. The quiet Daniels was a slender but muscular 6–9 workhorse who possessed a soft fallaway jumper. He averaged better than 20 points three times and won three ABA rebounding titles, never averaging less than 15 boards in any of his first six professional seasons. Daniels provided the blue-collar ethic for a flashy Indiana team that boasted such stars as George McGinnis, Roger Brown and Freddie Lewis. Daniels, a former University of New Mexico star, passed up an offer from the NBA's Cincinnati Royals in 1967 and signed with the Minnesota Muskies, earning Rookie of the Year honors. The seven-time All-Star spent his next six seasons with the Pacers, piling up most of his 11,739 career points (18.7) and

9,494 rebounds (15.1). Daniels spent his final ABA season in Memphis and played 11 NBA games for the New York Nets after the 1976 merger.

ADRIAN DANTLEY

Born: 2–28–56, at Washington, D.C.
Position: Guard/forward.
Teams: Braves, 1976–77, Pacers, 1977, Lakers, 1977–79, Jazz, 1979–86, Pistons, 1986–89, Mavericks, 1989–90, Bucks, 1990–91.

Dantley was probably the premier one-on-one scoring machine of his era. He played for seven teams over 15 seasons, averaged better than 20 points 11 times and won two scoring titles, with averages of 30.7 and 30.6. Amazingly, the 6–5, 210-pound Dantley, who divided time between small forward and guard, scored most of his points in the paint, defying centers who usually discouraged such activity. Dantley first jumped into the national consciousness in the mid-70s as a scoring phenom for Notre Dame and a 1976 Olympic hero. He averaged 20.3 points and 7.6 rebounds in 1976–77 for Buffalo, winning Rookie of the Year honors. But he was traded three times in his first four years before finally settling in Utah. Dantley played seven seasons with the Jazz before career-ending stints with Detroit, Dallas and Milwaukee. The six-time All-Star retired in 1991 with 23,177 points (24.3) and 5,455 rebounds (5.7).

BRAD DAUGHERTY

Born: 10–19–65, at Black Mountain, N.C.
Position: Center.
Team: Cavaliers, 1986–present.

Daugherty was a powerful force in Cleveland's middle for seven-plus seasons before undergoing major back surgery. The 7-foot former University of North Carolina star has not played since February 1994, when he left the lineup averaging 17 points and 10.2 rebounds. Daugherty was selected by the Cavaliers with the first overall pick of the 1986 draft and he didn't disappoint, stepping right into the lineup with rookie averages of 15.7 points and 8.1 rebounds. In 1990–91, he raised those averages to 21.6 and 10.9 and remained at that level for three straight seasons. Daugherty, not blessed with great jumping ability, relies on fundamentals and a deadly hook shot. The five-time All-Star also is one of the best passing centers in the game and a solid man-to-man defender. What Daugherty lacks in flash he makes up for with consistency. The big question: Will he be able to reclaim that consistency after his long layoff?

BOB DAVIES

Born: 1–15–20, at Harrisburg, Pa.
Position: Guard.
Team: Royals (NBL/BAA/NBA), 1945–55.

The 6–1 Davies was the premier playmaker of the early NBA. Content to help teammates carry the scoring load, he was a magician with the ball, performing behind-the-back, over-the-head and through-the-leg maneuvers that astounded conservative fans and players of his era. After leading Seton Hall University to 43 straight victories from 1939 to '41 and serving in World War II, Davies joined Rochester of the old National Basketball League and remained with the Royals for 10 seasons—seven of them in the BAA/NBA. Davies, who once held the single-game record of 20 assists, led the BAA with 321 in 1948–49 and helped the Royals capture the NBA championship in 1951. He was a four-time All-BAA/NBA first teamer and played in the league's first four All-Star Games. Davies, who retired in 1955, was elected to the Hall of Fame in 1969 and was selected to the NBA 25th Anniversary All-Time Team a year later.

WALTER DAVIS

Born: 9–9–54, at Pineville, N.C.
Position: Guard/forward.
Teams: Suns, 1977–88, Nuggets, 1988–91, 1991–92, Trail Blazers, 1991.

The graceful Davis was one of the purest long-range shooters the game has ever produced. At 6–6, the slender 195-pounder was a mismatch waiting to happen. If he played small forward, he was too fast and quick for the bigger opponents who tried to guard him. If he played shooting guard, he could post up smaller defenders. Either way, Davis was an offensive weapon who averaged more than 20 points six times and finished his 15-year career with 19,521—an 18.9 average. Davis, a University of North Carolina star and Olympic gold medal winner (1976), was drafted by Phoenix in 1977 and made an immediate impact, averaging 24.2 points and winning NBA Rookie of the Year honors. He spent 11 years in Phoenix, helping the Suns record four 50-

victory seasons and reach the 1984 Western Conference finals. Davis, a six-time All-Star, retired in 1992, at age 37, after short stints with Denver and Portland.

DAVE DEBUSSCHERE

Born: 10–16–40, at Detroit, Mich.
Position: Forward.
Teams: Pistons, 1962–68, Knicks, 1968–74.

DeBusschere earned a reputation as one of the game's all-time great defensive forwards, but he was no slouch on the offensive end, either. Over 12 NBA seasons with Detroit and New York, he scored 14,053 points (16.1 per game) and pulled down 9,618 rebounds (11.0). As a shooter, he was dangerous from inside or out. As a defender, he was a physical banger who could take the opposing team's best player out of the game. DeBusschere's versatile talents were wasted for a Detroit team that qualified for the playoffs twice in six-plus seasons. But the 6–6 DeBusschere was a perfect fit for a Knicks team that rolled to NBA championships in 1970 and '73. A six-time All-Defensive first-team selection, he held several NBA distinctions. At age 24, he was the youngest coach in NBA history (1964–67 with the Pistons). And for four seasons (1962–65), he doubled as a baseball pitcher in the Chicago White Sox organization. DeBusschere was elected to the Hall of Fame in 1982.

CLYDE DREXLER

Born: 6–22–62, at New Orleans, La.
Position: Guard.
Teams: Trail Blazers, 1983–95, Rockets, 1995–present.

Drexler might not be the most athletic and stylish performer in the Michael Jordan era, but he's

ROCKET MAN *Clyde Drexler finally found championship success with Houston*

close. "Clyde the Glide" plays on a different level of basketball sub-space. He slashes to the basket with aerial elegance, hangs majestically in the lane until it's safe to release a soft jumper and pops from long range. But the 6–7 Drexler is most dangerous on the break, where he can embarrass defenders with mouth-watering moves and no-look passes. Drexler, a first-round 1983 draft pick, gave Portland fans 11 exciting seasons, averaging better than 20 points six times and posting consistent assist and rebound numbers. He led the Trail Blazers to the NBA Finals in 1990 and '92, but his first championship did not come until 1995, after a late-season trade to Houston saw him reunited with his former University of Houston teammate Hakeem Olajuwon. Drexler, an eight-time All-Star and 1992 All-NBA first-teamer, was a member of the 1992 Olympic Dream Team.

JOE DUMARS

Born: 5–24–63, at Shreveport, La.
Position: Guard.
Team: Pistons, 1985–present.

The 6–3 Dumars has been one of the NBA's top shooting guards and classiest acts for more than a decade. Two of his Detroit seasons produced championships (1989 and '90) and another ended

NO ORDINARY JOE *Shooting guard Dumars was one of Detroit's top guns during the Pistons' 1989 and '90 championship seasons*

in the NBA Finals (1988). Most of Dumars' career was played along-side Isiah Thomas, one of the game's all-time best point guards. Thomas' leadership freed Dumars for the two things he does best: long-range shooting—he has averaged better than 20 points per game in three seasons—and tenacious defense, which earned him four NBA All-Defensive first-team citations during the Pistons' "Bad Boys" era. The former McNeese State University star can light up the scoreboard, as he did in a 1994 game when he hit a record-tying 10 3-pointers, and the 1989 NBA Finals when he earned MVP honors. The five-time All-Star has shown his versatility in recent years by switching to the Pistons' point.

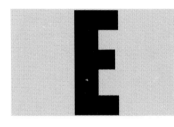

ALEX ENGLISH

Born: 1–5–54, at Columbia, S.C.
Position: Forward.
Teams: Bucks, 1976–78, Pacers, 1978–80, Nuggets, 1980–90, Mavericks, 1990–91.

English was the trigger man for Denver coach Doug Moe's high-powered 1980s offense—a free-lancing style that gave English the opportunity to showcase his uncanny scoring ability. The skinny 6–7 forward, a contradictory combination of graceful glides and awkward contortions, delivered his unorthodox jump shot, arms fully extended over his head, with a flick of his wrist. The shot was virtually unstoppable when he got within 12 feet of the basket. English, a former star at the University of South Carolina, was a long-shot second-round draft choice who spent four non-descript seasons with Milwaukee and Indiana before being traded to Denver. Over the next decade, he averaged better than 20 points

per game nine times, topped 2,000 points in a season eight times and won one scoring title. By the time he announced his retirement in 1991, English had accumulated 25,613 points (21.5), grabbed 6,538 rebounds (5.5) and played in eight All-Star Games.

JULIUS ERVING

See Legends of the NBA *page 65*

PATRICK EWING

See Legends of the NBA *page 66*

LARRY FOUST

Born: 6–24–28, at Painesville, Ohio.
Position: Forward/center;
Teams: Pistons, 1950–57, Lakers, 1957–60, Hawks, 1960–62.

Foust, one of the best big men in the early NBA, battled the George Mikans, Dolph Schayes and Arnie Risens of his era on even terms as the centerpiece of the Fort Wayne Pistons. Foust, a 6–9, 250-pound giant, entered the professional ranks in 1950 after four outstanding seasons at La Salle University. He made an immediate impact, averaging 13.5 points and 10 rebounds in his rookie season and showing an ability to match up defensively against his fellow big men. Foust was amazingly consistent, averaging from 12.2 to 17.0 points over his first 10 seasons while topping the 1,000-rebound barrier five times. He also was an eight-time All-Star and an All-NBA first-team selection in 1955. Foust, who helped the Pistons reach the NBA Finals in 1955 and '56, played briefly with Minneapolis and St. Louis before retiring in 1962 with 11,198 points (13.7 per game) and 8,041 rebounds (9.8).

WALT FRAZIER

See Legends of the NBA *page 67*

WORLD B. FREE

Born: 12–9–53, at Atlanta, Ga.
Position: Guard.
Teams: 76ers, 1975–78, 1986–87, Clippers, 1978–80, Warriors, 1980–82, Cavaliers, 1982–86, Rockets, 1987–88.

Free, a flashy, fast-shooting 6–3 guard, scored 17,955 points and averaged a lofty 20.3 over a 13-year NBA career that covered five cities. He was instant offense, from his deadly long-range jumper to his creative, whirling, spinning shot repertoire that confounded defenders and brought fans to their feet. But Free, who was drafted by Philadelphia in 1975 out of little Guilford College, had as many detractors as fans. He often was criticized as an undisciplined gunner, a hotdog who would play little defense. Conversely, he was praised as a charming man who brought personality and flair to the game. Free, who legally changed his first name from "Lloyd" to "World" in 1981, was all of the above. In retrospect, he was used as a hired gun by struggling teams in search of offensive and box-office help. Free never will be listed among the NBA's great team players, but as a pure offensive force he had few peers.

JOE FULKS

Born: 10–26–21, at Birmingham, Ky.
Position: Forward/center.
Teams: Warriors, 1946–54.

Fulks is credited as the first player to use a jump shot and he reigned as the early BAA/NBA's scoring sensation. The 6–5 Fulks, nicknamed "Jumpin' Joe," captured scoring championships in his first two Philadelphia seasons, averaging 23.2 points per game in 1946–47 and 22.1 a year later. Both figures were astounding for the period. But there was more to Fulks than just a pretty jump shot. He also was a rugged defensive rebounder and a three-time All-BAA first-team selection. Fulks' all-around play led the Warriors to the BAA's first

JUMP START *Joe Fulks, a shooting star*

championship and they advanced to the Finals in 1948 before falling to Baltimore. He finished his eight-year career with a 16.4-point average and his 63-point game in 1949 stood as an NBA record for 10 years. Fulks, who retired in 1954, was named to the NBA 25th Anniversary All-Time Team in 1970, and was elected to the Hall of Fame in 1977.

HARRY GALLATIN

Born: 4–26–27, at Roxana, Ill.
Position: Forward/center.
Teams: Knicks, 1948–57, Pistons, 1957–58.

The 6–6 Gallatin was a workhorse rebounder for a Knicks team that made three consecutive trips to the NBA Finals in the early 1950s, losing once to Rochester and twice to the powerful Minneapolis Lakers. Never a prolific scorer (13.0 over a 10-year career), he led the NBA in rebounding in 1953–54 (15.3) and ranked among the league's top 10 rebounders six times. Gallatin was nicknamed "Horse" because of his prolific work on the boards and a durability that allowed him to set a then-NBA record of 682 consecutive

games played. The former Missouri State Teachers College star was an All-NBA first-team selection in 1954 and the NBA's Coach of the Year for St. Louis in 1963, five years after his playing career had ended with a final season in Detroit. Gallatin, who was elected to the Hall of Fame in 1990, coached the Knicks in 1965 and '66.

GEORGE GERVIN

Born: 4–27–52, at Detroit, Mich.
Position: Guard.
Teams: Virginia Squires (ABA), 1972–74, Spurs (ABA/NBA), 1974–85, Bulls, 1985–86.

Gervin was one of the great scorers in NBA history. He seemed to glide around the court, delivering the ball to the basket with uncanny accuracy from the most impossible angles and positions. "The Iceman" was always cool and his shot assortment was as clever as his game was explosive. Gervin began his career with the ABA's Virginia Squires after his sophomore season at Eastern Michigan University. But it wasn't until he moved to the NBA with the Spurs in 1976 that it took off. Gervin averaged more than 20 points nine consecutive seasons and topped 30 twice en route to four scoring titles. When he retired in 1986 after one season in Chicago, Gervin had six 2,000-plus-point seasons, 26,595 combined ABA/NBA points and a 25.1 career average. He also had five All-NBA first-team citations and nine All-Star Game appearances, including a 34-point effort that netted him MVP honors in 1980.

ARTIS GILMORE

Born: 9–21–49, at Chipley, Fla.
Position: Center.
Teams: Kentucky Colonels (ABA), 1971–76, Bulls, 1976–82, 1987, Spurs, 1982–87, Celtics, 1988.

Gilmore, at 7–2 and 265 pounds, was a powerful center whose prolific numbers were overshadowed by contemporary Kareem Abdul-Jabbar. Gilmore was the polar opposite of Abdul-Jabbar—a

plodding, no-finesse inside bruiser who dominated with his powerful legs and legendary strength. And whereas Abdul-Jabbar played on six NBA championship teams, Gilmore never got close to a title in 12 NBA seasons with Chicago, San Antonio and Boston. But nobody can deny Gilmore his numbers, which were compiled over a 17-year career in the ABA and NBA: 24,041 points (18.1), 16,330 rebounds (12.3), 11 All-Star Games and one regular-season and playoff MVP (both in the ABA). When Gilmore retired in 1988, he was the NBA's all-time leader in field-goal percentage (.599), a product of his short left-handed hook, delivered for years from point-blank range. Gilmore, who earned just about every ABA honor imaginable in five years with Kentucky, played for the Colonels' 1975 ABA championship team.

ARTISTRY *Gilmore was a power source*

TOM GOLA

Born: 1–13–33, at Philadelphia, Pa.
Position: Guard/forward.
Teams: Warriors, 1955–62, Knicks, 1962–66.

The versatile Gola is one of two men to play on NIT, NCAA and NBA championship teams—and all came in Philadelphia, the city of his birth. The 6–6 Gola, a local high school hero, chose to play collegiate basketball at La Salle and his achievements there took on a storybook aura. En route to becoming college basketball's first four-time All-American, Gola averaged 20.9 points, grabbed an NCAA career-record 2,201 rebounds and earned 1955 College Player of the Year honors. He also led La Salle to the 1952 NIT and 1954 NCAA Tournament titles. When Philadelphia grabbed Gola with the first pick of the 1955 NBA draft, the Warriors got a quick, aggressive performer who could score, pass, rebound and play stifling defense. As a rookie, Gola teamed with Neil Johnston and Paul Arizin on the Warriors' 1956 championship team. He played 10 seasons with the Warriors and Knicks and performed in four All-Star Games. Gola was elected to the Hall of Fame in 1975.

GAIL GOODRICH

Born: 4–23–43, at Los Angeles, Calif.
Position: Guard.
Teams: Lakers, 1965–68, 1970–76, Suns, 1968–70, Jazz, 1976–79.

THE PHILADELPHIA STORY *Hal Greer (right) was a straight shooter for one of the NBA's greatest teams—the 1966-67 76ers*

Goodrich was a versatile little man who could swing effectively between the point and shooting guard positions. The 6–1 left-hander was a phenomenal scorer who always performed in an attacking mode. He would barrel through the lane, pull up for quick jumpers or create his own shots with deft one-on-one moves. Goodrich, also a good long-range shooter, had lightning-quick hands that allowed him to get off impossible shots over bigger defenders. After leading UCLA to NCAA Tournament titles in 1964 and '65, Goodrich spent his first three NBA seasons coming off the Los Angeles Lakers' bench and the next two as point guard for the expansion Phoenix Suns. When he was reacquired by the Lakers, Goodrich became the focal point of the offense, averaging 20 points or better four straight years. The five-time All-Star, a 1974 All-

NBA first-teamer who played his final three seasons in New Orleans, retired in 1979 with 19,181 points (18.6 per game) and 4,805 assists (4.7).

HORACE GRANT

Born: 7–4–65, at Augusta, Ga.
Position: Forward.
Teams: Bulls, 1987–94, Magic, 1994–present.

The 6–10 Grant is a highly respected blue-collar banger who provides the Orlando Magic with intensity, leadership, rebounding, interior defense and many of the little things that don't show up in box scores. The proof of Grant's value can be found in his three championship rings, reminders of seven glorious seasons in Chicago where he did the trenchwork for the three-peat Bulls of Michael Jordan and Scottie Pippen. Now he is being asked to take the

inside pressure off Magic center Shaquille O'Neal, a job he performed admirably in 1994–95 and 1995–96. He averaged 12.8 points and 9.7 rebounds for an Orlando team that reached the 1995 NBA Finals. Grant, a 1987 first-round draft pick out of Clemson University, complements his offensive work with a tenacious, clawing defense that limits intrusions into the paint. The 1994 All-Star, whose twin brother Harvey also plays in the NBA, signed with Orlando as a free agent in 1994.

HAL GREER

Born: 6–26–36, at Huntington, W. Va.
Position: Guard.
Team: Nationals/76ers, 1958–73.

Greer's sweet jump shot was a Syracuse and Philadelphia staple for 15 NBA seasons. Through good days and bad, the 6–2 guard pro-

vided consistent, durable, athletic play that made him one of the stars of his era. Greer joined the Syracuse Nationals as a second-round 1958 draft pick out of Marshall University and carved out a Hall of Fame career as one of the game's best outside shooters. He had the innate ability to dominate games—an ability that resulted in a career average of 19.2 and eight seasons of 20 or more points per game. Greer also recorded 4,540 career assists and played in 1,122 games—a record when he retired in 1973. But his most memorable season was 1966–67, when he averaged 22.1 points and teamed with Wilt Chamberlain, Billy Cunningham, Chet Walter, Lucious Jackson and Wali Jones on the 76ers team that ended Boston's eight-year championship reign. Greer, who played in 10 All-Star Games, was elected to the Hall of Fame in 1981.

DARRELL GRIFFITH

Born: 6–16–58, at Louisville, Ky.
Position: Guard.
Team: Jazz, 1980–91.

Griffith, alias "Dr. Dunkenstein," was a high-flying guard who excited fans with his acrobatic dunks and long-range bombs. From his first game for the University of Louisville through his 10 NBA seasons with the Utah Jazz, the 6–4 Griffith was an electrifying performer who kept fans, players and coaches on the edge of their seats. Griffith was blessed with a 4-foot vertical leap that was neutralized by knee problems. But he still could sky with the best of the game's top players and his outside shot was lethal. His only weakness was a preference for the perimeter game that kept him from using his inside ability. After leading Louisville to the 1980 NCAA Tournament championship and claiming national Player of the Year honors, Griffith averaged 20.6 points for Utah and was named NBA Rookie of the Year. He never enjoyed that level of success again, but he finished his productive career in 1991 with 12,391 points (16.2).

RICHIE GUERIN

Born: 5–29–32, at New York, N.Y.
Position: Guard.
Teams: Knicks, 1956–63, Hawks, 1963–67, 1968–70.

Guerin was an intense, up-tempo guard who doubled for five of his 13 NBA seasons as player-coach of the St. Louis/Atlanta Hawks. Guerin, one of the last two-handed set-shot artists, was most comfortable in the attack mode, using his speed to blow past defenders in his trademark dash to the basket. At 6–4, he was bigger than most guards and quick enough to badger them with his stubborn defense. Guerin, a six-time All-Star, dove for loose balls, battled for rebounds and speeded up the game with his very presence on the court. After four years at Iona College, Guerin played seven-plus seasons for the New York Knicks, averaging better than 20 points four times and twice topping 500 assists. Guerin began doubling as Hawks coach in 1964 and directed the team to 327 victories through 1971–72, two years after his retirement as a player. He finished his career with 14,676 points (17.3) and 4,211 assists (5.0).

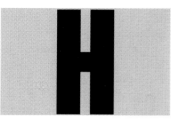

CLIFF HAGAN

Born: 12–9–31, at Owensboro, Ky.
Position: Forward.
Teams: Hawks, 1956–66, Dallas Chaparrals (ABA), 1967–70.

Hagan will forever be remembered as one of the two forwards traded by the Boston Celtics for the draft rights to Bill Russell. But Hagan forged a Hall of Fame career of his own—elected in 1977—using a deadly hook shot and a natural scoring prowess to amass 14,870 career points in 10 NBA seasons with St. Louis and three more with the ABA's Dallas Chaparrals. The 6–4 Hagan, a high-scoring collegiate star at the University of Kentucky under legendary Coach Adolph Rupp, teamed with Bob Pettit on a Hawks team that won five Western Division titles, captured the 1958 championship and reached the NBA Finals three other times. He averaged 18 points over his NBA career and played in five All-Star Games. The mobile Hagan, who once scored 26 points in a quarter, completed his career in 1970 as player-coach of the Chaparrals.

ANFERNEE HARDAWAY

Born: 7–18–72, at Memphis, Tenn.
Position: Guard/forward.
Team: Magic, 1993–present.

The athletic Hardaway, a 6–7 swingman, lights the fuse in Orlando's offense and makes life easier for center Shaquille O'Neal. "Penny" Hardaway has the Jordanesque inside-outside ability to carry an offense, but he prefers using his explosive talents to set up opportunities for others, especially O'Neal. Hardaway was drafted out of Memphis University after his junior season and quickly made his presence felt. He averaged 16.0 points, 5.4 rebounds and 6.6 assists as an NBA rookie and followed with averages of 20.9, 4.4 and 7.2, respectively, in 1994–95, earning All-NBA first-team honors and helping the Magic reach the NBA Finals. When O'Neal sat out the first quarter of the 1995–96 season with a broken thumb, Hardaway stepped up his offense and Orlando surprisingly jumped out to a 17–5 start. The bottom line: Hardaway's talent is so enormous he can simply plug himself into a game when and how he sees fit.

TIM HARDAWAY

Born: 9–1–66, at Chicago, Ill.
Position: Guard.
Team: Warriors, 1989–96, Heat, 1996–present.

Before a blown-out knee cost Hardaway one full season and parts of two others, he was penetrating the upper echelon of NBA point guards. Since he returned to action in 1994–95, he has lacked

JUST LIKE MAGIC *Anfernee Hardaway is Orlando's athletic trigger man*

FREQUENT FLYER *Elvin Hayes (11) was head and shoulders above most opponents*

that left fans and fellow players gasping. He left the University of Iowa after his freshman season and enjoyed short stints with the American Basketball League, the Harlem Globetrotters and the American Basketball Association. Hawkins was MVP for the champion Pittsburgh Pipers in the ABA's 1967–68 debut season, when he averaged 26.8 points and 13.5 rebounds. He signed with the NBA's Suns in 1969 and spent four-plus seasons in Phoenix, averaging more than 20 points three times and earning an All-NBA first-team citation in 1970 (24.6 points and 10.4 rebounds per game). The 6–8 "Hawk" played briefly with Los Angeles and Atlanta before retiring in 1976, and he was elected to the Hall of Fame in 1992.

ELVIN HAYES

Born: 11–17–45, at Rayville, La.
Position: Forward/center.
Teams: Rockets, 1968–72, 1981–84, Bullets, 1972–81.

"The Big E" was one of the NBA's most consistent scorers and rebounders over a 16-year career that included two stints with the Rockets (San Diego and Houston) and a glittering nine-year stretch with the Bullets. The 6–9 Hayes, who led the University of Houston to two NCAA Final Fours, brought his deadly turnaround jump shot to San Diego as the first overall pick of the 1968 draft and averaged a league-leading 28.4 points as a rookie. But the three-time All-NBA first-team selection enjoyed his greatest success in Washington, where he teamed with burly center Wes Unseld in a fierce frontcourt that led the Bullets to four Central Division titles, three NBA Finals and a 1978 championship. When Hayes retired in 1984 after a three-year return to Houston, he ranked in the all-time top five in points (27,313), games (1,303) and rebounds (16,279). The 12-time All-Star Game performer and two-time rebounding champion was elected to the Hall of Fame in 1990.

SPENCER HAYWOOD

Born: 4–22–49, at Silver City, Miss.
Position: Forward/center.
Teams: Denver Rockets (ABA), 1969–70, SuperSonics, 1970–75, Knicks, 1975–79, Jazz, 1979, Lakers, 1979–80, Bullets, 1981–83.

The 6–9 Haywood was a spectacular athlete who is best remembered for a landmark legal battle. He was an explosive leaper who could dominate games offensively and defensively. After his sophomore season at the University of Detroit, Haywood put together an incredible debut season for the ABA's Denver Rockets: He averaged 30 points and 19.5 rebounds per game, and claimed regular-season MVP, All-Star Game MVP and Rookie of the Year honors. But his 1970 jump to Seattle was interrupted by lawsuits that eventually gave NBA teams the right to draft underage college players as "hardship" cases. Haywood averaged better than 20 points in all five of his Sonics seasons, earned All-NBA first-team status twice and played in four All-Star Games before being traded to New York. His NBA career, which lasted seven more seasons before ending in 1983 at Washington, produced 14,592 points (19.2) and 7,038 rebounds (9.3). Haywood was a part-time player on the Lakers' 1980 championship team.

TOM HEINSOHN

Born: 8–26–34, at Jersey City, N.J.
Position: Forward.
Team: Celtics, 1956–65.

The 6–7 Heinsohn was a vital cog in the Boston Celtics' championship machine of the 1950s and '60s. When the two-time Holy Cross All-American arrived with Bill Russell via the 1956 draft, Boston began the greatest victory parade in team-sports history, a run that produced 11 championships in 13 years. The versatile Heinsohn, who led the star-studded Celtics in scoring from 1960 to '62, earned eight championship rings in his nine seasons

the explosiveness that once made him so difficult to defend. That quickness should gradually return, but in the meantime Hardaway must content himself with an outside-shooting and passing game that still ranks him high among the league's floor generals. At his best, the former University of Texas-El Paso star, Golden State's first-round 1989 draft pick, can blow past a defender, penetrate the lane and either dish off to a teammate or shoot. His assist averages have ranged from 8.7 to 10.6 and he consistently averages in the 20-point range. The 6-foot Hardaway, a three-time All-Star who was traded to Miami midway through the 1995–96 season, is one of those rare players who can beat you with the shot, the pass or a

steal that triggers his team's transition game.

JOHN HAVLICEK
See Legends of the NBA *page 68*

CONNIE HAWKINS

Born: 7–17–42, at Brooklyn, N.Y.
Position: Forward/center.
Team: Pittsburgh/Minnesota Pipers (ABA), 1967–69, Suns, 1969–73, Lakers, 1973–75, Hawks, 1975–76.

Hawkins, a New York City playground legend, was one of the most spectacular and flamboyant frequent fliers of the pre-Dr. J era. Although his career was disjointed, Hawkins nevertheless impressed contemporaries with an acrobatic, above-the-rim presence while amassing 12,194 points (18.6), 5,749 rebounds (8.8), six All-Star Game selections and a 1957 nod as NBA Rookie of the Year. The intense, competitive Heinsohn, who also enjoyed championship stature as a member of Holy Cross' 1954 NIT title team, later coached the Celtics to 427 regular-season victories and two more titles (1974 and '76). He retired in 1965 with a 19.8 career playoff scoring average (104 games) and he was elected to the Hall of Fame in 1986.

GRANT HILL

Born: 10–5–72, at Dallas, Tex.
Position: Forward.
Team: Pistons, 1994–present.

In his 1994–95 co-Rookie of the Year debut with Detroit, Hill was compared often to all-everything Chicago forward Scottie Pippen, in skills as well as poise and court presence. The 6–8 Hill, who played on two NCAA championship teams at Duke University, is an unusual talent: a playmaking forward who is as dangerous with the pass as the shot. He is at his best when he slashes to the basket, creating shots for teammates as well as himself. He will drive on anybody and he always finds a way to get the ball to the basket. The all-around strength of Hill's game is reflected by his two-season averages: 20.8 points, 8.2 rebounds and 6.0 assists per game. And he complements his offensive game with excellent defense. Hill, a two-time All-Star who needs only to expand his range, already rates as one of the game's more popular players. He is the son of former NFL running back Calvin Hill.

JEFF HORNACEK

Born: 5–3–63, at Elmhurst, Ill.
Position: Guard.
Teams: Suns, 1986–92, 76ers, 1992–94, Jazz, 1994–present.

Hornacek is a heady, fundamentally sound shooting guard who provides the perfect complement to Utah's "Big Two" of Karl Malone and John Stockton.

Having the 6–4 former Iowa State University player on the court with Stockton is like having two point guards at the same time. Hornacek will make the extra pass and he's an efficient shooter—50 percent from the floor, 87 percent from the free-throw line and an impressive 40 percent from 3-point range. He once hit a record-tying 11 consecutive 3-pointers. Hornacek also is a gritty defender whose only real deficiencies are rebounding and showmanship. The one-time All-Star was the 46th pick of the 1986 draft after an unspectacular college career and he played six solid seasons in Phoenix, followed by one and a half years in Philadelphia. Traded to Utah in 1994, Hornacek fit perfectly into Coach Jerry Sloan's team-first philosophy.

JUWAN HOWARD

Born: 2–7–73, at Chicago, Ill.
Position: Forward/center.
Team: Bullets, 1994–present

Howard is a team-oriented workhorse who can swing between the small and power forward positions. He led all rookies in rebounding (8.4 per game) in 1994–95 and followed with a 22.1-point and 8.2-rebound second season. His turnaround jumper is a polished, high-percentage shot. The 6–9, 250-pound Howard was a member of the University of Michigan's "Fab Five" team that lost in the NCAA Tournament championship game in 1992 and '93. His role for the Wolverines was much the same as it is for the Washington Bullets: pound the offensive and defensive boards, take high-percentage shots and

A SPEEDING BULLET *Washington's Juwan Howard is a young NBA workhorse*

play hard-nosed defense. Juwan Howard is not spectacular, but he makes up for any lack of athleticism with gritty trenchwork and all the little things he's willing to do. The coachable Howard left college after his junior season as the fifth overall draft pick in 1994.

BAILEY HOWELL

Born: 1–20–37, at Middleton, Tenn.
Position: Forward.
Teams: Pistons, 1959–64, Bullets, 1964–66, Celtics, 1966–70, 76ers, 1970–71.

Howell scored 17,770 points (18.7) and grabbed 9,383 rebounds (9.9) over a 12-year career as an NBA overachiever. "I don't have the ability of some of the players in this league," admitted Howell, who more than compensated with an all-out hustle that gave him status as a premier offensive and defensive forward. The 6–7 Howell used that hustle as a relentless offensive rebounder and developed a deadly jump shot from the wing. The former Mississippi State star broke into the NBA with Detroit in 1959 and played seven seasons with the Pistons and Bullets, averaging better than 20 points three times and recording double-digit rebounding totals six years in a row. But Howell's greatest fame would come as a member of Boston's 1968 and '69 championship teams, a perfect fit for the leadership and teamwork qualities he brought to the game. Howell, a six-time All-Star, retired in 1971 after one season in Philadelphia.

LOU HUDSON

Born: 7–11–44, at Greensboro, N.C.
Position: Guard/forward.
Teams: Hawks, 1966–77, Lakers, 1977–79.

Hudson, known for his sweet jumper and steady influence, was a versatile swingman for the St. Louis/Atlanta Hawks and Los Angeles Lakers for 13 NBA seasons. The 6–5 Hudson made a career out of mismatches and the perfectly-executed jump shot that earned him the nickname "Sweet Lou." If he played small forward, he was too quick for opposing defenders. If he played shooting guard, he was able to post up smaller opponents. He also had an explosive first step that gave him access to the lane and helped him defend quicker guards. Hudson, a University of Minnesota product, was drafted fourth overall by the Hawks in 1966. He assumed scoring responsibilities with the retirement of Bob Pettit and Cliff Hagan and averaged better than 20 points in seven of his 11 St. Louis/Atlanta seasons. When the six-time All-Star retired in 1979 after two seasons in Los Angeles, he had amassed 17,940 career points (20.2 per game) and 3,926 rebounds (4.4).

DAN ISSEL

Born: 10–25–48, at Batavia, Ill.
Position: Forward/center.
Teams: Kentucky Colonels (ABA), 1970–75, Nuggets (ABA/NBA), 1975–85.

What Issel lacked in style and grace he made up for with durability, intensity and a blue-collar work ethic. Nicknamed "Horse," the 6–9, 240-pounder played in 1,218 of a possible 1,242 career games over 15 ABA and NBA seasons. A 33.9-point scorer in his senior year at the University of Kentucky, Issel averaged 29.9 in 1970 for the ABA's Kentucky Colonels, winning co-Rookie of the Year honors and his only career scoring title. After helping the Colonels win the 1975 ABA championship, Issel was traded to Denver and began a successful 10-

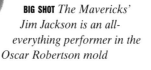

BIG SHOT *The Mavericks' Jim Jackson is an all-everything performer in the Oscar Robertson mold*

year run as one of the franchise's most prolific performers. He averaged better than 20 points per game in seven seasons for the Nuggets and completed his career in 1985 with combined ABA/NBA totals of 11,133 rebounds (9.1 per game) and 27,482 points (22.6), which ranks fifth on the all-time scoring list. Issel, who later coached the Nuggets for three years, was elected to the Hall of Fame in 1993.

JIM JACKSON

Born: 10–14–70, at Toledo, Ohio.
Position: Guard.
Team: Mavericks, 1992–present.

Jackson, a 6–6, 220-pound shooting guard, has the size, mobility, work ethic and leadership qualities to rank near the top of his position for years to come. He can produce points inside and out, he can help on the boards when needed and his passing and defense are getting better every game. The former Ohio State University star combines a will to win with a floor game that could rekindle flashes of Oscar Robertson. Jackson appeared to be on his way to that kind of stardom in 1994–95 when an ankle injury short-circuited his third professional season after 51 games. He was averaging 25.7 points, the fifth-best mark in the league, and 5.1 rebounds when he went down. Jackson came back to average 19.6 points in 1995-6; he was drafted by the Mavericks with the fourth overall pick of the 1992 draft after his junior season.

BUDDY JEANNETTE

Born: 9–15–17, at New Kensington, Pa.
Position: Guard.
Teams: Cleveland White Horses (NBL), 1938–39, Detroit Eagles (NBL), 1939–41, Sheboygan Redskins (NBL), 1942–43, Fort Wayne Pistons (NBL), 1943–46, Baltimore Bullets (BAA/NBA), 1947–50.

Jeannette, a classic playmaker and clutch shooter, was a pioneer of the professional game and one of the premier backcourt players of his era. At 5–11 and 175 pounds, Jeannette made up for his physical limitations with court savvy and a hard-nosed intensity that resulted in four career MVP awards. Three of these came in the old National Basketball League and the other in the American Basketball League, both predecessors of today's NBA. Jeanette's teams also won five league championships, including one that will always be significant in the NBA record books. Jeannette, player-coach of the ABL's Baltimore franchise, was invited to bring his team into the second-year BAA in 1947–48 and the surprising Bullets walked away with the championship. Jeannette continued in his role as player-coach for two more seasons and briefly coached the new-edition Baltimore Bullets in the mid-1960s. He was elected to the Hall of Fame in 1994.

DENNIS JOHNSON

Born: 9–18–54, at San Pedro, Calif.
Position: Guard.
Teams: SuperSonics, 1976–80, Suns, 1980–83, Celtics, 1983–90.

Johnson, a solid playmaker and scorer, was the premier defensive point guard of the 1980s and the stopper for one Seattle Super-Sonics and two Boston Celtics championship teams. The 6–4 former Pepperdine University star played in-your-face, man-to-man defense that resulted in six selections to the NBA All-Defensive first team. But he also was an outstanding passer and clutch shooter who could post big point totals when defenses began sagging off him. Johnson, a second-round 1976 draft pick, was the point man for a Seattle team that reached the NBA Finals in consecutive seasons and defeated Washington for the 1979 championship. Then, after three seasons in Phoenix, he blended perfectly into a talented Celtics team (containing superstars Larry Bird, Kevin McHale and Robert Parish) that reached the NBA Finals four times and captured championships in 1984 and '86. When he retired in 1990, the five-time All-Star had more than respectable totals of 15,535 points, 5,499 assists, 4,249 rebounds and 1,477 steals.

EDDIE JOHNSON

Born: 5–1–59, at Chicago, Ill.
Position: Guard/forward.
Teams: Kings, 1981–87, Suns, 1987–90, SuperSonics, 1990–93, Hornets, 1993–94, Pacers, 1995–present.

Johnson has built a solid 14-year career as a jump-shooting small forward for five NBA teams. The 6–7 former University of Illinois product is a pure outside shooter at a position that usually demands an inside game. Johnson makes up for his inside shortcomings with hard work and a defensive presence that has allowed him to extend his career beyond expectations. As a second-round 1981 draft pick, Johnson joined the Kansas City Kings and played sparingly his rookie season. But he blossomed over the next three campaigns, posting averages of 19.8, 21.9 and 22.9, respectively. By the time Johnson reached Phoenix in 1987, he was a solid role player who could come off the bench and provide instant offense. He earned the NBA Sixth Man Award in 1989 as a 21.5 scorer. Johnson, an 84 percent free throw shooter who is winding down his career in Indiana after stays in Seattle and Charlotte, has posted more than 18,000 points.

GUS JOHNSON

Born: 12–13–38, at Akron, Ohio.
Position: Forward.
Teams: Bullets, 1963–72, Suns, 1972, Indiana Pacers (ABA), 1972–73.

Johnson was a flamboyant, acrobatic forward who backed up his showboating with outstanding play. The 6–6, 235-pounder, a legend at the University of Idaho because of his amazing jumping ability, wore a gold star on his front tooth and spent a small fortune on clothing, shoes and jewelry. But over nine seasons with the Baltimore Bullets, the swashbuckling Johnson became a fan favorite who consistently delivered double-digit point and rebounding totals while earning

two selections to the NBA All-Defensive first team. Johnson, who reportedly could touch the top of the backboard, played through four knee surgeries before his NBA career ended with a 21-game season in Phoenix. The five-time All-Star signed with the ABA's Indiana Pacers and played a supporting role for the 1973 championship team. He retired with 9,944 NBA points (17.1) and 7,379 rebounds (12.7).

KEVIN JOHNSON

Born: 3–4–66, at Sacramento, Calif.
Position: Guard.
Teams: Cavaliers, 1987–88, Suns, 1988–present.

Johnson is a waterbug point guard who can dominate games with his explosive dashes to the basket. But he also has been a long-time source of Phoenix frustration because of his inability to stay in the lineup. When "K.J." is healthy,

GOOD POINT *Kevin Johnson keeps the Suns from setting in Phoenix*

he is the ultimate offensive and defensive instigator who lifts the Suns to championship-contender status. He has outstanding speed, a solid mid-range jump shot, excellent court vision and an ability to turn a game with his quickness and fast-break bursts. But the 6–1 former University of California star has never played an 82-game NBA season and twice has failed to suit up 50 times. Johnson, a 1987 Cleveland draft pick, was traded to Phoenix in 1988. He averaged better than 20 points in his first three full seasons with the Suns and reached double-digit assists in his first four. Johnson's only weakness is the 3-point shot, which he rarely takes.

LARRY JOHNSON

Born: 3–14–69, at Tyler, Tex.
Position: Forward.
Team: Hornets, 1991–96; Knicks, 1996–present.

Johnson is an offensive-minded power forward who has been robbed of quickness by serious back injuries. When he joined Charlotte out of the University of Nevada-Las Vegas as the first overall pick of the 1991 draft, the 6–7 Johnson was a lightning-quick 260-pounder who could run circles around most power forwards and post up the league's small forwards. Around the basket, Johnson was a whirling, twisting, thousand-move superstar who could score points in bunches. He did just that as the 1991–92 Rookie of the Year and a 22.1 second-year man, throwing in double-digit rebounding totals for good measure. But his 1993–94 season was cut to 51 games by back problems and he has been forced to rely more on his jumper while his rebounding totals have suffered. A two-time All-Star, Johnson still is capable of exciting numbers, but his game lacks the brute strength and confidence of the past. That's why the Hornets traded him to the Knicks after the 1995–96 season.

MAGIC JOHNSON

See Legends of the NBA *page 69*

MARQUES JOHNSON

Born: 2–8–56, at Natchitoches, La.
Position: Forward.
Teams: Bucks, 1977–84, Clippers, 1984–87, Warriors, 1989–90.

Johnson was an athletic forward who combined equal amounts finesse and power into a solid 11-year NBA career. The 6–7 Johnson, the 1977 College Player of the Year at UCLA, handled the ball like a guard and powered his way to the basket like a big man, often seeming to materialize out of nowhere for spectacular put-back slam dunks. The baseline was his playground, but he worked hard to develop a 20-foot jump shot that made him a complete player. Johnson, a Milwaukee first-round 1977 draft pick, averaged better than 20 points and 6 rebounds in five of his seven Milwaukee seasons and topped 300 assists three times. He also was a solid defensive player and shot-blocker who appeared in five All-Star Games. After leaving Milwaukee in 1984, Johnson played three seasons with the Clippers and a 10-game campaign with Golden State. He retired with 13,892 points (20.1 per game), 4,817 rebounds (7.0) and 2,502 assists (3.6).

NEIL JOHNSTON

Born: 2–4–29, at Chillicothe, Ohio.
Position: Center.
Team: Warriors, 1951–59.

Johnston, who was known for his baseball ability as a college player at Ohio State, became one of the NBA's offensive forces in the early 1950s. Armed with a deadly hook shot that he fired with a sweeping right arm, Johnston won three consecutive scoring titles, led the NBA in field-goal percentage three times and combined with Paul Arizin and Tom Gola on the Warriors' 1956 NBA championship team. Competing successfully as a 6–8 center in the George Mikan era, Johnston averaged 20 points or better in five of his eight NBA seasons and also captured the 1954–55 rebounding title with a 15.1 average. He was a four-time

All-NBA first-teamer, a six-time All-Star Game performer and a 19.4-point career scorer. Johnston's career was cut short in 1959 by a serious knee injury, but he remained as Warriors coach through 1960–61. He was elected to the Hall of Fame in 1990.

BOBBY JONES

Born: 12–18–51, at Charlotte, N.C.
Position: Forward.
Teams: Nuggets (ABA/NBA), 1974–78, 76ers, 1978–86.

The quiet, modest Jones was every coach's dream. Not only was he the premier defensive forward of the 1970s and '80s, he also was a troubleshooter who provided instant offense. If the 76ers needed points, Jones would go into his scoring mode. If they needed assists, rebounds, blocked shots, steals—it was Jones to the rescue. The 6–9 former North Carolina star could dominate without scoring points. Jones was at his best against the opponents' top scorer. He played two ABA seasons with Denver, two with the Nuggets in the NBA and his final eight with Philadelphia—and he was named to the All-Defensive first team an incredible 10 times. Jones also earned the NBA Sixth Man Award in 1983, the year he helped the 76ers win a championship. On a team that included Julius Erving and Moses Malone, Coach Billy Cunningham often singled out Jones as his MVP.

FAST HANDS *Bobby Jones (center) was the premier defensive forward of his era*

Jones, a four-time All-Star, retired in 1986 with 8,911 points (11.5 per game) and 4,256 rebounds (5.5).

K.C. JONES

Born: 5–25–32, at Taylor, Tex.
Position: Guard.
Team: Celtics, 1958–67.

Jones was a dependable playmaker during Boston's dynastic NBA reign and one of the greatest defensive guards ever to put on a uniform. Never an offensive force, Jones more than made up for it with court savvy, a ball-hawking presence and his ability to shut down high-scoring backcourt players like Jerry West and Hal Greer. The 6–1 Jones was a championship machine, playing on two title-winners with Bill Russell at the University of San Francisco, winning a gold medal with the 1956 U.S. Olympic team and capturing eight more championships in nine seasons with the Celtics. He later was assistant coach for two title teams and head coach for two more (with the Celtics in 1984 and '86). Jones compiled a 522–252 coaching mark over 10 seasons, including a 308–102 (.751) record in five Boston campaigns. He was elected to the Hall of Fame in 1989.

SAM JONES

Born: 6–24–33, at Laurinburg, N.C.
Position: Guard.
Team: Celtics, 1957–69.

Sam was half of Boston's championship-era "Jones Boys," combining with K.C. Jones in a perfectly balanced backcourt. Sam was the offensive force, K.C. the defensive wizard. Sam joined the Celtics as a first-round 1957 draft pick out of little North Carolina Central College and played a key role in a 12-season run that produced 10 NBA championships for the Celtics. Jones, one of the fastest players in the league, was known for his uncanny long-range bank shot and ability to perform in the clutch. He led the Celtics in scoring three times (including a 25.9 mark in 1964–65) and amassed 15,411 career points, averaging

17.7 per game. Jones also was a playoff force, averaging 18.9 points over 154 games. Jones, who was a five-time All-Star Game performer, was elected to the NBA 25th Anniversary All-Time Team in 1970 and the Hall of Fame in 1983.

MICHAEL JORDAN

See Legends of the NBA *page 70*

SHAWN KEMP

Born: 11–26–69, at Elkhart, Ind.
Position: Forward.
Team: SuperSonics, 1989–present.

Kemp is a highlight-film forward who has fought through the hype to become Seattle's physical and inspirational leader. From his rookie 1989–90 season to his current status as a three-time All-Star, Kemp has steadily improved his game. He still thrills fans with his swooping, acrobatic dunks and in-your-face rejections, but now he plays solid interior defense, relentlessly bangs the offensive boards and scores tough, critical points. All of which is not bad for a kid who was drafted in 1989, at age 20, with no college experience. Kemp struggled through his rookie season before jumping into the Sonics' rotation and averaging 15 points and 8.4 rebounds per game in his second year. The 1995–96 campaign was his best, producing averages of 19.6 points and 11.4 rebounds in a season that ended with an NBA Finals loss to Chicago. By the tender age of 26, Kemp already had scored more than 8,000 points and snared more than 5,000 rebounds.

JOHNNY (RED) KERR

Born: 8–17–32, at Chicago, Ill.
Position: Center.
Teams: Nationals/76ers, 1954–65, Bullets, 1965–66.

SONIC BOOM *Shawn Kemp is an explosive and acrobatic point producer*

Kerr was a fun-loving, hard-living center who once held the NBA's ironman streak. Kerr, a happy-go-lucky carouser whose 6–9 body resembled an enlarged Pillsbury Doughboy, more than compensated for his dalliances with spirited play and a willingness to play through injuries. In 11 seasons with Syracuse/Philadelphia and one with Baltimore, the red-headed wonder earned a reputation as the best passing center in the league and a crafty competitor who could beat an opponent with his head as well as his abilities. From his first 1954 game as a Syracuse rookie until November 1965 (his final season), Kerr played in 844 consecutive games, an NBA record that stood for 17 years. He also was part of an NBA championship team in that rookie season and his 12-year career produced 12,480 points (13.8 per game), 10,092 rebounds (11.2) and three All-Star Game appearances. Kerr later coached the Bulls and Suns for four years.

JASON KIDD

Born: 3–23–73, at San Francisco, Calif.
Position: Guard.
Team: Mavericks, 1994–present.

Kidd, a second overall draft pick by Dallas after his sophomore season at the University of California, was touted before his 1994–95 rookie season as the best pure point guard to come into the NBA since the Pistons' Isiah Thomas. He lived up to his lofty press clippings, averaging 11.7 points, handing out 607 assists (7.7) and earning co-Rookie of the Year honors. Kidd's second season produced even more impressive averages of 16.6 points and 9.7 assists. The 6–4 Kidd, who was called "the best passer on the planet" by Washington Bullets General Manager John Nash, is at his best when he penetrates the lane and sets up teammates for easy shots. But defenders who play the pass quickly discover Kidd has a proficient shot arsenal. He also is a fierce defender whose quick hands produce numerous steals that trigger the Mavericks' fast break. The bottom line: Kidd already is an NBA force and he'll only get better.

BERNARD KING

Born: 12–4–56, at Brooklyn, N.Y.
Position: Forward.
Teams: Nets, 1977–79, 1992–93, Jazz, 1979–80, Warriors, 1980–82, Knicks, 1982–87, Bullets, 1987–92.

King was an explosive scorer and underrated all-around player who defied odds and revived his career after reconstructive knee surgery. King wandered through New Jersey, Utah and Golden State before finding his niche with the New York Knicks in 1982. The scowling 6–7 forward won over Madison Square Garden fans with his intensity and creative shot-making, an ability fueled by a quick release and explosive first step. Before the injury, King was devastating with his back to the basket, spinning left or right. After the injury, he was more multi-dimensional, relying less on quickness and power. When King was injured in 1985, he was leading the league with a 32.9 scoring average. He returned to full-time action in 1987 with the Washington Bullets and played four more full seasons, averaging better than 20 points in three of them. King, a two-time All-NBA first-teamer who once enjoyed consecutive 50-point games, retired in 1993 with 19,655 points (22.5) and 5,060 rebounds (5.8).

BILL LAIMBEER

Born: 5–19–57, at Boston, Mass.
Position: Center.
Teams: Cavaliers, 1980–82, Pistons, 1982–94.

Laimbeer was a rough-and-tumble big man who centered the Detroit Pistons' back-to-back championship teams of 1989 and '90. The 6–11 former Notre Dame star performed with a physical flair that often drew accusations of "dirty play." But he never backed down and the Pistons embraced their "Bad Boys" image all the way to the bank. Laimbeer, who was drafted in 1979 by Cleveland and traded in 1982 to Detroit, was an unusual center who scored most of his points with a soft push shot from the perimeter. Laimbeer could not jump, he was slow afoot and he was not as athletic as the players he faced, but he got the job done, averaging 12.9 points and 9.7 rebounds over his 14-year career. During his 12 full Detroit seasons, the Pistons won three Central Division titles, topped 50 victories five times and reached the NBA Finals three years in a row. Laimbeer retired after the 1993–94 season.

BOB LANIER

Born: 9–10–48, at Buffalo, N.Y.
Position: Center.
Teams: Pistons, 1970–80, Bucks, 1980–84.

Lanier was one of the few NBA centers who could dominate inside and out. At 6–11, he could break down opponents with his short lefthanded hook shot, a deft perimeter scoring touch or a defensive presence that forced them away from the middle. Lanier's 19,248 points (20.1) and 9,698 rebounds (10.1) rank among the all-time career totals, but his contributions sometimes are overlooked. When Lanier was in his prime, he played for a weak Detroit team that had to struggle to reach the playoffs. Late in his career, he played for a good Milwaukee team that was overshadowed by Eastern Conference powers Philadelphia and Boston. Still, Lanier played in eight All-Star Games and averaged better than 20 points for eight consecutive years. After his 1984 retirement, he was honored numerous times for his citizenship and community contributions. Lanier was elected to the Hall of Fame in 1992.

JOE LAPCHICK

Born: 4–12–1900, at Yonkers, N.Y.
Position: Center.
Teams: Pre-NBA.

Lapchick was a pioneer of professional basketball and one of the NBA's first great coaches. At 6–5, he was an agile big man equally capable of passing, shooting and controlling the center jump—an important quality in the pre-1937 professional game. Lapchick became most prominent as a member of the mid-1920s Original Celtics, a barnstorming team credited with numerous innovations, particularly in the development of the pivot position (Lapchick's role) as the hub of an offense. As a coach, Lapchick built on those innovations from 1936–47 at St. John's University and for the next nine years with the New York franchise of the BAA/NBA. He coached the Knicks to 326 victories and three NBA Finals before returning to St. John's in 1956. By the time he retired in 1965, Lapchick had coached the Redmen to 334 victories and four NIT championships over 20 seasons. Lapchick was elected to the Hall of Fame in 1966.

FIRING ON ALL PISTONS *Bob Lanier (16) was the long-time centerpiece in Detroit*

A ROYAL PRESENCE *Cincinnati center Jerry Lucas was one of the great scorers/rebounders in NBA history*

Games and earned three All-NBA first-team citations. Lucas played on his only championship team in 1973, when he helped the Knicks to their second title in four years. He was elected to the Hall of Fame in 1979.

ED MACAULEY

Born: 3-22-28, at St. Louis, Mo.
Position: Forward/center.
Teams: Bombers, 1949–50, Celtics, 1950–56, Hawks, 1956–59.

The 6-8 Macauley was a gifted offensive player who could frustrate bigger defenders with his quickness and gliding moves around the basket. He combined for six seasons with guards Bob Cousy and Bill Sharman in a high-scoring run-and-gun Boston lineup that presaged the 24-second clock. Macauley, a two-time All-American at St. Louis University, will always be remembered as one of the two forwards the Celtics traded for the draft rights to center Bill Russell. But the trade sent him back to St. Louis, where he teamed with Bob Pettit and Cliff Hagan to lead the Hawks to their only NBA championship—a 1958 victory over the Celtics. Macauley, a three-time All-NBA first-team selection and a seven-time All-Star, was player-coach when he retired in 1959 with 11,234 career points (17.5 per game). He coached the Hawks to two Western Division titles. Macauley was elected to the Hall of Fame in 1960.

CLYDE LOVELLETTE

Born: 9-7-29, at Petersburg, Ind.
Position: Forward/center.
Teams: Lakers, 1953–57, Royals, 1957–58, Hawks, 1958–62, Celtics, 1962–64.

Lovellette was big (6-9), physical and capable of putting the ball in the basket. But he enhanced his natural center qualities with a one-handed set shot that allowed him to move outside and create problems for opposing centers. And during a career that included stints alongside George Mikan (Minneapolis) and Bill Russell (Boston), Lovellette often was asked to switch between both forward positions and the middle. No problem. Lovellette had honed his offensive game under Phog Allen at the University of Kansas, where

he led the Jayhawks to the 1952 NCAA Tournament championship. He complemented that with an Olympic gold medal (1952) and three NBA championships—1954 with the Lakers and 1963 and '64 with the Celtics. Over 11 seasons with four teams, the versatile Lovellette scored 11,947 points (17.0) and grabbed 6,663 rebounds (9.5). The three-time All-Star retired in 1964 and was elected to the Hall of Fame in 1988.

JERRY LUCAS

Born: 3-30-40, at Middletown, Ohio.
Position: Forward/center
Teams: Royals, 1963–69, Warriors, 1969–71, Knicks, 1971–74.

From the moment he put on his first uniform at Middletown High

School, Lucas was one of the most celebrated players in history. And by the time he was drafted by the NBA's Cincinnati Royals out of Ohio State in 1962, his resume showed why: two state titles, three appearances in the NCAA Finals, one national championship, two College Player of the Year awards, numerous records and an Olympic gold medal. Lucas, who combined with Oscar Robertson as one of the game's best inside-outside combinations, put his distinctive over-the-shoulder shooting style and aggressiveness to quick work for the Royals, averaging 17.7 points and 17.4 rebounds in a Rookie of the Year debut. Over an 11-year NBA career that included stints in San Francisco and New York, he averaged 17 points and 15.6 rebounds, played in eight All-Star

JEFF MALONE

Born: 6-28-61, at Mobile, Ala.
Position: Guard.
Teams: Bullets, 1983–90, Jazz, 1990–94, 76ers, 1994–96.

Malone was a catch-and-shoot guard who piled up more than 17,000 points in a 13-year career with Washington, Utah and Philadelphia. The 6-4 shooting guard could provide fast-and-furious offense with an assortment of jump shots that he liked to launch in the 15- to 20-foot range. He was adept at moving without the ball, coming off picks and shooting a soft fadeaway while going either right or left. Malone, who also played solid defense, was selected by the Bullets out of Mississippi State University with the 10th overall pick of the 1983 draft. By his third season, he was a consistent 20-point scorer who would earn two All-Star Game invitations. After seven seasons in Washington, he was traded to Utah and spent three and a half years as an offensive alternative to Jazz teammates Karl Malone and John Stockton. Malone ended his career in January 1996, after an injury-plagued 1994–95 season in Philadelphia.

KARL MALONE

Born: 7–24–63, at Summerfield, La.
Position: Forward.
Team: Jazz, 1985–present.

Karl Malone, a.k.a. "The Mailman," is the prototypical power forward. For more than a decade, he has used his 6-9, 256-pound body to brutalize opponents who dare to venture into the paint. Malone is a scorer, rebounder, defender and leader for the Utah Jazz, the team he joined in 1985 as a first-round draft pick out of Louisiana Tech University. Since his 1985–86 rookie season, he has formed the NBA's top inside/outside combination with point guard John Stockton. Malone is capable of taking over games, especially when he uses his powerful body to get the ball down low, where he's unstoppable. He also can post up

for the short jumper and he's devastating on the boards, having topped 11 rebounds per game in six seasons. Malone, an eight-time All-Star, has averaged better than 25 points nine times and earned eight All-NBA first-team citations. He also was a member of the Dream Team at Barcelona in the 1992 Olympics. Malone has the heart of a champion, although that is one honor that has eluded him.

MOSES MALONE

See Legends of the NBA *page 71*

DANNY MANNING

Born: 5–17–66, at Hattiesburg, Miss.
Position: Forward.
Teams: Clippers, 1988–94, Hawks, 1994, Suns, 1994–present.

When healthy, Manning is a mobile 6-10 small forward who knows how to use his size advantage. But he has missed considerable time with torn anterior cruciate ligaments in both knees and the injuries have reduced his explosiveness. Manning was taken by the Los Angeles Clippers with the first overall draft pick of 1988, shortly after he had led Kansas University to an NCAA championship. But he was uncomfortable in his go-to offensive role for a weak Clippers team, although he did enjoy two All-Star seasons. When he was signed by the Suns as a free-agent in 1994, he stepped into a situation where he could exploit team-oriented skills that relied on superior ballhandling, passing vision, post-up abilities and mid-range shooting to complement Charles Barkley and Kevin Johnson. The Suns were 36–10 when Manning hurt his left knee. The injury cost him the rest of the season and more than half of 1995–96.

PETE MARAVICH

Born: 6–22–47, at Aliquippa, Pa.
Position: Guard.
Teams: Hawks, 1970–74, Jazz, 1974–80, Celtics, 1980.

"Pistol Pete" will be remembered as the most prolific offensive

force in college basketball history and a creative, prime-time performer for 10 pro seasons. When Maravich was drafted by the Atlanta Hawks out of Louisiana State University in 1970, he owned three national scoring titles and held numerous NCAA offensive records, including career average (44.2) and points (3,667). It wasn't so much that Maravich scored points in bunches, it was how he did it—with the most dazzling repertoire of offensive moves ever assembled. From no-look passes to double-clutching 20-foot jumpers, he played the game creatively and made both fans and players gasp. The 6–5 Maravich averaged 23.2 points as an NBA rookie and scored 15,948 points (24.2 per game) over a career that included one scoring title (New Orleans 1976–77), two All-NBA first-team selections and five All-Star Game performances. He was elected to the Hall of Fame in 1987.

SLATER MARTIN

Born: 10–22–25, at Houston, Tex.
Position: Guard.
Teams: Lakers, 1949–56, Knicks, 1956, Hawks, 1956–60.

The 5–10 Martin was a crafty playmaker who provided the steadying influence for five NBA championship teams. Always under control and ever dangerous in the clutch, Martin compensated for his diminutive size with a scrappy, hard-nosed style that brought out the best in his teammates. After a colorful career at the University of Texas, Martin joined George Mikan, Jim Pollard and Vern Mikkelsen in Minneapolis and quarterbacked the Lakers to their second consecutive championship in 1950. Three more followed in 1952, '53 and '54 and Martin enjoyed a fifth title in 1958, as a teammate of Bob Pettit, Ed Macauley and Cliff Hagan with the St. Louis Hawks. Statistically, Martin does not raise eyebrows with his 9.8-point and 4.2-assist per game career averages, but numbers don't always

PETE RE-PETE *The ever-creative Maravich (44) soared for the Hawks in 1972*

SETTING THE PACE *George McGinnis was an ABA scourge in his early career*

tell the story. Martin's success can be measured by NBA championships and his membership in the Hall of Fame.

JAMAL MASHBURN

Born: 11–29–72, at New York, N.Y.
Position: Forward.
Team: Mavericks, 1993–present.

Mashburn is a talented 6–8 forward who should rank consistently among the league's scoring leaders. His versatility allows him to fire from 3-point range or challenge the big men inside with a pull-up jumper or a creative slash to the basket. He is explosive, as his 24.1 and 23.4 second- and third-season scoring averages might suggest, and he has worked hard to improve his passing, rebounding and defense. Mashburn declared for the 1993 draft after his junior season at the University of Kentucky and was

grabbed by Dallas with the fourth overall pick. He averaged 19.2 points and 4.5 rebounds in 1993–94, earning a spot on the NBA All-Rookie first team. The youthful trio of Mashburn, Jim Jackson and Jason Kidd—Dallas' three Js—forms the heart and soul of the Mavericks.

BOB McADOO

Born: 9–25–51, at Greensboro, N.C.
Position: Forward/center.
Teams: Braves, 1972–76, Knicks, 1976–79, Celtics, 1979, Pistons, 1979–81, Nets, 1981, Lakers, 1981–85, 76ers, 1985–86.

The 6–9 McAdoo was a sweet-shooting forward who spent his early NBA years winning scoring titles and his later career as a valuable extra on two Lakers championship teams. McAdoo, a University of North Carolina

product, was one of the best pure outside shooters the game has ever produced. After winning Rookie of the Year honors in 1973, he exploded into NBA consciousness with consecutive scoring averages of 30.6, 34.5 and 31.1, winning scoring titles each year and a regular-season MVP in 1975. But the Braves' top gun was inexplicably traded to the Knicks in 1976 and he bounced around the league, piling up points and new teams. It wasn't until he reached Los Angeles that he rediscovered success—as a low-scoring role player for the Lakers' 1982 and '85 title teams. McAdoo ended his career in 1986 at Philadelphia with 18,787 points (22.1) and an impressive .503 field-goal percentage.

GEORGE McGINNIS

Born: 8–12–50, at Indianapolis, Ind.
Position: Forward.
Teams: Pacers (ABA/NBA), 1971–75, 1980–82, 76ers, 1975–78, Nuggets, 1978–80.

McGinnis was a bruising inside force who could beat you with his rebounding or scoring. The 6–8, 235-pound forward, who signed an ABA contract after his sophomore season at Indiana University, literally muscled his way to the top of the offensive charts, throwing in some acrobatic derring-do for good measure. McGinnis' best years were in the ABA, where he won a scoring title, earned one MVP citation and helped the Indiana Pacers to consecutive championships in 1972 and '73. One year before the ABA/NBA merger, McGinnis signed with Philadelphia, where he earned All-NBA first-team honors in 1976 and averaged more than 20 points and 10 rebounds for three straight years. He later played for the Nuggets before returning to the Pacers to finish his career. When the three-time NBA All-Star retired in 1982, he owned combined ABA/NBA totals of 17,009 points (20.2 per game) and 9,233 rebounds (11.0).

DICK McGUIRE

Born: 1–25–26, at Huntington, N.Y.
Position: Guard.
Teams: Knicks, 1949–57, Pistons, 1957–60.

In the NBA's formative years, the clever McGuire ranked as one of the league's premier point guards. He seldom scored in double figures, but he was a master ball-handler and his court vision was outstanding. McGuire, a former St. John's star, was at his best when penetrating the lane and drawing defenders, leaving a teammate open for one of his slick passes. He led the league with 386 assists as a Knicks rookie in 1949–50 and he averaged 6.3 assists his second season, tying for the league lead. With "Tricky Dick" running the offense, the Knicks reached the NBA Finals in 1951, '52 and '53, losing once to Rochester and twice to Minneapolis. He played eight seasons in New York and three more in Detroit, earning seven All-Star Game selections before retiring in 1960. In 1993, McGuire joined Al McGuire, a former college coach, as the first brother combination in the basketball Hall of Fame.

KEVIN McHALE

Born: 12–19–57, at Hibbing, Minn.
Position: Forward/center.
Team: Celtics, 1980–93.

McHale spent his early career as a Boston sixth man and the rest as one of the top power forwards in the NBA. The 6–10 former University of Minnesota star had the ability to step off the bench and provide instant offense and defense, a traditional role in Celtics history. But he became even more valuable as a starter alongside Larry Bird and center Robert Parish, providing an all-around consistency that helped Boston win three championships. McHale had exceptionally long arms that allowed him to get off inside shots and an explosive first step to the basket. He was an outstanding rebounder, a three-time All-Defensive first-team stopper

INSIDE MAN *Boston's Kevin McHale*

and an intimidating, shot-blocking presence in the middle. McHale, a seven-time All-Star and a 1987 All-NBA first teamer, averaged better than 20 points five times and ended his career in 1993 with 17,335 (17.9 per game). He also pulled down 7,122 rebounds (7.3).

GEORGE MIKAN

See Legends of the NBA *page 72*

VERN MIKKELSEN

Born: 10–21–28, at Fresno, Calif.
Position: Forward/center.
Team: Lakers, 1949–59.

Mikkelsen, a prototypical power forward at 6–7 and 230 pounds, was one of the cornerstones of the Minneapolis Lakers championship dynasty that also featured center George Mikan, forward Jim Pollard and point guard Slater Martin. Mikkelsen was an intense competitor who did not give up space or rebounds without a serious elbow or two. As a double-figure scorer and rebounder, he was a charter member of one of the greatest frontcourts in basketball history. A six-time All-Star, Mikkelsen used his superior strength and size to muscle his way to totals of 10,063 career points (14.4 per game) and 5,940 rebounds (8.4). Those numbers

probably would have been higher in a lineup without the 6–10 Mikan. Mikkelsen, a former star at Hamline University, spent his entire 10-year career with the Lakers and retired in 1959 with four championship rings. He was elected to the Hall of Fame in 1995.

REGGIE MILLER

Born: 8–24–65, at Riverside, Calif.
Position: Guard.
Team: Pacers, 1987–present.

Miller is a trash-talking, in-your-face shooting guard who owns the fastest gun in the Midwest. His range is well beyond the 3-point line and his confidence is as high as the jump shots he drops through the net. The slender 6–7 Miller won't bang for the rebounds or pile up assists, but, oh, how he can shoot. He has averaged better than 20 points per game five times and most of them come from the perimeter. The former UCLA star, Indiana's 1987 first-round draft pick, is probably the most explosive performer in the game. Once, he scored eight points in 16.4 seconds. In a 1994 playoff game against the Knicks, he erupted for an amazing 25 fourth-quarter points. With the help of 7–4 center Rik Smits, Miller carried the Pacers to within a game of the NBA Finals in 1994 and '95. Miller, a three-time All-Star and 88-percent free-throw shooter, is at his best when a game is on the line.

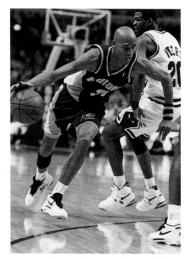

LONG SHOT *Pacers bomber Reggie Miller*

SLICK KNICK *Smooth Earl Monroe helped New York win a championship*

SIDNEY MONCRIEF

Born: 9–21–57, at Little Rock, Ark.
Position: Guard.
Teams: Bucks, 1979–89, Hawks, 1990–91.

The silky-smooth Moncrief was a near-perfect blend of offense and defense. He could score 20 points while shutting down a high-scoring opponent—a double talent not many players could claim. The 6–3 Moncrief was the glue for a Milwaukee team that posted seven straight 50-victory seasons, won seven consecutive Midwest and Central Division titles and advanced three times to the Eastern Conference finals in the 1980s. Twice he was voted the NBA's Defensive Player of the Year and he was a four-time member of the league's All-Defensive first team. But in each of those four seasons, Moncrief also averaged better than 20 points. His versatil-

ity was best illustrated in 1981–82, when he became the first player since Boston's Dave Cowens (in 1975–76) to lead his team in scoring (19.8), rebounding (6.7) and assists (4.8). The former University of Arkansas star retired after one season in Atlanta with 11,931 points (15.6 per game) and 2,793 assists (3.6).

EARL MONROE

Born: 11–21–44, at Philadelphia, Pa.
Position: Guard.
Teams: Bullets, 1967–71, Knicks, 1971–80.

The 6–3 Monroe played with a flair that earned him a place among the game's most popular players. "Earl The Pearl" was instant offense, a perpetual fountain of whirling, spinning, double-pumping moves that produced 17,454 points (18.8) and 3,594 assists (3.9) over a 13-year career with the Baltimore Bullets and New York Knicks. Monroe, who had averaged a small-college record 41.5 points as a Winston-Salem State College senior, made a quick impact on the NBA with a 24.3-point average that earned him 1968 Rookie of the Year honors. He combined with center Wes Unseld to lead the Bullets into the 1971 NBA Finals and he meshed with Walt Frazier in a classy New York backcourt that led the Knicks to the 1973 championship. Monroe, a four-time All-Star who averaged more than 20 points six times, was forced to the sideline in 1980 by a knee injury. He was elected to the Hall of Fame in 1990.

ALONZO MOURNING

Born: 2–8–70, at Chesapeake, Va.
Position: Center.
Teams: Hornets, 1992–95, Heat, 1995–present.

Mourning rates among the ˙top five NBA centers and his improving all-around game is fueled by a fiery intensity. At 6–10, the former Georgetown University star is undersized in his matchups against Hakeem Olajuwon, Shaquille O'Neal, Patrick Ewing and David Robinson, but he battles the boards, blocks shots, moves with agility around the basket and even steps out for an accurate jump shot. Mourning was selected with the second overall pick of the 1992 draft and tabbed as the man who would lead the 4-year-old Hornets out of the expansion wilderness. He was everything he was expected to be—passionate, tough and coachable—qualities he exhibited in his first three seasons with averages of 21.0, 21.5 and 21.3 points and 10.3, 10.2 and 9.9 rebounds. But the Charlotte love affair ended before the 1995–96 season when the three-time All-Star was traded to Miami after a bitter contract dispute. Mourning averaged 23.2 points and 10.4 rebounds in his debut performance for the Heat.

CHRIS MULLIN

Born: 7–30–63, at New York, N.Y.
Position: Forward.
Team: Warriors, 1985–present.

Mullin is a high-scoring small forward who has battled through personal problems and injuries in a career that spans more than a decade with the Golden State Warriors. The savvy lefthander has won many games with a 3-point shot he hits with 36 percent frequency and he is an excellent passer and free-throw shooter. Mullin is not a physical player, but he will get his rebounds and he

GOLDEN BOY *Veteran guard Chris Mullin is an NBA Warrior, both in name and personality*

defends with a nice combination of hard work and instincts. Mullin, a 1992 All-NBA first-teamer, came out of St. John's University in 1985 and averaged better than 25 points and 5 rebounds for five straight seasons from 1988–93. Although alcohol rehabilitation and injuries have limited his effectiveness in recent years, Mullin remains one of the game's best pure shooters and most respected performers. The five-time All-Star is a two-time Olympic gold medalist, as a member of the 1984 amateur U.S. team and the 1992 Dream Team.

CALVIN MURPHY

Born: 5–9–48, at Norwalk, Conn.
Position: Guard.
Team: Rockets, 1970–83.

The 5–9 Murphy, the most popular player in Rockets history, zipped around the NBA hardcourts for 13 seasons, dazzling fans with his oversized heart and never-ending enthusiasm. What he lacked in size, he more than made up for with a quickness that allowed him to penetrate, pull out of a sprint for a quick jumper and play aggressive, chest-to-chest defense against bigger opponents. Murphy was a five-time 20-point scorer and one of the most deadly free-throw shooters in the game. A 33.1-point scorer over three varsity seasons at Niagara University and one of the legendary players of college basketball history, Murphy was a key player on Houston's 1980–81 team that advanced to the NBA Finals. He finished his career in 1983 with 17,949 points (17.9) and his 4,402 assists still rank as a Rockets record. Murphy was elected to the Hall of Fame in 1993.

DIKEMBE MUTOMBO

Born: 6–25–66, at Kinshasa, Zaire.
Position: Center.
Team: Nuggets, 1991–1996; Hawks, 1996– present.

Mutombo, a Zaire native who is still learning the finer arts of basketball, comes from a line of intimidating Georgetown centers. At 7–2, he is an inside force who ruled Denver's paint as the NBA's 1995 Defensive Player of the Year. No shot is safe from the long reach of a soaring Mutombo, who led the league in blocks in 1994, '95 and '96. He also is one of the NBA's best rebounders, grabbing more than 1,000 in two of his first five seasons. Mutombo's weakness is on offense, where he operates mechanically with a shooting range of five feet. His only shots are the dunk and the jump hook. Mutombo arrived in Denver as the fourth overall pick of the 1991 draft and averaged 16.6 points as a rookie. But that average dropped in each of his first five years. If the three-time All-Star can expand his offensive game as a new member of the Hawks, he will jump into the upper echelon of NBA centers.

LARRY NANCE

Born: 2–12–59, at Anderson, S.C.
Position: Forward/center.
Teams: Suns, 1981–88, Cavaliers, 1988–94.

Nance was an athletic power forward who created severe matchup problems with his 6–10 height and quickness off the ball. The former Clemson University star was one of the game's great leapers and 1984 winner of the NBA's All-Star Slam-Dunk Championship. That leaping ability made him dangerous on spectacular alley-oop lobs as well as on the offensive and defensive boards. Nance, who could run the floor and defend either centers or small forwards, was a 20th-pick steal for Phoenix in the 1981 draft and rose to prominence after an unspectacular rookie debut. Over the next 11 seasons, he never averaged under 16 points or 8 rebounds while making 54.6 percent of his shots. Over a 13-year career with the Suns and Cavaliers, Nance qualified for three All-Star Games and earned a spot on the 1989 NBA All-Defensive first team. He retired in 1994 with 15,687 points (17.1) and 7,352 rebounds (8.0).

NORM NIXON

Born: 10–10–55, at Macon, Ga.
Position: Guard.
Teams: Lakers, 1977–83, Clippers, 1983–89.

Nixon was a pure point guard who played in the shadow of Lakers stars Kareem Abdul-Jabbar, Magic Johnson and James Worthy on Los Angeles' 1980 and '82 championship teams. The 6–2 former Duquesne University star was at his best when running the offense, setting up easy baskets for teammates, leading the fast break and penetrating the lane. But Nixon also was a dangerous shooter, a dimension that set him apart from many other point guards. The popular playmaker, a late 1977 first-round draft pick, enjoyed six solid seasons with the Lakers before a stunning trade sent him to the San Diego Clippers, clearing the way for Johnson to operate exclusively at the Lakers' point. Nixon, who played on three Pacific Division winners for the Lakers, spent his final six injury-plagued seasons with a team that never even posted a winning record. He retired after the 1988–89 season with 12,065 points (15.7 per game) and an impressive 6,386 assists (8.3).

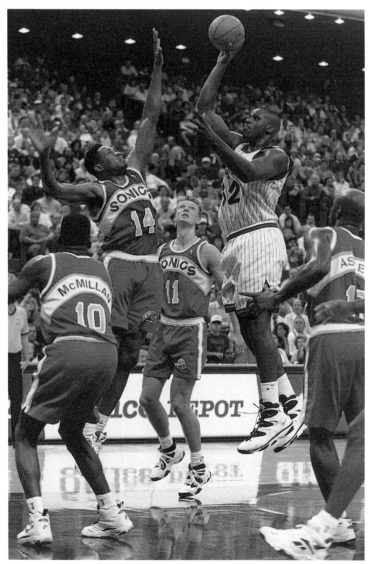

SHAQ ATTACK *Lakers center Shaquille O'Neal is one of the league's rising stars*

HAKEEM OLAJUWON

See Legends of the NBA *page 73*

SHAQUILLE O'NEAL

Born: 3–6–72, at Newark, N.J.
Position: Center.
Team: Magic, 1992–96; Lakers, 1996–present.

O'Neal is a powerful, 300-pound center who does most of his damage close to the basket. When the 7–1 Shaq gets the ball down low, nobody is strong enough to challenge his rim-rattling dunks. While other NBA centers are more polished, none can match the low-post domination O'Neal brings to a game—as an offensive weapon and an intimidating shot-blocker. O'Neal, who left Lousiana State University after his junior season, was drafted by Orlando in 1992. He quickly became the NBA's most marketable athlete behind Michael Jordan. O'Neal earned Rookie of the Year honors in 1992–93 and won an NBA scoring title (29.3) while leading the Magic to the NBA Finals two years later. After the 1995–96 season, he took his game to Los Angeles as the most expensive free agent in history. Opponents have discovered the best defense against Shaq is a foul—he shoots just over 50 percent from the line. O'Neal was a member of Dream Team II and III.

ROBERT PARISH

Born: 8–30–53, at Shreveport, La.
Position: Center.
Teams: Warriors, 1976–80, Celtics, 1980–94, Hornets, 1994–present.

As one of two 20-year players in NBA history, the 7–1 Parish holds the record for games played and he ranks among the career leaders in many other categories. The former Centenary star has performed his double-decade feat with a workmanlike precision that places him in the company of the game's all-time great centers. There has never been anything flashy about "The Chief," but his career numbers (more than 23,000 points and 14,000 rebounds) and contributions as a member of three Boston championship teams will someday pique the interest of Hall of Fame voters. From his 1976–77 rookie

HAIL TO THE CHIEF *Former Celtics star Robert Parish is one of two double-decade NBA performers*

season with Golden State through a 14-year run in Boston and two final seasons in Charlotte, Parish has provided quiet leadership with his solid defense, offensive and defensive rebounding, unselfish passing and deadly turnaround jumpers that always seem to come at the right moments. A nine-time All-Star, Parish averaged double-digit rebounds 10 times.

GARY PAYTON

Born: 7–23–68, at Oakland, Calif.
Position: Guard.
Team: SuperSonics, 1990–present.

Payton, a nice blend of offense and defense, has steadily worked his way into the upper echelon of NBA point guards. There never was anything wrong with Payton's ball-hawking, pressure defense, which created havoc for opposing guards and set the pace for Seattle's transition attack. But the former Oregon State University star entered the NBA in 1990 without an outside shot, giving defenders the option of dropping back into double teams. Payton averaged a meager 7.2 points as a rookie, but he worked hard on his shot and watched his averages climb to 9.4, 13.5, 16.5 and 20.6. With defenders now forced to respect him outside, Payton uses his quickness to create shots and passes off the dribble and his assist totals are consistently respectable. Payton, a notorious trash-talker, is a three-time All-Defensive first-team selection and the NBA's 1995–96 Defensive Player of the Year. He also is a three-time All-Star.

BOB PETTIT

See Legends of the NBA *page 74*

ANDY PHILLIP

Born: 3–7–22, at Granite City, Ill.
Position: Guard.
Teams: Stags (BAA/NBA), 1947–50, Warriors, 1950–53, Pistons, 1953–56, Celtics, 1956–58.

Phillip ranked alongside Slater Martin, Bob Cousy and Dick McGuire as one of the premier passing guards of the early years of the NBA. He had quick hands and a peripheral vision that allowed him to spot passing lanes and thread the ball to spots other guards would never consider. The 6-2 Phillip, a member of the University of Illinois' "Whiz Kids" of the early 1940s, began his 11-year BAA/NBA career with the Chicago Stags and enjoyed later stints with Philadelphia, Fort Wayne and Boston. A five-time All-Star Game performer, Phillip holds the distinction of being the first NBA player to record more than 500 assists in a single season (1951–52). When Boston Coach Red Auerbach needed a play-maker for a title run in 1956, he talked Phillip out of retirement and he helped the Celtics win their first championship. Phillip, who finished his outstanding career in 1958 with 3,759 assists (5.4 per game), was elected to the Hall of Fame in 1961.

SCOTTIE PIPPEN

Born: 9–25–65, at Hamburg, Ark.
Position: Guard/forward.
Team: Bulls, 1987–present.

Pippen, a 1987 first-round draft pick, is part of the two-headed monster that rules professional basketball in Chicago. The former Central Arkansas star, like teammate Michael Jordan, is an athletic force who gives the Bulls a powerful presence on both ends of the court. If you like offense, Pippen can provide it with a soft outside jumper, a pull-up runner or a spectacular dunk. If you prefer defense, he can go chest-to-chest with anybody in the game. The 6–7 swingman is a three-time All-NBA first-team selection and a five-time NBA All-Defensive first-teamer. But more importantly, he was a valuable cog on Chicago's 1991, '92, '93 and '96 championship teams. To illustrate Pippen's all-around abilities, consider 1994–95: He led the Bulls in scoring (21.4), rebounding (8.1), assists (5.2), steals (2.94), blocks (1.13) and minutes (38.2). The six-time All-Star was in the 1992 and 1996 Olympic Dream Teams.

JIM POLLARD

Born: 7–9–22, at Oakland, Calif.
Position: Forward.
Team: Lakers (NBL/NBA), 1948–55.

Pollard, a 6–5 leaper, was the perfect complement to George Mikan and Vern Mikkelsen in a vaunted Minneapolis Lakers frontcourt that otherwise lacked finesse and athleticism. Pollard was a deadly outside shooter who could bang inside and perform dazzling aerial displays. The "Kangaroo Kid," a former college star at Stanford, began his professional career in the American Basketball League before joining Mikan and the newly formed Lakers in the National Basketball League. The Lakers rolled to an NBL championship in 1948 and followed with BAA/NBA titles in 1949, '50, '52, '53 and '54. The Minneapolis frontcourt, with point guard Slater Martin directing traffic, was simply unstoppable and Pollard was a major factor. When he retired in 1955, he had scored 6,522 points (13.1) and played in four All-Star Games. Pollard, an All-NBA first-team selection in 1950, was elected to the Hall of Fame in 1977.

KEVIN PORTER

Born: 4–17–50, at Chicago, Ill.
Position: Guard.
Teams: Bullets, 1972–75, 1979–83, Pistons, 1975–77, 1978–79, Nets, 1978.

Porter was a classic NBA point guard who used his outstanding quickness and clever passing to set

A LOT OF BULL *Scottie Pippen is part of Chicago's two-headed monster*

up teammates for easy baskets. Porter, who played his college ball at St. Francis of Pennsylvania, worked with a cockiness, aggressiveness and in-your-face attitude that made him an unpopular figure among NBA opponents. But he was a master at the fast break and teammates had to constantly beware of pinpoint passes seemingly coming from nowhere. The ever-scowling Porter began his career in Baltimore and blossomed into a big-time assist man. In 1974–75, he averaged 8.0 and a year later he raised that average to 10.2 in Detroit. Porter's big season was 1978–79, when he became the NBA's first 1,000-assist man and also averaged a career-high 15.4 points. Porter, who spent his first three seasons with the Bullets and returned to Washington for his last three, retired in 1983 with 7,645 points (11.6) and 5,314 assists (8.1).

MARK PRICE

Born: 2-15-64, at Bartlesville, Okla.
Position: Guard.
Teams: Cavaliers, 1986–95, Bullets, 1995–present.

Price is living, dribbling proof there's still a place for the little man in the NBA. The 6-foot former Georgia Tech point guard has thrived for a decade, mystifying critics who said he was too slow, too small and too deliberate for a high-level game. Price, a second-round 1986 pick by Dallas, was acquired by Cleveland in a draft-day trade that helped turn the Cavaliers into an Eastern Conference power. Through hard work and gritty determination, he developed into a first-class floor general, a nice combination of shooter, penetrator and defender who can step up his game at critical moments. One of the best 3-point marksmen in the league, Price also is a career 90-percent free-throw shooter who has ranked consistently among the assist leaders. The two-time Long Distance Shootout champion and four-time All-Star has been

plagued by injuries, a factor in his trade to Washington before the 1995–96 season.

FRANK RAMSEY

Born: 7-13-31, at Corydon, Ky.
Position: Guard.
Team: Celtics, 1954–64.

Ramsey carved a Hall of Fame career out of his nine seasons as a substitute guard for the powerful Boston Celtics. Never a starter, the 6–3 Ramsey had the ability to come off the bench in pressure situations and ignite an offense, a trump card Celtics Coach Red Auerbach played to perfection. Time after time, the heady and steady Ramsey came through in the clutch, never complaining about playing time and earning the respect of appreciative Boston fans. Ramsey, a former star under Adolph Rupp at the University of Kentucky, was rewarded with seven championship rings as he piled up 8,378 points (13.4) and a surprising 3,410 rebounds (5.5). His averages in 98 postseason games were mirror images of the regular season. Ramsey, who played through 1964 without ever performing in an All-Star Game, was elected to the Hall of Fame in 1981.

WILLIS REED

Born: 6-25-42, at Hico, La.
Position: Center.
Team: Knicks, 1964–74.

Reed was the physical and inspirational leader of a Knicks team that captured championships in 1970 and '73. The hard-working center, who suffered a series of knee injuries, scored 12,183 points (18.7 per game) and grabbed 8,414 rebounds (12.9) over a 10–year career that ended in 1974. The 6–10, 240-pound Reed, a former Grambling State University star,

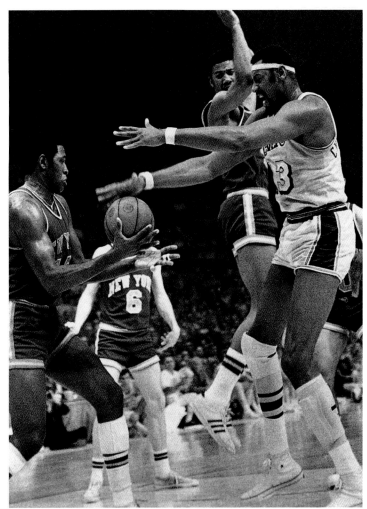

MY BALL *Knicks' Willis Reed (left) claims a rebound from Wilt Chamberlain*

earned Rookie of the Year honors in 1964–65 while battling tenaciously against the likes of Wilt Chamberlain and Bill Russell. His physical presence was complemented by an ability to move outside for a soft lefthanded jump shot. Reed was at his best in 1969–70, when he became the first player to earn All-Star Game, regular-season and NBA Finals MVP citations in the same season while leading the Knicks to their first championship. Injuries destroyed his 1971–72 season, but he returned to ignite another title run in 1972–73. Reed, a seven-time All-Star, was elected to the Hall of Fame in 1981.

GLEN RICE

Born: 5-28-67, at Flint, Mich.
Position: Guard/forward.
Teams: Heat, 1989–95, Hornets, 1995–present.

Rice is one of the game's pure outside shooters. When the 6–8 small forward goes into his zone, he can produce points in bunches from any place and angle on the court. Rice, whose long-range bombing helped the University of Michigan win the 1989 NCAA Tournament championship, was drafted by the Miami Heat with the fourth overall pick of the 1989 draft. He averaged 13.6 points as a rookie and jumped his average to 22.3 two years later, when he also grabbed 5.0 rebounds per game. Rice was the focus of the struggling Heat's offense for six seasons before a blockbuster 1995 trade sent him to Charlotte, where he averaged 21.6 points in his first season. Critics have labeled Rice a one-dimensional shooter, but he has worked hard to develop a floor game that could expand his offensive horizons. If he can add that dimension, the 1995 Long Distance Shootout champion could become one of the most explosive scorers in the game.

MITCH RICHMOND

Born: 6–30–65, at Fort Lauderdale, Fla.
Position: Guard.
Teams: Warriors, 1988–91, Kings, 1991–present.

Richmond is the well-rounded shooting guard who carries the scoring load for the Sacramento Kings. The 6–5 former Kansas State University star is difficult to defend because he can fire from 3-point range, drive the lane, finish the fast break and post up smaller guards. Richmond, the fifth over-all pick of the 1988 draft, averaged 22 points and 5.9 rebounds in 1988–89 en route to Rookie of the Year honors. Over his first eight seasons, his scoring average never dipped below 21, putting him in select NBA company. Richmond spent three seasons with Golden State before a 1991 trade brought him to lowly Sacramento. With Richmond providing the center-piece for a franchise badly in need of one, the Kings began making the slow trip to respectability. One of the highlights of Richmond's career was the 1995 All-Star Game, when he came off the bench for the West team and scored 23 points, earning MVP honors.

ALVIN ROBERTSON

Born: 7–22–62, at Barberton, Ohio.
Position: Guard.
Teams: Spurs, 1984–89, Bucks, 1989–93, Pistons, 1993, Raptors, 1995–present.

Robertson has operated as a do-everything big guard for more than a decade. The 6–4 former University of Arkansas star is a hard-working offensive and defen-sive player who can influence a game in many ways. During his prime, Robertson was a double-digit scorer, a hard-nosed rebounder and an outstanding passer, whether operating in a half-court game or on the break. He also was a two-time All-Defensive first-teamer who topped 200 steals in a season six times. Robertson, a first-round 1984 draft pick by San Antonio, played five seasons with the Spurs, averaging better than 17 points four times and posting consistent rebounding and assist totals. He spent the next three seasons in Milwaukee before splitting 1992–93 with the Bucks and Detroit Pistons. Robertson, a four-time All-Star and 10,000-point scorer, sat out the 1993–94 and 1994–95 seasons with back problems, resurfacing in 1995–96 with the expansion Toronto Raptors.

OSCAR ROBERTSON

See Legends of the NBA *page 75*

DAVID ROBINSON

Born: 8–6–65, at Key West, Fla.
Position: Center.
Team: Spurs, 1987–present.

Robinson, the NBA's 1994–95 MVP, is the perfect center. He can score, pass, shoot free throws, run the floor and guard the basket with a Bill Russell-like intensity. His 18-foot jumper is deadly, his first-step quickness is explosive and his shot-blocking defense is stifling. The San Antonio Spurs were so taken with the 7–1 U.S. Naval Academy senior that they drafted him with the first overall pick of 1987 and waited two years while he fulfilled his military com-mitment. "The Admiral" blos-somed quickly, averaging 24.3 points and 12.0 rebounds en route to 1989–90 Rookie of the Year honors. His scoring and rebound-ing averages have never dropped under 23 and 10, respectively, and in 1993–94 he led the league in scoring (29.8) while leading the Spurs in assists. Robinson, a left-hander who averaged an NBA-leading 4.49 blocks in 1992, is a four-time All-NBA and All-Defensive first-teamer and he was 1992 Defensive Player of the Year. Robinson was a member of the 1992 gold medal-winning Olympic Dream Team.

GLENN ROBINSON

Born: 1–10–73, at Gary, Ind.
Position: Forward.
Team: Bucks, 1994–present.

Milwaukee's "Big Dog" will be a big offensive force for years to come. The 6–7 small forward is an explosive scoring machine, a mobile shotmaker who can get his points going to the basket or firing from 3-point range. He entered the NBA in 1994, and quickly picked up where he left off in a spectacular three-year college career at Purdue. After a national-best 30.3-point scoring average in his junior season, Robinson was drafted with the first overall pick and forged a 21.9 rookie average while grabbing 6.4 rebounds per game. He averaged 20.2 points in a solid second season. Some observers predict a scoring title in his future and players who have tried to defend his quick pull-up jumpers or post-up turnarounds will not argue the point. If he has a weakness, it's on the defensive end, but he is willing to work. Robinson and teammate Vin Baker form a formidable young frontcourt tandem.

GUY RODGERS

Born: 9–1–35, at Philadelphia, Pa.
Position: Guard.
Teams: Warriors, 1958–66, Bulls, 1966–67, Royals, 1967, Bucks, 1968–70.

Rodgers, a lefthanded version of NBA idol Bob Cousy, was a flashy point guard with great passing

THE ADMIRAL *San Antonio's David Robinson is the perfect NBA center*

and ball-handling skills. He was at his best when running the fast break for the Philadelphia/San Francisco Warriors. But he also was the creative force who found ways to get the ball low to scoring machine Wilt Chamberlain, his Warriors teammate for five-plus seasons. The 6-foot Rodgers was drafted out of Temple University in 1958, and quickly unveiled his bag of tricks—behind-the-back dribbles, no-look passes and dazzling scoop shots—that made him an instant fan favorite. Three times he averaged double figures in assists, leading the league twice, and he once recorded 28 in a single game, tying Cousy's then-NBA record. Rodgers, a four-time All-Star, spent eight of his 12 seasons with the Warriors and retired in 1970 after short stints in Cincinnati, Chicago and Milwaukee. He finished with career totals of 10,415 points (11.7 per game) and 6,917 assists (7.8).

DENNIS RODMAN

Born: 5–13–61, at Trenton, N.J.
Position: Forward.
Teams: Pistons, 1986–93, Spurs, 1993–95, Bulls, 1995–present.

In a world where teamwork and attitude are keys to success, the 6–8 Rodman stands out like a sore thumb. He dyes his hair in pastel colors, pouts, refuses to get in sideline huddles and ignores his coach. But the positives Rodman brings to the court far outweigh his idiosyncracies. Simply stated, Rodman is one of the most explosive rebounders in history and a smothering defender. Period. He does not have, or want, an offensive game. But that's all right for teams that already have enough firepower. Rodman was drafted out of Southeast Oklahoma State in 1986 and played seven seasons for a Detroit team that won two championships. He followed with two seasons in San Antonio before moving on to a 1995–96 Chicago team that will rank among the best of all time. Rodman, a two-time Defensive Player of the Year and seven-time All-Defensive first-

NATIONALS TREASURE *Syracuse's Dolph Schayes was one of the more athletic and consistent performers of the early NBA*

teamer, has led the league with incredible rebounding averages of 18.7, 18.3, 17.3, 16.8 and 14.9. He's an intense bulldog, Chicago's perfect complement to Michael Jordan and Scottie Pippen.

BILL RUSSELL

See Legends of the NBA *page 76*

DOLPH SCHAYES

Born: 5–19–28, at New York, N.Y.
Position: Forward/center.
Teams: Nationals, 1949–63, Warriors, 1963–64.

The durable Schayes was one of the more athletic players of the early NBA and one of its most consistent performers. The former New York University star played 15 NBA seasons, all but one for Syracuse, and retired with a then-record 1,059 games played, 706 consecutively from 1952 to '61. Over his long career, Schayes

opened up defenses with his ability to hit long-range set shots and penetrate to the basket. He also dominated the boards, posting 11 straight double-digit rebounding seasons and leading the league in 1950–51 (16.4). Schayes, a deadly free throw shooter, led the Nationals to the NBA Finals in 1950 and '54 and their only championship in 1955. A six-time All-NBA first-team selection and a 12-time All-Star, Schayes finished his career in 1964 with 19,247 points (18.2) and 11,256 rebounds (10.6). He was named to the NBA 25th Anniversary All-Time Team in 1970 and elected to the Hall of Fame in 1972.

DETLEF SCHREMPF

Born: 1–21–63, at Leverkusen, Germany.
Position: Forward.
Teams: Mavericks, 1985–89, Pacers, 1989–93, SuperSonics, 1993–present.

Schrempf, a German native and a four-year star for the University of Washington, has developed into one of the NBA's better all-around players. Schrempf is the complete offensive package, a 6–10 small or

power forward who can pass, shoot, rebound and play defense. He is an unselfish player who makes the most of his opportunities. In 1994–95 for Seattle, he connected on 93 of 181 3-point shots (51.4 percent) while averaging 19.2 points, 6.2 rebounds and 3.8 assists. In 1995–96, he averaged 17.1 points and helped the Sonics advance to the NBA Finals. Schrempf was selected by Dallas with the eighth pick of the 1985 draft and was used sparingly by the Mavericks. He didn't blossom until a 1989 trade to the Pacers increased his minutes and he really stepped up after Seattle acquired him in 1993. Schrempf, a two-time NBA Sixth Man Award winner while with Indiana, has become a major figure in Seattle's high-powered attack.

BYRON SCOTT

Born: 3–28–61, at Ogden, Utah.
Position: Guard.
Teams: Lakers, 1983–93, Pacers, 1993–95, Grizzlies, 1995–present.

The 6–4 Scott spent most of his 10 Los Angeles seasons providing outside firepower as a complement to Magic Johnson's penetrating dish-off game. It was a perfect match for the former Arizona State University star, whose catch-and-shoot talent requires a point guard who can push the ball to the basket and draw away defenders. Scott was drafted by the Los Angeles Clippers in 1983 and his draft rights were traded to the Lakers, who watched him blossom in a solid rookie season. From 1984 through 1992, Scott's scoring average ranged from 14.5 points to 21.7. In 1985, he led the league in 3-point shooting with a .433 percentage and he helped the Lakers win championships in 1985, '87 and '88. Scott, a ballhawking defender with quick hands, was signed by Indiana in 1993 and he spent his 13th NBA season with the expansion Vancouver Grizzlies in 1995–96, averaging 10.2 points.

BILL SHARMAN

Born: 5–25–26, at Abilene, Tex.
Position: Guard.
Teams: Capitols, 1950–51, Celtics, 1951–61.

Sharman teamed with Bob Cousy for 10 years in one of the great backcourts of basketball history. Cousy provided the flash and glitter, while Sharman was the straight shooter for a Boston Celtics team that introduced the run-and-gun offense. Sharman, who starred at the University of Southern California, spent one year with the Washington Capitols before moving into Boston's backcourt of the future. While Cousy was dazzling fans and opponents with no-look passes and fancy dribbling, Sharman was scoring in double figures and doing the little things that don't show up in the box scores. He was named All-NBA first team four times and played in eight All-Star Games, winning MVP honors in 1955. Sharman finished his career in 1961 with 12,665 points (17.8 per game) after playing on four championship teams as a charter member of the Celtics' 13-year basketball dynasty. He was named to the NBA 25th Anniversary All-Time Team in 1970 and elected into the Hall of Fame in 1975.

JACK SIKMA

Born: 11–14–55, at Kankakee, Ill.
Position: Forward/center.
Teams: SuperSonics, 1977–86, Bucks, 1986–91.

The 7-foot Sikma was an outstanding all-around center and the most popular player in Seattle's NBA history. Drafted out of little Illinois Wesleyan University in 1977, Sikma spent nine of his 14 seasons in Seattle, leading the SuperSonics to NBA Finals appearances in his first

JUMPING JACK *Seattle enforcer Sikma*

two campaigns and a 1979 championship. Sikma was a 250-pounder who thrived offensively inside the lane with an ugly, overhead jumper that was virtually unstoppable and a short hook. He was an aggressive rebounder who averaged in double figures eight times and a coachable, tireless worker who steadily improved his game, both offensively and defensively. The seven-time All-Star was traded to the Bucks in 1986, and spent his final five seasons in Milwaukee without an appreciable drop in production. Sikma retired in 1991 with 17,287 points (15.6) and 10,816 rebounds (9.8).

PAUL SILAS

Born: 7–12–43, at Prescott, Ariz.
Position: Forward.
Teams: Hawks, 1964–69, Suns, 1969–72, Celtics, 1972–76, Nuggets, 1976–77, SuperSonics, 1977–80.

Silas, a physical 6–7 battler, built a 16-year career around his ability to grab rebounds and play intense, chest-to-chest defense. Never a headline or attention grabber, Silas valiantly performed behind-the-scenes trenchwork for three NBA champions. The former Creighton University star was drafted by the St. Louis Hawks in 1964, but it wasn't until a 1969 trade to Phoenix that he blossomed into a valuable role player. Over the next seven seasons, Silas averaged better than 11 rebounds per game and he anchored Boston's 1974 and '76 title teams as Dave Cowens, John Havlicek and Jo Jo White garnered the headlines. When Seattle acquired an aging Silas in 1977, the Sonics made consecutive NBA Finals appearances, winning a championship in 1979. Silas, a two-time All-Defensive first-team selection, retired in 1980 with only a 9.4 scoring average, but his 12,357 rebounds (9.9) rank among the all-time leaders.

JERRY SLOAN

Born: 3–28–42, at McLeansboro, Ill.
Position: Guard/forward.
Teams: Bullets, 1965–66, Bulls, 1966–76.

The hard-nosed Sloan was the guts of a Chicago Bulls team that advanced to the Western Conference finals twice in the mid-1970s. The 6–5 Sloan, an Evansville University product, was an intense, in-your-face defensive stopper who frustrated opponents with a rugged physical presence that drew charges of "dirty play." But the only thing dirty about Sloan was his uniform after games in which he bumped bodies under the basket, hit the floor after taking charges and

dove relentlessly into every ball scramble on the court. He was emotional, he was dedicated and he knew only one speed—full throttle. Sloan played one season for Baltimore before joining the Bulls in the 1966 expansion draft. He spent the next 10 seasons averaging 14 points and 7.4 rebounds while claiming four NBA All-Defensive first-team citations. After retiring in 1976, Sloan took his intensity to the bench as a successful coach for the Bulls and the current-edition Utah Jazz.

JOE SMITH

Born: 7–26–75, at Norfolk, Va.
Position: Forward.
Team: Warriors, 1995–present.

The hard-working Smith will climb the NBA talent ladder quickly and help Warriors fans forget the team's shaky recent past. He entered the league in the 1995 draft at age 19 and quickly displayed the talents that could help him become one of the game's top swing forwards. Smith, who was grabbed by the Warriors with the draft's first overall pick after his sophomore season at Maryland, showed agility around the basket in his rookie season while averaging 15.3 points and 8.7 rebounds.. He can use either hand and his shooting range goes to 18 feet. Smith also will run the court, he will battle the offensive and defensive boards and his interior defense will improve because he is coachable. The best thing about Smith, who averaged 20.8 points and 10.6 rebounds in his final season at Maryland, is that he will give a great effort every time he steps on the court.

RIK SMITS

Born: 8–23–66, at Eindhoven, Holland.
Position: Center.
Team: Pacers, 1988–present.

Smits, a 7–4 center who didn't discover basketball until age 15, is still feeling his way around the professional game. He has the tools—size, agility, soft shooting touch and bulk—to play with the NBA's big boys and he is blossoming with every new season. Smits, who was born and raised in Holland, was selected by Indiana with the second overall pick of the 1988 draft after four seasons at Marist College. He earned a spot on the NBA All-Rookie first team in 1988–89, but his game had a lot of holes and intensity was in short supply. Smits has worked hard to correct his shortcomings and now rates as a top-line center, capable of matching up with any of the game's best pivot men on a given night. As Smits improves, so do the Pacers, who came up one game short in their bid to reach the NBA Finals in 1994 and '95.

LATRELL SPREWELL

Born: 9–8–70, at Milwaukee, Wis.
Positon: Guard.
Team: Warriors, 1992–present.

Sprewell can score. He can pass. And he can play chest-to-chest, pressure defense. The question is whether he wants to. Since an outstanding 1993–94 second season when Sprewell averaged 21 points, 4.9 rebounds and 4.7 assists for the Golden State Warriors, bickering and silent brooding have been more definitive of his game than the explosive slams, the long-range jump shots and pinpoint passes that earned him a 1994 All-NBA first-team citation. Although his numbers remain excellent, the 6–5 Sprewell has transformed into a scoring guard who looks for his shot as a first, second and third option. That's not all bad because he does possess a special talent for creating shots, especially off the dribble. But it also results in a lower shooting percentage. A two-time All-Star who played at the University of Alabama, Sprewell is at his best when he exhibits the all-around talents that were so prominent in 1993–94.

JERRY STACKHOUSE

Born: 11–5–74, at Kinston, N.C.
Position: Guard/forward.
Team: 76ers, 1995–present.

Stackhouse has been followed by the Michael Jordan spotlight through two college seasons at North Carolina and his rookie campaign with the Philadelphia 76ers. As an athletic, acrobatic shooting guard who played at Jordan's alma mater, the comparisons were natural. And Stackhouse lived up to early billing with a solid rookie performance that produced 19.2 points per game. Stackhouse, who opted for the NBA draft after his sophomore season with the Tar Heels, plays with a charisma and intensity that bodes well for 76ers fans. He's explosive to the basket, his outside jump shot is improving and he's capable of scoring points in bunches. Scouts expect Stackhouse to emerge as the best rebounding shooting guard in the game and his defensive quickness should translate into easy points. The bottom line: Stackhouse will soar into the NBA stratosphere as a Jordanesque star.

JOHN STOCKTON

Born: 3–26–62, at Spokane, Wash.
Position: Guard.
Team: Jazz, 1984–present.

The 6–1 Stockton, the most prodigious assist and steal man in NBA history, is Utah's outside answer to Karl Malone. Nobody makes off-the-dribble bullet passes like the former Gonzaga University star, who locates the open man with an instinctive, radar-like sixth sense. Stockton also is an accomplished 3-point shooter, a durable performer and a floor general who seldom makes a bad decision. After spending his first three sea-sons on the Utah bench, Stockton became a starter in 1987–88 and began piling up impressive numbers. Over his first five seasons as a starter, he averaged 1,134 assists, 11 more than Isiah Thomas' previous one-season record. The eight-time All-Star has led the league eight straight seasons, has a career average of better than 11 per game and holds virtually every assist record imaginable. Stockton also holds the NBA career record for steals and has led the league in that category twice. A two-time All-NBA first-team selection, he was a member of the 1992 Olympic Dream Team.

ALL THAT JAZZ
The multi-talented John Stockton holds the NBA all-time records for assists and steals

REGGIE THEUS

Born: 10–13–57, at Inglewood, Calif.
Position: Guard.
Teams: Bulls, 1978–84, Kings, 1984–88, Hawks, 1988–89, Magic, 1989–90, Nets, 1990–91.

The 6–7 Theus was an offensive-minded point guard who might have been better off as a shooting guard—a position that would have better utilized his long-range shooting and inside scoring capabilities. But he played most of his 13-year career with Chicago and Kansas City/Sacramento teams that needed him to be a play-maker—a role he filled reluctantly at first. But as Theus matured into a less point-conscious team leader, his assist totals rose and his game took on a new dimension. Theus was most comfortable in a running-style offense, the kind he played for three run-and-gun seasons at the University of Nevada Las Vegas. He could be acrobatic at times and his shooting range was somewhere beyond the sidelines. Theus, a two-time All-Star, retired in 1991, after one-season stays in Atlanta, Orlando and New Jersey. He left with 19,015 points (18.5) and 6,453 assists (6.3).

ISIAH THOMAS

Born: 4–30–61, at Chicago, Ill.
Position: Guard.
Team: Pistons, 1981–94.

Thomas, the ultimate point guard, treated the basketball court as his personal playground for 13 amazing seasons in Detroit. He penetrated, he passed, he shot, he cajoled and he led the Pistons to consecutive championships in 1989 and '90. By the time he was finished, in 1994 the lightning-quick, 6–1 Thomas had scored 18,822 points (19.2), handed out

NEAR PERFECTION *Isiah Thomas was the prototype NBA point guard*

9,061 assists (9.3) and appeared in 11 All-Star Games, winning MVP honors in two of them. He was a three-time All-NBA first-team selection and MVP of the 1990 NBA Finals, when he averaged 27.6 points and 7.0 assists in a scintillating performance. Thomas, the Pistons' all-time leader in points, steals and assists, made his NBA debut in 1981, after leading Indiana University to an NCAA Tournament championship in his sophomore season. Thomas set a then-NBA record in 1984–85 with 1,123 assists (13.9) and he currently ranks fourth on the all-time list.

DAVID THOMPSON

Born: 7–13–54, at Shelby, N.C.
Position: Guard/forward.
Teams: Nuggets (ABA/NBA), 1975–82, SuperSonics, 1982–84.

Thompson, one of the most athletically gifted players the game has ever produced, struggled through a controversial career that was short-circuited by substance abuse and personal problems. Thompson, who used his 44-inch vertical leap to skywalk North Carolina State University to the 1974 NCAA Tournament championship, burst upon the ABA scene in 1975 as one of the most heralded players in history. He didn't disappoint, thrilling Denver fans with above-the-rim acrobatics that produced averages of 26 points and 6.3 rebounds and the ABA's Rookie of the Year award. The amazing Thompson could score from anywhere with his smooth jump shot or dazzling aerial explosions. After the 1976 merger, the 6–5 Thompson brought his high-wire act to the NBA, averaging better than 21 points per game in five consecutive seasons and earning two All-NBA first-team berths. But his career quickly unraveled amid rumors of drug problems and he played only three more seasons, one with the Nuggets and two with the SuperSonics. The four-time NBA All-Star finished with a combined ABA/NBA total of 13,422 points (22.7).

NATE THURMOND

Born: 7–25–41, at Akron, Ohio.
Position: Center.
Teams: Warriors, 1963–74, Bulls, 1974–75, Cavaliers, 1975–77.

The 6–11 Thurmond was the perfect blend of offense and defense. He was physical around the basket, whether claiming rebounds or blocking shots, and he was smooth from the perimeter, where he could hit a soft jumper or feed a cutting teammate. The former Bowling Green State star was drafted by San Francisco in 1963 and played power forward because Wilt Chamberlain was dominating the middle. But the Warriors thought so highly of Thurmond, they traded Chamberlain in 1965. Over a 14-year career that included short stints with Chicago and Cleveland, Thurmond averaged 15 points (14,437) and 15 rebounds (14,464) per game. He also was a two-time All-Defensive first-teamer and a seven-time All-Star. The best illustration of Thurmond's versatility is that he was the first player to record a quadruple-double—22 points, 14 rebounds, 13 assists and 12 blocked shots in a 1974 game. He was elected to the Hall of Fame in 1984.

JACK TWYMAN

Born: 5–11–34, at Pittsburgh, Pa.
Position: Guard/forward.
Team: Royals, 1955–66.

Twyman will be remembered as one of the best pure-shooting forwards in the 1950s and '60s. The 6–6 University of Cincinnati product, who spent his entire 11-year professional career with the Royals—first in Rochester then in Cincinnati—averaged 31.2 points in 1959–60 and topped the 25-point barrier three times. When he finished his career in 1966, Twyman had scored 15,840 points (19.2) and grabbed 5,424 rebounds (6.6). Twyman, who played in six All-Star Games, was most comfortable from the corner, where he punished sagging defenses. But he also could score inside and he formed a lethal offensive combination with Cincinnati teammates Oscar Robertson and Jerry Lucas for three exciting seasons. Twyman's efforts off-court in humanitarian activities were also well-known, especially his long-time legal guardianship of former teammate Maurice Stokes, who was paralyzed in a 1958 game. Twyman was elected to the Hall of Fame in 1982.

WES UNSELD

Born: 3–14–46, at Louisville, Ky.
Position: Center.
Team: Bullets, 1968–81.

The 6–7, 245-pound Unseld was an enforcer-like center who ruled the boards and helped the Bullets reach four NBA Finals during the 1970s. Never a prolific scorer, Unseld made up for it with his leadership, intensity and unflagging dedication to rebounding. The physical Unseld, a two-time Louisville All-American, was especially adept at pulling down missed shots and triggering the fast break with strong outlet passes. Over his 13 NBA seasons, all spent with the Bullets, he grabbed 13,769 rebounds (14.0) and scored 10,624 points (10.8). Unseld had a memorable debut season in 1968–69 at Baltimore, becoming only the second NBA player to be named Rookie of the Year and MVP in the same season. Over the next decade, Unseld's Bullets would win seven Central and Atlantic Division titles, four Eastern Conference titles and one championship (1978). The five-time All-Star, who later coached the Bullets for seven seasons, was elected to the Hall of Fame in 1988.

NICK VAN EXEL

Born: 11–27–71, at Kenosha, Wis.
Position: Guard.
Team: Lakers, 1993–present.

Van Exel is a point guard with an attitude. He's cocky, brash, arrogant and so aggressive his Los Angeles Lakers teammates don't dare take their eyes off the ball. The 6–1 waterbug fired up a team-record 511 3-point shots in his 1994–95 second season, but he's just as likely to explode to the basket with athletic, lightning-quick dashes. In Van Exel's 1993–94 rookie season, most of those dashes ended up with him taking a shot. In his second and third seasons, he dished off more and raised his assist totals among the leaders. Van Exel's career numbers of 15.1 points and 7.0 assists per game might be just the tip of the iceberg. He was a 1993 second-round steal for the Lakers, who ignored reports of attitude problems at the University of Cincinnati. As valuable as his explosiveness and range is the fire Van Exel lights under the team with his aggressiveness.

KIKI VANDEWEGHE

Born: 8–1–58, at Wiesbaden, West Germany.
Position: Forward.
Teams: Nuggets, 1980–84, Trail Blazers, 1984–89, Knicks, 1989–92, Clippers, 1992–93.

Vandeweghe was an offensive-minded small forward who thrived in Denver Coach Doug Moe's run-and-gun attack of the early 1980s. The 6–8 former UCLA star knew one speed—fast forward—and he never stopped running in a 13-year NBA career that produced 15,980 points and an impressive 19.7 per game average. Vandeweghe, the son of former NBA guard Ernie Vandeweghe, was not blessed with great speed or leaping ability. But he possessed a first-step quickness that allowed him to blow past defenders with either hand and a quick release that permitted him to get off shots in heavy traffic. His shoulder fake threw defenders off balance and his 20-foot jumper was soft and accurate. Vandeweghe averaged better than 20 points seven times, including a 26.9 mark for Portland in 1986–87, when he led the NBA in 3-point shooting (48.1 percent). The two-time All-Star retired in 1993, after short stints with the Knicks and Clippers.

CHET WALKER

Born: 2–22–40, at Benton Harbor, Mich.
Position: Guard/forward.
Teams: Nationals/76ers, 1962–69, Bulls, 1969–75.

"Chet The Jet" was one of the best one-on-one players the game has produced. The 6–6 former Bradley University star had an incredible knack for creating shots, pumping two or three times while in the air and either making the basket or drawing a foul that he usually turned into two points. Because of those instinctive offensive abilities and a natural 20-foot jump shot, Walker was the late-game go-to man for the Philadelphia 76ers and Chicago Bulls over a 13-year NBA career that produced 18,831 points (18.2) and 7,314 rebounds (7.1). Walker was a key figure for the 76ers' 1966–67 championship team that won a regular-season-

RAW POWER *Burly Wes Unseld created space in Washington's middle*

record 68 games and ended the Boston Celtics' eight-year title reign. He averaged 19.3 points and 8.1 rebounds for a squad that included Wilt Chamberlain, Billy Cunningham and Hal Greer. Walker played in seven All-Star Games and averaged 18.2 points over 13 postseason appearances.

BILL WALTON

Born: 11–5–52, at La Mesa, Calif.
Position: Center.
Teams: Trail Blazers, 1974–79, Clippers, 1979–85, Celtics, 1985–87.

Any search for the prototypical center begins and ends with Walton, who will be best remembered for his brilliant college career at UCLA. The 6–11 Walton could do everything: score, rebound, defend, block shots and trigger the fast break. Only a series of foot and knee injuries kept the big redhead from joining the Wilt Chamberlains, Bill Russells and Kareem Abdul-Jabbars on the list of all-time great professional pivot men. Even though he lost four full seasons and numerous partial seasons to injuries, Walton still ranked among the best. In 1976–77, he averaged 18.6 points and 13.2 rebounds while leading Portland to its first NBA championship. A year later, Walton averaged 18.9 points, 14.4 rebounds, 5.0 assists and 2.5 blocks en route to regular-season MVP honors. He managed only one more healthy season— 1985–86, when he came off Boston's bench and helped the Celtics win a championship. Walton was elected to the Hall of Fame in 1993.

BOBBY WANZER

Born: 6–4–21, at New York, N.Y.
Position: Guard.
Team: Royals, 1948–57.

Wanzer was one of the best shooting guards of his era and a perfect backcourt mate for Bob Davies in Rochester. But the 6-foot former Seton Hall star was much more than a proficient point scorer.

Wanzer handled the ball, passed and played chest-to-chest defense, never giving less than 100 percent effort. Wanzer, Davies and big man Arnie Risen were an NBA force in the early 1950s, winning one championship (1951) and challenging for numerous others. But the Royals were blocked by the formidable Minneapolis Lakers machine that won five titles in six seasons. Wanzer, a five-time All-Star, was the first free-throw shooter to average better than 90 percent for a season (90.4 in 1951–52) and he topped 80 percent for his career. Wanzer, who retired in 1957 with 6,924 points,

served as Rochester player-coach in 1955–56 and 1956–57 and coach only in 1957–58. He was elected to the Hall of Fame in 1987.

CHRIS WEBBER

Born: 3–1–73, at Detroit, Mich.
Position: Forward.
Teams: Warriors, 1993–94, Bullets, 1994–present.

Webber is a do-everything power forward with triple-double potential. The 6–10 former University of Michigan star has extraordinary ballhandling ability for a big man and the inside skills to produce a lot of points. Webber is not a

BLAZE OF GLORY *When healthy, Bill Walton (32) was a dominating NBA center*

strong outside shooter, but there's no reason for him to wander beyond 18 feet. The only thing standing between him and stardom is a questionable attitude that already has forced one trade. Webber was drafted by Orlando with the first overall pick in 1993 and the Magic traded him immediately to Golden State for Anfernee Hardaway and a package of future draft picks. He averaged 17.5 points and 9.1 rebounds per game in 1993–94 en route to Rookie of the Year honors, but his constant bickering with Coach Don Nelson finally forced a trade to Washington. Now he's maturing in a talented young frontcourt that includes Rasheed Wallace, 7–7 Romanian center Gheorghe Muresan and former Michigan teammate Juwan Howard.

JERRY WEST

See Legends of the NBA *page 77*

JO JO WHITE

Born: 11–16–46, at St. Louis, Mo.
Position: Guard.
Teams: Celtics, 1969–79, Warriors, 1979–80, Kings, 1980–81.

White was the ever-cool point guard who led Boston to five straight Atlantic Division titles and a pair of championships in the 1970s. The 6–3 White, a think-and-react floor general who could provide equal parts offense and defense, performed his duties quietly and efficiently while flashier teammates like Dave Cowens and John Havlicek garnered the recognition. He seldom tried to perform beyond his capabilities and he never tried to draw attention, something that finally came because of his reliability in the clutch. The former Kansas University star was a fine outside shooter who averaged 17.2 points over his 12-year career, but he also was a fine passer who could open up and tighten the Celtics' offense with crafty change-of-pace maneuvers. White was at his best in the 1976 postseason, when he averaged 22.7 points and 5.4 assists and claimed NBA Finals

MVP honors. The seven-time All-Star retired in 1981, after short stints with Golden State and Kansas City.

LENNY WILKENS

Born: 10–28–37, at Brooklyn, N.Y.
Position: Guard.
Teams: Hawks, 1960–68, SuperSonics, 1968–72, Cavaliers, 1972–74, Trail Blazers, 1974–75.

Wilkens will always be remembered as the winningest coach in NBA history, but his playing career also was Hall of Fame-caliber. He was an outstanding point guard who scored 17,772 points (16.5) and handed out 7,211 assists (6.7) over 15 seasons with four teams. Wilkens, who made his first national impact with Providence College, was a first-round 1960 draft pick of the St. Louis Hawks and he went on to average double-digit points in each of his first 14 seasons. He also played in nine All-Star Games, claiming the MVP award in 1971. It was during a four-year stay in Seattle that Wilkens got his first taste of coaching, directing the Sonics from 1969 to '72 as player-coach. He performed the same duty for one year at Portland before retiring in 1975 to devote full time to coaching. The 6-1 Wilkens, who played in 1,077 regular-season games, was elected to the Hall of Fame in 1988.

DOMINIQUE WILKINS

Born: 1–12–60, at Paris, France.
Position: Forward.
Teams: Hawks, 1982–94, Clippers, 1994, Celtics, 1994–95.

Wilkins was a high-scoring, high-soaring forward who played above NBA rims for 13 seasons with the Hawks, Clippers and Celtics. The acrobatic 6–8 shotmaker could produce points from anywhere on the court and he did it with stylish flair. Wilkins left the University of Georgia after his junior season and became one of the most prolific scorers in NBA history over the next 11-plus seasons in Atlanta. From 1983–84 to 1993–94,

DYNAMIC DUO *Dominique Wilkins (left) and Mookie Blaylock formed a solid combination for the 1992–93 Atlanta Hawks*

115

Wilkins never averaged less than 20 points or 6 rebounds and he captured a scoring title in 1985–86 with a 30.3 mark. With Wilkins leading the charge, the Hawks thrived on the court, but they never had the accessory talent to advance deep into the playoffs. Wilkins was a nine-time All-Star, a 1986 All-NBA first-teamer and a two-time winner of the All-Star Slam Dunk Championship. After short stays with the Los Angeles Clippers and Boston, Wilkins finished his career in 1995 with 25,389 points (25.8) and 6,696 rebounds (6.8).

BUCK WILLIAMS

Born: 3–8–60, at Rocky Mount, N.C.
Position: Forward.
Teams: Nets, 1981–89, Trail Blazers, 1989–96.

Williams was a power forward who carved an outstanding 15-year career out of rebounding and defense. The 6–8, 225-pounder was a tireless worker who pounded the boards relentlessly and earned two All-Defensive first-team selections. Williams averaged better than 12 rebounds per game over his first six seasons with New Jersey, and helped Portland reach the NBA Finals in two of his first three seasons after a 1989 trade to the Trail Blazers. Williams, who left the University of Maryland after his junior season, was selected by New Jersey with the third overall pick of the 1981 draft. He made a quick impact, earning 1981–82 Rookie of the Year honors with averages of 15.5 points and 12.3 rebounds. Those numbers did not vary much over the years as Williams settled into his role as one of the league's most consistent performers. He retired after the 1995–96 season with more than 16,000 points and 12,000 rebounds.

GUS WILLIAMS

Born: 10–10–53, at Mount Vernon, N.Y.
Position: Guard.
Teams: Warriors, 1975–77, SuperSonics, 1977–84, Bullets, 1984–86, Hawks, 1986–87.

MAN WORKING *Relentless Buck Williams led the Trail Blazers to the NBA Finals after the 1989–90 and 1991–92 seasons*

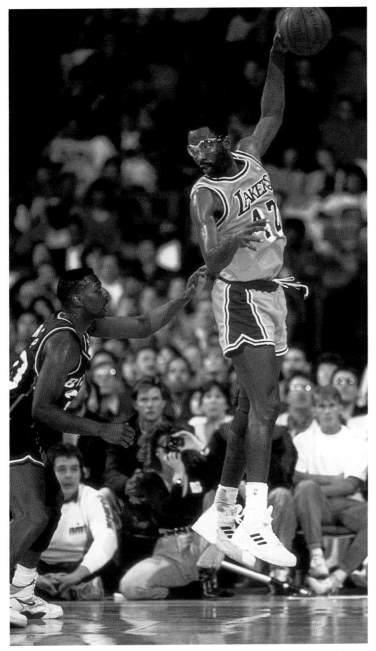

QUICK STUDY *James Worthy was overshadowed in 12 seasons with the Lakers*

Williams was described by contemporaries as the best open-court player in the game. The 6–2 blur was devastating on the fast break, where he could knife between defenders for a basket, whip a no-look pass to a streaking teammate or stop and pop a long-range jumper. The former University of Southern California star, who played his first two seasons with the Golden State Warriors before finding his niche with Seattle in 1977–78, formed an outstanding backcourt combination with defensive-minded point man Dennis Johnson. With their guards pulling a heavy load and Jack Sikma manning the middle, the SuperSonics powered their way to the 1978 NBA Finals and captured their first championship in 1979. But Williams enjoyed his best season in 1981–82, when he averaged 23.4 points and 6.9 assists while earning All-NBA first-team honors. When the two-time All-Star ended his career in 1987, after short stays in Washington and Atlanta, he had piled up 14,093 points (17.1) and 4,597 assists (5.6).

JAMES WORTHY

Born: 2–27–61, at Gastonia, N.C.
Position: Forward.
Team: Lakers, 1982–94.

Worthy was the quiet enforcer for the Los Angeles Lakers' 1980s championship machine. Because he was overshadowed by Kareem Abdul-Jabbar and Magic Johnson most of his 12-year career, the 6–9 Worthy toiled in relative obscurity as one of the best small forwards in the NBA. He was one of the quickest big men the game has ever produced, which explained his explosive power drives through the lane or along the baseline. Worthy also could bury the outside jumper and play the kind of chest-to-chest defense that produces championships. The former North Carolina star, who helped the Tar Heels win the 1982 NCAA Tournament, played on three championship teams for the Lakers and four more that lost in the Finals. He averaged 22.0 points, 7.4 rebounds and 4.4 assists in the 1988 Finals, claiming MVP honors. The seven-time All-Star retired in 1994 with 16,320 points (17.6)—not bad for a team's third-option star.

GEORGE YARDLEY

Born: 11–23–28, at Hollywood, Calif.
Position: Forward.
Teams: Pistons, 1953–59, Nationals, 1959–60.

Yardley, a.k.a. "The Bird," was an early NBA scoring machine for the Fort Wayne Pistons and Syracuse Nationals. The 6–5 Yardley was an unlikely looking basketball star who stood out because of a prematurely balding head, knobby elbows and knees and a loping run that made him look like an ostrich tip-toeing through a minefield. But there was nothing amusing to NBA defenders about his ability to put the ball in the basket. Yardley could score from anywhere on the court, which he did at a 19.2-point clip through his seven-year career, and he was an aggressive rebounder, twice averaging in double figures. He had an instinctive knack for being in the right spot at the right time. Yardley, a six-time All-Star, won a scoring title in 1957–58 when he averaged 27.8 and became the first player to top 2,000 points in a season. Yardley finished his career in 1960, after a short stay at Syracuse.

MAX ZASLOFSKY

Born: 12–7–25, at Brooklyn, N.Y.
Position: Guard/forward.
Teams: Stags, 1946–50, Knicks, 1950–53, Bullets, 1953, Hawks, 1953, Pistons, 1953–56.

Zaslofsky was one of the most feared outside shooters in a BAA/NBA career that lasted from 1946 to '56. The former St. John's star could score with a two-hand set or a running one-hand jumper, shots he got away with one of the quickest releases in the game. His cat-like quickness made him a dangerous defender and he was known for his diving, ball-hawking intensity. Zaslofsky averaged 21.0 and 20.6 points over the 1947–48 and 1948–49 seasons for the Chicago Stags, impressive totals for the period. Not surprisingly, he was an All-BAA first-team selection in each of his first three seasons. But it wasn't until the Stags franchise folded in 1950 that Zaslofsky enjoyed the team success he longed for. He led the Knicks and Pistons to the 1951, '52, '53 and '55 NBA Finals, but couldn't quite get a championship ring. Zaslofsky retired in 1956 with 7,990 points (14.8).

THE GREAT COACHES

He's an architect, strategist, motivator, screamer and father confessor. He cracks the whip one day, holds hands and consoles shattered egos the next. A coach is the glue that binds a team's individual parts into a unit. But most of all, he is a teacher who provides young and impressionable players with a framework for winning.

"Winning" is the ultimate goal for any coach, but how he accomplishes that end is open to interpretation. Red Auerbach, the master builder of the Boston Celtics dynasty, was a volatile personality, aggressive and passionate at practice as well as during games. John Kundla, who coached the Minneapolis Lakers to five championships, was a quiet, calm sideline presence. Don Nelson was a basketball version of Dr Jekyll and Mr Hyde, a ferocious bulldog during games, a patient teacher during practice. Jack Ramsay was the ultimate teacher, Billy Cunningham the ultimate motivator.

For every coach, style is simply a means to the end—winning games and championships. So are the more mundane qualities he must possess: evaluation of talent, framing that talent within the proper system, communicating with players, handling adversity and executing game strategy.

He must be flexible and willing to adapt. Pat Riley was able to dominate in Los Angeles with a wide-open running attack and in New York with a slower, half-court offense. He fit the system to his players.

While often different in style and approach, every good coach has one common denominator: a commitment to defense. Few championships have been won—and few coaches have survived—without it.

WHAT TO DO *When Seattle Coach George Karl talks, his Sonics players listen*

RED AUERBACH

Architect of a dynasty

SEEING RED *Auerbach and his traditional victory cigar*

His name weaves through the NBA history books like a road through the countryside. Arnold (Red) Auerbach has dominated the game from his early days as coach and master builder of the Boston Celtics dynasty, to his current status as evaluator of talent, advisor and elder statesman of basketball's most storied and successful franchise.

The always volatile Auerbach can trace his coaching roots back to 1946, the year the Basketball Association of America began play as the forerunner to the NBA. A brash, self-assured 29-year-old, Auerbach guided the Washington Capitols to a 49–11 first-year record and the Eastern Division championship.

Two more seasons in Washington produced another division title and one year with the Tri-Cities Blackhawks set the stage for a more permanent move. When Auerbach took the Celtics reins in 1950, he immediately began pouring the foundation for a basketball dynasty.

In retrospect, Auerbach's genius was in his vision. He wanted a slicker, faster offense with racehorse guards who could get out on the fast break and a dominating center who could feed them the ball. Ball-handling magician Bob Cousy arrived in 1950 and off-guard Bill Sharman a year later. The dominating center, Bill Russell, was acquired in 1956 at a stiff draft-day price—high-scoring forwards Cliff Hagan and Ed Macauley, two future Hall of Famers.

With the pieces in place and a steady stream of supporting players (Tom Heinsohn, Sam Jones, K.C. Jones, John Havlicek, Tom Sanders, Don Nelson) parading through Boston Garden, the cigar-chomping Auerbach concentrated on coaching the powerhouse he had assembled. And from 1957 through 1966, the Celtics won nine Eastern Division titles and nine NBA championships—including a team sports-record eight in a row. The only miss came in 1958, when the Celtics lost to St. Louis in the NBA Finals.

Auerbach's sideline presence was anything but passive. He was aggressive, demanding and ready to explode at a moment's notice. Referees were an easy target and his sharp tongue irritated and provoked thin-skinned opponents. He fought for every call, every break, and he pushed his players to the limit, espousing the principles of teamwork and breakneck defense.

The players understood and readily accepted Auerbach's passion for winning and his devotion to the game.

"I've never known anybody who has played under Red Auerbach who didn't like him," Russell once said. "Of course, I've never known anybody who has played against him who did like him."

Auerbach stepped down after the 1966 championship and turned the team over to Russell, who directed the Celtics to titles in 1968 and '69. Auerbach finished his outstanding career with a 938–479 regular-season record, a 99–69 playoff mark and one Coach of the Year citation (1965). His 938 wins stood as an NBA milestone until 1995.

True to his nature, Auerbach did not submit to a passive retirement. He served in various front-office capacities and continued building teams that claimed five more titles in the 1970s and '80s. Auerbach was named NBA Executive of the Year in 1980, the same year he was selected by the Professional Basketball Writers Association as the "Greatest Coach in the History of the NBA."

> **❝ I've never known anybody who has played under Red Auerbach who didn't like him. ❞**
>
> *Bill Russell*

Facts and Figures

Personal	Born: September 20, 1917, at Brooklyn, N.Y.
Teams	Capitols, 1946–49, Blackhawks, 1949–50, Celtics, 1950–66
NBA Coach of the Year	1965
NBA Finals Appearances	1957, 1958, 1959, 1960, 1961, 1962, 1963, 1964, 1965, 1966
NBA Championships	1957, 1959, 1960, 1961, 1962, 1963, 1964, 1965, 1966

Coaching Record	G	W	L	Pct.
Regular Season	1,417	938	479	.662
Playoffs	168	99	69	.589

BILLY CUNNINGHAM

The legend of Billy C

Billy Cunningham coached only eight NBA seasons and he spent all of them with the Philadelphia 76ers—the team he represented for nine years as a player. He never tore down and rebuilt rosters, he never rescued forlorn franchises and he never jumped from team to team in search of more money and a longer career.

Cunningham's short tenure casts him as a misfit among the game's all-time great coaches, but his 454–196 career record yielded a .698 winning percentage, the second-best mark in NBA history; his .629 playoff winning percentage ranks sixth all-time; he reached the 300- and 400-victory plateaus faster than any coach except Pat Riley; and his teams won one championship (1983) and lost in the NBA Finals twice (1980 and '82).

Cunningham was not your typical Xs-and-Os coach. His sideline demeanor was much like his playing style: foot-stomping, emotional and intense. He battled referees, chastised malingering players and demanded hustle and a commitment to defense—qualities he never lacked as a jumping-jack forward who averaged more than 20 points and 10 rebounds over a career that also included two ABA seasons.

Critics point out that he inherited a loaded roster with Julius (Dr. J) Erving, George McGinnis and Doug Collins when he left the broadcast booth in 1977 to replace Gene Shue. But Cunningham coaxed the 76ers into maximum effort that produced three Atlantic Division titles and at least 52 victories in seven of his eight seasons. And he did it while learning on the job.

"He's as good as any coach in the league," Erving said in 1982. "He's not a totalitarian kind of coach, but he's quite good."

McGinnis was more succinct. "If I had to give a one-word description of Billy," he said, "it would be 'intense.'"

Cunningham, a key player for the 76ers' 1967 championship team, carried that intensity over to a team that battled the Boston Celtics for Eastern Conference supremacy in the 1980s. Dr. J remained as its heart and soul through Cunningham's coaching regime, but McGinnis, Collins and Darryl Dawkins gave way to Maurice Cheeks, Andrew Toney and Bobby Jones.

The 76ers won their battles against Boston in 1980 and '82, but they lost both NBA Finals wars to Western Conference power Los Angeles. It wasn't until the arrival of 6-foot-11 center Moses Malone, immediately following the second loss to the Lakers, that Cunningham and the 76ers could claim a championship, which was punctuated by a shocking four-game Finals sweep of the Lakers.

Cunningham lasted two more seasons, winning 110 games. After taking the 76ers to the 1985 Eastern Conference finals (a loss to the Celtics) he retired, saying he needed time off and the players needed to hear a new voice.

Surprisingly, Cunningham has never returned to the sideline, although he did resurface in 1987, as the driving force behind a successful effort to get an expansion franchise for the city of Miami.

Facts and Figures

Personal	Born: June 3, 1943, at Brooklyn, N.Y.			
Teams	76ers, 1977–85			
Coach of the Year	None			
NBA Finals Appearances	1980, 1982, 1983			
NBA Championships	1983			
Coaching Record	G	W	L	Pct.
Regular Season	650	454	196	.698
Playoffs	105	66	39	.629

SIXER FIXER *Emotion was a big part of Cunningham's coaching style*

> **❝He has gone from being a real student of the game and coaching the way a player might do it, to one who is making the moves and organizing the club.❞**
>
> *Julius Erving*

CHUCK DALY

Better late than never

DALY ROUTINE *His Pistons thrived under a defensive philosophy*

For a man who didn't even land his first NBA head coaching job until age 51, Chuck Daly traveled a long road very fast. In 12 whirlwind seasons, he piled up 564 victories, a .598 winning percentage, two NBA championships and an Olympic gold medal as coach of the greatest basketball team ever assembled.

Daly's meandering career stretched through eight seasons as a high school coach and six more as an assistant at Duke University. His first contact with the national spotlight came in 1969, when he became head coach at Boston College and he raised eyebrows from 1971 to '77 when he coached an overachieving University of Pennsylvania team to four Ivy League titles and four NCAA Tournament berths.

When Daly took a job as assistant to Philadelphia coach Billy Cunningham in 1978, it appeared to be a brief diversion from the college basketball wars. But Daly helped Cunningham carve out two division titles in four-plus seasons and when the Cleveland Cavaliers came calling in 1981, he jumped at the chance for an NBA head job—a decision he would regret.

The Cleveland organization was in shambles, thanks to the wheeling and dealing of owner Ted Stepien. Daly's first NBA test ended in disaster—he was fired with a 9–32 record at midseason and spent the next season as a broadcaster.

When Detroit beckoned in 1983, Daly was better prepared. The Pistons, who had not qualified for postseason play in six seasons, compiled a 49–33 record and earned the first of nine consecutive playoff berths under Daly.

The 1980s were exciting for long-suffering Detroit fans. The new coach began assembling a talented lineup around point guard Isiah Thomas and 6-foot-11 center Bill Laimbeer. Shooting guard Joe Dumars came aboard in 1985 and high-scoring Adrian Dantley arrived a year later. Vinnie Johnson, Mark Aguirre, John Salley, Dennis Rodman and James Edwards filled out a championship-caliber roster.

Daly molded the Pistons into a defensive machine that bumped, bruised and pounded opponents into physical and mental mistakes. His players embraced the philosophy. "He's a player's coach," Laimbeer said. "He realizes it's a player's game, not a coach's game. A coach's job is to guide the team to get it in position to win and that's what he does."

With Thomas, Dantley and Dumars handling the scoring load, Detroit's "Bad Boys" posted five consecutive 50-win seasons, won three straight Central Division titles and reached the NBA Finals in 1988, '89 and '90. With consecutive title-series victories over Los Angeles (1989) and Portland (1990), the Pistons became only the second repeat NBA champions in more than two decades.

Daly took his defense-first philosophy to New Jersey in 1992, guiding the Nets to their first winning record (43–39) since 1984–85. After another winning season, he retired with a 564–379 regular-season mark and a .607 playoff winning percentage.

Even more than his Detroit championship teams, Daly will be remembered as the man who coached the original Dream Team that stormed through the 1992 Olympic Games at Barcelona.

The greatest team ever assembled featured Michael Jordan, Magic Johnson, Larry Bird, David Robinson, Patrick Ewing, Charles Barkley and numerous other NBA superstars. And, of course, one of the greatest coaches—Chuck Daly.

> **"He's a player's coach. He realizes it's a player's game, not a coach's game."**
>
> *Bill Laimbeer,*
> *former Detroit center*

Facts and Figures

Personal	Born: July 20, 1930, at St. Mary's, Pa.		
Teams	Cavaliers, 1981–82, Pistons, 1983–92, Nets, 1992–94		
Coach of the Year	None		
NBA Finals Appearances	1988, 1989, 1990		
NBA Championships	1989, 1990		
Coaching Record	**G**	**W**	**L**	**Pct.**
Regular Season	943	564	379	.598
Playoffs	122	74	48	.607

RED HOLZMAN

New York, New York

For 18 years, Red Holzman worked his coaching magic in cities around the National Basketball Association. He pushed, he cajoled and he introduced his players to the principles of teamwork and defense. And when he was finished, he stepped proudly off the court with 696 career victories and a .547 playoff winning percentage that ranked among the best in history.

But for all of his accomplishments, Holzman will always be remembered for one magical season and one beautifully sculptured team that lifted New York to the top of the professional basketball world. The 1969–70 Knicks not only captured the heart of the Big Apple, they did it with a presence, a strut that gave them status among the NBA's all-time great teams.

Holzman arrived in New York in 1957, after four years as coach of the Milwaukee and St. Louis Hawks. The Knicks, still looking for their first NBA championship in their 22nd season, were stumbling under Dick McGuire when Holzman took the reins and guided them to a 28–17 finish. The team jumped to 54 victories in

Facts and Figures				
Personal	Born: August 10, 1920, Brooklyn, N.Y.			
Teams	Hawks, 1953–57, Knicks, 1967–77, 1978–82			
Coach of the Year	1970			
NBA Finals Appearances	1970, 1972, 1973			
NBA Championships	1970, 1973			
Coaching Record	G	W	L	Pct.
Regular Season	1,300	696	604	.535
Playoffs	106	58	48	.547

1968–69, a portent of things to come.

The 1969–70 Knicks were a perfect blend of Holzman's philosophies. Willis Reed, a 6-foot-10 bulldog, manned the middle, Bill Bradley and Dave DeBusschere controlled the wings and Dick Barnett and Walt Frazier dominated the backcourt. The Knicks could play up-tempo or half court, they were smart, they could shoot and they played outstanding defense. Frazier, one of the best defensive guards ever to play the game, was the Knicks' go-to scorer.

With Holzman dictating the team's pace from his familiar sideline crouch, the Knicks rolled to a 60–22 record, an Eastern Division title and playoff victories over Baltimore and Milwaukee. They culminated their special season and brought bedlam to Madison Square Garden with a seven-game NBA Finals victory over the Los Angeles Lakers.

Holzman, a former player with a Rochester Royals team that passed through the NBL, BAA and NBA in the 1940s and '50s, was the toast of New York. And he didn't stop there. The 1970–71 Knicks won another division title, the 1971–72 team advanced to the NBA Finals before losing to the Lakers and the 1972–73 Knicks returned to the championship circle with a five-game triumph over the Lakers. Reed, Bradley,

DeBusschere, Frazier and newcomers Earl Monroe and Jerry Lucas never deviated from Holzman's winning credo: "If you play good, hard defense, the offense will take care of itself."

Although there were to be no more championships under Holzman, the New York fans remained fiercely loyal to the man who had brought the Knicks their only two NBA successes. He would remain a familiar figure on the Knicks' sideline until 1982, when he retired at age 62. His New York success was recognized later by the Basketball Writers Association of America, which voted him NBA Coach of the Decade for the 1970s.

Holzman, the man and the coach, probably was captured best by the words of Bradley, who went on to greater fame as a United States Senator: "His contribution to the game helped revive respect for team play and, in particular, team defense."

> **❝His contribution to the game helped revive respect for team play and, in particular, team defense.❞**
>
> *U.S. Senator Bill Bradley, former Knicks forward*

THE KNICK OF TIME *Red Holzman put some bite in the Big Apple*

PHIL JACKSON

Chicago's free spirit

Nothing about Phil Jackson's early career suggested basketball life beyond retirement. As a 1960s and '70s forward for the New York Knicks, Jackson was a gangly, 6-foot-8 NBA hippie, complete with long hair, beard and a free spirit.

But everybody should have suspected there was more to the man than met the eye. Especially when he parlayed an awkward lefthanded jumper and an ugly hook shot into a 12-year playing career. Jackson survived the NBA wars because he understood that he could make up for his offensive shortcomings with hard work and defense.

"He's a very, very intelligent guy, about basketball and about other things," said Red Holzman, who coached Jackson when he played for the Knicks. "He has a great feel for the game, a great feel for people and he has a knack for keeping everybody happy."

Those qualities became very important in 1989, when Jackson, who had spent five seasons coaching in the Continental Basketball Association and two as a Chicago assistant under Doug Collins, was hired to guide a Bulls team that seemingly had everything, starting, of course, with Michael Jordan and Scottie Pippen, one of the greatest one-two punches in the history of

> ## He has a great feel for the game, a great feel for people and he has a knack for keeping everybody happy.

Red Holzman,
former New York
Knicks coach

the game.

So how does a rookie coach handle the best basketball player in the world? Jackson crossed his fingers and installed a triangle offense, which would require Jordan to play a more team-oriented role. The three-time scoring champion resisted briefly, but finally embraced Jackson's philosophies as the victories began piling up. The Bulls won 55 games and Jordan won another scoring title in Jackson's first season, setting the stage for the most dominant title run in a quarter of a century.

The 1990–91 Bulls were a study in precision. Jackson relaxed team rules, gave his players a freer rein and asked only that they act like professionals and dedicate themselves to winning. During the games, he sat quietly in his chair, seldom raising his voice and never losing his cool.

There really wasn't much reason to. With a lineup featuring Jordan, Pippen, Horace Grant and John Paxson, the Bulls rolled to 61 victories, a Central Division title and an NBA Finals date with Los Angeles. The Bulls capped the season by winning Chicago's first-ever championship with a five-game romp past the Lakers.

In 1991–92, Chicago was even more dominating. The Bulls posted a franchise-record 67 victories, repeated as division champs and defeated Portland in a six-game Finals. The following season, the Bulls made it three straight championships with another six-game Finals victory, this time over Phoenix. They also became the first team to win three consecutive titles since the Boston Celtics of 1964–66.

But Jackson's best coaching jobs came in 1993–94, when he led

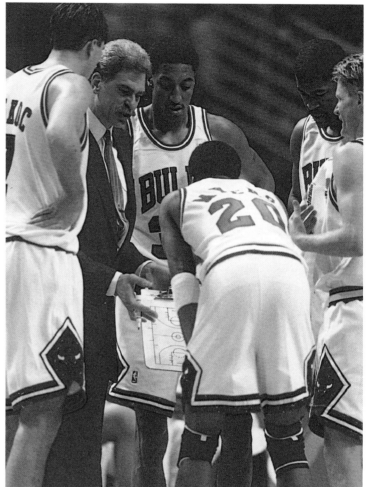

SMOOTH TALKER *Phil Jackson is the guiding force for the Bulls*

a Jordanless team to 55 victories, and 1995–96, when he guided the Bulls, with Jordan, to an unprecedented 72–10 regular-season record, a 15–3 playoff run and the franchise's fourth championship in six years. Chicago defeated Seattle in a six-game NBA Finals.

Jackson finished 1995–96, his seventh Chicago season, with 414 career victories and a playoff winning percentage of .723, the highest in league history. Not bad for a former NBA hippie.

Facts and Figures

Personal	Born: September 17, 1945, at Deer Lodge, Mont.			
Teams	Bulls, 1989–present			
Coach of the Year	None			
NBA Finals Appearances	1991, 1992, 1993			
NBA Championships	1991, 1992, 1993			
Coaching Record	G	W	L	Pct.
Regular Season	574	414	160	.721
Playoffs	112	81	31	.723

JOHN KUNDLA

Johnny on the spot

George Mikan looms over the Minneapolis Lakers record book like a massive redwood. At 6-foot-10 and 245 pounds, the powerful and relentless Mikan brutalized smaller opponents as the centerpiece for the first dynasty in National Basketball Association history.

But lost in the shadow of Mikan's accomplishments are several outstanding players—Jim Pollard, Vern Mikkelsen and Slater Martin—and the man who choreographed Mikan's NBA career. John Kundla was the guiding force for a Lakers team that won five NBA championships in six seasons and gave the NBA its first appearance in the national spotlight.

Kundla was an up-and-coming coach at St. Thomas College in Minnesota when the Lakers were organized to compete in the 1947–48 National Basketball League. Young, bright and articulate, the 31-year-old Kundla was the perfect choice for a young team that would require patience and a steady hand.

But before the first season opened, Kundla and the Lakers got a giant surprise—literally. With the disbanding of the Chicago Gears franchise, players rights were distributed around the league and Mikan was awarded to Minneapolis.

The Mikan–Kundla combination proved lethal. The Lakers rolled to a first-year NBL championship, then jumped to the two-year-old Basketball Association of America and won another. They made it three straight in 1949-50 when the BAA officially became the NBA. After missing out in 1950-51, the Lakers came back and rattled off three more championships, giving them five NBA titles in six years.

Kundla, a perfectionist, pushed his players to the limit of their skills while remaining in the background. "The players do the work; they should get the public-ity," he told one reporter in the midst of the Lakers' championship run.

But not everybody bought into that modesty. "Kundla has devised one of the finest series of plays (cuts and blocks) I've ever seen to make full use of George

HAPPY TOGETHER *John Kundla and players celebrate a 1959 playoff victory*

Mikan," marveled New York Knicks coach Joe Lapchick in the 1952–53 season.

Lapchick was referring to Minneapolis' innovative motion offense, which Kundla redesigned when the league widened the foul lane from 6 to 12 feet, attempting to minimize Mikan's growing dominance by getting him away from the basket. But instead of neutralizing Mikan's power game, the maneuvering opened up the lane for Kundla's streamlined cutting-and-passing attack.

First he experimented with a double pivot, with players cutting to the basket in intricate and confusing weaves. Then he positioned Mikan high and created room for his adept passing and elbow-clearing drives to the basket. Shortly after the wider lane was introduced, Mikan exploded for a 61-point game.

But Kundla preached more than power offense. In three of their first four NBA seasons, the Lakers led the league in fewest points allowed. Even after Mikan's 1954 retirement, the Lakers remained an NBA force because of their commitment on the defensive end.

Kundla coached the Lakers through 1958–59, a season that culminated with another visit to the NBA Finals. This time, however, the Lakers, featuring rookie Elgin Baylor, lost to the rising Boston Celtics. Kundla, who left the team with a 423–302 career mark and a lofty .632 playoff winning percentage, coached nine more seasons at the University of Minnesota.

> **“Kundla has devised one of the finest series of plays I've ever seen to make full use of George Mikan. ”**
>
> *Joe Lapchick,*
> *former New York*
> *Knicks coach*

Facts and Figures

Personal	Born: July 3, 1916, at Star Junction, Pa.			
Teams	Lakers, 1948–59			
Coach of the Year	None			
NBA Finals Appearances	1949, 1950, 1952, 1953, 1954, 1959			
NBA Championships	1949, 1950, 1952, 1953, 1954			
Coaching Record	G	W	L	Pct.
Regular Season	725	423	302	.583
Playoffs	95	60	35	.632

DON NELSON

The basketball guru

Everything about his sideline demeanor belied the real Don Nelson. He paced, bounded, yelled instructions to players and complained to officials. His complaints often were vociferous enough to draw technicals and his temperament in defeat was not congenial.

But away from the court or during practice, Nelson became a teacher, a basketball guru who molded young minds and bodies into the ways of the NBA. He was patient, he treated players and fans with respect and he built winners.

"He's the perfect coach," Philadelphia Coach John Lucas once said. "You know he cares about you by the way he deals with you." Lucas played two seasons under Nelson at Milwaukee.

Nelson "dealt" with players for almost two decades after finishing his outstanding 14-year playing career in 1976 with the Boston Celtics. In 11 seasons with the Bucks, seven with the Golden State Warriors and part of one with the New York Knicks, he compiled 851 coaching victories, won seven division titles and delivered nine seasons of 50 or more wins.

The only thing missing from Nelson's coaching resume is an

> ## 44 He's the perfect coach. You know he cares about you by the way he deals with you. 77

John Lucas,
a former NBA coach and
Milwaukee player

NBA championship, an honor he enjoyed five times as a Boston player. "What burns inside of me is that … I've never won a title as a coach," he said when he took the Knicks job in 1995. "It's something I would like to do before I hang up my sneakers."

That dream died quickly as a veteran New York team refused to buy into Nelson's up-tempo offensive philosophy, forcing a midseason parting of the ways. Nelson went into retirement without his championship, but not without the league-wide respect he had earned over two decades.

Nelson's coaching career began in 1976 when he was invited to become coach Larry Costello's Milwaukee assistant. When Costello unexpectedly resigned 17 games into the 1976-77 season, Nelson was thrust into the spotlight—a career move he had not anticipated. Unprepared and overwhelmed, Nelson "worked on two very simple priorities: Teach good defense and run like hell on offense."

That philosophy served him well as his Bucks, featuring Sidney Moncrief, Marques Johnson and Junior Bridgeman, rolled to 540 victories and seven consecutive Central Division titles in 11 seasons in Milwaukee. But the Bucks' road to the NBA Finals always traveled through Boston or Philadelphia, cities that ruled the Eastern Conference throughout the decade.

Unable to get the Bucks past the conference finals, Nelson moved to Golden State as the team's executive vice president in 1987 and took the coaching reins

in 1988–89. The long-suffering Warriors perked up under his direction and compiled a 277–260 record over seven seasons, topping the 50-win barrier twice.

One of the highlights of Nelson's West Coast stay was a 1994 trip to the Toronto World Championships as coach of Dream Team II. Nelson and the

U.S. came away with a gold medal.

Nelson holds two NBA distinctions that say a lot about his love for the game and his ability to motivate players: He appeared in more games (more than 2,800) as a player and head coach than anybody except Lenny Wilkens and he earned an unprecedented three Coach of the Year citations.

CALM BEFORE THE STORM *Don Nelson in an uncharacteristically mellow mood*

Facts and Figures

Personal	Born: May 15, 1940, at Muskegon, Mich.			
Teams	Bucks, 1976–87, Warriors, 1988–95, Knicks, 1995–96			
Coach of the Year	1983, 1985, 1992			
NBA Finals Appearances	None			
NBA Championships	None			
Coaching Record	**G**	**W**	**L**	**Pct.**
Regular Season	1,480	851	629	.575
Playoffs	112	51	61	.455

JACK RAMSAY

The ultimate teacher

There was no big secret to Jack Ramsay's success. Ramsay was the ultimate teacher, an education Ph.D. who conducted his classes in National Basketball Association arenas around the country. As a coach for four teams over 21 seasons, he taught basic skills, shaped character and gave his players a chance to succeed.

"Teaching," Ramsay once said, "is something that has been rewarding to me. Victories are produced by a team. Defeats, I take personally, because it means I didn't get my job done."

When Ramsay retired in November 1988, his resume suggested a job well done: an 864–783 record, 16 playoff appearances, 14 winning records, one NBA championship and a .525 winning percentage. He still ranks in the top five of most major all-time coaching categories and his record doesn't even include the 234 victories he compiled as coach at St. Joseph's College, his Philadelphia-based alma mater.

It was during his 11 seasons at St. Joseph's that Ramsay earned his Ph.D. and determined his life course. Unable to shake the basketball bug that had bitten him during his years as a college coach and educator, he left St. Joseph's

in 1966 to become general manager of the Philadelphia 76ers and found himself back on the sidelines two years later, coaching the team to a 55–27 record and second-place finish in the NBA's Eastern Division.

He would not leave the sidelines again for 20 years. After another three seasons in Philadelphia, Ramsay took over the 2-year-old Buffalo Braves in 1972–73 and suffered through a 21–61 disaster. But with Bob McAdoo scoring points and Randy Smith directing the offense, Ramsay's Braves posted their first winning record in 1973–74 and earned the first of three playoff berths—the only three in franchise history until the relocated Los Angeles Clippers qualified in 1991–92.

But Ramsay's real genius would not be displayed until 1976–77, when he took the helm of the 6-year-old Portland Trail Blazers, another franchise that had never experienced a winning season or qualified for the playoffs. With a healthy Bill Walton at center and burly Maurice Lucas at forward, Ramsay's Blazers recorded a 49–33 record and won 14 of 19 playoff games en route to one of the great Cinderella championships in NBA history. Ironically, the

Blazers beat the 76ers in a six-game Finals.

Portland followed that success with a 58–24 record and reached the playoffs in nine of Ramsay's 10 seasons there. But there would be no more serious championship runs. In 1986, Ramsay headed for Indianapolis and a new challenge—a team that had not won more than 26 games in four years and had made one postseason appearance in the last 10.

The 1986–87 Pacers perked up under Ramsay, recording a 41–41 record and reaching the playoffs. But in 1988–89, when Indiana got off to an 0–7 start, the 63-year-old Ramsay resigned, citing lack of enjoyment and concern about not getting the job done.

"All I can say is that he is a great basketball coach," said Bob Whitsitt, SuperSonics President at the time of Ramsay's resignation. "He has done a lot of good for the game. His record speaks for itself."

> **" Victories are produced by a team. Defeats, I take personally, because it means I didn't get my job done. "**
>
> *Jack Ramsay*

TEACHER, TEACHER *The basketball court was Ramsay's classroom*

Facts and Figures

Personal	Born: February 21, 1925, at Philadelphia, Pa.			
Teams	76ers, 1968–72, Braves, 1972–76, Trail Blazers, 1976–86, Pacers, 1986–88			
Coach of the Year	None			
NBA Finals Appearances	1977			
NBA Championships	1977			
Coaching Record	**G**	**W**	**L**	**Pct.**
Regular Season	1,647	864	783	.525
Playoffs	102	44	58	.431

PAT RILEY

The fire burns deep

He sits on the sideline, gazing distantly through the frenzied action on the court. His hair, as always, is perfectly coiffed and his expensive suit partially covers his shiny, unmarked shoes. Pat Riley is at work, a calm presence amid the NBA storm.

Calm, at least, on the surface. But those who have played or worked for Riley know different. The inner fire burns intensely and his demands for organization and perfection are obsessive, explaining one of the most amazing coaching records ever compiled.

Over 14 seasons, Riley's teams have a winning percentage of .702, the best in professional sports history among 10-year coaches. Riley has coached and won more playoff games than any other NBA boss and his teams have won four championships and reached the NBA Finals on four other occasions. His 798 regular-season victories rank among the all-time top 10 and he could

challenge Lenny Wilkens' all-time record before he is finished.

Ironically, Riley did not have coaching ambitions in 1976, when he finished a nine-year playing career in Phoenix. He was working in the broadcast booth three years later when Lakers coach Jack McKinney suffered severe head injuries in a bicycle accident and was replaced by Paul Westhead. Westhead invited Riley to be his assistant.

When Westhead butted heads two years later with team owner Jerry Buss and star player Magic Johnson, Riley took over and guided the Lakers to the 1982 championship.

"When I got the head coaching job in 1981, I was looked at as a lucky guy who just walked into a situation where I had talented players," Riley said. "As the team continued to win, it was taken for granted. Now, everything's gone beyond my imagination."

Blessed with a lineup that included Johnson at the point, Kareem Abdul-Jabbar at center and James Worthy at forward, Riley opened up the Lakers' offense and the team cruised through the 1980s. He coached the Lakers to nine straight Pacific Division titles and a record four consecutive 60-victory seasons, winning three more championships in six NBA Finals appearances.

Riley left Los Angeles after the 1989–90 season for a television job with NBC, but he returned to the court in 1991 as

STANDING PAT *Riley has introduced his winning formula to three NBA teams*

coach of the New York Knicks— an underachieving team in need of a philosophy and direction.

Riley provided both, molding a physical team around Patrick Ewing, his intimidating center. While the Lakers ran opponents off the court with their "Showtime" offense, the Knicks bullied, bumped and bruised them with a physical defense that kept scores under triple figures. Riley's Knicks were criticized for being a throwback to the boring game of yesteryear, but they topped 50 victories four consecutive seasons, won three Atlantic Division titles and reached the NBA Finals in 1994, losing to Houston in seven games.

Riley moved to Miami in 1995 as coach and team president, a role that allowed him to build quickly with a trade for 6-foot-10

Charlotte center Alonzo Mourning, a dominating shot-blocker. Before his first Miami season was half over, Riley had performed a thorough makeover of the Heat roster and had the former expansion team on course for its third playoff appearance.

And maybe, Miami fans hope, on course for its first championship. With Riley at the controls, the odds are in their favor.

> **❝As the team (the Los Angeles Lakers) continued to win, it was taken for granted.❞**
>
> *Pat Riley*

Facts and Figures

Personal	Born: March 20, 1945, at Rome, N.Y.			
Teams	Lakers, 1981–90, Knicks, 1991–95, Heat, 1995–present			
Coach of the Year	1990, 1993			
NBA Finals Appearances	1982, 1983, 1984, 1985, 1987, 1988, 1989, 1994			
NBA Championships	1982, 1985, 1987, 1988			
Coaching Record	G	W	L	Pct.
Regular Season	1,137	798	339	.702
Playoffs	215	137	78	.637

LENNY WILKENS

Out of the shadows

He's the NBA's quiet man, always under control and never speaking without careful consideration. Nothing about him is spectacular, demonstrative or exciting. And for the better part of two decades, Lenny Wilkens has been lost in the shadows of the game's more dominant personalities, unwilling to dramatize his case as professional basketball's most underrated coach.

But that changed on January 6, 1995, when Wilkens was thrust into the spotlight by the enormity of his own accomplishment.

When his Atlanta Hawks posted a 112–90 victory over Washington, Wilkens earned his 939th career victory and moved past the legendary Red Auerbach into first place on the all-time list.

Wilkens' victory total has since topped 1,000 and he hasn't even turned the corner on age 60 yet. The passion is still there, the ability to motivate and communicate with players is still intact and the competitive instincts are still strong, suggesting the victory record could climb out of sight.

"Lenny is always under control," said Chuck Daly, coach of the 1989 and '90 Detroit championship teams and a long-time admirer. "His teams are always prepared and his players trust him. He is one of the great coaches of our time."

When Wilkens, a skinny point guard, began an outstanding 15-year playing career with the Hawks in 1960, he never dreamed of extending that career to the sideline. But coaches and management took note of his cool, intelligent, unselfish and mistake-free playing style, qualities that would push him into his career calling. From 1969–72, Wilkens served as player-coach for the expansion Seattle SuperSonics and in 1974–75 he performed the same role for Portland. Those seasons were merely warmups for the long road into the record books.

Wilkens returned to Seattle in 1977 and coached the Sonics for eight seasons, producing six winning records, three 50-victory

EYES LIKE A HAWK *Lenny Wilkens, the NBA's all-time winningest coach*

> ❝He is one of the great coaches of our time.❞
>
> *Chuck Daly, former NBA coach*

campaigns and two NBA Finals appearances. The 1978 Sonics, featuring Jack Sikma, Gus Williams and Dennis Johnson, lost to Washington in seven games, but the 1979 team beat the Bullets in five. The championship would be the first and last on Wilkens' resume.

Wilkens moved to Cleveland in 1986 and undertook a major rebuilding job for a demoralized organization. In his third season, the Cavs posted a franchise-record 57 victories and the team qualified for the playoffs in five of his seven years. The 1991–92 team, featuring Brad Daugherty, Mark Price and Larry Nance, won 57 games and reached the Eastern Conference finals, losing to eventual champion Chicago.

As he had in Seattle and Cleveland, Wilkens brought instant credibility to the Hawks when he took the reins in 1993. His first team jumped from 43 to 57 victories, won the Central Division and defeated Miami in a first-round playoff series.

"Lenny transformed one of the worst defensive teams in the league into one of the best," said Hawks President Stan Kasten. That fix-it job earned him his first NBA Coach of the Year citation and set the stage for the record-setting 1994–95 campaign. Punctuating that dream was Wilkens' selection as coach for the Dream Team III club that would compete in the Atlanta Olympic Games.

Facts and Figures

Personal	Born: October 28, 1937, at Brooklyn, N.Y.			
Teams	SuperSonics, 1969–72, 1977–85, Trail Blazers, 1974–76, Cavaliers, 1986–93, Hawks, 1993–present			
Coach of the Year	1994			
NBA Finals Appearances	1978, 1979			
NBA Championships	1979			
Coaching Record	G	W	L	Pct.
Regular Season	1,864	1,014	850	.544
Playoffs	134	64	70	.478

THE NBA'S SECOND SEASON

It happens every spring. The NBA's regular-season preliminaries come to a merciful end, 16 teams move into a more competitive dimension and re-energized players intensify their chase for basketball's Holy Grail.

It's called the "Second Season," but many who compete consider the playoffs the "Only Season." The first 82 games are the appetizer; the 15 to 26 it might take to win a championship are the main course and dessert.

The NBA's 29 teams spend the six-month regular season fighting for one of the 16 playoff berths, jockeying for home-court advantage and trying to make their journey through the postseason maze as easy as possible. The regular season does have its perks—division championships, scoring titles, awards—but nothing has

meaning until the first postseason elbow is delivered—and received.

How, who, where and when

The NBA's playoff format is a logical succession that begins with the eight most successful regular-season teams from the Eastern and Western Conferences qualifying for postseason play. The qualifiers are seeded one through eight, with the two division winners getting the top positions and the rest of the teams lining up according to their record. The first seed pairs off against the eighth, second against seventh, third against sixth, and

fourth against fifth in first-round best-of-five series. The higher ranked teams always benefit from home-court advantage. In the first round they are home in games one, two and five, if necessary.

A slightly different format is used in the Conference semi-finals and finals. The first-round winners advance to the best-of-seven semi-final series and the winners to the Conference finals. The format for home-court advantage in these series is 2–2–1–1–1; Conference semi-finalists with the best regular-season record—not division winners—host games one, two, and if

necessary, five and seven.

The Eastern and Western Conference champions battle in the NBA Finals for supremacy. The title series is set up in a 2–3–2 format with the better regular-season team assured of games one, two, six and seven at home, if the series goes the full distance.

The following pages offer a 50-year glimpse of the NBA Finals and the coronation of each season's champion.

INSIDE SCOOP *Orlando's Shaquille O'Neal (32) and Houston's Hakeem Olajuwon in the 1995 NBA Finals*

1947

Warriors Surprise Stags Behind No Ordinary Joe

Like a newborn colt taking its first uneasy steps, the Basketball Association of America tottered through its first professional season, groping for steadying hands and the hope of firmer footing just around the corner.

Nothing had come easy in its debut campaign and every decision had been made with uncertainty and bottom-line accountability. But every team official understood one basic fact: The league needed appealing events and players—and it needed them fast.

So it was not without some measure of satisfaction that the Philadelphia Warriors, a team that had staggered through much of the season before meshing over the final month, reached the league's first championship series. The Warriors, owned and coached by Eddie Gottlieb, had the league's most marketable star, a high-scoring Kentucky hillbilly named Joe Fulks.

Jumpin' Joe was the man who popularized the jump shot, a scoring maneuver he executed from unusual angles while leaning, running or standing alone on the perimeter. Fulks was an offensive marvel to the conservative Eastern basketball fans and he averaged a league-best 23.2 points in 1946–47, an unsightly total in the pre-shot clock game.

Fulks was at his best during the BAA's first playoff season, and the Warriors' drive to a championship was enhanced by an awkward system that did not benefit the

DRIVING FORCE *Joe Fulks (10) powered the Warriors to the first NBA championship*

1947 NBA Finals

Philadelphia	84	Chicago	71	at Philadelphia
Philadelphia	85	Chicago	74	at Philadelphia
Philadelphia	75	Chicago	72	at Chicago
Chicago	74	Philadelphia	73	at Chicago
Philadelphia	83	Chicago	80	at Philadelphia

league's best regular-season teams. Philadelphia had finished 14 games behind the Eastern Division-champion Washington Capitols, who were coached by young Red Auerbach. But BAA

officials set up a strange format that matched division winners, second-place finishers and third-place teams in the opening round. Auerbach's Capitols were upset by Western Division champion Chicago while the Warriors defeated the St. Louis Bombers and New York Knickerbockers to advance to the Finals.

And the Warriors got an additional break when scheduling problems at Chicago Stadium forced the first game of the final series to be played at a packed Philadelphia Arena, where Fulks unleashed a 37-point shooting blitz that buried the Stags, 84–71. Fans and reporters marveled at one of the greatest shooting exhibitions ever staged.

Fulks was quiet in Game 2 at Philadelphia, but the Warriors still claimed an 85–74 victory and a 2–0 series advantage, thanks to Howie Dallmar (18 points) and center Art Hillhouse, who scored 7 of his team's final 10 points.

By the time the series shifted to Chicago, the Warriors were riding an unstoppable wave of momentum—and Fulks was doing the driving. Jumpin' Joe fired in 26 points in Game 3 as the Warriors held off a frantic Chicago rally in a 75–72 decision.

The Stags delayed elimination in Game 4 on the combined 38-point scoring of Max Zaslofsky and Don Carlson in a 74–73 victory, but the Warriors rode Fulks' 34-point explosion to a title-clinching 83–80 Game 5 victory before the home fans at Philadelphia.

The BAA had its first champion, its first superstar and its first Cinderella in a memorable NBA Finals upset.

1948

Welcome to the Big Time

The Baltimore Bullets were a late, late addition to the Basketball Association of America—a team taken from the regional American Basketball League to fill out the BAA lineup when four of the circuit's 11 charter franchises folded

after one season.

But the Bullets were more than an afterthought in the young league's second postseason. Led by player/coach Buddy Jeannette, they tied for second in the Western Division and zipped past Chicago in a semifinal playoff. When the defending-champion Warriors posted a 71–60 victory

1948 NBA Finals

Philadelphia	71	Baltimore	60	at Philadelphia
Baltimore	66	Philadelphia	63	at Philadelphia
Baltimore	72	Philadelphia	70	at Baltimore
Baltimore	78	Philadelphia	75	at Baltimore
Philadelphia	91	Baltimore	82	at Philadelphia
Baltimore	88	Philadelphia	73	at Baltimore

in the championship series opener and stormed to a 41–20 halftime lead in Game 2, it appeared Cinderella was about to lose her glass sneaker.

Not so. Recoveries from 21-point deficits in the pre-shot clock era were inconceivable, but that's exactly what the Bullets did. They pulled within 48–40 at the end of three quarters, forged ahead late in the game and secured victory on Paul Hoffman's tip-in with four seconds remaining. The 66–63 victory, the biggest comeback in NBA Finals history, gave the Bullets the momentum they needed.

When the series returned to Baltimore, they scored 72–70 and 78–75 victories. The Warriors recovered for a 91–82 Game 5 triumph at Philadelphia, but the Bullets closed out the shocking series with an 88–73 blowout at Baltimore.

The "minor leaguers" were BAA champions.

1949

A Dynasty Takes Shape

The Minneapolis championship reign opened as the Lakers rode the broad shoulders of 6–10 center George Mikan to a 44–16 regular-season record, playoff sweeps of Chicago and Rochester and a six-game NBA Finals victory over Red Auerbach's Washington Capitols.

The Lakers, one of four National Basketball League teams to jump to the BAA, captured the first three games against Washington. The opener, an 88–84 thriller that featured Mikan's 42-point outburst, was not decided until Don Carlson broke an 84–84 deadlock with two last-minute free throws.

The Capitols worked hard to keep the ball away from Mikan in Game 2 and he scored only 10 points, but Carlson poured in 16 and Herm Schaefer added 13 in a 76–62 Lakers' romp. Mikan rebounded for 35 points in Game 3 at Washington, and the Lakers rolled to a 94–74 victory.

The Lakers' 3–0 advantage was fortunate because Mikan hit the floor hard during the Capitols' 83–71 Game 4 victory, breaking his wrist. But playing with a cast, the Minneapolis big man scored 22 points in a 74–66 loss before keying the Lakers' title-clinching 77–56 victory at Minneapolis.

Mikan, the regular-season scoring champion with a 28.3 average, finished the playoffs with 303 points (30.3).

1949 NBA Finals

Minneapolis	88	Washington	84	at Minneapolis
Minneapolis	76	Washington	62	at Minneapolis
Minneapolis	94	Washington	74	at Washington
Washington	83	Minneapolis	71	at Washington
Washington	74	Minneapolis	66	at Washington
Minneapolis	77	Washington	56	at Minneapolis

SCORING MACHINE *George Mikan guided the Lakers' championship journey*

1950

Another Title, by George

The Lakers, with rookies Slater Martin (guard), Tiger Harrison (guard) and Vern Mikkelsen (power forward) bolstering a starting lineup that already featured Jim Pollard and George Mikan, squared off against Syracuse and Dolph Schayes in the NBA Finals.

The Nationals had forged the best regular-season record (51–13) in the bulky 17-team "National Basketball Association," but they were no match for Minneapolis in the title series. John Kundla's Lakers won the opener at Syracuse, 68–66, on Harrison's 40-foot set shot and claimed Games 3 and 4 with 14 and 8-point victories before their home fans.

The Nationals' only breakthroughs came on their home court—91–85 and 83–76 decisions in Games 2 and 5. In both victories, Syracuse guard Paul Seymour held Pollard to low point totals, leaving Mikan to handle the offensive load. He scored 60 points in the two losses.

Seymour's defense had no impact on Game 6 as Mikan's 40-point explosion carried the Lakers to a 110–95 title-clinching, fight-filled victory at Minneapolis Auditorium. The powerful Mikan averaged 32.2 points in the six games as the Lakers became the first team to win consecutive BAA/NBA championships.

1950 NBA Finals

Minneapolis	68	Syracuse	66	at Syracuse
Syracuse	91	Minneapolis	85	at Syracuse
Minneapolis	91	Syracuse	77	at St. Paul
Minneapolis	77	Syracuse	69	at St. Paul
Syracuse	83	Minneapolis	76	at Syracuse
Minneapolis	110	Syracuse	95	at Minneapolis

1951
New York, New York

An all-New York NBA Finals that pitted Rochester against the upstart Knicks developed into the first seven-game battle in league history. Amazingly, the Knicks, third-place Eastern Division finishers during the regular season, almost triumphed after losing the first three games.

The Royals, who had advanced to the Finals by beating the injury-plagued Minneapolis Lakers in the Western Division finals, handled the Knicks with 92–65, 99–84 and 78–71 series-opening victories behind the inspired play of center Arnie Risen and guard Bob Davies. The 6–9 Risen dominated inside, scoring 27 points in the Game 3 victory at New York's Armory.

But just as quickly as the Knicks had fallen into their deep hole they pulled themselves out. They blew a 17-point lead in

ROYALTY *Rochester stars (l to r): Red Holzman, Bobby Wanzer, Bob Davies, Arnie Johnson, Jack Coleman, Arnie Risen*

1951 NBA Finals

Rochester	92	New York	65	at Rochester
Rochester	99	New York	84	at Rochester
Rochester	78	New York	71	at New York
New York	79	Rochester	73	at New York
New York	92	Rochester	89	at Rochester
New York	80	Rochester	73	at New York
Rochester	79	New York	75	at Rochester

Game 4 but managed to pull out a 79–73 victory. Then they rode the combined 50-point scoring of Connie Simmons and Max Zaslofsky to a 92–89 upset at Rochester. Zaslofsky's 23-point Game 6 outburst carried the Knicks to an 80–73 series-tying triumph at New York.

The Knicks fell behind by 14 points early in the finale at Rochester, but they rallied in the second half and edged in front, 74–72, with two minutes remaining. The game was tied 75–75 with less than a minute to play when Davies delivered the killing blows—a pair of free throws. Jack Coleman's last second layup clinched the Royals' 79–75 victory. Risen led Rochester scorers with 24 points and Davies added 20.

1952
Return of the King

The Minneapolis Lakers, who had fallen in the 1951 playoffs when George Mikan broke a bone in his ankle, returned to the NBA throne—but not without a seven-game scare from the Knicks.

New York advanced to the Finals for the second straight season after finishing third in the NBA's Eastern Division. But unlike 1951, when they lost the first three games to Rochester, the Knicks took the Lakers to overtime in an 83–79 opening game loss at St. Paul and pulled off an 80–72 second-game upset as they held Mikan to 18 points and Jim Pollard to 13.

The Lakers stormed back for an 82–77 victory at New York, but they suffered a double loss in Game 4—the Knicks held Mikan to 11 points in a 90–89 overtime victory, but Pollard, a 34-point scorer in the opener, was sidelined with a back injury.

It didn't seem to matter as Mikan and Vern Mikkelsen each scored 32 points in a 102–89 Game 5 rout, but the Knicks bounced back for a third time with a 76–68 sixth-game triumph that knotted the series at 3–3.

As usual, the Lakers' fortunes were tied to Mikan's coattails and the big center came through in the decisive seventh game. He scored 22 points and grabbed 19 rebounds as Minneapolis clinched its third championship in four years. Pollard came off the injured list and provided a clinching spark in the Lakers' 82–65 victory. He scored all 10 of his points in the fourth quarter.

1952 NBA Finals

Minneapolis	83	New York	79 (OT)	at St. Paul
New York	80	Minneapolis	72	at St. Paul
Minneapolis	82	New York	77	at New York
New York	90	Minneapolis	89 (OT)	at New York
Minneapolis	102	New York	89	at St. Paul
New York	76	Minneapolis	68	at New York
Minneapolis	82	New York	65	at Minneapolis

1953
Four out of Five

It was a 1952 rematch and for the first time the NBA Finals featured division champions. New York was making its third straight title-series appearance and the Lakers were making their fourth in five years. But Minneapolis had won in each of its Finals; the Knicks had lost their previous two.

The New Yorkers served notice they had every intention of changing that when they marched into Minneapolis, scored 30 points in an impressive fourth quarter and walked away with a surprising 96–88 opening victory.

Minneapolis stormed back for a 47–30 halftime lead in Game 2, but the Knicks staged a frantic rally that tied the game and turned it into a late free throw-shooting contest. The Lakers finally prevailed, 73–71.

Under a new playoff format, the next three games would be played at New York—and this series was decided there. The Lakers claimed their fourth title in five years with a Big Apple

HIGH BALL *George Mikan (right) powered his way over and around the Knicks*

1953 NBA Finals

New York	96	Minneapolis	88	at Minneapolis
Minneapolis	73	New York	71	at Minneapolis
Minneapolis	90	New York	75	at New York
Minneapolis	71	New York	69	at New York
Minneapolis	91	New York	84	at New York

sweep that featured 90–75, 71–69 and 91–84 victories.

Game 4 was decided by Whitey Skoog's two last-minute baskets, and Game 5 was secured by George Mikan's late three-point play after the Lakers had almost frittered away a 20-point lead.

1954
Lakers Win Again As Mikan Era Ends

When the NBA's 1953–54 season opened, Minneapolis forward Jim Pollard was 31 and center George Mikan was closing in on 30. Pollard's athletic skills were deteriorating and Mikan's powerful body was showing the ravages of physically relentless defenders. A dynasty was showing signs of decay.

That first NBA dynasty would crumble after the 1954 playoff season when the 6–10, 245-pound Mikan announced the end of his outstanding career. The Lakers star retired a body that had endured two broken legs, broken bones in its feet, wrist, nose, thumb and fingers and cuts and slashes that required more than 150 stitches.

But Mikan was not the injured party when his final title series opened at Minneapolis. The Syracuse Nationals had emerged from a bruising round-robin Eastern Division playoff battle against New York and Boston,

paying a heavy price. Star forward Dolph Schayes entered the Finals with a broken wrist, guard Paul Seymour had a broken thumb and forward Earl Lloyd had a broken hand. Then guard George King suffered a broken wrist in Game 2 of the Finals when Mikan tried to block his shot.

It only figured that the Nationals, who had tied for second place in the Eastern Division during the regular season, would provide easy prey for the Lakers' third consecutive championship and fifth in six seasons. But Syracuse had shown plenty of heart in the experimental round-robin preliminary and it showed plenty more against the Lakers.

Minneapolis claimed first blood in the opener when backup center Clyde Lovellette, filling in for the foul-plagued Mikan, scored 16 points and the Lakers' defense held the injured Schayes and Lloyd to a combined three points in a 79–68 victory. But the Lakers' mystique took a serious blow in a Game 2 thriller that ended on a 40-foot Seymour set shot that produced a 62–60 Syracuse victory

with seven seconds remaining. The playoff loss was the first for the Lakers at Minneapolis Auditorium in seven seasons.

But with Schayes and Lloyd still playing at half speed and King sitting out, Mikan took control of Game 3—a 30-point, 15-rebound performance in which he connected on 11 of 18 shots. The 81–67 victory at Syracuse was a lesson in power basketball, with Mikan, Vern Mikkelsen and Lovellette throwing their weight and elbows, while Slater Martin directed traffic from the perimeter.

The Nationals, however, refused to back down and evened the series four nights later with an 80–69 victory, keyed by Seymour's

25-point effort. But again they paid a price, this time losing guard Billy Gabor to a knee injury.

The Lakers reasserted their inside dominance during an 84–73 victory in Game 5 at Syracuse, but the Nationals stunned them again at Minneapolis, 65–63, when unlikely hero Jim Neal, a backup center, connected on a 25-foot buzzer-beating shot.

Syracuse's magic finally ran out. With Pollard scoring 22 points, the Lakers grabbed a big Game 7 lead and cruised to a title-clinching 87–80 triumph, despite an heroic 18-point effort by the cast-hindered Schayes.

The Lakers were kings for one last glorious season.

1954 NBA Finals

Minneapolis	79	Syracuse	68	at Minneapolis
Syracuse	62	Minneapolis	60	at Minneapolis
Minneapolis	81	Syracuse	67	at Syracuse
Syracuse	80	Minneapolis	69	at Syracuse
Minneapolis	84	Syracuse	73	at Syracuse
Syracuse	65	Minneapolis	63	at Minneapolis
Minneapolis	87	Syracuse	80	at Minneapolis

1955

A Clockwork Victory

With Minneapolis weakened by the retirement of George Mikan and Syracuse Owner Danny Biasone's shot-clock innovation speeding up a foul-plagued game, the NBA opened a faster-paced era. Ironically, Biasone's Nationals benefited from both developments and engaged Fort Wayne in an exciting seven-game Finals.

Play opened at Syracuse and the Nationals rolled to a quick 2–0 advantage with 86–82 and 87–84 victories. Red Rocha sparked the Game 1 win with 19 points and hit a clinching 25-foot set shot in the final seconds of Game 2.

But the tide turned quickly when the Nationals traveled to Indianapolis, the Pistons' post-season home because of scheduling problems at Fort Wayne. The Pistons, led by Mel Hutchins' 22 points, won the third game 96–89 and evened the series with a 109–102 verdict, despite 28-points from Dolph Schayes. Frank Brian hit two late free throws to give a the Pistons a 74–71 Game 5 victory and a 3–2 series edge.

But Syracuse wouldn't die. The Nationals survived George Yardley's 31 points and pulled even with a 109–104 victory—their 27th consecutive triumph over the Pistons at Syracuse. No. 28 would come in Game 7.

Syracuse had to wipe out a 17-point Fort Wayne lead in the finale and survive a late-game scare. The clincher in the Nationals' 92–91 victory wasn't delivered until 12 seconds remained when George King sank a tiebreaking free throw.

King, who finished with 15 points, was one of seven Syracuse scorers in double figures. Larry Foust led the Pistons with 24.

1955 NBA Finals

Syracuse	86	Fort Wayne	82	at Syracuse
Syracuse	87	Fort Wayne	84	at Syracuse
Fort Wayne	96	Syracuse	89	at Indianapolis
Fort Wayne	109	Syracuse	102	at Indianapolis
Fort Wayne	74	Syracuse	71	at Indianpolis
Syracuse	109	Fort Wayne	104	at Syracuse
Syracuse	92	Fort Wayne	91	at Syracuse

1956

The Philadelphia Story

The NBA's first decade ended just like it started—with the Philadelphia Warriors sitting atop the basketball world. The Warriors, featuring the high-scoring tandem of center Neil Johnston and forward Paul Arizin, cruised to the league's best record (45–27), defeated Syracuse in an Eastern Division playoff and eased past Fort Wayne in a five-game NBA Finals.

The Pistons, making their second consecutive Finals appearance, were no match for the Warriors, even with high-scoring George Yardley firing from all over the court. And that became clear in the Philadelphia opener when the Warriors fell behind by 15, rallied behind the inspired play of reserve forward Ernie Beck (23 points) and scored a 98–94 victory.

The Pistons battled back in Game 2 for an 84–83 win, the decisive points coming on two of Yardley's 30 points. But that was Fort Wayne's last hurrah.

Arizin and Johnston combined for 47 points in Philadelphia's 100–96 Game 3 victory, and Arizin was unstoppable in Game 4, contributing 30 points in the Warriors' 107–105 triumph.

The Game 5 clincher was decided by a late third-quarter Philadelphia rush that broke open a 64–60 battle. Fort Wayne never got closer than seven points the rest of the way and the Warriors coasted to their 99–88 victory. Joe Graboski scored 29 points and Arizin added 26 for Philadelphia, more than offsetting Yardley's 30-point effort.

The Warriors, winners of the BAA's first title in 1947, were champions for a second time.

1956 NBA Finals

Philadelphia	98	Fort Wayne	94	at Philadelphia
Fort Wayne	84	Philadelphia	83	at Fort Wayne
Philadelphia	100	Fort Wayne	96	at Philadelphia
Philadelphia	107	Fort Wayne	105	at Fort Wayne
Philadelphia	99	Fort Wayne	88	at Philadelphia

1957

Here Come the Celtics

Two first-timers matched up in the NBA Finals—the first of four dramatic meetings over five years. And the intensity was illustrated by two 125–123 double-overtime thrillers—St. Louis' Game 1 victory and Boston's Game 7 clincher.

The opener, which featured a 37-point performance by St. Louis' Bob Pettit and a 36-point effort by Boston's Bill Sharman, was decided in the second extra period when Jack Coleman hit a long jumper. But the Celtics held Pettit to 11 points in the second game and rolled to a 119–99 triumph.

When the series moved to St. Louis, the teams traded victories with St. Louis winning 100–98 on Pettit's last-second jumper and Boston responding with a 123–118 victory keyed by Bob Cousy's 31 points. The Celtics took a 3–2 series edge with a 124–109 victory at Boston Garden and the Hawks fought back at St. Louis when Cliff Hagan tipped in a last-second shot for a 96–94 win.

Game 7 was a classic. Cousy and Sharman shot a combined 5 for 40, but rookies Bill Russell and Tom Heinsohn picked up the slack with a combined 56 points and 55 rebounds. The game was not decided until the second over-time when Jim Loscutoff hit a clinching free throw and the Hawks just missed on a desperate last-second tip attempt. The game ended when St. Louis player/coach Alex Hannum threw a half-court pass off the Hawks' back-board to Pettit, who missed the point-blank tip.

The Celtics' 13-year championship run was underway.

1957 NBA Finals

St. Louis	125	Boston	123 (2 OT)	at Boston
Boston	119	St. Louis	99	at Boston
St. Louis	100	Boston	98	at St. Louis
Boston	123	St. Louis	118	at St. Louis
Boston	124	St. Louis	109	at Boston
St. Louis	96	Boston	94	at St. Louis
Boston	125	St. Louis	123 (2 OT)	at Boston

SPECIAL DELIVERY *Boston point guard Bob Cousy dazzled St. Louis with his clever passing, but the Hawks got the last laugh in the 1958 Finals*

1958
Pettit Roars, Hawks Soar Past Outmanned Celtics

It was basketball's version of a heavyweight boxing championship rematch: the power-packed St. Louis Hawks against the jab-and-run Boston Celtics. Bob Pettit, Cliff Hagan, Ed Macauley and Slater Martin versus Bill Russell, Bob Cousy, Tom Heinsohn, Bill Sharman and newcomer Sam Jones.

The Celtics, laying the foundation for the championship mystique that would engulf the NBA for more than a decade, had scored a 1957 seven-game decision that produced the franchise's first title. The Hawks, who were looking for a little mystique of their own behind the high-scoring tandem of Pettit (24.6 points per game) and Hagan (19.9), were hoping for a quick 1958 knockout.

It wasn't quick, but it was decisive. The series matched the early pattern of 1957 as the Hawks marched into Boston Garden and pulled off a 104–102 first-game upset and the embarrassed Celtics recovered with style in a 136–112 Game 2 rout. Little did anybody realize that Game 3, at St. Louis' Kiel Auditorium, would provide the series turning point—by accident.

The Hawks won the game, 111–108, but the Celtics lost the series when the 6–10 Russell tore ankle ligaments, an injury that put pressure on Heinsohn and aging Arnie Risen to stop St. Louis' powerful frontcourt. Russell tried to play with a heavily taped ankle, but without him in top form, Boston was overmatched. Still, the Hawks had to work for every inch of their championship journey.

Boston Coach Red Auerbach used the Russell injury to inspire his team in a surprising 109–98 Game 4 victory. But the Hawks struck back for a 102–100 fifth-game triumph that set up Boston for the knockout punch.

Game 6 ranks among the great games in NBA Finals history and most of the dramatics were provided by Pettit, St. Louis' classy power forward. As 10,218 fans howled their approval at Kiel Auditorium, Pettit scored 50 points, single-handedly held off a late Boston rally and delivered St. Louis its only NBA title.

The 110–109 sixth-game victory began taking shape when the Hawks surged ahead 95–93 on a Pettit field goal with 6:16 remaining. Three times the Celtics pulled to within a point and three times Pettit answered with a critical basket. His final two-pointer gave the Hawks a 110–107 lead with 16 seconds to play and Sharman's uncontested layup determined the final margin.

After Martin dribbled away the final seconds, the St. Louis players lifted Pettit onto their shoulders and carried him around the floor. Pettit, who connected on 19 of 34 field goals and 12 of 19 free throws, scored 19 of St. Louis' final 21 points. His 50 points were a record for a regulation playoff game and he finished the series with a 29.3 average.

Sharman scored 26 points in the finale and Heinsohn added 23.

1958 NBA Finals

St. Louis	104	Boston	102	at Boston
Boston	136	St. Louis	112	at Boston
St. Louis	111	Boston	108	at St. Louis
Boston	109	St. Louis	98	at St. Louis
St. Louis	102	Boston	100	at Boston
St. Louis	110	Boston	109	at St. Louis

1959
A Sweeping Change

A funny thing happened on the way to another Boston–St. Louis NBA Finals masterpiece. The Hawks, who had finished 16 games ahead of the 33–39 Lakers in the Western Division, were upset by surprising Minneapolis in a six-game division finals series.

Boston versus Minneapolis was a masterpiece only in the eyes of championship-hungry Celtics fans. Boston had defeated the Lakers 18 consecutive times over two seasons and had buried them 173–139 in a late February meeting that set numerous NBA point-scoring records. To say that the Lakers were overmatched, even with rookie scoring sensation Elgin Baylor, was an understatement.

The series opened in Boston and the Celtics rolled to 118–115 and 128–108 victories. When the action moved to Minneapolis, the Celtics continued their domination with a 123–110 triumph that set Minneapolis up for the kill.

Game 4, a 118–113 Boston clincher, belonged to the Celtics trio of Bill Sharman (29 points), Frank Ramsey (24) and Tom Heinsohn (23).

The game, like the series, was a testimony to Boston's front-line talent and depth. How overpowering were the Celtics?

They scored 487 points (at an average of 121.8 per game), an NBA Finals record for a four-game series. Center Bill Russell intimidated Minneapolis shooters and averaged an amazing 29.5 rebounds, grabbing 30 in three straight outings. Guard Bob Cousy, who handed out 19 assists in Boston's Game 3 rout, averaged 12.8 for the series.

The championship was Boston's second in three seasons and the four-game sweep was the first in NBA Finals history.

1959 NBA Finals

Boston	118	Minneapolis	115	at Boston
Boston	128	Minneapolis	108	at Boston
Boston	123	Minneapolis	110	at St. Paul
Boston	118	Minneapolis	113	at Minneapolis

1960
Firing on All Cylinders

Boston's burgeoning juggernaut rolled to an NBA-record of 59 regular-season victories en route to a championship series rematch with St. Louis. And true to past Celtics–Hawks encounters, this one went the distance.

The teams traded early punches. The Celtics earned a 140–122 Game 1 victory at Boston and a 102–86 Game 3 win at St. Louis behind the backcourt play of Bob Cousy, Bill Sharman and Frank Ramsey and the inside domination of Bill Russell. The Hawks countered with 113–103 and 106–96 road and home victories behind the three-pronged frontcourt attack of Bob Pettit, Cliff Hagan and Clyde Lovellette, who had combined to average 71.7 points per game during the regular season.

The Celtics regained the advantage with a 127–102 Game 5 rout at Boston, but the Hawks knotted the series with a 105–102 win at St. Louis. Boston's hopes for a second consecutive championship would be decided in a seventh game at Boston Garden.

It was no contest. Russell scored 22 points and grabbed 35 rebounds, sixth man Ramsey amassed 24 and 13, Tom Heinsohn had 22 and 8, and Cousy scored 19 points and handed out 14 assists in a 122–103 Boston victory. The championship machine was in full gear.

1960 NBA Finals

Boston	140	St. Louis	122	at Boston
St. Louis	113	Boston	103	at Boston
Boston	102	St. Louis	86	at St. Louis
St. Louis	106	Boston	96	at St. Louis
Boston	127	St. Louis	102	at Boston
St. Louis	105	Boston	102	at St. Louis
Boston	122	St. Louis	103	at Boston

LOOSE BALL *Boston's Bob Cousy (right) battles Johnny McCarthy during Game 4 of the 1960 NBA Finals*

1961
A Balancing Act

The Boston team that swept to 57 regular-season victories and advanced to its fifth straight NBA Finals featured dominating center Bill Russell and had six players who averaged 15 or more points per game—Tom Heinsohn (21.3), Bob Cousy (18.1), Russell (16.9), Bill Sharman (16.0), Frank Ramsey (15.1) and Sam Jones (15.0).

That balance was too much for a frontcourt-heavy St. Louis team that went down quietly in its fourth NBA Finals appearance in five years—the last for Hall of Fame forward Bob Pettit.

The Celtics demonstrated their dominance in a 129–95 Game 1 rout that would stand for 17 years as the NBA Finals record for the largest margin of victory. Russell grabbed 31 rebounds en route to a series average of 28.5.

St. Louis forward Cliff Hagan exploded for 40 points in Game 2, and Pettit matched that total in Game 4, but the Celtics still pulled off 116–108 and 119–104 victories. The Hawks' only tri- umph came in a 124–120 Game 3 thriller at the Kiel Auditorium in St. Louis.

Russell was at his ferocious best in the Celtics' 121–112 Game 5 clincher at Boston Garden. He grabbed 38 rebounds and intimi- dated St. Louis shooters with his inside defense. Boston's third straight championship was accom- plished with an impressive 121- point average.

1961 NBA Finals

Boston	129	St. Louis	95	at Boston
Boston	116	St. Louis	108	at Boston
St. Louis	124	Boston	120	at St. Louis
Boston	119	St. Louis	104	at St. Louis
Boston	121	St. Louis	112	at Boston

1962
Lakers' Shot at Destiny Comes Up Inches Short

In the minds of Los Angeles bas- ketball fans, it always will be remembered as "The Shot."

Game 7 of the NBA Finals. Score tied 100–100. Lakers' ball with five seconds remaining. A dream about to crumble at Boston Garden in mid-dynasty.

For Los Angeles fans, this was the opportunity for their Lakers to ascend to the NBA throne in just their second season after moving from Minneapolis. They were young, they were talented and they were blessed with one of the greatest superstar tandems in league history—forward Elgin Baylor and guard Jerry West.

For Boston fans, this was the opportunity for their Celtics to do something no other professional basketball team—and few other sports teams—had ever accom- plished: four consecutive champi- onships. Red Auerbach's Celtics were experienced, they were deep and they were poised.

The crucial five seconds unfolded with Hot Rod Hundley dribbling near the top of the key, looking for the well-defended Baylor and West. He settled for Frank Selvy, who was open on the baseline, about eight feet from the basket. Selvy, a hero only moments earlier when he scored two baskets to tie the score, launched his poten- tial winner and watched it bounce short off the rim.

"I would trade all my points for that last basket," a dejected Selvy told reporters after the game.

Given a reprieve, the Celtics stormed back in overtime for a dramatic 110–107 victory. Sam Jones keyed the charge, scoring 5 of his 27 points, and sixth man Frank Ramsey punctuated the effort with 23 points. But more importantly, the Boston title streak was intact.

Nothing about this champi- onship was easy. The Celtics, who had cruised through the regular season with 60 victories, won the opener at Boston Garden, 122–108, but the Lakers evened matters the next day when West scored 40 points in a 129–122 ver- dict and took a 2–1 edge two nights later in a thriller at Los Angeles.

The Lakers' 117–115 Game 3 triumph, which was decided at the final buzzer when West stole a Boston inbounds pass and dribbled uncontested for a layup, sent the record crowd of 15,180 at the Los Angeles Sports Arena into a frenzy. But if the Celtics felt the jolt of that last-second heartbreaker, they did not show it during a methodical 115–103 Game 4 victory that knot- ted the series.

The stage was set for Baylor, who confounded the double- teaming Celtics and a full house at Boston Garden with a 61-point, 22-rebound Game 5 performance that keyed a 126–121 Lakers vic-

CELEBRATION TIME *Happy Celtics enjoy the fruits of their fourth straight title*

tory. Baylor's 61 points still stand as an NBA Finals record.

But just when it appeared the Celtics were staggering, the Boston mystique took over. Defying the law of averages, the Celtics stunned another sellout Sports Arena crowd and knotted the series with a 119–105 victory, setting up the sev- enth-game drama.

The Celtics posted their title- clinching victory despite another big performance by Baylor—41 points. Boston center Bill Russell countered that with an NBA Finals-record 40 rebounds.

1962 NBA Finals

Boston	122	Los Angeles	108	at Boston
Los Angeles	129	Boston	122	at Boston
Los Angeles	117	Boston	115	at Los Angeles
Boston	115	Los Angeles	103	at Los Angeles
Los Angeles	126	Boston	121	at Boston
Boston	119	Los Angeles	105	at Los Angeles
Boston	110	Los Angeles	107 (OT)	at Boston

1963

Five and Counting...

The Celtics had survived a 1962 scare and Coach Red Auerbach was looking for the inspiration that might carry them to a fifth consecutive championship. He got it when veteran guard Bob Cousy announced he would retire after the season.

Winning one for the "Cooz" became the battle cry as the Celtics rolled to 58 regular-season victories, advanced through a difficult seven-game divisional playoff series against Cincinnati and settled in for a rematch with the

1963 NBA Finals

Boston	117	Los Angeles	114	at Boston
Boston	113	Los Angeles	106	at Boston
Los Angeles	119	Boston	99	at Los Angeles
Boston	108	Los Angeles	105	at Los Angeles
Los Angeles	126	Boston	119	at Boston
Boston	112	Los Angeles	109	at Los Angeles

Los Angeles Lakers. Auerbach's job became even easier when the Celtics opened with 117–114 and 113–106 victories at Boston Garden.

The Lakers revived briefly in Game 3 at Los Angeles, posting a 119–99 decision behind Jerry West's 42-point outburst. But Boston moved within a game of another title two days later with a 108–105 victory.

Los Angeles got 43 points from Elgin Baylor and 32 from West

and staved off elimination in a 126–119 Game 5 win at Boston. But the Lakers were just delaying the inevitable.

John Havlicek scored 11 straight points as Boston built a 14-point halftime lead in Game 6 and Tom Heinsohn secured the victory with four late free throws that closed out his 22-point effort.

Fittingly, Cousy, who scored 18 points and overcame a fourth-quarter ankle injury, dribbled away the final seconds of Boston's 112–109 title-securing victory.

West (32) and Baylor (28) combined for 60 points in the Lakers' losing cause.

1964

Six and Counting...

The Celtics, playing their first season without inspirational leader Bob Cousy, took the best shot of another would be champion. But, like all challengers before them, the San Francisco Warriors and high-scoring Wilt Chamberlain were unable to derail Boston's title express.

Bill Russell vs. Chamberlain took center stage in an intriguing battle that fell short of expectations. The 7-1 Chamberlain did have his spectacular moments— 38 rebounds in Game 4, 30 points in Game 5—but the victory clearly went to Russell and another title, the record sixth in a row, to the Celtics.

Russell was a defensive animal as Boston took quick control of the series with 108–96 and 124–101 victories at Boston Garden. A 115–91 thrashing in Game 3 when the series moved to San Francisco proved to be only a temporary setback for the

Celtics, who rebounded for a 98–95 win behind the 25-point scoring of Tom Heinsohn and a 23-point effort by Sam Jones. The Celtics were poised for the kill as the series moved back to Boston.

Russell held Chamberlain scoreless in the first six minutes of Game 5 and Heinsohn, Sam Jones and Frank Ramsey combined for 55 points in the 105–99 clincher. When Russell secured victory with an emphatic last-minute jam, exuberant fans rushed the court, hoisting triumphant Boston players and Coach Red Auerbach on their shoulders.

The Celtics' six straight titles have never been matched by any major professional sports team. In the National Hockey League, the Montreal Canadiens claimed a record five consecutive Stanley Cups and in baseball the New York Yankees won five World Series in a row. No National Football League team has ever managed to win more than three consecutive championships.

1964 NBA Finals

Boston	108	San Francisco	96	at Boston
Boston	124	San Francisco	101	at Boston
San Francisco	115	Boston	91	at San Francisco
Boston	98	San Francisco	95	at San Francisco
Boston	105	San Francisco	99	at Boston

OVER THE TOP *Wilt Chamberlain won this battle, but Bill Russell (6) won the war*

1965
Seven and Counting...

After the Celtics escaped a seven-game division finals upset bid by Philadelphia, they braced for a title-series meeting with old rival Los Angeles. But Boston's pursuit of a seventh straight championship lacked drama, thanks to a knee injury suffered by Elgin Baylor in a playoff game.

With only Jerry West to carry the Lakers' offensive banner, the Celtics rolled off quick 142–110 and 129–123 victories at Boston Garden. Boston defensive wizard K.C. Jones "held" West to 26 points in the opener, far below the prolific 40.6 average he would compile in the series.

West scored 43 points and 6–10 LeRoy Ellis added 29 as the Lakers recovered for a 126–105 Game 3 victory at Los Angeles. But a 37-point performance by Sam Jones propelled to Celtics to a 112–99 triumph that pushed them to within a game of another title.

The Celtics didn't waste time finishing off the overmatched Lakers. With Bill Russell controlling the boards (30 rebounds), the Celtics ran off 20 unanswered fourth-quarter points and coasted to a 129–96 clincher.

1965 NBA Finals

Boston	142	Los Angeles	110	at Boston
Boston	129	Los Angeles	123	at Boston
Los Angeles	126	Boston	105	at Los Angeles
Boston	112	Los Angeles	99	at Los Angeles
Boston	129	Los Angeles	96	at Boston

1966
Lakers See Red As Celtics Win Again

The announcement came like a bolt of lightning. Arnold (Red) Auerbach, the 48-year-old cigar-chomping architect of Boston's NBA championship dynasty, was retiring after the 1966 playoffs. But that wasn't all. Auerbach also announced that 10-year center Bill Russell would become player/coach—the first black coach in NBA history.

True to Auerbach's nature, the timing of the announcement served a more subtle purpose. His Celtics had just lost a 133–129 overtime game to Los Angeles in the opener of the NBA Finals and the wily veteran needed something to spark an aging team in its pursuit of an eighth straight title.

As usual, Auerbach's psychological ploy worked. With the Lakers' Game 1 success (Jerry West scored 41 points, Elgin Baylor 36) obscured by Boston's changing of the guard, the Celtics exploded behind Russell, John Havlicek and Sam Jones for consecutive 129–109, 120–106 and 122–117 victories—the second and third at the Los Angeles Sports Arena. Boston won Game 4 despite West's 45-point performance.

But just when it appeared Auerbach had successfully orchestrated his grand finale, the Lakers struck back. Baylor, who was still fighting the effects of a serious 1965 knee injury, kept them alive

BIG SIX *Bill Russell powers his way through the Lakers' defense*

1966 NBA Finals

Los Angeles	133	Boston	129 (OT)	at Boston
Boston	129	Los Angeles	109	at Boston
Boston	120	Los Angeles	106	at Los Angeles
Boston	122	Los Angeles	117	at Los Angeles
Los Angeles	121	Boston	117	at Boston
Los Angeles	123	Boston	115	at Los Angeles
Boston	95	Los Angeles	93	at Boston

in Game 5 with a 41-point outburst that produced a 121–117 victory at Boston Garden. Then Los Angeles evened the count at Los Angeles with a 123–115 victory that featured Gail Goodrich's 28-point effort. The series returned to Boston Garden for another seventh-game classic.

It appeared the Celtics were going to win easily when they bolted to a big early lead and Baylor was held to two first-half points. They led by 19 two minutes into the third quarter when the Lakers began chipping away. West, who scored a game-high 36 points, led the comeback that pulled Los Angeles to within six points with 25 seconds remaining.

Auerbach, as had been his trademark for 16 Boston seasons, lit his cigar, signaling victory to the 13,909 Garden fans. But in this case, his confidence was ill-advised. The Lakers pulled within two points with four seconds remaining and Auerbach had to sweat a little before the clock finally ran out on the 95–93 victory.

Fittingly, the key figure in Boston's Game 7 triumph was Russell, who scored 25 points, grabbed 32 rebounds and then officially took the coaching baton from Auerbach. Sam Jones added 22 points and Tom Sanders and Don Nelson combined to hold Baylor to 18 points.

Auerbach finished his coaching career in fine style—eight consecutive championships, nine in 10 seasons and nine Eastern Division titles.

1967

Chamberlain, 76ers End Boston's Title Reign

For the first seven seasons of his prolific career, Wilt Chamberlain was an offensive machine. He won seven scoring titles, led the NBA in rebounding five times, averaged an incredible 50.4 points for an entire season and never fell below 33.5 points or 22.3 rebounds in any campaign. The numbers, like his powerful 7-foot-1 body, were intimidating.

But something was missing. Over those seven seasons, a Chamberlain team never won a championship. The 1963–64 San Francisco Warriors reached the NBA Finals, but they were shackled by the Boston Celtics in five games. While Boston center Bill Russell collected championship rings, Chamberlain collected critics who labeled him a "me-first" prodigy.

But the sniping stopped in 1966–67, as did the Celtics' relentless title machine. Chamberlain, at the urging of Coach Alex Hannum, put less emphasis on offense, defended with Russell-like intensity and became the middle man for one of the most talented lineups ever assembled.

This Philadelphia 76ers outfit was no ordinary team. Joining Chamberlain in an All-Star cast were forwards Billy Cunningham, Chet Walker and Lucious Jackson and guards Hal Greer, Wali Jones and Larry Costello. Six 76ers averaged in double figures, led by Chamberlain (24.1) and Greer (22.1), and Wilt led the league with a phenomenal .683 shooting percentage while finishing third with 7.8 assists per game.

This well-balanced attack averaged 125.2 points, played stifling defense and rolled to an unprecedented 68–13 record, easily winning the Eastern Division title over a Boston team that won 60 times. But the ultimate test was passed in the division finals when the 76ers blew past the Celtics in a five-game storm, ending Boston's eight-year championship reign.

SIXER FIXER *Wilt Chamberlain (13) outduels San Francisco's Nate Thurmond (left) for a Game 5 rebound*

The last order of business was an NBA Finals matchup with San Francisco, a team that featured high-scoring Rick Barry, 6–11 center Nate Thurmond and guard Jeff Mullins. But Philadelphia's biggest opponent after Boston was complacency.

That became apparent in the title-series opener when the 76ers built a 19-point first-half lead, frittered it away in the final minutes and were forced into overtime on Mullins' two late free throws. They finally prevailed, 141–135, as Greer finished with 32 points, Jones 30, Cunningham 26 and Walker 23—more than countering Barry's 37.

Game 2 was all 76ers as Chamberlain grabbed 38 rebounds and Greer connected for 30 points in a 126–95 rout. But the Warriors bounced back in a 130–124 third-game explosion set off by Barry's 55 points and Thurmond's 27 boards.

Philadelphia all but settled the issue with a 122–108 Game 4 decision as Greer scored 38 and Walker 33. And after the Warriors had claimed a 117–109 fifth-game verdict, the 76ers closed out their first championship the next day with a 125–122 victory at San Francisco.

Chamberlain, fittingly, was a Game 6 hero and he did it with rebounding and defense. All six of his blocked shots and 8 of his 23 rebounds came in the final quarter when he shared the spotlight with Cunningham, who scored 13 straight points.

It was a sweet victory for Chamberlain—and exoneration—for the NBA's top gun.

1967 NBA Finals

Philadelphia	141	San Francisco	135 (OT)	at Philadelphia
Philadelphia	126	San Francisco	95	at Philadelphia
San Francisco	130	Philadelphia	124	at San Francisco
Philadelphia	122	San Francisco	108	at San Francisco
San Francisco	117	Philadelphia	109	at Philadelphia
Philadelphia	125	San Francisco	122	at San Francisco

1968
Boston Baked Revenge

The Philadelphia 76ers, who had dethroned the Boston Celtics in 1967, returned to the top of the 1967–68 Eastern Division standings with 62 victories and cruised to a 3–1 edge in a division finals rematch. But in a dramatic turnaround sparked by the fierce determination of player/coach Bill Russell, Boston shocked the 76ers by winning the next three games and advanced to its 11th NBA Finals in 12 years—and its sixth against the Lakers.

The Celtics held the high-scoring tandem of Elgin Baylor and Jerry West to a combined 18-of-55 shooting in the first game and claimed a 107–101 victory, but the Lakers answered with a 123–113 Game 2 win at Boston Garden.

The alternating victory pattern continued in Los Angeles with Boston winning, 127–119, and the Lakers responding, 118–105, behind West's 38 points. The series returned to Boston for the pivotal fifth game.

The Celtics bounded to a 19-point first-half lead, but a frantic rally pulled the Lakers close and last-minute baskets by West (35 points) and Baylor forced overtime. The Celtics, who got 31 points from John Havlicek and 26 from Don Nelson, finally prevailed, 120–117.

Buoyed by that success, Boston wrapped up another championship two days later at Los Angeles when Havlicek scored 40 points and Bailey Howell added 30 in a 124–109 victory.

1968 NBA Finals

Boston	107	Los Angeles	101	at Boston
Los Angeles	123	Boston	113	at Boston
Boston	127	Los Angeles	119	at Los Angeles
Los Angeles	118	Boston	105	at Los Angeles
Boston	120	Los Angeles	117 (OT)	at Boston
Boston	124	Los Angeles	109	at Los Angeles

1969
One Last Fling

With player/coach Bill Russell fighting age and leg problems in his final season, the Boston Celtics had slipped to fourth place in the Eastern Division. Only pride had carried them through three playoff rounds, setting up a seventh NBA Finals battle with the Lakers.

The Lakers, who had been bolstered by the addition of center Wilt Chamberlain, finally had reason for optimism. Veteran guard Jerry West made that clear in the Finals opener when he scored 53 points, handed out 10 assists and personally delivered a 120–118 Los Angeles message.

West fired another 41 points at the Celtics in Game 2, but John Havlicek countered with 43. The verdict was decided by Lakers forward Elgin Baylor, who scored his team's final 12 points in a 118–112 victory.

Havlicek scored 34 as the Celtics broke through for a Game 3 victory, 111–105, and they pulled even two days later when Sam Jones hit an off-balance 18-foot jumper that bounced around the rim as the final buzzer sounded, finally falling through for an 89–88 victory. West scored 39 points as Los Angeles pulled back in front with a 117–104 win, but the Celtics forced a seventh game with a 99–90 decision at Boston.

With thousands of balloons positioned in the rafters of the Los Angeles Forum in anticipation of a Lakers championship, the Celtics took a 17-point lead into the fourth quarter. With Chamberlain sitting the final 5½ minutes with a knee injury and West frantically carrying a team on his shoulders (42 points, 13 rebounds, 12 assists), the Celtics barely held on for a 108–106 title-clinching victory.

COMING THROUGH *Celtics star John Havlicek spots an opening between two 76ers during a division semifinal battle*

1969 NBA Finals

Los Angeles	120	Boston	118	at Los Angeles
Los Angeles	118	Boston	112	at Los Angeles
Boston	111	Los Angeles	105	at Boston
Boston	89	Los Angeles	88	at Boston
Los Angeles	117	Boston	104	at Los Angeles
Boston	99	Los Angeles	90	at Boston
Boston	108	Los Angeles	106	at Los Angeles

MVP: Jerry West, Los Angeles

1970
New Era Begins

The roar from the Madison Square Garden crowd was deafening. All eyes focused on a lone figure hobbling out of the shadows. The New York Knicks stopped their warmups and watched with admiration. The Los Angeles Lakers stopped and scrutinized the monumental challenge the basketball gods had thrown into their path.

Without a word, with no sign of emotion, Willis Reed stepped onto the court and gave New York its first NBA championship. Never mind the seventh-game victory that would be needed to confirm it. The game was over before it started. Reed, his leg heavily bandaged because of a muscle tear he had suffered in Game 5, already

1970 NBA Finals

New York	124	Los Angeles	112		at New York
Los Angeles	105	New York	103		at New York
New York	111	Los Angeles	108 (OT)	at Los Angeles
Los Angeles	121	New York	115 (OT)	at Los Angeles
New York	107	Los Angeles	100		at New York
Los Angeles	135	New York	113		at Los Angeles
New York	113	Los Angeles	99		at New York

MVP: Willis Reed, New York

REJECTION *Jerry West is blocked by Knicks backup center Nate Bowman*

had given his teammates everything they would need to win.

The 6-foot-10 center didn't even contest the opening jump against Los Angeles center Wilt Chamberlain, but he did contest everything else Chamberlain tried to do. And the crowd roared again when Reed scored New York's first two baskets. For a full half, Reed gave it everything he had, finishing with four points, three rebounds and respectable defense against Chamberlain.

Emotionally charged, the Knicks were unbeatable. With guard Walt Frazier scoring 36 points, handing out 19 assists and playing his usual stifling defense, the Knicks rolled to a 61–37 halftime lead and powered to a 113–99 title-clinching victory. Reed capped a marvelous season in which he recorded an unprecedented regular-season, All-Star Game and NBA Finals MVP sweep.

Reed was merely one cog in New York's 1970 title machine. The big lefthander, who could confound less mobile centers with his ability to move outside, was the centerpiece in a lineup that included forwards Bill Bradley and Dave DeBusschere and guards Dick Barnett and Frazier. The lineup was short on stars but long on teamwork and defense— Coach Red Holzman's trademark.

The Knicks started their title run with a league-best 60 victories and advanced through the playoffs with only a second-round scare. The Knicks entered the title series as three-time NBA Finals losers; the Lakers, featuring aging Jerry West, Elgin Baylor and Chamberlain, had lost seven straight Finals—all to the Boston Celtics.

New York drew first blood when Reed, moving his game to the perimeter to counter Chamberlain, scored 37 points and grabbed 16 rebounds in a 124–112 victory. The Lakers answered as West scored 34 points and hit a pair of free throws that decided a 105–103 win.

The victory-trading pattern continued. The Lakers forced a Game 3 overtime when West hit a 60-foot basket as time expired, but the Knicks came back to claim a 111–108 victory behind Reed's 38 points and 17 rebounds. Game 4 also went into overtime before the Lakers prevailed, 121–115, behind West's 37 points and 18 assists.

Game 5 long will be remembered for Reed's injury and the Knicks' inspiring play without him en route to their 107–100 victory. Reed crumpled to the floor on a first-quarter drive, writhing in pain. The Knicks trailed 25–15 as their center was helped to the sideline and the Madison Square Garden crowd fell into a stunned silence. But that changed quickly as the Knicks scratched and clawed their way back into the game, forced 19 second-half Los Angeles turnovers and posted their shocking victory.

But there was nothing inspiring about Game 6 as Chamberlain, unimpeded with Reed on the sideline, scored 45 points and grabbed 17 rebounds in a 135–113 rout, setting the stage for Reed's heroics in Game 7.

A BASKETBALL SANDWICH *No matter who the Bucks played, young center Lew Alcindor (with ball) merited double and triple-team attention*

1971
Young Bucks Grow Horns In Championship Season

He was the perfect blend of basketball talents. Oscar Robertson could thread the perfect pass, grab the clutch rebound, hit the outside shot, penetrate to the basket and play defense against smaller guards or bigger forwards.

When the basketball gods drew up a blueprint for the perfect player, they used a Big O. And from the moment Robertson entered the NBA as a three-time NCAA scoring champion from the University of Cincinnati, nobody doubted the incredible impact he would have on the game. He scored almost at will. He set assist records and challenged the league's giants for rebounds. He turned the Cincinnati Royals into an instant winner.

But one important line was missing from Robertson's resume. He was never a champion, from his collegiate days with Cincinnati through his 10-year professional career with the Royals. When he was traded to the 3-year-old Milwaukee Bucks in 1970, Robertson looked at his new assignment with a sense of purpose.

The 1970–71 Bucks were unlike any expansion team in league history. The 1969 draft had yielded a 7-foot-2 prize and the normal building process was pushed into fast forward. Lew Alcindor, who had led UCLA to three straight NCAA titles and an 88–2 three-year record, was the ticket to quick success and Robertson was asked to become a guiding force.

He took the challenge seriously. Robertson ran the show, sacrificing shots to get teammates more involved, scolding when he thought somebody needed a push and cajoling when he thought somebody needed a tender nudge. Coach Larry Costello encouraged his veteran star and young players like Alcindor, forwards Bobby Dandridge and Greg Smith and guard Lucius Allen thrived.

Operating with mechanical precision, the Bucks began rolling off victory after victory, including an NBA-record 20 straight at one point. When the season ended, the Bucks were 66–16 and Alcindor was league scoring champion (31.7) and MVP. The Bucks rolled through two quick playoff series before squaring off against Eastern Conference-champion Baltimore in the NBA Finals.

The banged-up Bullets were no match for the healthy Bucks. Alcindor, who later converted to the Islamic faith and change his name to Kareem Abdul-Jabbar, dominated 245-pound Wes Unseld, who was playing on a badly sprained ankle. Robertson was too much for Earl Monroe, who was fighting pulled muscles. And Baltimore forward Gus Johnson, battling knee problems, played in only two games.

Alcindor fired in 31 points and the Bucks opened the final series with a 98–88 victory at Milwaukee. Robertson sparked a 102–83 second-game rout at Baltimore by scoring 22 points and holding Monroe to 11. When the series returned to Milwaukee, Dandridge scored 29 points in a 107–99 victory and the Bucks pulled to within a game of the second sweep in Finals history.

The series ended in fitting fashion with Robertson, Milwaukee's father figure, pouring in 30 points in a 118–106 clincher. The Big O finally had a ring and the NBA had a 3-year-old champion.

1971 NBA Finals

Milwaukee	98	Baltimore	88	at Milwaukee
Milwaukee	102	Baltimore	83	at Baltimore
Milwaukee	107	Baltimore	99	at Milwaukee
Milwaukee	118	Baltimore	106	at Baltimore

MVP: Lew Alcindor, Milwaukee

1972
Dominating Lakers End West Coast Frustration

Jerry West's first 11 professional seasons were bittersweet. His Lakers pairing with Elgin Baylor had been fruitful, his reputation as one of the game's great shooters had spread far and wide and the road to the NBA championship had passed consistently through Los Angeles.

And that was the source of his frustration. The road passed through Los Angeles—and on to Boston and New York. Seven times West had played in the NBA Finals and seven times he had experienced defeat. Four times West's Lakers had fallen in excruciating seventh games. His personal Finals ledger was phenomenal; his team's was much less.

So it was with some suspicion that West viewed the incredible 1971–72 season as it unfolded. He relinquished some of his scoring responsibilities to backcourt mate Gail Goodrich for more of a point guard role. Baylor, his knees no longer able to withstand the rigors of playing in the NBA, retired after playing nine games. Center Wilt Chamberlain was 35 years old. West himself was 33.

The day Baylor announced his retirement, the Lakers won a game. They also won their next game, the one after that and 30 more over a two-month span. When defending-champion Milwaukee handed the Lakers a 120–104 setback on January 9, they ended an incredible 33-game winning streak—the longest ever compiled by a professional sports team.

The loss left Los Angeles at 39–3 and the Lakers went on to post an unprecedented 69–13 record. The table was set for the city's first championship and the Lakers passed a big test with a six-game conference finals victory over the Milwaukee Bucks, who sported a 63–19 regular-season mark. The last challenge would come from the Knicks, who had posted a seven-game Finals victory over the Lakers in 1970.

SMOTHERING DEFENSE *Lakers defenders surround New York guard Walt Frazier during action in the Game 5 clincher*

The 1970 Knicks had received inspired play from center Willis Reed, who could not play in this series because of aching knees.

So it was all the more shocking when Jerry Lucas scored 26 points, Bill Bradley connected on 11 of 12 field-goal attempts and the Knicks won the Finals opener 114–92—at Los Angeles.

Happy Hairston, known for his rugged rebounding, gave the Lakers a Game 2 spark when he scored 12 second-half points and Los Angeles evened the series with a 106–92 victory. Then the Lakers took control of the series and bolted to a 2–1 edge with a 107–96 triumph at New York.

Game 4 brought back memories of 1970—in reverse. This time it was Chamberlain (not Reed) who fell to the floor in the first quarter, severely spraining his wrist. But Chamberlain refused to leave the game and blocked several key shots in overtime, helping the Lakers to a key 116–111 victory. Chamberlain's inspiration was complemented by the relentless scoring of Goodrich and West.

The Knicks got another dose of their own 1970 medicine in Game 5 when Chamberlain, his aching wrist numbed by painkillers, incited the Los Angeles crowd with a heroic 24-point, 29-rebound performance. The 114–100 victory gave the Lakers their long-awaited championship and the best combined regular season/playoff record in league history—81 victories, 16 defeats.

For West, it ended more than a decade of frustration.

1972 NBA Finals

New York	114	Los Angeles	92	at Los Angeles
Los Angeles	106	New York	92	at Los Angeles
Los Angeles	107	New York	96	at New York
Los Angeles	116	New York	111 (OT)	at New York
Los Angeles	114	New York	100	at Los Angeles

MVP: Wilt Chamberlain, Los Angeles

1973
In the Knick of Time

The Knicks versus the Lakers—it was beginning to sound like a broken record. The Knicks had defeated Los Angeles in 1970, giving New York its first NBA championship. The Lakers had returned the favor in 1972, giving Los Angeles its long-awaited first title. The rubber match, featuring two aging teams, followed a different script.

The Lakers took quick advantage of the tired Knicks, who had only one day of rest between their seventh-game conference finals victory over Boston and the title-series opener in Los Angeles. When New York stumbled out of the blocks, the Lakers rolled up a 20-point lead en route to a 115–112 victory.

But the fatigue so evident in Game 1 was lost in a second-game defensive haze. New York guards Walt Frazier and Earl Monroe turned up the pressure on Jerry West and Gail Goodrich and a limping Willis Reed combined with Jerry Lucas to stop Wilt Chamberlain inside, sparking a 99–95 series-knotting triumph. The biggest offensive blow was delivered by backup Phil Jackson, who came off the Knicks bench to score 17 points.

Games 3, 4 and 5 were more of the same—a stifling New York defense that held Chamberlain to 22 total field goals and refused to let Los Angeles top 100 points.

Reed sparked the 87–83 Game 3 victory at New York's Madison Square Garden with 22 points and Dave DeBusschere exploded for 33 points two nights later in a 103–98 triumph. Five Knicks reached double figures in a 102–93 Game 5 triumph that completed the five-game blitz.

1973 NBA Finals

Los Angeles	115	New York	112	at Los Angeles
New York	99	Los Angeles	95	at Los Angeles
New York	87	Los Angeles	83	at New York
New York	103	Los Angeles	98	at New York
New York	102	Los Angeles	93	at Los Angeles

MVP: Willis Reed, New York

1974
Return of the King

The script for Game 7 was simple: The Boston Celtics, making their first NBA Finals appearance since 1969, had to find an answer for Milwaukee's Kareem Abdul-Jabbar—the NBA's ultimate team against its ultimate player.

But a funny thing happened on the way to a championship. Boston's David dropped the Bucks' Goliath with a spectacular 28-point, 14-rebound performance and the Celtics claimed their 12th championship in 18 years with a 102–87 victory at Milwaukee.

Boston's David had the last name of Cowens. The 6–9 center combined with John Havlicek (16 points) in a late Celtics surge that broke open a 71–68 battle. Boston defenders spent the game sagging on Abdul-Jabbar, who finished

BUCKING THE ODDS *Kareem Abdul-Jabbar (33) and Milwaukee stopped Chicago before losing to Boston in the NBA Finals*

1974 NBA Finals

Boston	98	Milwaukee	83	at Milwaukee
Milwaukee	105	Boston	96 (OT)	at Milwaukee
Boston	95	Milwaukee	83	at Boston
Milwaukee	97	Boston	89	at Boston
Boston	96	Milwaukee	87	at Milwaukee
Milwaukee	102	Boston	101 (2 OT)	at Boston
Boston	102	Milwaukee	87	at Milwaukee

MVP: John Havlicek, Boston

with 26 points—below his 32.5 series average.

The series was a tug of war that pitted the scoring punch of Abdul-Jabbar against the more balanced attack of Havlicek, Cowens and Jo Jo White. Boston won Games 1 and 5 at Milwaukee and the third contest at Boston Garden. The Bucks countered with victories in Games 2 and 4 and forced Game 7 with a 102–101 victory at Boston in a thriller

that went to double-overtime.

Milwaukee took a two-point lead into the final seconds of Game 6, but Boston tied at 86–86, when Havlicek hit a long jumper. The first overtime ended when Havlicek missed a jumper over Abdul-Jabbar, grabbed his own rebound and converted, forcing a second extra session. Abdul-Jabbar ended the game with a buzzer-beating skyhook, giving the Bucks a series-extending victory.

1975

The Little Team That Could

It was not surprising that the 1975 postseason produced the third NBA Finals sweep in league history. But it was a major shock to see the broom being wielded by the unheralded Golden State Warriors instead of the powerful Washington Bullets.

If Golden State's victory wasn't the greatest upset in NBA Finals history, it was close. And Al Attles' overachievers—48-game winners during the regular season—performed their little miracle with pressure defense, fierce hustle and the machine gun-like firepower of star forward Rick Barry.

The series opened at the Capital Centre in Washington and the Warriors quickly set the series tone. They jumped to a 14-point halftime lead, held off the Bullets down the stretch and rode the

ELVIN HAYES *towers over Jamaal Wilkes*

play of backup guard Phil Smith (20 points) to a 101–95 victory. Barry's jumper with 38 seconds remaining secured the outcome.

Games 2 and 3 were played in San Francisco because of scheduling conflicts and Golden State took quick advantage. Barry scored 36 points in a tense 92–91 second-game victory, and 38 in a 109–101 triumph that gave the Warriors a shocking 3–0 advantage.

Game 4 at Washington was typical Warriors. They trailed by 14 points early and 8 in the final five minutes but wiped away both deficits before clinching a 96–95 victory. Barry was high scorer with 20, but Butch Beard scored his team's final seven points.

Golden State's unsung hero was Jamaal Wilkes, who held high-scoring Washington forward Elvin Hayes to 44 points in the series.

1975 NBA Finals

Golden State	101	Washington	95	at Washington
Golden State	92	Washington	91	at San Francisco
Golden State	109	Washington	101	at San Francisco
Golden State	96	Washington	95	at Washington

MVP: Rick Barry, Golden State

1976

Celtics Make Suns Set in Game That Will Never Die

For the young and ambitious Phoenix Suns, Game 5 of the NBA Finals offered a ticket to immortality—the opportunity for a basketball frog to turn into a king. For the aging and experienced Boston Celtics, Game 5 offered a different kind of challenge—the opportunity for a last championship hurrah before reconstructive surgery.

Both teams had scratched and clawed their way to a pair of victories, the Celtics winning Games 1 and 2 at Boston Garden and the Suns holding serve in the third and fourth contests at Phoenix. The time was right for both teams to seize the moment in a fifth-game classic that became an indelible entry in NBA lore.

There was nothing classic about the opening minutes of Game 5 as the Celtics raced to a 32–12 lead and entered the intermission with a 15-point advantage. But the Suns, inspired by the halftime pleadings of Coach John MacLeod, stepped up their defensive pressure, got the ball to guard Paul Westphal and center Alvan Adams, and crawled back into the game.

The dramatics started at the end of regulation when the Suns forced a 95–95 tie and both teams blew opportunities to win at the free throw line. Curtis Perry missed a pair of foul shots for Phoenix; John Havlicek missed two for Boston.

When the first overtime ended, the game was knotted at 101–101, and Phoenix coaches were arguing vehemently that they should be awarded a technical foul because Boston forward Paul Silas had tried to call an illegal timeout in the waning seconds. The referees chose to ignore Silas' miscall.

The second overtime was even more controversial. The Celtics held a three-point lead with 15 seconds remaining and chants of "We're No. 1" filled Boston Garden. But the chants died quickly when Dick Van Arsdale cut the lead to one and Perry connected off a Westphal steal, giving the Suns a shocking 110–109 advantage.

With four seconds left, Havlicek raced upcourt and banked in a dramatic 18-foot shot, putting the Celtics back on top as ecstatic fans raced onto the court. Mayhem prevailed as players were swarmed, fights broke out and trash was thrown while the referees tried to restore

order. A single second remained on the clock.

After a long delay, the fans were pushed to the edges of the court and the Suns called an illegal timeout, taking an intentional technical foul that Boston's Jo Jo White, a 33-point scorer, hit for a two-point lead. But Phoenix now got the ball at halfcourt and inbounded it to Garfield Heard, who fired up a 25-foot miracle jumper that swished through the net. Another overtime.

With fans now in an ugly mood and harassing Phoenix players from close quarters, the game proceeded and took still another turn. Several Boston players had fouled out and seldom-used 6-6 forward Glenn McDonald stepped into the spotlight. He scored six overtime points, the final two giving the Celtics a dramatic 128–126 win. The greatest game in Finals history was over—finally.

Demoralized, the Suns lost an anticlimactic sixth game at Phoenix, 87–80. Charlie Scott scored 25 points for the winning Celtics, who procured their 13th championship in 20 years and second in three seasons.

1976 NBA Finals

Boston	98	Phoenix	87	at Boston
Boston	105	Phoenix	90	at Boston
Phoenix	105	Boston	98	at Phoenix
Phoenix	109	Boston	107	at Phoenix
Boston	128	Phoenix	126 (3 OT)	at Boston
Boston	87	Phoenix	80	at Phoenix

MVP: Jo Jo White, Boston

1977
Blazing to a Championship

The 1977 NBA Finals produced another Cinderella champion—a Portland expansion franchise competing in its seventh season. And it produced a title-series first—a team coming back to win four straight games after losing the first two.

The prospects for a Portland championship appeared bleak when the Philadelphia 76ers rode the combined 63-point scoring of Julius Erving and Doug Collins to a 107–101 Game 1 victory and stormed to a 107–89 second-game rout that was marred by a late brawl.

But when the series moved to Portland three days later, the only brawling was done by the riled-up Trail Blazers, who stepped up the pace, defended tenaciously and rolled to a 129–107 momentum-reversing victory. Power forward Maurice Lucas and center Bill Walton bullied the 76ers for a combined 47 points and 30 rebounds.

It was more of the same in Game 4 as Walton dominated the middle and Lucas powered his way for easy baskets. The 130–98 victory sent the series back to Philadelphia with a sense of inevitability.

The 76ers got 37 points from Dr. J in Game 5, but the Blazers continued to dominate behind Walton (24 rebounds), Lucas (20 points, 13 rebounds) and Bobby Gross (25 points). The 110–104 victory touched off a wave of Blazermania that engrossed the city of Portland.

The Game 6 finale at Portland was both entertaining and tense right down to the final buzzer. The Blazers express appeared to be chugging relentlessly toward victory with a 12-point lead and only six minutes to play, but success seldom comes easily.

Philadelphia refused to die and cut the deficit to three with 51 seconds remaining. Lucas hit a Portland free throw, but a George McGinnis basket cut the lead to two. The 76ers regained possession

in the final seconds and Erving, Lloyd Free and McGinnis missed potential game-tying jumpers before time expired on Portland's 109–107 victory.

Walton, appropriately, put the finishing touches on the championship with 20 points, 23 rebounds, 8 blocked shots and 7 assists in the title-clincher. Gross added 24 points. Erving scored 40 points in a losing cause.

BLAZE OF GLORY *Bill Walton (32) and the inspired Trail Blazers overpowered Julius Erving (6) and the 76ers in an upset*

1977 NBA Finals

Philadelphia	107	Portland	101	at Philadelphia
Philadelphia	107	Portland	89	at Philadelphia
Portland	129	Philadelphia	107	at Portland
Portland	130	Philadelphia	98	at Portland
Portland	110	Philadelphia	104	at Philadelphia
Portland	109	Philadelphia	107	at Portland

MVP: Bill Walton, Portland

1978
Sleepless in Seattle

In a continuation of its rags-to-riches script, the 1978 NBA Finals featured two underdog teams looking for their first championships. Washington had finished the regular season as the third-best team in the East and Seattle had advanced through the playoffs after compiling the fourth-best mark in the West. What the series lacked in marquee appeal, it made up for with drama and intensity.

The SuperSonics grabbed the early momentum with a 106–102 Game 1 victory at Seattle and a tense 93–92 third-game win at

Washington. The Bullets had their backs against the wall when they tipped off for a Game 4 showdown at Seattle's Kingdome—a game that was witnessed by an NBA Finals record crowd of 39,547.

Guard Dennis Johnson gave Seattle fans a 33-point performance and the Sonics held a 15-point advantage late in the third period. But the Bullets raced back,

finally taking a 106–104 lead on a Bob Dandridge three-point play. Seattle tied again on Fred Brown's long jumper, forcing overtime.

The extra period belonged to Bullets guard Charles Johnson and Washington went on to claim a series-squaring 120–116 triumph. After the teams traded home-court victories, Game 7 was played at Seattle Coliseum, where the Sonics had won 22 consecutive games.

That streak would end. Charles Johnson and Dandridge scored 19 points apiece and center Wes Unseld hit two critical free throws as the Bullets clinched with a 105–99 win. Washington became only the third NBA Finals team to win a seventh game on the road.

1978 NBA Finals

Seattle	106	Washington	102	at Seattle
Washington	106	Seattle	98	at Washington
Seattle	93	Washington	92	at Washington
Washington	120	Seattle	116 (OT)	at Seattle
Seattle	98	Washington	94	at Seattle
Washington	117	Seattle	82	at Washington
Washington	105	Seattle	99	at Seattle

MVP: Wes Unseld, Washington

1979
Dodging More Bullets

By the time Washington and Seattle squared off in an NBA Finals rematch, they had discarded their Cinderella labels. The Bullets had begun defense of their 1978 crown with an Atlantic Division title and the SuperSonics, winners in the Pacific Division, had outspoken designs on removing the Bullets from their throne.

This battle pitted Washington's outstanding frontcourt of Elvin Hayes, Bob Dandridge and Wes Unseld against Seattle's classy backcourt of Dennis Johnson, Gus Williams and Fred Brown. And the big guys drew first blood with a series-opening 99–97 victory on Larry Wright's two free throws after time had expired.

But the little guys ruled the rest of the way as Seattle raced to four straight victories and its first championship. Game 2 was a 92–82 momentum-grabber at Washington and Game 3 was a 105–95 celebration at the massive Kingdome, where 35,928 Seattle fans basked in a coronation-like atmosphere. Williams scored 31 points and the defensive-minded Johnson added 17.

The Bullets showed life in Game 4 when they forced an overtime on Unseld's layup, but the

Sonics recovered for a 114–112 victory. Williams and Johnson, who scored more than half of Seattle's points in the series, combined for 68 in this game and center Jack Sikma added 20 with 17 rebounds.

Seattle finished its impressive title run in Washington with a 97–93 victory that was sealed by Brown's four late baskets.

1979 NBA Finals

Washington	99	Seattle	97	at Washington
Seattle	92	Washington	82	at Washington
Seattle	105	Washington	95	at Seattle
Seattle	114	Washington	112 (OT)	at Seattle
Seattle	97	Washington	93	at Washington

MVP: Dennis Johnson, Seattle

SWEET VICTORY *Seattle's bench celebrates as guard Gus Williams dribbles away the final seconds of Game 5*

1980
Magic Saves the Day
For Inspired Lakers

The news was disconcerting for Los Angeles Lakers fans. Center Kareem Abdul-Jabbar, a scoring machine through the first five games of the NBA Finals, would not be available for Game 6 at Philadelphia's Spectrum because of a severely sprained ankle.

Suddenly the 76ers' 3–2 deficit didn't seem so ominous. The powerful Lakers with a 7-foot-2 hole in their middle were not so daunting and proper strategy seemed obvious: Try not to get embarrassed in Game 6 and return home to Los Angeles for the clincher, hopefully with Abdul-Jabbar in the lineup.

But somebody forgot to tell the Lakers to lay down. And nobody envisioned the powerful Magic spell Coach Paul Westhead would cast over his young team. Magic, as in Earvin (Magic) Johnson, the 6–9 rookie with an effervescent smile and the amazing ability to play any position on the court—including, as everybody would quickly discover, center.

Johnson's teammates understood the mesmerizing control he could exhibit on a basketball court—his no-look passes, court sense, clever penetrations to the basket and ability to quarterback the fast break. They had watched him dominate opponents as a point guard, a small forward and a power forward, averaging 18 points, 7.7 rebounds and 7.3 assists over the regular season. But when Westhead announced that the 20-year-old former Michigan State

star would fill in at center for the stricken Abdul-Jabbar, even his closest friends shook their heads in disbelief.

For the record, Magic lost the center jump to 6–11 Darryl Dawkins. But that's just about the only thing he lost in a game viewed by a captivated national television audience. Johnson bounced, boxed out, shot, defended and charmed the nation while scoring 42 points, grabbing 15 rebounds and handing out 7 assists in an unfamiliar position against players three inches taller.

With the 37-point help of Jamaal Wilkes, who keyed a third-quarter surge that enabled the Lakers to pull away, Johnson dominated the 76ers and Los Angeles closed out its second West Coast championship with a 123–107 victory.

Before Johnson's "Showtime" rescue, the series had belonged to Abdul-Jabbar. The Lakers' big man scored 33 points, grabbed 14 rebounds and blocked six shots in a 109–102 Game 1 victory at the Los Angeles Forum and he scored 38 points in Game 2, 33 in Game 3 and 40 in Game 5—before and after he sprained his ankle.

And the Lakers needed every one of those points against the stubborn 76ers. Dawkins, Julius Erving and Maurice Cheeks combined for 71 points in Philadelphia's 107–104 Game 2 victory. And after the Lakers had pulled back in front with a 111–101 Game 3 win, the

76ers answered 105–102 as Dawkins scored 26 and Erving 23.

The Lakers held a two-point third-quarter lead in Game 5 when Abdul-Jabbar sprained his ankle and retired to the locker room. He returned early in the fourth quarter, scored 14 invaluable points down the stretch and converted a three-point play that secured a 108–103 victory.

Then, like millions of fans, he watched an extraordinary Game 6 on television—probably, like everybody else, in disbelief.

MAGIC MOMENT
Los Angeles Lakers star Magic Johnson (32) provided numerous match-up problems for Lionel Hollins and his Philadelphia teammates

1980 NBA Finals

Los Angeles	109	Philadelphia	102	at Los Angeles
Philadelphia	107	Los Angeles	104	at Los Angeles
Los Angeles	111	Philadelphia	101	at Philadelphia
Philadelphia	105	Los Angeles	102	at Philadelphia
Los Angeles	108	Philadelphia	103	at Los Angeles
Los Angeles	123	Philadelphia	107	at Philadelphia

MVP: Magic Johnson, Los Angeles

1981
Back in the Spotlight

The Boston Celtics, out of the spotlight since 1976, claimed the franchise's 14th championship with a six-game triumph over the Houston Rockets. The Celtics survived despite a five-game scoring slump by second-year forward Larry Bird.

Bird struggled through most of Game 1 at Boston Garden, but still came up with the key play in a 98–95 victory. It came late in the fourth quarter when Bird launched a long jump shot, realized immediately it was off target and darted inside for the rebound. He grabbed the ball before it hit the floor near the baseline, switched it to his left hand as he was falling out of bounds and swished a 15-footer. It was one of the greatest shots in the history of the NBA Finals.

Down but hardly out, the Rockets fought back in Game 2 for a 92–90 victory behind the 31 points of center Moses Malone. But the Celtics answered with a stifling defensive effort that keyed a 94–71 masterpiece at Houston. The Rockets held Bird to eight points for the second straight game and evened the series one day later with a 91–86 win.

The momentum turned in Game 5 and it wasn't Bird making the big plays. Cedric Maxwell exploded for 28 points and 15 rebounds in a 109–80 romp that set the Rockets up for the kill.

The Game 6 clincher marked the offensive rejuvenation of Bird, who scored 27 points and hit his only series 3-point basket in the stretch run of a 102–91 victory.

1981 NBA Finals

Boston	98	Houston	95	at Boston
Houston	92	Boston	90	at Boston
Boston	94	Houston	71	at Houston
Houston	91	Boston	86	at Houston
Boston	109	Houston	80	at Boston
Boston	102	Houston	91	at Houston

MVP: Cedric Maxwell, Boston

FLYING HIGH *Larry Bird scores two of his 27 Game 6 points against Houston*

1982
Showtime: Another L.A. Hit

The Los Angeles Lakers returned their "Showtime" attack to center stage and captured their second championship in three seasons—another six-game decision over Philadelphia. But this series lacked the Game 6 dramatics of 1980 as the Lakers won three of the first four contests and wrapped up their third West Coast title before a full house at the Los Angeles Forum.

When the Lakers put together a 40–9 second-half blitz that wiped out a 15-point Game 1 deficit en route to a 124–117 victory, it seemed like business as usual. Los Angeles had used its devastating fast break and tenacious zone-trap defense to roll past Phoenix and San Antonio in unprecedented playoff sweeps. The first-game NBA Finals victory was their ninth in a row.

That streak ended three days later when the 76ers, behind Julius Erving's 24 points and 16 rebounds, ran off a 110–94 victory at Philadelphia. But the Lakers rolled off consecutive wins at the Forum and put the 76ers' hopes on the critical list.

Point guard Norm Nixon keyed the 129–108 third-game victory with 29 points, offsetting a 36-point outburst by Philadelphia guard Andrew Toney. Magic Johnson and Jamaal Wilkes both scored 24 points and Kareem Abdul-Jabbar added another 22 in the Lakers' 111–101 Game 4 triumph.

The 76ers staved off elimination thanks to the strong Game 5 play of Darryl Dawkins. The center held Abdul-Jabbar to a shocking six points and scored 20 himself in a 135–102 romp.

But the Lakers rebounded emphatically in Game 6. Wilkes scored 27 and Johnson performed a "13 triple"—13 points, 13 rebounds and 13 assists—in Los Angeles' 114–104 championship clincher.

1982 NBA Finals

Los Angeles	124	Philadelphia	117	at Philadelphia
Philadelphia	110	Los Angeles	94	at Philadelphia
Los Angeles	129	Philadelphia	108	at Los Angeles
Los Angeles	111	Philadelphia	101	at Los Angeles
Philadelphia	135	Los Angeles	102	at Philadelphia
Los Angeles	114	Philadelphia	104	at Los Angeles

MVP: Magic Johnson, Los Angeles

1983
Moses Finds Promised Land

The 76ers, three times a brides-maid since their lone Philadelphia championship in 1967, finally broke through—and they did it in style against an old nemesis. The 76ers recorded the fourth sweep in NBA Finals history, defeating the same Los Angeles Lakers who had handed them Finals losses in 1980 and 1982, and they completed the postseason with an unprecedented 12–1 record.

Amazingly, Philadelphia won each game after trailing at the half and the 76ers did it behind the inside/out domination of center Moses Malone, guard Andrew Toney and forward Julius Erving. Malone, who had been acquired in an offseason trade to firm up the team's soft middle, averaged 25.8 points and tenaciously pounded the boards, outrebounding Lakers center Kareem Abdul-Jabbar 72–30. Toney averaged 22 points and Erving 19.

The injury-plagued Lakers entered the series without forward James Worthy and with point guard Norm Nixon and backup forward Bob McAdoo at less than full strength. And their vulnerability quickly became evident.

Malone set the tone for the series when he scored 27 points and grabbed 18 rebounds in a 113–107 opening victory at Philadelphia. And he finished in style, scoring 24 points and pulling down 23 rebounds in the 115–108 title-clincher at the Los Angeles Forum. In between, the 76ers recorded a 103–93 victory at Philadelphia's Spectrum and a 111–94 triumph at the Forum.

Final statistics suggest Philadelphia won the series in the four fourth quarters, when they outscored the Lakers 124–79.

1983 NBA Finals

Philadelphia	113	Los Angeles	107	at Philadelphia
Philadelphia	103	Los Angeles	93	at Philadelphia
Philadelphia	111	Los Angeles	94	at Los Angeles
Philadelphia	115	Los Angeles	108	at Los Angeles

MVP: Moses Malone, Philadelphia

HARD BODY *Moses Malone (2) led the 76ers past the outmanned Lakers*

1984
A Long-Awaited Rematch

The Boston Celtics continued their NBA Finals mastery over the Los Angeles Lakers in a bitter seven-game battle that pitted Larry Bird against Magic Johnson for the first time. The Celtics had recorded seven Finals victories over Lakers teams from 1959 to 1969 and the renewal of that rivalry after 15 years was memorable.

The teams split the first four games, Los Angeles posting lopsided 115–109 and 137–104 victories and Boston answering with two overtime thrillers the Lakers probably should have won.

The Game 2 overtime was forced when Celtics guard Gerald Henderson stole a James Worthy pass in the final seconds and converted a game-tying layup. Boston won, 124–121, on a Scott Wedman jumper. Game 4 was pushed into overtime when Johnson missed a pair of late free throws and Boston went on to win 129–125.

With the series tied at 2–2, the Celtics really turned up the heat in Game 5—literally. The contest was played in a sweltering 98 degrees at Boston Garden and the Lakers wilted as Bird soared. While overheated fans swooned in the stands and the Lakers gulped down oxygen on the side-line, Bird connected on 15 of 20 field-goal attempts, scored 34 points and sparked a memorable 121–103 victory.

The Lakers recovered in the cool of the L.A. Forum for a 119–108 win behind Kareem Abdul-Jabbar's 30 points, but the balanced Celtics were too much in Game 7. Cedric Maxwell finished with 24 points and 8 assists, Bird had 20 points and 12 rebounds and defensive-minded Dennis Johnson scored 22 points in a 111–102 victory.

The Celtics were champions for a 15th time.

1984 NBA Finals

Los Angeles	115	Boston	109	at Boston
Boston	124	Los Angeles	121 (OT)	at Boston
Los Angeles	137	Boston	104	at Los Angeles
Boston	129	Los Angeles	125 (OT)	at Los Angeles
Boston	121	Los Angeles	103	at Boston
Los Angeles	119	Boston	108	at Los Angeles
Boston	111	Los Angeles	102	at Boston

MVP: Larry Bird, Boston

1985

Sweet Revenge: Lakers End Long Celtics Hex

The Boston Celtics had taken great delight in their 1984 NBA Finals victory over the Lakers—maybe a little too much. Their comments were arrogant, their attitude was cavalier and their post-series shots were stinging and sarcastic.

Los Angeles players had not forgotten M. L. Carr entering Boston Garden before Game 7 wearing goggles, in a mocking imitation of the Lakers center Kareem Abdul-Jabbar; or Cedric Maxwell's choke signal to James Worthy as he prepared to shoot a free throw late in Game 4; or Larry Bird's insinuations that Magic Johnson's inept play had helped the Celtics win; or Kevin McHale's joking reference to "Tragic Johnson."

And the Lakers were well aware of the franchise's inability to beat the Celtics in the NBA Finals: eight tries, eight failures. Never had a coach entered a championship series with more motivational weapons than Lakers Coach Pat Riley in 1985— and never has a team responded in a more negative fashion: Celtics 148, Lakers 114.

The Memorial Day Massacre, coming off the bitter 1984 loss, was humiliating and hard to believe. Abdul-Jabbar, 38 years old, looked every bit his age as he tried to keep up with Boston center Robert Parish. The "Showtime" running game was slowed to a crawl and the final spread probably could have been even bigger.

On the Boston side, Scott

AWARD WINNER *Lakers center Kareem Abdul-Jabbar shows off his Finals MVP trophy*

Wedman hit all 11 of his shots and guard Danny Ainge shared the spotlight. Everything the Celtics did worked and the game ended with Coach K.C. Jones in a suspicious mood.

And rightly so. In retrospect,

Game 1 might have been the best thing that could have happened to the Lakers. Embarrassed and determined to make the pain go away, they got 30 points, 17 rebounds and 8 assists from Abdul-Jabbar and 22 points from Michael Cooper en route to a 109–102 victory at Boston. Game 3 at Los Angeles was a 136–111 Lakers blowout, sparked by Worthy's 29 points.

The Celtics, down but not out, responded in Game 4 with a 107–105 victory that was decided by Dennis Johnson's buzzer-beating jump shot. With the fifth game scheduled for the Forum under the league's new 2–3–2 format, the Lakers revved up their Showtime

engines for a big finish.

Worthy, Abdul-Jabbar and Magic combined forces in a 120–111 victory that put the Lakers within a game of their fourth West Coast championship. Abdul-Jabbar scored 36 points, Worthy added 33 and Johnson scored 26 while handing out 17 assists.

Game 6 was a Lakers' landmark. Not only did they defeat the Celtics for the first time, they did it on the parquet floor of Boston Garden where the Celtics had never lost a title-clinching game. The 111–100 victory was posted behind the firepower of Abdul-Jabbar (29 points), Worthy (28) and Johnson (a 14–10–14 triple-double).

1985 NBA Finals

Boston	148	Los Angeles	114	at Boston
Los Angeles	109	Boston	102	at Boston
Los Angeles	136	Boston	111	at Los Angeles
Boston	107	Los Angeles	105	at Los Angeles
Los Angeles	120,	Boston	111	at Los Angeles
Los Angeles	111	Boston	100	at Boston

MVP: Kareem Abdul-Jabbar, Los Angeles

1986

Celtics Blast Rockets

Boston Coach K.C. Jones had the perfect solution for the problems posed by Houston's Twin Towers. He simply let his Bird fly over, under and around the imposing Ralph Sampson and Hakeem Olajuwon in a six-game NBA Finals that produced the Celtics' 16th championship.

With Larry Bird and center Robert Parish in top form, the 7–4 Sampson and 7-foot Olajuwon did not pose a serious problem for the Celtics. Bird averaged 24 points, 9.7 rebounds, 9.5 assists and 2.7 steals as Boston duplicated its six-game 1981 victory over Houston and matched Los Angeles as a three-time champion in the 1980s.

The Celtics rolled to an easy 112–100 Game 1 victory at Boston Garden as Parish scored 23 points, Bird and Kevin McHale scored 21 and Bird handed out 13 assists, more than compensating for Olajuwon's 33 points. Bird's 31-point effort keyed Boston's 117–95 second-game rout.

But any thoughts of a sweep dissolved quickly in Houston when Sampson exploded for 24 points and 22 rebounds and the Rockets held off a late Boston charge for a 106–104 win. The Celtics regained control, however, when Bird and backup center Bill Walton hit key last-minute baskets that produced a 106–103 Game 4 triumph.

Ahead 3–1, the Celtics dropped a 111–96 decision in Houston when Olajuwon scored 32 points, grabbed 14 rebounds and blocked 8 shots. But they wrapped up the series in Boston, 114–97, behind Bird's triple-double: 29 points, 11 rebounds and 12 assists.

1986 NBA Finals

Boston	112	Houston	100	at Boston
Boston	117	Houston	95	at Boston
Houston	106	Boston	104	at Houston
Boston	106	Houston	103	at Houston
Houston	111	Boston	96	at Houston
Boston	114	Houston	97	at Boston

MVP: Larry Bird, Boston

1987

Settling an Old Score

In the rubber match of a bitter 1980s rivalry, the Lakers prevailed in a six-game NBA Finals romp over the Celtics. Magic Johnson did most of the damage, but he got plenty of help from Kareem Abdul-Jabbar, James Worthy, Michael Cooper and the rest of the Lakers cast.

The tone was set at the Los Angeles Forum where the fast-breaking Lakers pounded out 126–113 and 141–122 victories. Worthy scored 33 points in the opener and Magic totaled 51 points and 33 assists in the two games. The wounded Celtics returned to Boston Garden looking for a dose of that old championship pride.

They found some in Game 3, a 109–103 face-saving victory. Larry Bird scored 30 points and Dennis Johnson added 26. But their fate would not be determined until the waning seconds of Game 4.

The Celtics appeared headed for a series-evening victory as time ticked away in another classic Lakers-Celtics battle. Bird's 3-point basket had given them a 106–104 lead with 12 seconds remaining, but an Abdul-Jabbar free throw cut the margin to one. When Abdul-Jabbar missed the second free throw, Boston's Kevin McHale grabbed the rebound and lost the ball out of bounds. Johnson delivered a championship-crushing blow when he connected on a "junior, junior skyhook" as time expired.

Boston held serve one more time at Boston Garden 123–108, but the Lakers wrapped things up at the Forum as Abdul-Jabbar (32 points) and Magic (19 assists) keyed a 106–93 victory.

1987 NBA Finals

Los Angeles	126	Boston	113	at Los Angeles
Los Angeles	141	Boston	122	at Los Angeles
Boston	109	Los Angeles	103	at Boston
Los Angeles	107	Boston	106	at Boston
Boston	123	Los Angeles	108	at Boston
Los Angeles	106	Boston	93	at Los Angeles

MVP: Magic Johnson, Los Angeles

FIRING RANGE *Celtics center Robert Parish takes a free throw-line jumper as Lakers defenders watch helplessly*

1988
Lakers Fight Off "Bad Boys," Fulfill Guarantee

Not long after Los Angeles' 1987 championship-clinching victory over Boston, somebody asked Coach Pat Riley if the Lakers could become the first team to win back-to-back titles since the Celtics of 1968 and 1969. "Not only can the Lakers win again," Riley responded, "I'll guarantee it."

With those bold words, Riley set the tone for the 1987–88 season. The Lakers, with 40-year-old Kareem Abdul-Jabbar still manning the middle, were talented enough to pull off Riley's prediction, but like all wanna-be repeat champions before them, they

would have to overcome many obstacles: complacency, injuries, hungry challengers and, of course, Lady Luck.

The luck factor was minimized during a 62–20 regular season that insured the Lakers of home-court advantage throughout the playoffs. That was fortunate because they were extended to seventh games at the Los Angeles Forum by conference rivals Utah and Dallas during an exhausting postseason run.

Not surprisingly, that seven-game pattern continued in a rough-and-tumble NBA Finals against Detroit's Pistons—the "Bad Boys" of the Eastern Conference. The Pistons, a rising NBA power, featured the super backcourt of Isiah

Thomas and Joe Dumars and a confrontational frontcourt with bruisers Bill Laimbeer, Rick Mahorn, John Salley, Dennis Rodman and James Edwards. Frontcourt scoring was provided by the slashing Adrian Dantley.

Any thoughts that the glitzy Lakers would run right past the defensive-minded Pistons were discarded during an eye-opening first game at the Forum. After best friends Thomas and Magic Johnson exchanged center-court kisses before tipoff, Dantley connected on 14 of 16 field-goal attempts and Detroit defenders pushed the Lakers all over the court in a 105–93 victory.

The Lakers, facing a must-win Game 2 on their home court, showed heart with a 108–96 win as James Worthy scored 26 points. Game 3 was played before 39,188 Detroit fans at the Pontiac Silverdome and Los Angeles escaped with a 99–86 victory.

The Pistons did not make another misstep before their home fans. Dantley scored 27 points in a 111–86 Game 4 victory and 25 two nights later in a 104–94 win that gave Detroit a 3–2 series advantage. Game 5 was played before a crowd of 41,732,

the largest in NBA Finals history.

Game 6 at the L.A. Forum was the series classic. With his team trailing 56–48 early in the third quarter, Thomas went on a scoring spree that almost delivered Detroit its first NBA championship. He scored the next 14 points, suffered a severely sprained ankle that forced him to the sideline for half a minute and still finished the period with 11-of-13 shooting for 25 points—an NBA Finals one-quarter record. The Pistons rode that momentum into the final minute carrying a 102–99 edge.

But the Lakers responded in championship fashion. Byron Scott's basket cut the deficit to one point and two Abdul-Jabbar free throws with 14 seconds remaining decided the Lakers' 103–102 victory. Thomas finished with 43 points and 8 assists.

Having cut the heart out of Detroit's title hopes, Los Angeles closed out the series with a 108–105 victory that featured Worthy's first career triple-double (36 points, 16 rebounds, 10 assists).

The Lakers were champions for a fifth time in the 1980s—this time guaranteed.

1988 NBA Finals

Detroit	105	Los Angeles	93	at Los Angeles
Los Angeles	108	Detroit	96	at Los Angeles
Los Angeles	99	Detroit	86	at Detroit
Detroit	111	Los Angeles	86	at Detroit
Detroit	104	Los Angeles	94	at Detroit
Los Angeles	103	Detroit	102	at Los Angeles
Los Angeles	108	Detroit	105	at Los Angeles

MVP: James Worthy, Los Angeles

1989
A Changing of the Guard

While the 1988 Detroit Pistons were losing a championship to Los Angeles in a bitter seven-game NBA Finals, they were learning a valuable lesson—how to win. They did a little teaching of their own when they squared off with the aging Lakers in a 1989 rematch, a

battle that ended 40 years of franchise frustration dating back to their early life as the Fort Wayne Pistons.

En route to their first championship, Detroit's "Bad Boys" had won 63 regular-season games and generated dislike around the league for their brutish style. But the Pistons laughed at critics all the way through an easy playoff

run and a shocking Finals sweep that closed out 42-year-old Lakers center Kareem Abdul-Jabbar's outstanding career and snapped the Los Angeles championship streak at two. The Lakers had won five of the last nine NBA titles.

Detroit's victory was decided by its rugged frontcourt and the scoring of guards Isiah Thomas, Joe Dumars and Vinnie Johnson, who combined for 65 points in a 109–97 Game 1 victory at Detroit.

Game 2 was more competitive, but the Lakers' fate was sealed when Magic Johnson pulled a hamstring in the third quarter, an injury that was to restrict him the rest of the way. The Lakers, already playing without injured Byron Scott, scored just 13 fourth-quarter points and fell 108–105 as

Dumars connected for 33.

Dumars continued his hot shooting with 31 points in Game 3 (21 in the third quarter) and Detroit moved ahead 3–0 with a 114–110 victory. That set the stage for only the fifth sweep in NBA Finals history.

The Pistons fell behind by 16 points early in the second quarter of Game 4. But they chipped away at the deficit and got a fourth-quarter boost from backup center James Edwards, who scored all 13 of his points in the period. Dumars finished with 23 in the 105–97 title-clinching victory.

The series ended with the Los Angeles Forum crowd chanting, "Kareem, Kareem, Kareem" as the Pistons hugged and celebrated on the court.

1989 NBA Finals

Detroit	109	Los Angeles	97	at Detroit
Detroit	108	Los Angeles	105	at Detroit
Detroit	114	Los Angeles	110	at Los Angeles
Detroit	105	Los Angeles	97	at Los Angeles

MVP: Joe Dumars, Detroit

LITTLE BIG MAN

Isiah Thomas provided the spark for Detroit's second straight championship

1990
Detroit's Little Big Man

One season after breaking their 40-year championship jinx, the Detroit Pistons became only the third franchise to win consecutive titles. The five-game victory over the Portland Trail Blazers was signed, sealed and delivered by point guard Isiah Thomas, who averaged 27.6 points and made a number of big plays just when it appeared that the Pistons were down and out.

Thomas sent a message in Game 1. The Blazers held a 90–80 lead with seven minutes remaining and appeared to be coasting when he suddenly stepped up. With Thomas leading the charge, the Pistons pulled closer and closer, finally forcing a 94–94 tie en route to a 105–99 victory. Thomas finished with 33 points, including 10 in a row down the stretch.

Portland fought back in Game 2 with a 106–105 overtime victory that was decided on Clyde Drexler's two free throws. But the Pistons shocked the Blazers by winning the next three games at Portland—a place where they had not won since 1974.

Joe Dumars keyed the 121–106 Game 3 triumph with 33 points and the three guards—Dumars, Thomas and Vinnie Johnson—combined for 78 points in a 112–109 fourth-game win. The Thomas-Johnson combo clicked again in a shocking Game 5 clincher.

The Blazers, on the verge of forcing a sixth game, carried a 90–83 lead into the final two minutes. But Johnson suddenly caught fire, Portland went cold and Detroit scored nine straight points in a shocking conclusion to a 92–90 victory. Thomas, who scored 29 points, set up Johnson's 15-foot winner with 0.7 seconds remaining after a Portland turnover. The basket capped a marvelous 15-point final quarter for Johnson, who scored seven of the final nine.

1990 NBA Finals

Detroit	105	Portland	99	at Detroit
Portland	106	Detroit	105 (OT)	at Detroit
Detroit	121	Portland	106	at Portland
Detroit	112	Portland	109	at Portland
Detroit	92	Portland	90	at Portland

MVP: Isiah Thomas, Detroit

1991

Bulls End 25-Year Drought

The Chicago Bulls ended a quarter century of frustration when Scottie Pippen, Michael Jordan and John Paxson combined for 82 points in a 108–101 Game 5 victory over Los Angeles and clinched the franchise's first NBA championship.

The Bulls, who lost the NBA Finals opener at Chicago Stadium when the Lakers' Sam Perkins hit a three-point shot with 14 seconds remaining, completed their four-game comeback blitz at the Los Angeles Forum and ended their playoff run with a 15–2 record. The Bulls simply smothered the Lakers defensively while Jordan, Pippen and Paxson glistened in the offensive spotlight.

Jordan collected 30 points and 10 assists in the clincher and finished the series with a 31.2-point average. Pippen upstaged his teammate with a 32-point, 13-rebound, 7-assist, 5-steal effort in the finale. But the Lakers' real thorn was Paxson, who hit 29 of his final 42 NBA Finals shots. The hot-shooting guard scored 20 Game 5 points, eight in a key fourth-quarter Chicago run that decided the game.

After losing the opener despite Jordan's 36-point effort, the Bulls bounced back for a 107–86 second-game rout and claimed Game 3 in overtime, 104–96. A Jordan jump shot tied the game with 3.4 seconds left in regulation and he scored six points in the extra period. Game 4 was a 97–82 mismatch.

The Bulls, who held the Lakers to a record-low 458 points, could not stop Magic Johnson, who averaged 18.6 points and 12.4 assists in a losing cause.

The Lakers played the finale without injured starters James Worthy and Byron Scott.

1991 NBA Finals

Los Angeles	93	Chicago	91	at Chicago
Chicago	107	Los Angeles	86	at Chicago
Chicago	104	Los Angeles	96 (OT)	at Los Angeles
Chicago	97	Los Angeles	82	at Los Angeles
Chicago	108	Los Angeles	101	at Los Angeles

MVP: Michael Jordan, Chicago

STAR POWER *It was Magic Johnson vs. Michael Jordan (left) in the 1991 Finals*

1992

Bulls Give an Encore

It took the Chicago Bulls 25 years to win their first NBA championship, but just one year to win a second. It was the Michael Jordan show as the Bulls posted a 97–93 Game 6 victory over the Portland Trail Blazers and became only the fourth NBA franchise to claim consecutive titles.

Jordan, who averaged 35.8 points and claimed his unprecedented second straight MVP award, scored 33 in the finale and combined with Scottie Pippen (26) to score the Bulls' final 19 points. The Trail Blazers held a seemingly safe 79–64 lead entering the final period but were outscored, 14–2, in the opening minutes.

The amazing comeback climaxed a series in which the Bulls seemed to toy with fate. After Jordan sparked a 122–89 opening-game romp with an NBA Finals-record 35-point first half, the Blazers showed a little comeback spark of their own. They wiped out Chicago's 10-point fourth-quarter Game 2 lead with a 15–5 spurt and won the game in overtime, 115–104. Clyde Drexler scored 26 points for Portland, but guard Danny Ainge provided the victory spark by scoring nine points in the extra period.

The teams split the next two games, Chicago winning 94–84 at Portland and losing 93–88 when the Trail Blazers scored 19 of the game's final 27 points. But Jordan came to the rescue with a 46-point effort in the fifth game that sparked a 119–106 victory and set the stage for the dramatic Chicago finale.

Only the Minneapolis (1940s and '50s) and Los Angeles Lakers (1987–88), the Boston Celtics (1960s) and Detroit Pistons (1989–90) had won consecutive championships before the Bulls.

1992 NBA Finals

Chicago	122	Portland	89	at Chicago
Portland	115	Chicago	104 (OT)	at Chicago
Chicago	94	Portland	84	at Portland
Portland	93	Chicago	88	at Portland
Chicago	119	Portland	106	at Portland
Chicago	97	Portland	93	at Chicago

MVP: Michael Jordan, Chicago

1993

Three Titles Are a Charm For Jordan-Powered Bulls

The "three-peat" talk started shortly after Chicago's 1992 NBA Finals victory over Portland. Everybody agreed: The Bulls, fueled by the incredible Michael Jordan, were capable of winning a third consecutive championship. It hadn't happened for 27 years, but nothing, it seemed, was beyond Jordan's extensive reach.

And virtually everything in his career had come in such multiples. Seven scoring titles; three regular-season MVPs; two NBA Finals MVPs; seven All-NBA first-team citations; six All-NBA Defensive first-team selections; three steals titles. The "three-peat" fantasy provided a noble challenge for the basketball player who had everything.

The idea began gathering momentum when the Bulls won their third straight Central Division title, advanced unscathed through the first two rounds of the playoffs and recovered from a 2–0 deficit to defeat the New York Knicks in the Eastern Conference finals. The only remaining obstacle was a Phoenix team featuring Charles Barkley, Dan Majerle and Kevin Johnson—a team that had posted a league-best 62 wins.

The Suns' championship hopes took a severe blow when the Bulls charged into America West Arena and grabbed 100–92 and 111–108 series-opening victories. Chicago pulled away in the fourth quarter of the opener when Jordan scored 14 of his 31 points. Jordan (42 points, 12 rebounds) and Barkley (42, 13) offset each other in Game 2, but the Bulls got 26 points from Horace Grant and a triple-double from Scottie Pippen.

Game 3 at Chicago Stadium was a 3-hour, 20-minute marathon that matched the longest game in NBA Finals history—three overtimes. A three-point play by Horace Grant tied the game at 103, forcing the first extra session, and the teams battled fiercely before Phoenix finally prevailed,

1993 NBA Finals

Chicago	100	Phoenix	92	at Phoenix
Chicago	111	Phoenix	108	at Phoenix
Phoenix	129	Chicago	121 (3 OT)	at Chicago
Chicago	111	Phoenix	105	at Chicago
Phoenix	108	Chicago	98	at Chicago
Chicago	99	Phoenix	98	at Phoenix

MVP: Michael Jordan, Chicago

129–121. Barkley, Johnson and Majerle (six 3-pointers) combined for 77 points, more than offsetting the combined 70 of Jordan (44) and Pippen (26).

Game 4 was a case of too much Jordan, who exploded for 55 points and keyed a 111–105 victory. But Johnson and Richard Dumas scored 25 points apiece and the Suns broke serve again in Game 5 with a 108–98 win that sent the series back to Phoenix.

The Bulls, their backs planted firmly against the wall, built an 87–79 lead through three quarters of Game 6 but suddenly went ice cold—a drought that produced a record-low 12 fourth-quarter points. They were blanked for six minutes as Phoenix raced to a shocking 98–94 lead.

But Jordan cut the deficit to two with less than a minute to play and the Bulls got the ball back in the final seconds. The pass went low to Grant, who flipped it out to John Paxson unattended beyond the 3-point line. Paxson drilled the championship-winning shot with 3.9 seconds remaining.

BIG SHOTS *There was nothing funny about the show staged by Michael Jordan (23) and Charles Barkley in the 1993 Finals*

1994
Rockets Dismantle Knicks

It wasn't pretty, but the Houston Rockets showed what it takes to win a championship: defense, defense and more defense—and a large dose of Hakeem Olajuwon.

The Rockets' seven-game victory over the New York Knicks was a titanic defensive struggle in which the winners scored a seven-game record-low 603 points— New York totaled 608. Neither team broke 100 during the series and no game was decided by more than nine. In the end, Olajuwon won his head-to-head battle with New York's Patrick Ewing and the Rockets won the first championship in franchise history.

The 7-foot Olajuwon scored 28 points and grabbed 10 rebounds as the Rockets won the opener at Houston, 85–78. But the Knicks bounced back for a 91–83 Game 2 victory and the next two games followed script, the Rockets winning the New York opener and the Knicks prevailing in Game 4.

But the Knicks broke pattern in Game 5 at Madison Square Garden when Ewing scored 25 points and grabbed 12 rebounds and John Starks added 19 points in a 91–84 victory that put the Knicks on the brink of their first title since 1973. But that was not to be.

Returning to Houston, the Rockets rode Olajuwon's 30-

JUST REWARD *Smiling NBA Commissioner David Stern presents the championship trophy to the victorious Rockets*

point, 10-rebound effort to an 86–84 victory. The outcome was not decided until Olajuwon blocked Starks' three-point attempt with two seconds remaining. Starks scored 16 of his 27 points in the fourth quarter.

Olajuwon, who averaged 26.9 points, took center stage in the 90–84 finale, scoring 25 points and grabbing 10 rebounds. Vernon Maxwell broke out of his series-long slump to score 21.

1994 NBA Finals

Houston	85	New York	78	at Houston
New York	91	Houston	83	at Houston
Houston	93	New York	89	at New York
New York	91	Houston	82	at New York
New York	91	Houston	84	at New York
Houston	86	New York	84	at Houston
Houston	90	New York	84	at Houston

MVP: Hakeem Olajuwon, Houston

1995
A Dream Come True

The Houston Rockets, maligned as a fluke champion in 1994, shot down critics with a surprising sweep of the Orlando Magic and joined the growing list of repeat title winners.

The Rockets, who needed 27 years to win their first championship, rode the inspired play of center Hakeem Olajuwon, who had averages of 32.8 points, 11.5 rebounds and 5.5 assists per game. His counterpart, 7-foot-1, 300-pound Shaquille O'Neal, averaged 28 points and 12.5 rebounds but Olajuwon's team-

mates won the long-distance war. The teams combined to attempt 210 3-pointers, a record for a four-game Finals series.

The turning point might have occurred in a wild first game as the Magic did a late disappearing act before their home fans. The Magic had a 20-point first-half lead, led 110–107 in the final moments of regulation and lost a golden opportunity to secure victory when Nick Anderson missed four free throws in the final 10 seconds. Houston's Kenny Smith buried a dramatic 3-point shot with 1.6 seconds left to force overtime and the Rockets finally won, 120–118, when Olajuwon tipped

in a missed shot as time expired.

Olajuwon scored 34 points and backup guard Sam Cassell fired in 31 as Houston completed its surprising Orlando sweep with a 117–106 victory. Game 3 at Houston, a 106–103 Rockets win, was decided by Robert Horry's 3-

point bomb with 14.1 seconds showing on the clock.

The Rockets joined the Celtics, Lakers, Pistons and Bulls as repeat champions with a 113–101 win in the finale. Olajuwon scored 35 points and Mario Elie added 22.

1995 NBA Finals

Houston	120	Orlando	118 (OT)	at Orlando
Houston	117	Orlando	106	at Orlando
Houston	106	Orlando	103	at Houston
Houston	113	Orlando	101	at Houston

MVP: Hakeem Olajuwon, Houston

1996

Chicago Delivers Crowning Blow to 87–13 Season

The Chicago Bulls, putting an exclamation point behind their claim as the greatest single-season team ever assembled, closed out their fourth championship in six years with a six-game NBA Finals victory over Seattle and brought their final 1995–96 ledger to 87–13.

The Father's Day clincher before an emotional crowd at Chicago's United Center dropped the curtain on a regular season that produced a 72-10 record—the first 70-win regular season in NBA history—and a 15–3 playoff run that could have been even better. The Bulls won the first three games of their NBA Finals series and threatened to close the season with an unprecedented 15-1 play-off run, but the SuperSonics spoiled that dream by winning the next two games on their home court.

The centerpiece for the Bulls was the incomparable Michael Jordan, who earned his record eighth NBA scoring title and punctuated his season with his fourth regular-season and NBA Finals MVP awards. But Jordan got plenty of help from high-scoring forward Scottie Pippen, rebounding monster Dennis Rodman and such role players as Ron Harper, Luc Longley, Toni Kukoc and Steve Kerr.

Jordan scored 28 points, Pippen added 21 and Kukoc 18 as the Bulls, coming off two series sweeps and a five-game triumph over the Knicks, got a jump on the Sonics with a 107–90 victory at the United Center. Only power forward Shawn Kemp showed any life for Seattle, scoring 32 points.

Game 2 was not so easy. The Sonics, 64-game regular-season winners who were known for their quickness and ability to pressure defensively, stepped up their game and made a late run that fell just short in Chicago's 92-88 victory. Seattle trailed by 11 after three

quarters, but Kemp (29 points) was dazzling in a 23–16 final-period surge. Jordan scored 29 points, but Chicago's difference might have been Rodman, who grabbed 20 rebounds, 11 in a monster third quarter, and chipped in an unexpected 10 points.

The Bulls stepped to the edge of another long-standing NBA record—Philadelphia's best-ever 12–1 playoff run in 1983—when they traveled to Seattle, lifted their game up several notches and blew away the startled Sonics, 108–86, in Game 3. But any thoughts of a Finals sweep dissolved in the early moments of Game 4, a 107–86 Seattle victory.

The Sonics were in fine form as Kemp powered his way for 25 points and guard Gary Payton, the NBA's Defensive Player of the Year, held Jordan to 6-of-19 shooting and added 21. Re-energized and buoyed by their Game 4 effort, the Sonics put another chink in the Bulls' armor with an 89–78 Game 5 victory.

But Seattle was only delaying the inevitable. A return to Chicago was the perfect prescription and the 87–75 series-ending victory contained all the elements of success that had carried the Bulls through the regular season—intense, stifling defense, a combined 39 points from Jordan and Pippen, nine points and 19 rebounds from Rodman, and an outstanding supporting effort from Harper, Longley and Kukoc. Only Detlef Schrempf (23 points), Payton (19) and Kemp (18) kept the Sonics from wilting before the fourth quarter.

When all the shouting had ended and another championship trophy had been handed to Coach Phil Jackson (the Bulls had won in 1991, '92 and '93), the only remaining question was where the Bulls belonged in the context of team history. "We never decided to give ourselves the best team label from Day 1," Jordan said. "If we're (judged) to be the best team in history, it's not our decision."

BULL MARKET *Michael Jordan helped deliver a fourth championship to Chicago fans*

1996 NBA Finals

Chicago	107	Seattle	90	at Chicago
Chicago	92	Seattle	88	at Chicago
Chicago	108	Seattle	86	at Seattle
Seattle	107	Chicago	86	at Seattle
Seattle	89	Chicago	78	at Seattle
Chicago	87	Seattle	75	at Chicago

MVP: Michael Jordan, Chicago

THE NBA ALL-STAR GAME

See Michael slam. See Charles jam. Watch Larry shoot and Magic pass. In its most basic element, its simplest form, the NBA All-Star Weekend is a spectacular parade of one-name basketball superstars who strut their most creative stuff for adoring fans and a growing global audience.

The Greatest Show Off Earth

It is Michael Jordan winning the 1987 Slam-Dunk Championship with a magnificent leap from the free-throw line. It is Larry Nance's 1984 two-ball, windmill slam and Cedric Ceballos' 1992 "Hocus-Pocus" blindfolded jam. It is Larry Bird firing in a stream of 3-point baskets in rapid-fire succession to win the first AT&T Long Distance Shootout. It is Craig Hodges connecting on a crowd-silencing 19 straight 3-pointers en route to the second of a record-tying three consecutive Shootout titles.

And, of course, it's the All-Star Game, which remains the cornerstone of what is now a weekend-long extravaganza that promotes the individual creativity players are asked to harness during regular-season play. For one game every year, the best of the NBA's best are allowed to use their sweetest one-on-one moves, throw their most dazzling no-look passes, test their hang time both inside and outside the paint and perform their most artistic slams.

It is a prime-time basketball show that has gained status as one of the year's most popular sports attractions.

ALL THAT JAZZ *Utah's 1993 Co-MVPs John Stockton (left) and Karl Malone*

In the Beginning

When NBA Public Relations Director Haskell Cohen proposed his idea for an NBA All-Star Game, he was sitting in the league office on the 80th floor of New York's Empire State Building. It was an appropriate setting for a lofty idea.

But lofty was in the eye of the beholder. Even though the 1950 NBA was in desperate need of respect and publicity, President Maurice Podoloff and the bottom-line conscious league owners were skeptical that such a game would draw enough interest and worried that a public relations flop would do more harm than good.

Fortunately for the NBA, Boston Owner Walter Brown did not accept their misgivings. Not only did he disagree, he enthusiastically embraced the idea of a midseason classic that would rival the success of baseball's All-Star Game. Brown was so sure the game would provide a boost to the NBA's image that he offered Boston Garden as a free venue and said he would pay all expenses and incur any losses.

Thanks to Brown's persever-

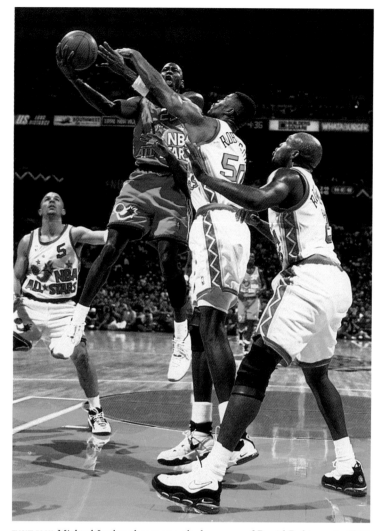

FLIGHT PLAN *Michael Jordan shoots over the long arm of David Robinson in 1996*

dous pride. All you have to do is wake up that competitive instinct and they're ready to go."

For three decades, that pride and competitive instinct were enough to make the All-Star Game a successful midseason fixture. The Wilt Chamberlains, Oscar Robertsons, Elgin Baylors, Bob Pettits and Bill Russells could be counted on to provide an exciting and memorable show. But when the NBA enjoyed an incredible popularity explosion in the early 1980s, its All-Star classic developed a personality of its own.

A major chunk of that personality is provided by players who now are eager to compete in a status-enhancing hoopfest that begins on Thursday and continues to entertain throngs of fans and television viewers through the crowning of an MVP following the Sunday All-Star Game.

The growth and blossoming of All-Star Weekend in the 1980s mirrored the explosion of professional basketball as a worldwide phenomenon, taking root with the addition of fan-friendly events that would build to the main course.

Slams, Bombs and Other Things

The rise of the All-Star Game to super-event status started in 1984, when marketing-conscious David Stern took the reins as NBA Commissioner and introduced All-Star Saturday. As a preliminary to the Sunday game, players were brought in to compete in a crowd-pleasing slam-dunk competition and two teams of former NBA stars competed in the Legends Classic, which has since been replaced by a Rookie All-Star Game.

The competitions were an immediate success. Phoenix forward Larry Nance rose into prominence with the whirling jam that gave him an exciting victory over the 76ers' Julius Erving in 1984 and Atlanta's Dominique Wilkins won the second competition a year later. The 1986 festivities included the popular 3-point-shooting contest that was dominated by Boston's Bird for the first three years.

Buoyed by those successes and ever mindful of the unconquered worlds that lay at its fingertips, the NBA continued an All-Star expansion that would transcend anything baseball, football or any other sport had to offer. In 1990,

ance, the NBA unveiled its All-Star Game on March 2, 1951, before 10,094 fans at Boston Garden. The Eastern Conference, featuring the offensive-minded starting lineup of Joe Fulks, Dolph Schayes, Ed Macauley, Bob Cousy and Andy Phillip, rolled to an easy 111–94 victory over the George Mikan-led Western Conference. The game was an unqualified success and Brown's status as a basketball visionary was insured.

High-Rising Fortunes

The early All-Star Game was a marvelous showcase for the prime NBA talent that went unnoticed by a large segment of the sports-viewing public. The game attracted television interest that helped boost the NBA's image, but it lacked the glitz and glitter that

would lift it into worldwide prominence in the 1980s and '90s. Players were selected and brought in for the one-night show and sent back to their appointed cities to resume the regular-season grind. In the 1950s and '60s NBA, many underpaid players viewed the classic as an unnecessary extension of an already too-long season.

"It's true that most players were pretty blasé when they were first selected," conceded former Celtics Coach Red Auerbach, an 11-time coach of the Eastern Conference Stars. "They like to make you think they don't care. But once they walk inside that arena on the night of the game, see the size of the crowd and feel the electricity, their whole attitude changes.

"One thing about the great ones: They've got that tremen-

A Little Bit of Heaven

In the big, bigger, biggest world of the NBA, the 1986 All-Star show was stolen by two of the game's littlest warriors—Atlanta's 5-foot-7 Spud Webb and Detroit's 6–1 point guard Isiah Thomas.

Webb became the media darling during the All-Star Saturday festivities when he outpointed seven other players in the Slam-Dunk competition. Performing before family and friends in his hometown of Dallas, Webb gave away 10 inches to his shortest rival and walked away with the trophy.

With the crowd at Reunion Arena giving him rousing support, Webb started the competition with a twisting, reverse

dunk that was slammed so hard it bounced off his head and back through the basket cylinder. He also performed two 360-degree jams and finished with a put-back dunk that he slammed home after bouncing the ball off the floor and backboard.

"It gives hope to everybody under 5–11 that you can play," marveled West Coach Pat Riley. Thomas took center stage for the East team the next day with a 30-point, 10-assist, 5-steal effort that earned him a second All-Star MVP honor. Thomas scored 12 of his points in the fourth quarter when the East pulled away for a 139–132 victory.

the NBA added a Friday night "Stay in School Celebration" that offered All-Star city students an appetizing dose of NBA stars, musical and television performers and other entertainers. Since 1993, the All-Star Weekend has started on Thursday, thanks to the Jam Session hoop festival that offers four days of interactive booths, exhibits and 3-on-3 competitions in a theme park-like atmosphere.

So, just how popular has this All-Star basketball frenzy become? Consider: The All-Star Game has been played before crowds of 44,735 (Houston's Astrodome), 43,146 (Indianapolis' Hoosier Dome) and 34,275 (Seattle's Kingdome); the 1996 game was viewed in more than 200 million homes around the world and covered by about 1,600 American and foreign reporters and broadcasters; TNT Sports previewed All-Star Saturday on Friday night and presented three prime-time hours of live coverage on Saturday; and NBC Sports punctuates its All-Star Game broadcast with long pre-game and halftime shows.

The All-Star Game has become fan-friendly in every sense. Starting lineups are selected by fans and the contest is rotated among the 28 NBA cities. Coaches, who select the reserves to fill out their rosters, are determined by the teams with the best conference records at the three-month stage of the season.

Down Memory Lane

Over the years, the All-Star Game has produced a little of everything: five overtimes, a 70-foot desperation bomb, an 87-point half, a buzzer-beating 20-foot game-winner and a player coming out of retirement to win MVP honors.

There are two things fans can depend on when the star-studded lineups take the court: The game will be wide open with lots of points and it will be filled with razzle-dazzle and free-wheeling offense. And, of course, the cream usually will rise to the top.

East-West All-Star Games
March 2, 1951, at Boston, East 111, West 94
Celtics forward Ed Macauley rewarded 10,094 Boston Garden fans with a 20-point, 6-rebound performance that earned him MVP honors in the first All-Star classic. Macauley, who received 19-point support from the Warriors' Joe Fulks, also excelled defensively, holding Lakers center George Mikan to four field goals and 12 points. Indianapolis' Alex Groza led the West with 17 points.

February 11, 1952, at Boston, East 108, West 91
A 16–3 East run, in the final five minutes, settled a contest that was dominated by two players— the Warriors' Paul Arizin (26 points, 6 rebounds) and Lakers center George Mikan (26 points, 15 boards). Arizin, who hit 9 of 13 field-goal attempts and all eight of his free throws, earned MVP honors.

January 13, 1953, at Fort Wayne, West 79, East 75
Rochester guard Bob Davies scored eight of his nine points in the final quarter to help the West hold on for its first All-Star victory. But the real damage was inflicted by 6–10 Lakers center George Mikan, who earned MVP honors with a 22-point, 16-rebound effort. It was the lowest-scoring game in All-Star history.

January 21, 1954, at New York, East 98, West 93 (OT)
Celtics guard Bob Cousy scored 10 of his 20 points in the first All-Star overtime period and the East thrilled 16,487 Madison Square Garden fans with its third victory in four years. The West, which got 23 points from Lakers forward Jim Pollard, forced the extra period on two last-second George Mikan free throws.

January 18, 1955, at New York, East 100, West 91
The Boston backcourt of Bob Cousy and Bill Sharman combined for 35 points as the East recovered from a third-quarter deficit in a game that featured 20 lead changes. MVP Sharman scored 10 of his 15 points in the decisive final period as the East won for the fourth time in five years.

January 24, 1956, at Rochester, West 108, East 94
St. Louis forward Bob Pettit scored 20 points and sparked a 41-point third-quarter explosion that carried the West to its second All-Star victory. Pettit, the game's MVP, also grabbed 24 rebounds, keying the West's whopping 79–53 rebounding advantage. Rochester's Maurice Stokes thrilled the home crowd with 10 points and 16 rebounds.

January 15, 1957, at Boston, East 109, West 97
Warriors center Neil Johnston scored 15 of his 19 points in the third quarter and Boston guard Bob Cousy earned his second MVP award with a 10-point, 7-assist effort. But the play of the game was provided by Celtics guard Bill Sharman, who connected on a 70-foot, buzzer-beating bomb just before halftime.

January 21, 1958, at St. Louis, East 130, West 118
Philadelphia's Paul Arizin scored 24 points and Boston's Bob Cousy added 20 points and 10 assists to key the East victory. But Bob Pettit put on a show for his home-town fans with a monster 28-point, 26-rebound effort that gave him the distinction of becoming the first member of a losing team to capture MVP honors.

January 23, 1959, at Detroit, West 124, East 108
Co-MVPs Bob Pettit (St. Louis) and Elgin Baylor (Minneapolis) combined for 49 points and 27 rebounds and the West pulled away in the final period for its third All-Star victory. Pettit finished with 25 points and 16 rebounds while Baylor, an NBA rookie, totaled 24 and 11.

January 22, 1960, at Philadelphia, East 125, West 115
Rookie Philadelphia center Wilt Chamberlain delighted his home fans with a 23-point, 25-rebound MVP effort as the East coasted to its seventh victory in 10 classics. Tom Gola, Chamberlain's teammate at Philadelphia, helped preserve the victory with three third-quarter steals and four straight fourth-quarter baskets.

January 17, 1961, at Syracuse, West 153, East 131
Cincinnati rookie Oscar Robertson scored 23 points and handed out an All-Star record 14 assists as the West exploded to a 47–19 first-quarter lead and never looked back. Robertson claimed MVP honors over teammate Bob Pettit (St. Louis), who set an All-Star record with 29 points. Five players topped 20 points in the game.

January 16, 1962, at St. Louis, West 150, East 130
The West won its second straight All-Star Game, despite a record 42-point effort by the East's Wilt Chamberlain. Hawks forward Bob Pettit claimed his fourth All-Star MVP with 25 points and a record 27 rebounds, but he got plenty of help from Elgin Baylor (32 points), Oscar Robertson (26 points, 13 assists) and Walt Bellamy (23 points, 17 rebounds).

January 16, 1963, at Los Angeles, East 115, West 108
Boston center Bill Russell scored 19 points, pulled down 24 rebounds and outdueled West big man Wilt Chamberlain in the first classic on the West Coast. Russell, the game's MVP, got 21-point support from Cincinnati guard Oscar Robertson while St. Louis' Bob Pettit led the West with 25 points.

January 14, 1964, at Boston, East 111, West 107
A contest that was threatened by a potential players' strike was decided by the double-barreled combination of East guard Oscar Robertson (Cincinnati) and center Bill Russell (Boston). Robertson,

the game's MVP, scored 26 points, grabbed 14 rebounds and handed out 8 assists. Russell scored 13 points and pulled down 21 rebounds.

January 13, 1965, at St. Louis, East 124, West 123

The East squandered most of a 16-point fourth-quarter lead but held on behind the efforts of two Cincinnati stars. Oscar Robertson scored a game-high 28 points and Jerry Lucas grabbed MVP honors with 25 points and 10 rebounds. Baltimore's Gus Johnson led West scorers with 25 points.

January 11, 1966, at Cincinnati, East 137, West 94

Cincinnati guard Adrian Smith, the least heralded of the talented All-Star contingent, delighted his home fans with a 24-point outburst that keyed the East's easy victory and earned him an MVP trophy. The outcome was never in doubt as the East raced to a 63–36 halftime advantage and coasted to its 11th All-Star victory.

COMING THROUGH *East guard Lenny Wilkens drives for two in the 1973 classic*

January 10, 1967, at San Francisco, West 135, East 120

Forward Rick Barry, playing on his home court, connected on 16 of 27 field-goal attempts and scored 38 points to help the West end its four-game All-Star losing streak. Barry's MVP effort got plenty of support from Detroit forward Dave DeBusschere (22 points) and Lakers forward Elgin Baylor (20).

January 23, 1968, at New York, East 144, West 124

Philadelphia guard Hal Greer connected on all eight of his field-goal attempts, scored 21 points and led the East to an easy victory before an All-Star record crowd of 18,422 at Madison Square Garden. Greer, the game's MVP, scored 19 of his points in a third-quarter run that helped the East pull away. East guard John Havlicek (Boston) led all scorers with 26 points.

January 14, 1969, at Baltimore, East 123, West 112

Cincinnati guard Oscar Robertson claimed his third MVP trophy with

a 24-point performance that helped the East to its 13th All-Star victory. The East grabbed a 16-point first-quarter advantage but needed a 37-point final period to nail down the triumph. Earl Monroe, playing on his home court, added 21 points for the East.

January 20, 1970, at Philadelphia, East 142, West 135

The West staged a frantic, record-setting 50-point fourth-quarter rally, but it was too little too late to salvage victory in the 20th All-Star Game. New York's Willis Reed earned MVP honors with 21 points and 11 rebounds, but San Diego's Elvin Hayes took game honors with 24 points and 15 boards.

January 12, 1971, at San Diego, West 108, East 107

Young Milwaukee center Lew Alcindor completed a three-point play with 48 seconds remaining to lift the West to an exciting one-point victory. Alcindor finished with 19 points, but Seattle guard Lenny Wilkens claimed MVP honors by sinking 8 of 11 field-goal attempts, scoring 21 points and sparking a late 14–1 surge that made victory possible.

January 18, 1972, at Los Angeles, West 112, East 110

Lakers guard Jerry West, playing on his home court, brought a sudden end to the most exciting game in All-Star history when he sank a running 20-foot jumper as time expired. West, the game's MVP, scored 13 points and was one of seven West players to score in the 10- to 13-point range.

January 23, 1973, at Chicago, East 104, West 84

Boston center Dave Cowens scored 15 points and grabbed 13 rebounds in the East's easy victory at Chicago Stadium. Cowens, the game's MVP, sparked a third-quarter 19–6 run that broke a 57–57 tie. Kansas City-Omaha guard Nate Archibald finished with a game-high 17 points for the West.

Here are some All-Star facts worth noting:

- Kareem Abdul-Jabbar played in a record 18 All-Star Games and scored a record 251 points (13.9 per game). But Michael Jordan (21.9) and Oscar Robertson (20.5) were more prolific All-Star scorers.

- Former St. Louis great Bob Pettit earned a record four MVP citations, one more than Robertson. One came in 1962, when the ever-intense Hawks forward grabbed a record 27 rebounds and added 25 points for good measure.

- Wilt Chamberlain set the All-Star single-game record with 42 points in that same 1962 classic, two points better than Jordan managed in 1988 while playing in front of his home Chicago fans. Both Chamberlain and Jordan connected on 17 of 23 shots.

- Larry Bird, fittingly, scored the first 3-point basket in All-Star history with 1:40 left in a 1980 overtime period.

- Utah's John Stockton and Karl Malone became the first teammates to share an MVP award after leading the West to an overtime victory in 1993.

January 15, 1974, at Seattle, West 134, East 123

West reserves Bob Lanier (Detroit) and Spencer Haywood (Seattle) combined to make 21 of 32 field-goal attempts, score 47 points and pull down 21 rebounds in a convincing West victory. The West jumped out to a 25-point first-half lead and was never threatened. Lanier claimed MVP honors with 24 points and 10 rebounds in 26 minutes.

January 14, 1975, at Phoenix, East 108, West 102

In a game dominated by opposing

guards Walt Frazier (Knicks) and Nate Archibald (Kings), the East prevailed for its 16th All-Star victory. Frazier made 10 of 17 field-goal attempts and scored 30 points en route to MVP honors. Archibald sank 10 of 15 shots and led the West with 27 points.

February 3, 1976, at Philadelphia, East 123, West 109

Washington guard Dave Bing scored all of his 16 points after intermission as the East overcame a five-point halftime deficit and won easily. Bing earned MVP honors, but Bob McAdoo (Buffalo) scored 22 points and Dave Cowens (Boston) pulled down 16 rebounds for the East. The game was played in Philadelphia as part of the city's Bicentennial celebration.

February 13, 1977, at Milwaukee, West 125, East 124

Phoenix guard Paul Westphal made a pair of baskets and a key steal in the closing minutes to preserve the West's one-point victory. Westphal finished with 20 points, but game scoring honors were claimed by East stars Julius Erving (Philadelphia) and Bob McAdoo (New York), who finished with 30 apiece. Erving became the second player from a losing team to win MVP honors.

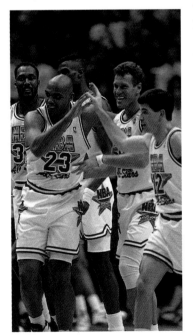

OVERTIME WIN *The West celebrates in 1993*

February 5, 1978, at Atlanta, East 133, West 125

The East, sparked by hot-shooting Buffalo guard Randy Smith, staged a frantic 41–25 fourth-quarter rally that secured a shocking come-from-behind victory. Smith, who connected on 30- and 40-foot bombs to end the first and second quarters, hit 11 of 14 shots and scored a game-high 27 points en route to MVP honors.

February 4, 1979, at Detroit, West 134, East 129

The West, in danger of blowing an 80–58 halftime lead, held off a furious East rally to claim victory before a record All-Star crowd of 31,745 at Detroit's Pontiac Silverdome. David Thompson of Denver earned MVP honors with 25 points, but Philadelphia's Julius Erving (29 points) and San Antonio's George Gervin (26) sparked the comeback effort that came up just short.

February 4, 1980, at Landover, East 144, West 136 (OT)

Boston rookie Larry Bird sank the first All-Star 3-point field goal with 1:40 left in overtime, breaking a 136–136 tie and sending the East on to victory. Houston's Moses Malone contributed to the triumph with five overtime points, but East teammate George Gervin (San Antonio) claimed MVP honors with a game-high 34.

February 1, 1981, at Cleveland, East 123, West 120

Boston playmaker Nate Archibald scored nine points, handed out nine assists and short-circuited a West comeback with his excellent late-game ballhandling to claim MVP honors. Seattle guard Paul Westphal (19 points) and Phoenix guard Dennis Johnson (19) led a spirited West comeback from a 113–99 deficit.

January 31, 1982, at East Rutherford, East 120, West 118

Larry Bird scored 12 of his 19 points in the final 6½ minutes to claim MVP honors and Boston teammate Robert Parish scored a team-high 21 as the East won for the third consecutive year. Bird and Parish were a combined 16 of 24 from the field while Seattle's Gus Williams scored a game-high 22 for the West.

February 13, 1983, at Los Angeles, East 132, West 123

High-flying Philadelphia forward Julius Erving scored a game-high 25 points and the East rolled to its fourth straight All-Star victory. The East needed Erving's MVP performance to overcome the double-edged heroics from Los Angeles Lakers stars, Magic Johnson (a record 16 assists) and Kareem Abdul-Jabbar (9-of-12 shooting, 20 points).

January 29, 1984, at Denver, East 154, West 145 (OT)

Detroit guard Isiah Thomas scored all 21 of his points after intermission as the East overcame a 14-point halftime deficit for its fifth straight All-Star victory and its 23rd overall in 34 midseason classics. The third overtime classic featured a 34-point explosion by Philadelphia's Julius Erving and a record-setting 22-assist performance by Los Angeles point guard Magic Johnson.

NBA Slam-Dunk Championship

The following players have won the Slam-Dunk competition, which became a popular feature of All-Star Weekend in 1984:

Year	Player	Team	Height
1984	Larry Nance	Phoenix	6–10
1985	Dominique Wilkins	Atlanta	6–8
1986	Spud Webb	Atlanta	5–7
1987	Michael Jordan	Chicago	6–6
1988	Michael Jordan	Chicago	6–6
1989	Kenny Walker	New York	6–8
1990	Dominique Wilkins	Atlanta	6–8
1991	Dee Brown	Boston	6–1
1992	Cedric Ceballos	Phoenix	6–7
1993	Harold Miner	Miami	6–5
1994	Isaiah Rider	Minnesota	6–5
1995	Harold Miner	Miami	6–5
1996	Brent Barry	L.A. Clippers	6–6

February 10, 1985, at Indianapolis, West 140, East 129

The West snapped its five-game All-Star losing streak as 7–4 Houston center Ralph Sampson claimed MVP honors with 24 points and 10 rebounds. San Antonio's George Gervin chipped in 23 points and Lakers guard Magic Johnson thrilled the record All-Star crowd of 43,146 at the Hoosier Dome with 21 points and 15 assists.

February 9, 1986, at Dallas, East 139, West 132

Detroit point guard Isiah Thomas claimed his second MVP award in three years with an outstanding 30-point, 10-assist, 5-steal performance. The West team held a two-point lead after three quarters, but Thomas and Boston's Larry Bird, a 23-point scorer, were too much down the stretch.

February 8, 1987, at Seattle, West 154, East 149 (OT)

Rolando Blackman hit two free throws after regulation time had expired to force overtime and the West went on to record its second All-Star victory in three years. Seattle forward Tom Chambers, a late addition to the West squad, scored 34 points to claim MVP honors while Dallas guard Blackman added 29.

BULL MARKET *1994 All-Star MVP Scottie Pippen, a 29-point scorer*

February 7, 1988, at Chicago, East 138, West 133

Bulls guard Michael Jordan gave Chicago fans a highlight-film performance, scoring 16 of his game-high 40 points in the final 5:51 to secure the East victory. Jordan, who also grabbed 8 rebounds and made 4 steals, stole the spotlight from the West's Kareem Abdul-Jabbar, who registered 10 points and became the highest scoring player in All-Star Game history.

February 12, 1989, at Houston, West 143, East 134

The West's victory in the 39th All-Star classic was delivered by Utah's Mailman, Karl Malone, who scored 28 points and pulled down 9 rebounds. But Malone got plenty of help from elsewhere. Seattle's Dale Ellis provided 27 points and Jazz teammate John Stockton handed out 17 assists. The game was played before a record All-Star crowd of 44,735 at Houston's Astrodome.

February 11, 1990, at Miami, East 130, West 113

The East squad shot 54.3 percent and had seven scorers reach double figures as it posted an easy victory in the 40th All-Star Game. But Los Angeles Lakers point guard Magic Johnson, who scored 22 points and grabbed 6 rebounds, became only the third player from a losing team to capture the MVP award. The triumph lifted the East's overall All-Star advantage to 26–14.

February 10, 1991, at Charlotte, East 116, West 114

The 41st classic was the Michael and Charles show. The Bulls' Michael Jordan scored 26 points, but Philadelphia's Charles Barkley earned the MVP award with a crowd-pleasing 17-point, 22-rebound performance. Five players scored in double figures for a balanced West team, but it fell just short in its attempt to come back from a nine-point halftime deficit.

February 9, 1992, at Orlando, West 153, East 113

Magic Johnson came out of retirement to put on a dazzling performance in the West's easy victory. Johnson connected on 9 of 12 field-goal attempts, made all three of his 3-point shots, scored 25 points, handed out 9 assists and grabbed 5 rebounds.

February 21, 1993, at Salt Lake City, West 135, East 132 (OT)

The West captured the NBA's fifth All-Star overtime game behind the 1–2 Utah punch of forward Karl Malone and point guard John Stockton. Malone scored 28 points and pulled down 10 rebounds while Stockton distributed 15 assists. Malone and Stockton became only the second duo to share All-Star MVP honors.

February 13, 1994, at Minneapolis, East 127, West 118

The East rebounded from consecutive losses behind the 29-point effort of Chicago's Scottie Pippen. Pippen, who punctuated his MVP performance with five 3-point baskets and 11 rebounds, received 20-point support from East teammates Patrick Ewing (Knicks) and Mark Price (Cavaliers).

February 12, 1995, at Phoenix, West 139, East 112

Mitch Richmond, Sacramento guard and the game's MVP, came off the bench to hit 10 of 13 shots, score a game-high 23 points and lead the West to an easy victory. Utah's Karl Malone scored 13 of his 15 points in a 41-point second-quarter explosion that gave the West a lead it never relinquished.

February 11, 1996, at San Antonio, East 129, West 118

Chicago's Michael Jordan scored 10 of his 20 points in a third-quarter explosion that carried the East to a double-digit lead and set the tone for an easy victory. Jordan, who claimed his second MVP award in his first All-Star appearance since 1993, got 25-point, 10-rebound support from Orlando center Shaquille O'Neal.

SONIC TONIC *Shawn Kemp soars high*

The AT&T Long Distance Shootout

The following players have won the NBA's 3-point shooting competition, which became a regular All-Star Saturday feature in 1986:

Year	Player	Team	Position
1986	Larry Bird	Boston	forward
1987	Larry Bird	Boston	forward
1988	Larry Bird	Boston	forward
1989	Dale Ellis	Seattle	guard/forward
1990	Craig Hodges	Chicago	guard
1991	Craig Hodges	Chicago	guard
1992	Craig Hodges	Chicago	guard
1993	Mark Price	Cleveland	guard
1994	Mark Price	Cleveland	guard
1995	Glen Rice	Miami	forward
1996	Tim Legler	Washington	guard

THE NBA DRAFT

Philosophically, theoretically and fundamentally, nothing about the NBA Draft has changed over the last 50 years. Cosmetically, physically and socially, almost everything about the Draft is different.

The search for parity

In its purest form, the NBA Draft remains what it always has been: an opportunity for weaker teams to get the first shots at the best available college and amateur players in the league's perennial quest for parity. Since July 1, 1947—the humble beginning of the annual selection process—teams have taken turns picking players in inverse order of their previous season's position in the final standings, theoretically closing the gap between top and bottom.

In its most flamboyant form, the draft has turned into a media monster, a prime-time extravaganza that has graduated from the smoky back rooms of anonymity to the noisy fan-filled arenas of today's NBA. Television cameras capture the pomp and circumstance of a frill-covered proceeding that includes center-stage introductions, draft-pick interviews and the intrigue of watching team officials try to change the direction of long-suffering franchises.

Simply stated, the NBA Draft is a case study in short-term evolution. It's a phenomenon, a fascinating example of how an embryonic process can get from there to here.

Calling All Czars

The early NBA was almost an afterthought for the sports-conscious American. Baseball, college football and boxing captured the daily headlines and even professional football, still groping for recognition and respect, received

NEW BLOOD *Warriors officials preside over the signing of 1950 draftee Paul Arizin*

more attention. Not surprisingly, the annual NBA Draft was nothing more than an agate listing on the back pages of NBA-city newspapers.

For obvious reasons, the league conducted its draft in quiet anonymity, making a conference call from its New York headquarters to team representatives who made their selections in the comfort of their own offices. For most

teams, the process was a guessing game. Few franchises had the money for full-time scouts, some didn't even have assistant coaches and talent often was evaluated by word-of-mouth reports and newspaper accounts of college games.

Typical of the period was Boston Coach Red Auerbach's discovery and acquisition of center Bill Russell, who would eventually lead the Celtics to 11 NBA cham-

pionships in 13 seasons in a brilliant Hall of Fame career. Auerbach's fascination with the 6-10 University of San Francisco star was born from his need for a rebounder and defender to center his fast-paced attack. He had never seen him play.

"I had to have somebody who could get me the ball," Auerbach said. "Bill (Reinhart) said Russell was the greatest defensive player and greatest rebounder he'd ever seen."

Reinhart, Auerbach's former George Washington University coach, was right. And Auerbach trusted his judgement so much that he swung a 1956 draft-day trade with St. Louis, giving up Ed Macauley and Cliff Hagan, two future Hall of Famers.

Auerbach also demonstrated the value of another early-draft rule in 1956, when he grabbed Holy Cross forward Tom Heinsohn, another important piece to his championship puzzle, with a territorial pick. The rule permitted any team, in an attempt to boost box-office appeal, to precede the regular draft by selecting a player from a college in its immediate geographic area. Any team using a territorial pick would forfeit its first-round selection.

Before the territorial rule was dropped after the 1965 draft, such all-time stars as Vern Mikkelsen (Lakers), Macauley (Bombers), Heinsohn (Celtics), Paul Arizin (Warriors), Guy Rodgers (Warriors), Oscar Robertson

WARRIOR PRINCE *Point guard Guy Rodgers, a 1958 territorial draft pick, became Philadelphia's guiding force*

Hakeem Olajuwon, leaving Portland with second choice Sam Bowie. The third pick of that 1984 Draft belong to Chicago, and the Bulls took Michael Jordan.

The NBA further distanced its teams from the possibility of late-season maneuvering with the 1985 institution of a draft lottery, which threw the names of its seven non-playoff qualifiers into a hat and drew lots for first-round positioning. The New York Knicks won the first lottery and they drafted Georgetown center Patrick Ewing.

The league refined its lottery process in 1990, heavily weighting its drawing in favor of the teams with the worst records. With 11 teams competing in the drawing because of expansion, the weakest team was given 11 lots, the second-worst team received 10 lots, and so on. In 1994, the lottery system was weighted even more in favor of the weaker teams.

From No-Show to Showtime

But the NBA Draft's most dramatic advance has been in packaging, mirroring the global explosion of the game itself. From the back-

(Royals) and Jerry Lucas (Royals) had entered the league as territorial picks. Wilt Chamberlain became territorial property of the Warriors in 1959, even though he played his college ball at Kansas University. The Warriors were granted permission to sign him because he was born and raised in Philadelphia.

With the 1965 demise of the territorial rule, the NBA began tinkering with other methods of insuring parity—and integrity.

Heads or Tails

As scouting procedures and communication became more sophisticated and teams became more aware of the impact the draft could have on their roster, the process began undergoing changes—and the movement toward national recognition inched forward.

From 1966 through 1984, the league determined its first and second overall picks through an annual coin flip, a process designed to protect the system from teams intentionally losing end-of-season games to enhance their draft position. The teams with the worst records from the Eastern and Western conferences

"flipped" for No. 1 status, an important consideration in years when one player stood out as a franchise-turning prospect.

Such was the case in 1969, when the one-year-old Milwaukee Bucks won the flip over the

Phoenix Suns and drafted UCLA center Lew Alcindor, who led them to a 1971 championship. In 1979, the Los Angeles Lakers beat out Chicago for the chance to draft Magic Johnson and in 1984, the Houston Rockets grabbed

On the Flip of a Coin

The NBA began using a coin flip in 1966 to determine its first and second draft positions. The following chart illustrates the annual winners and losers:

Year	Winner	Selection	Loser	Selection
1966	Knicks	Cazzie Russell	Pistons	Dave Bing
1967	Pistons	Jimmy Walker	Bullets	Earl Monroe
1968	Rockets	Elvin Hayes	Bullets	Wes Unseld
1969	Bucks	Lew Alcindor	Suns	Neal Walk
1970	Pistons	Bob Lanier	Rockets	Rudy Tomjanovich
1971	Cavaliers	Austin Carr	Trail Blazers	Sidney Wicks
1972	Trail Blazers	LaRue Martin	Braves	Bob McAdoo
1973	76ers	Doug Collins	Cavaliers	Jim Brewer
1974	Trail Blazers	Bill Walton	76ers	Marvin Barnes
1975	Hawks	David Thompson	Lakers	Dave Meyers
1976	Rockets	John Lucas	Bulls	Scott May
1977	Bucks	Kent Benson	Kings	Otis Birdsong
1978	Trail Blazers	Mychal Thompson	Kings	Phil Ford
1979	Lakers	Magic Johnson	Bulls	David Greenwood
1980	Warriors	J.B. Carroll	Jazz	Darrell Griffith
1981	Mavericks	Mark Aguirre	Pistons	Isiah Thomas
1982	Lakers	James Worthy	Clippers	Terry Cummings
1983	Rockets	Ralph Sampson	Pacers	Steve Stipanovich
1984	Rockets	Hakeem Olajuwon	Trail Blazers	Sam Bowie

Odds and Ends – Strange Draft Facts

● The ABA signing war claimed a major NBA casualty in 1975, when the Atlanta Hawks selected North Carolina State's David Thompson and Morgan State's Marvin Webster with the first and third overall picks of the draft—and lost both. Thompson and Webster signed with the ABA's Denver Nuggets.

● Prior to 1967, no NBA team had ever signed a player before the draft. But both Detroit and Baltimore, which owned the first and second overall picks, entered the selection process with contracts already signed, sealed and delivered. The Pistons announced the signing of Providence's Jimmy Walker the day before the draft and the Bullets said they had signed Winston-Salem State star Earl Monroe when they made their choice.

● To say that the 1979 draft was conducted in a state of confusion is an understatement. Only eight of the 22 franchises selected in their fixed positions

and 14 first-round choices were peddled back and forth 21 times. Six teams did not make first-round picks.

● The shocker of the 1987 draft was Washington's first-round pick (12th overall) of 5-foot-3 point guard Tyrone (Muggsy) Bogues, who went on to a nice career with the Charlotte Hornets.

● The NBA conducted 19 coin flips to determine the No. 1 and No. 2 draft positions, and eight times the coin flip loser landed the league's Rookie of the Year. Lew Alcindor (1969) and Ralph Sampson (1983) were No. 1s who attained top-rookie status. But award winners Dave Bing (Detroit, 1966), Earl Monroe (Baltimore, 1967), Wes Unseld (Baltimore, 1968), Sidney Wicks (Portland, 1971), Bob McAdoo (Buffalo, 1972), Phil Ford (Kansas City, 1978), Darrell Griffith (Utah, 1980) and Terry Cummings (San Diego, 1982) were all No. 2s. Bing, Monroe and Unseld also are Hall of Famers.

TWIN TOWERS *Houston grabbed 7-footers Hakeem Olajuwon (34) and Ralph Sampson (50) with back-to-back No. 1 overall picks in 1983 and '84*

room, conference-call atmosphere of the early years, the draft has become a media-hyped, well-choreographed show that entertains thousands of fans in huge arenas as well as international television audiences.

With the proliferation of the college game, the scouting of star players, postseason all-star tournaments, pre-draft camps, cable television and other sources of information, rabid fans and "draftniks" are almost as knowledgeable about today's players and team needs as the teams themselves. But still the draft retains a mystique and charm, thanks to the unpredictability of a process that encourages draft-day trades and maneuvering that is guaranteed to distort everybody's best-laid plan.

That mystique was reflected by the league's 1992 decision to move the draft out of New York and turn it into a veritable traveling show. Now it hops from city to city every June, attracting huge crowds and more and more publicity. A record throng of 21,268 attended the 1995 show at Toronto's SkyDome—the first draft held outside the United States.

The modern selection process is like a major party, complete with cheers and jeers from fans and the presence of high draft picks who revel in the opportunity to be showcased in front of a huge audience. Teams that make bad judgements or come unprepared risk international humiliation.

Two other important developments have helped to shape the draft. A 1971 court decision sup-

ported Spencer Haywood's right to become eligible for the draft before his college eligibility had expired, opening the door for future players to leave school early. Now underclassmen can declare themselves available for the draft simply by sending written notice to the league office. Such stars as Magic Johnson, Isiah Thomas, Michael Jordan, James Worthy, Dominique Wilkins, Hakeem Olajuwon and Karl Malone have all successfully

made the jump, but many others have tried and failed. A record 10 underclassmen were chosen in the first round of the 1995 draft.

One of the most obvious differences between then and now is the length of the draft. Early drafts had no limit and the 1960 process extended a record 21 rounds. But in 1974, the league restricted its draft to 10 rounds and it was subsequently reduced to seven in 1985, to three in 1988, and to the present two rounds in 1989.

Patching Up Those First-Round Cracks

The young man sits nervously, watching the show unfold amid the cheers and jeers of thousands of fans in one of 29 NBA arenas. One name is called, then another and another. Each announcement sends a cold shiver down his spine as he waits. Finally, his name is called. He makes the triumphant strut to center stage to be greeted by NBA Commissioner David Stern. At that moment, a lifetime's dream is fulfilled. This is followed by interviews, pats on the back, questions and, finally, the inevitable self doubts as the young man realizes the difficult tasks that face him as a first-round draft pick.

That scenario unfolds 29 times every year on a special June day. Television cameras and reporters deliver the moment to viewers and readers worldwide. By the time he steps on that stage, the young man has been tested, analyzed, questioned, prodded and pressured for months by teams that cannot afford a first-round mistake.

It's getting harder and harder for that to happen. Team officials are armed with dossiers and film on hundreds of college players they have spent many hours and thousands of dollars evaluating for months, if not years. They have gleaned additional information from postseason all-star tournaments, pre-draft camps and interviews that give them a strong feel for personality and attitude, as well as players' desire to perform in their city.

Today's sophisticated, computerized, high-tech scouting methods are light years removed from the word-of-mouth, one-quick-look, take-a-chance draft techniques of yesteryear. But there were fewer rosters to stock in the early NBA and the elite talents were always easy to spot, even if teams were not blessed with large scouting staffs.

Still, in any era, there are players who manage to slip through the first-round cracks. Sometimes the key to success can be found in the second or third rounds—usually the blue-collar players who make up for talent deficiencies with hard work and dedication.

The Waiting Game

Those who believe good things come to those who wait can find two solid examples in the NBA Draft. Master Celtics architect Red Auerbach was roundly criticized in 1978, when he used Boston's first-round pick (sixth overall) on Indiana State forward Larry Bird, a junior-eligible selection who already had announced he would stay in school for his senior year. The Celtics, who were coming off a 32–50 season and needed immediate help, would have to struggle through another campaign without any. But Auerbach and the Celtics persevered during a 29–53 1978–79

NICK OF TIME *The Lakers stole point guard Van Exel with the 37th overall pick*

Slipping Through the Net

Many players have enjoyed (or are enjoying) highly successful careers despite not being drafted in the first round. Here are some examples:

Player	Year Drafted	Round	Overall Pick	Team
Jack Twyman	1955	2nd	10th	Royals
K.C. Jones	1956	2nd		Celtics
Hal Greer	1958	2nd	14th	Nationals
Doug Moe	1961	2nd	22nd	Packers
Chet Walker	1962	2nd	14th	Nationals
Willis Reed	1964	2nd	10th	Knicks
Paul Silas	1964	2nd	12th	Hawks
Ron Boone	1968	11th	147th	Suns
Nate Archibald	1970	2nd	19th	Royals
Dan Issel	1970	8th	122nd	Pistons
Calvin Murphy	1970	2nd	18th	Rockets
George Gervin	1974	3rd	40th	Suns
World B. Free	1975	2nd	23rd	76ers
Alex English	1976	2nd	23rd	Bucks
Dennis Johnson	1976	2nd	29th	SuperSonics
Maurice Cheeks	1978	2nd	36th	76ers
Bill Laimbeer	1979	3rd	65th	Cavaliers
Danny Ainge	1981	2nd	31st	Celtics
Eddie Johnson	1981	2nd	29th	Kings
Spud Webb	1985	4th	87th	Pistons
Jeff Hornacek	1986	2nd	46th	Suns
Dennis Rodman	1986	2nd	27th	Pistons
Cedric Ceballos	1990	2nd	48th	Suns
Nick Van Exel	1993	2nd	37th	Lakers

It's a Lottery

The NBA began its draft lottery system in 1985, with seven non-playoff qualifiers gaining first-round position through a lottery system. The following chart traces the history of the lottery with the order of teams selecting and their first picks:

Year	Team	Player	Year	Team	Player
1985	New York	Patrick Ewing	1991	Charlotte	Larry Johnson
	Indiana	Wayman Tisdale		New Jersey	Kenny Anderson
	L.A. Clippers	Benoit Benjamin		Sacramento	Billy Owens
	Seattle	Xavier McDaniel		Denver	Dikembe Mutombo
	Atlanta	Jon Koncak		Miami	Steve Smith
	Sacramento	Joe Kleine		Dallas	Doug Smith
	Golden State	Chris Mullin		Minnesota	Luc Longley
				Denver	Mark Macon
1986	Cleveland	Brad Daugherty		Atlanta	Stacey Augmon
	Boston	Len Bias		Orlando	Brian Williams
	Golden State	Chris Washburn		Cleveland	Terrell Brandon
	Indiana	Chuck Person			
	New York	Kenny Walker	1992	Orlando	Shaquille O'Neal
	Phoenix	William Bedford		Charlotte	Alonzo Mourning
	Dallas	Roy Tarpley		Minnesota	Christian Laettner
				Dallas	Jimmy Jackson
1987	San Antonio	David Robinson		Denver	LaPhonso Ellis
	Phoenix	Armon Gilliam		Washington	Tom Gugliotta
	New Jersey	Dennis Hopson		Sacramento	Walt Williams
	L.A. Clippers	Reggie Williams		Milwaukee	Todd Day
	Seattle	Scottie Pippen		Philadelphia	Clarence Weatherspoon
	Sacramento	Kenny Smith		Atlanta	Adam Keefe
	Cleveland	Kevin Johnson		Houston	Robert Horry
1988	L.A. Clippers	Danny Manning	1993	Orlando	Chris Webber
	Indiana	Rik Smits		Philadelphia	Shawn Bradley
	Philadelphia	Charles Smith		Golden State	Anfernee Hardaway
	New Jersey	Chris Morris		Dallas	Jamal Mashburn
	Golden State	Mitch Richmond		Minnesota	J.R. Rider
	L.A. Clippers	Hersey Hawkins		Washington	Calbert Cheaney
	Phoenix	Tim Perry		Sacramento	Bobby Hurley
				Milwaukee	Vin Baker
1989	Sacramento	Pervis Ellison		Denver	Rodney Rogers
	L.A. Clippers	Danny Ferry		Detroit	Lindsey Hunter
	San Antonio	Sean Elliott		Detroit	Allan Houston
	Miami	Glen Rice			
	Charlotte	J.R. Reid	1994	Milwaukee	Glenn Robinson
	Chicago	Stacey King		Dallas	Jason Kidd
	Indiana	George McCloud		Detroit	Grant Hill
	Dallas	Randy White		Minnesota	Donyell Marshall
	Washington	Tom Hammonds		Washington	Juwan Howard
				Philadelphia	Sharone Wright
1990	New Jersey	Derrick Coleman		L.A. Clippers	Lamond Murray
	Seattle	Gary Payton		Sacramento	Brian Grant
	Denver	Chris Jackson		Boston	Eric Montross
	Orlando	Dennis Scott		L.A. Lakers	Eddie Jones
	Charlotte	Kendall Gill		Seattle	Carlos Rogers
	Minnesota	Felton Spencer			
	Sacramento	Lionel Simmons			
	L.A. Clippers	Bo Kimble			
	Miami	Willie Burton			
	Atlanta	Rumeal Robinson			
	Golden State	Tyrone Hill			

Year	Team	Player
1995	Golden State	Joe Smith
	L.A. Clippers	Antonio McDyess
	Philadelphia	Jerry Stackhouse
	Washington	Rasheed Wallace
	Minnesota	Kevin Garnett
	Vancouver	Bryant Reeves
	Toronto	Damon Stoudamire
	Portland	Shawn Respert
	New Jersey	Ed O'Bannon
	Miami	Kurt Thomas
	Milwaukee	Gary Trent
	Dallas	Cherokee Parks
	Sacramento	Corliss Williamson
1996	Philadelphia	Allen Iverson
	Toronto	Marcus Camby
	Vancouver	Shareef Abdur-Rahim
	Milwaukee	Stephon Marbury
	Minnesota	Ray Allen
	Boston	Antoine Walker
	L.A. Clippers	Lorenzen Wright
	New Jersey	Kerry Kittles
	Dallas	Samaki Walker
	Indiana	Erick Dampier
	Golden State	Todd Fuller
	Cleveland	Vitaly Potapenko
	Charlotte	Kobe Bryant

LUCKY 13 *Milwaukee won the 1994 draft lottery and selected Glenn Robinson*

season. And when Bird arrived, Auerbach came away looking like a genius. Bird led Boston to a 61–21 first-year record, eight Atlantic Division titles in his first nine seasons and three NBA championships in the 1980s.

The San Antonio Spurs took a similar gamble in 1987 when they selected 7-1 Navy center David Robinson with the first overall pick—even though Robinson would have to fulfill two years of military duty before he could play. The Spurs suffered through 31–51 and 21–61 seasons while waiting for Robinson, who quickly turned them into Midwest Division champions. With Robinson, the 1995 league MVP, in the post, San Antonio won division titles in three of his first six seasons and posted 62-, 56-, 55- and 55-victory records.

How important would Lew Alcindor have been to the health and well-being of the ABA? Perhaps the answer can be found in the NBA Draft.

The NBA was so worried the ABA would pick off the biggest player plum in many years that it conducted the first two rounds of its 1969 selection process (29 picks) over the telephone a month ahead of its final 18 rounds. That allowed the Milwaukee Bucks time to pursue Alcindor (later Kareem Abdul-Jabbar) while other NBA teams raced to sign the rest of the year's best players. The Bucks, of course, signed Alcindor, ruining the ABA's chance for a major off-court victory.

The expansion Orlando Magic got rich quick and exposed a major flaw in the draft lottery system in 1992 and '93 when they walked away with consecutive No. 1 overall picks that produced center Shaquille O'Neal and swingman Anfernee Hardaway.

There was nothing strange about the Magic's 1991–92 season, which produced a 21–61 third-year record and seventh place in the Atlantic Division. That losing record was a winning formula in the draft lottery, which gave the Magic the first overall pick and franchise center O'Neal.

With O'Neal manning the middle in 1992–93, the Magic improved to 41–41, and missed qualifying for the playoffs by a single game. That earned them a 1-in-66 shot at another No. 1 pick in the weighted lottery—and, amazingly, they won again. That made them the first team since the 1983 and '84 Houston Rockets to make No. 1 selections in consecutive seasons.

The Magic selected Michigan forward Chris Webber, sent him to Golden State for No. 3 pick Hardaway and three future No. 1s and moved into position to challenge for a championship. The embarrassed NBA re-weighted its lottery system, making it very unlikely—but not impossible—that such a situation will ever occur again.

THE STORIED ARENAS

There's no place like home, whether it be in Kansas or the NBA. The great basketball venues, past and present, provide a nostalgic mix of charm, inspiration, fan appeal and glorious memories.

GATE 4

OLD GLORY Venerable Chicago Stadium, the loud and raucous home of the Bulls and Blackhawks for generations of fans, gave way to the modern United Center in 1994.

GARDEN PARTY *The banner-filled rafters and parquet floor were unique features in the dank, musty atmosphere of Boston Garden*

BOSTON GARDEN
Mystique, Memories and Championships

It was dank, musty, smelly, dark and either uncomfortably cold or swelteringly hot, depending on the time of year and the weather outside. It housed rats the size of rabbits, cockroaches the size of rats and memories bigger than all the oversized vermin combined. The fans who worshiped there were loud, raucous, belligerent, obnoxious and borderline fanatical.

Boston Garden was not your typical high-tech, see-and-be-seen, follow-the-bouncing cheerleader arena. It was a no-nonsense, blue-collar architectural dinosaur that changed little from its 1928 opening to its 1995 last hurrah. Sports-hardened New England hockey and basketball fans did not go there to socialize. They took their teams seriously and supported them with enthusiasm and loyalty.

That's just as well because the Garden was as hard on them as it was the opposing players who tried to ignore and penetrate its mystique. There was no air-conditioning to defend against the oppressive summer heat; there was minimal heat to fend off the bitterly cold winter temperatures; the slatted wooden mustard-yellow seats were hard and uncomfortable and some were positioned behind huge support pillars; there was no instant replay, no high-tech scoreboard, no scantily-clad dancing girls, no courtside celebrities. For sports events, Boston Garden was all business.

The Garden was born in a pre-Depression boom as a hockey facility and remained true to that calling for 68 years. It was first and foremost home of the Bruins, but the NBA's Celtics, co-tenants since 1946, gave the building a championship aura the Bruins could not. The green-and-white clad Celtics, coached by the colorful and very Irish Red Auerbach, ran their distinctive parquet floor in black high-top sneakers, winning championship after championship and the begrudging support of skeptical hockey fans. When the Garden ended its reign as dean of U.S. sports arenas after the 1994-95 season, it did so with 16 Celtics and five Bruins championship banners hanging majestically from its rafters.

The banners and the teams were passed on to Boston's new 18,600-seat FleetCenter before the 1995–96 hockey and basketball seasons, but the aura and the memories — the heart and soul of the Boston Garden mystique — were retired with the rats and roaches. They survive only in the telling and retelling of stories by those who were there and the NBA records that confirm the invincibility of the team that gave the building respect and personality.

Some of the Garden's subtle images are of opposing players and referees getting blasted by ice cold water in the middle of a shower; or showered visitors trying to dry themselves with already damp towels; or complaints of tiny, hole-in-the-wall dressing rooms with roaches running rampant and little heat; or dead spots on the parquet floor that the Celtics used to great advantage— or the belligerent Boston fans positioned precariously close to the court and in balconies overhanging the floor. But the basketball images are more vivid:

● Auerbach lighting up a cigar in the final minute of a game, signaling official confirmation of another Celtics victory.

● Bill Russell versus Wilt Chamberlain.

● Excited fans storming onto the floor to celebrate one of Boston's 11 NBA championships in a 13-year span from 1957–69.

● The Celtics versus Jerry West, Elgin Baylor and the Lakers in the NBA Finals.

● John Havlicek running … and running … and running … and running some more.

● Bob Cousy making another no-look, behind-the-back pass to a surprised teammate.

● Sam Jones connecting on a 20-foot bank shot.

● Frank Ramsey, Havlicek, Don Nelson, Larry Siegfried, Kevin McHale—all successful Celtics "Sixth Men."

● The Celtics versus Magic Johnson, Kareem Abdul-Jabbar, James Worthy and the Lakers in the NBA Finals.

● Larry Bird firing in a 3-point jumper.

For those who prefer the incredible games, performances and plays that graced the Celtics' parquet, there's plenty to choose from. A good starting point is Game 7 of the 1957 NBA Finals— a 125–123 double-overtime victory over the St. Louis Hawks that produced Boston's first championship and started a winning legacy that would gain legendary status. That game ended on an incredible note when the Hawks' Alex Hannum made a half-court pass to Bob Pettit—off the backboard—and Pettit, apparently surprised that such a maneuver could work, missed the point-blank, game-tying tip-in.

Another Boston championship was the product of a missed shot. The Lakers, six-time NBA Finals losers to Boston in the 1960s, lost a golden opportunity to interrupt the Celtics' eight-year title run in Game 7 of the 1962 Finals when Frank Selvy missed a last-second, wide-open 10-foot jumper in regulation play. Given a reprieve, the Celtics posted a 110–107 victory in overtime.

One of the most famous Boston victories was recorded three years later in Game 7 of the Eastern Conference finals when Havlicek preserved a 110–109 vic-

tory over Philadelphia with a last-second steal. Long-time Boston announcer Johnny Most immortalized the moment with his classic radio call: "Havlicek stole the ball." The words were delivered with such force and urgency by Most's distinctive voice that the game became an immediate classic.

Perhaps more significant in the Celtics' long success story was the off-balance 18-foot leaner that Sam Jones threw toward the basket with time running out in Game 4 of the 1969 Finals. As the buzzer sounded, the ball rolled tantalizingly around the rim before falling through. The 89–88 victory over the Lakers propelled the Celtics to their final title of the "Bill Russell era."

The Celtics really turned up the heat for Game 5 of the 1984 NBA Finals in another Garden classic. With temperatures rising over 100 degrees outside, Boston Garden thermostats reached a sweltering 98 as both players and fans battled heat exhaustion and dehydration. As the Lakers gulped oxygen on their sideline and dozens of fans swooned in the stands, a seemingly refreshed Bird soared for 34 points in a 121–103 victory.

The NBA's first All-Star Game was played at Boston Garden in 1951 and Chicago's Michael Jordan dented the Celtics for a playoff-record 63 points in a 1986 double-overtime thriller, but most long-time Celtics watchers insist that Game 5 of the 1976 NBA Finals was the greatest game in Garden history—maybe the greatest basketball game ever.

That 128–126 triple-overtime win over Phoenix was full of dramatic turning points and plays, none more memorable than the 22-foot game-tying desperation heave by the Suns' Garfield Heard at the end of the second overtime. Heard's miraculous shot was delivered off a Phoenix inbounds pass with one second remaining on the clock and Boston fans ringing the court,

ready to storm the floor for a victory celebration. It set off a fan melee that held up play for several minutes and it set up the third-overtime heroics of Boston reserve Glenn McDonald. The loss demoralized the exhausted Suns and the Celtics went on to easily claim another championship.

The personalities (P.R. man Howie McHugh, organist John Kiley, trainer Buddy LeRoux, former owners Walter Brown, Marvin Kratter and Paul Gaston, Auerbach), the decaying building, the players, the banners, the parquet floor and even the rats—they all were part of a Boston Garden atmosphere that stretched above and beyond the worlds of hockey and basketball.

In its long, glorious history, the Garden played host to political rallies, religious revivals, ice shows, concerts, circuses, rodeos, poultry shows, home shows, conventions and various sports events—bicycle races, wrestling, Roller Derby, lacrosse, tractor pulls, boxing and even indoor baseball. It truly was a building for all seasons, but none more special than the one that ran from November to May or June—the time required for each of the Celtics' 16 championships.

When Boston Garden played host to its final basketball game in 1995, the Celtics had posted an incredible 1,291–424 home record there. The moss-covered building with one elevator and 10 bathrooms quietly gave way to the modern FleetCenter with its seven elevators, 13 escalators, 34 bathrooms, 104 luxury boxes and numerous other conveniences never experienced before by the hard-core, no-nonsense Boston sports fans.

It was a familiar transition. Boston Garden was neither the first nor last of the NBA's storied arenas to give way to the recent obsession for modernistic, space-aged facilities with all the conveniences of home. The following profiles describe some of the most engaging structures, both past and present.

CHICAGO STADIUM
Loud, Proud and Rowdy

The old barn on Madison Street closed its doors after the 1993–94 season with a combination of sadness and relief.

Like Boston Garden, 65-year-old Chicago Stadium had become dirty, dingy and decayed, a former state-of-the-art facility that had fought valiantly against the ravages of time. Right up to the end, its dedicated fans were the loudest and rowdiest in sports and the old building still could generate the emotion and electricity that influence championships. But everyone agreed: it was time to go.

So the once-venerable Stadium was turned into a parking lot and the NHL's Blackhawks and NBA's Bulls moved into the 21,711-seat United Center, with its more than 200 luxury suites and high-tech, fill-every-need conveniences. It took less than a minute inside the new building to see that sports, Chicago-style, could never be quite the same.

Chicago Stadium was built in the pre-Depression boom (1929) as a hockey arena and fans had to ease into professional basketball after the expansion Bulls became tenants in 1967. While hockey, basketball and boxing have provided the main entertainment, the old barn could never be called one or two-dimensional. In its 65 years, Chicago Stadium hosted political conventions (Franklin D. Roosevelt coined his "New Deal" slogan there), rodeos, circuses, ice shows, concerts, jitterbug contests and sports events ranging from bicycle races and roller derby to indoor track and soccer.

It also will be remembered as the site of the first indoor professional football game—an NFL championship-deciding contest that was hastily staged on a makeshift 80-yard imported-dirt field because of a driving Chicago snowstorm. The Bears won that historic 1932 title, 9–0, over the Portsmouth Spartans.

Part of the Stadium's enduring charm was the trademark Barton Organ that kept the building rocking, rolling and swaying through good times and bad. The organ's pipes, which would have measured more than a city block if laid end to end, were built into the foundation of the building and thus couldn't be moved to the United Center. The ear-pounding organ provided the background music for many of the building's most dramatic moments.

The best recent memories were provided by the Bulls—most of them since the 1984 arrival of Michael Jordan. Not only did Jordan mesmerize Chicago fans with his high-flying artistry and phenomenal scoring, he led the Bulls to three consecutive NBA titles from 1991–93—the first "three-peat" since the 1960s Celtics won eight championships in a row.

Bulls announcer Red Kerr, a veteran of Chicago Stadium as a player and coach, fondly recalled his favorite moment—the Bulls' championship ring ceremony after their second title—for the *Chicago Tribune*: "One of the great thrills was to see the players come back up out of the bowels of the stadium. It was fantastic. I've heard the Stadium is loud, but after everyone else was on the floor and there was only one more, the announcer said, 'And now, the greatest basketball player this planet will ever see …' Nobody heard it, but they all knew Michael was the only guy not out there. That was the loudest the Stadium has ever been."

Perhaps the most fitting epitaph was offered by Bulls Coach Phil Jackson before the Stadium's final hurrah in 1994.

"You get a wonderful feeling in this building," he said. "Boston Garden or other places like that aren't even close to this place. The noise, closeness to the playing floor, the connection among the fans in each section with the players all contribute to the warmth, the heartiness of the place."

HOT HOUSE *The United Center is the new home for Chicago's indoor sports*

SQUARE ROOT OF ENTERTAINMENT *Hockey, basketball and figure skating—the sports were diverse and plentiful in the Madison Square Garden of 1948 New York*

MADISON SQUARE GARDEN
The Granddaddy of All Sports Arenas

Madison Square Garden cannot claim distinction as America's oldest existing arena, but it has survived in name for more than a century in the sports capital of North America. Four Madison Square Gardens have existed on three different sites since 1879, offering New York patrons every kind of entertainment venue imaginable.

Madison Square Garden I and II were constructed on the same site at Madison Square bordering 26th Street and Madison Avenue. The first building was demolished in 1890 and replaced by a bigger, better Garden that endured until 1925.

Madison Square Garden III

Indoor sports as we know it today took its New York foothold in 1925 when promoter Tex Rickard oversaw the construction of an 18,000-seat arena at 49th Street and Eighth Avenue. Rickard's principal attraction was the NHL's Rangers, but it didn't take long for the new Garden to be recognized as America's premier recreational showplace.

The Rangers and boxing ruled the professional sports venue in the early years, but the Garden soon became known as the "Mecca of Basketball" under the expert direction of Ned Irish, another outstanding promoter. Irish became well known for his college basketball doubleheaders and he was the primary moving force behind the prestigious National Invitation Tournament, an annual Garden event that overshadowed the up-and-coming NCAA Tournament in the late 1930s and '40s.

Professional basketball took its place in the Garden showcase when the Basketball Association of America, the predecessor to the NBA, was formed in 1946. The Knickerbockers' presence in the country's No. 1 sports market helped legitimize the NBA during its painful early years and, although the Knicks never won an NBA championship in the build-ing, they grew into one of the game's venerable franchises while playing there. And the league itself grew in stature.

Madison Square Garden IV

When New York officials bill the current Garden as "The World's Most Famous Arena," it's hard to argue the point.

Opened in 1968 as a huge multi-purpose complex, Garden IV featured a circular cable-suspended roof that covered a 19,000-seat arena, 5,000-seat Felt Forum, the 48-lane Bowling Center, a 500-seat cinema, the Hall of Fame Club, the National Art Museum of Sport, a 50,000-square-foot Exposition Rotunda and a 29-story office building with a pedestrian mall.

The new Garden, located between 31st and 33rd Streets and Seventh and Eighth Avenues on Manhattan's West Side, cost $43 million and opened for business when Bob Hope and Bing Crosby hosted a USO salute. The Knicks played their first basketball game there three days later—appropriately, on Valentine's Day.

It was love at fourth site for the up-and-coming Knicks, who captured their first NBA championship in 1970 when they defeated the Lakers in a memorable NBA Finals Game 7 at the Garden. The Knicks added another title in 1973.

Almost three decades of memories have flooded through the hallowed building—Ali vs. Frazier, the Rangers ending 54 years of Stanley Cup frustration, Hope and Crosby, Frank Sinatra, the Rolling Stones, Elvis Presley, Michael Jackson, Elton John, Luciano Pavarotti, Billy Joel, Bruce Springsteen, Barbra Streisand, political conventions and famous personalities ranging from future U.S. presidents and a Pope to the Harlem Globetrotters and the Muppets.

And through its more than a quarter of a century, the Garden has moved steadily forward with state-of-the-art scoreboards, instant replay equipment, numerous renovations, dramatic facility updates and even an upscale surge of clientele.

In its bid to keep up with the Los Angeles Forum of the '80s, the Madison Square Garden of the '90s even boasts its own celebrity row, featuring such high-profile fans as Spike Lee, Woody Allen, Dustin Hoffman, Donald Trump and special guests like Madonna and Arnold Schwarzenegger.

BIGGER AND BETTER *Madison Square Garden IV remarkably has lived up to its New York responsibilities, with its modern look and state-of-the-art advancements*

THE GREAT WESTERN FORUM
Glitz, Glamour and Showtime

Basketball, Los Angeles-style, is more than a game. It's an event, a social experience and a theatrical production, expertly wrapped in Hollywood glitz and complete with celebrities, dancing girls and high-tech scoreboards and replay screens.

NBA images of the Forum include actors Jack Nicholson and Dyan Cannon at courtside, the "Showtime" Lakers, Magic and Kareem, the Laker Girls and, of course, the championships—one in 1972 and five in the glorious 1980s. From its grand opening in December 1967 to its current status as the league's "Showtime" arena, the Forum and its upscale patrons have changed the ambience of professional basketball.

When Jack Kent Cooke, then owner of the Lakers and NHL Kings, built his Forum at an unbelievable cost of $16 million, he envisioned a social atmosphere that would contrast the fan intensity of such facilities as Boston Garden and New York's Madison Square Garden. His $16 million cost would dwarf the $5 million of Philadelphia's new Spectrum and it would give L.A. fans such luxuries as fully upholstered, extrawide, theater-style seats set in rows with plenty of legroom.

Cooke billed the Forum as a modern-day version of the Colosseum of Ancient Rome and newcomers still gawk at the 80 support columns that stand 57 feet high and weigh 55 tons. Cooke outfitted male ushers in togas, usherettes in short pants and his Lakers in purple and gold uniforms. He realigned courtside seating, charging hefty fees for season tickets that were snapped up by celebrity fans like Nicholson and Walter Matthau.

The building remained the "Forum" through the 1979 sale of the building and its teams to Jerry Buss and all of the Lakers' six championships. It was changed to "The Great Western Forum" in 1988 as part of a major advertising agreement.

Everything about the Forum is upscale, clean and fast, from its celebrity patronage and 17,505 theater-friendly basketball seats to the Lakers' run-and-gun style. The Forum will be best remembered as the home of Pat Riley's "Showtime" Lakers featuring Magic Johnson, Kareem Abdul-Jabbar and James Worthy. But it also plays host to more than 200 events per year and has showcased some of sports' greatest athletes and the entertainment world's top performers. And in 1984, the Forum served as the venue for all basketball competition in the Los Angeles Olympic Games.

Not surprisingly, the Lakers have won more than 75 percent of their games in the building.

MEMORIAL COLISEUM
Everything's Coming Up Roses

When the Trail Blazers ended their stay in the 35-year-old Coliseum in May 1995 with a 117–109 playoff loss to Phoenix, they also completed a string of 810 consecutive sellouts—the longest string in the NBA.

The sellout string was both good and bad. It certainly proved that Portland fans were loyal to their only professional sports franchise. But it also was a reflection of the arena's 12,888 seating capacity—the smallest in the NBA. The last Coliseum game that was not sold out was April 5, 1977, when 12,359 showed up to see the Blazers play Detroit.

Unlike many of the players who fretted about life away from Chicago Stadium and Boston Garden when those arenas were abandoned, Portland welcomed the 1995 move into the 21,500-seat Rose Garden. Coliseum facilities were cramped, warmup jackets often were required for winter practices and power outages were not uncommon. And players often complained that fans were so quiet during games you could hear a sneaker drop.

That wasn't always the case. Portland fans were as noisy as any in the league during the early years and they helped the Blazers through their unlikely 1977 championship run. But there was virtually no turnover in season tickets as the years passed and the Coliseum crowd got old. The fans also grew mellow and serene, a generational characteristic that didn't sit well with the young players.

In the 25 years of Trail Blazers basketball, the Coliseum hosted three NBA Finals, a college basketball Final Four, Dream Team exhibitions and the first NBA game attended by a U.S. chief executive. President Gerald Ford dropped in for a 1974 contest against Buffalo.

The Rose Garden joined the growing list of glitzy new arenas before the 1995–96 season, a trend that's likely to continue.

THE PHILADELPHIA SPECTRUM
A $5-Million Fortress

The Spectrum, which joined the growing list of defunct sports facilities at the end of the 1995–96 seasons, was part of a late 1960s arena blitz that also produced the Los Angeles Forum and the fourth edition of New York's Madison Square Garden. But whereas the vast Garden complex was constructed at a cost of $43 million and the Forum was built for $16 million, the Spectrum came in at the bargain price of $5 million.

The Wilt Chamberlain and Hal Greer-led 76ers, coming off a 1966–67 championship season, played their first game in the new building on October 18, 1967, and posted an impressive 103–87 victory over the Los Angeles Lakers. They went on to win 62 games and advanced to the Western Conference finals before losing a tough seven-game series to Boston.

Over the building's 29 years, the 76ers won five more division titles, advanced to four NBA Finals and won one more championship. The NHL's Flyers added to the legacy with Stanley Cup championships in 1974 and '75 and four losses in the Cup Finals.

The 1982–83 76ers, coached by former star Billy Cunningham and featuring Julius Erving, Moses Malone, Maurice Cheeks, Andrew Toney and Bobby Jones, gave the Spectrum its greatest basketball memory by posting 65 regular-season victories and a 12–1 playoff run that ended with a Finals sweep of the Lakers. Fittingly, players from that team were the honored guests when the 76ers played their last game there in April 1996.

"This homecourt became a fortress for us," Dr. J told a crowd of 18,168 during halftime ceremonies of the basketball finale. "The other teams felt that we were running downhill and they were running uphill. If the walls could talk, they would have some great stories to tell."

Some of them not so positive. The great 76ers teams of the 1980s were countered by some not-so-great teams of the 1970s and 1990s. The 1972–73 Sixers struggled through a 9–73 season—the worst record in NBA history. The 1995–96 Sixers struggled to an 18–64 mark, the NBA-record sixth consecutive season in which they had lost more games than the previous year. But the Sixers finished with an impressive 745–402 record at the Spectrum.

The multi-purpose building was replaced by the CoreStates Center, a 21,000-seat facility that was built 100 yards to the south.

HOME COOKIN' *The Palace at Auburn Hills played host to consecutive Detroit championships*

OTHER ARENAS

Convention Hall, Philadelphia

Before the Spectrum, there was Convention Hall, home of the former Philadelphia Warriors and the 76ers. The Warriors, who played part of their schedule at the Philadelphia Arena, won the 1956 championship there. But the Hall's most memorable tenant was the 1966–67 76ers, who posted a then-unprecedented 68–13 record and broke Boston's championship stranglehold. That Sixers team, hailed by many as the best in history, featured center Wilt Chamberlain, forwards Billy Cunningham and Chet Walker and guards Hal Greer and Wali Jones. The 76ers, who had already spent 14 NBA seasons in Syracuse—as the Nationals—before moving to Philadelphia, played four years in Convention Hall before moving to the Spectrum.

The Los Angeles Sports Arena

The Sports Arena is the current home of the Clippers and the former home of the Lakers, who played seven seasons there after moving from their 12-season NBA home of Minneapolis in 1960. The Lakers played in four NBA Finals from 1962 to '66 before moving into their new home at the Los Angeles Forum. The Clippers have played there since moving from San Diego in 1984. They have posted only one winning record and qualified for two postseason series as tenants of the building.

Minneapolis Auditorium

Home of the Lakers from 1948 to 1960—when they moved to the West Coast—the 10,000-seat facility provided an intimidating atmosphere for the George Mikan-led champions. The Lakers won five NBA titles as tenants of the venerable building and were nearly invincible there during the Mikan years.

The Summit, Houston

The Rockets posted a 582–278 record over their first 21 seasons in the 16,611-seat facility. They also made four NBA Finals appearances and joined an elite group of teams in 1994 and '95 when they recorded back-to-back NBA championships.

Palace of Auburn Hills, Detroit

This relatively new arena opened in August 1988—just in time to play host for the Pistons' back-to-back NBA championships. The 21,454-seat building replaced the Pontiac Silverdome—home of the NFL's Detroit Lions—where the Pistons had played for 10 NBA seasons.

The Current NBA Arenas

Team	Arena	Capacity	First Game
Atlanta Hawks	The Omni	16,378	1972
Boston Celtics	FleetCenter	18,600	1995
Charlotte Hornets	Charlotte Coliseum	24,042	1988
Chicago Bulls	United Center	21,711	1994
Cleveland Cavaliers	Gund Arena	20,562	1994
Dallas Mavericks	Reunion Arena	17,502	1980
Denver Nuggets	McNichols Sports Arena	17,171	1976
Detroit Pistons	The Palace of Auburn Hills	21,454	1988
Golden State Warriors	Oakland Coliseum Arena	15,025	1966
Houston Rockets	The Summit	16,611	1975
Indiana Pacers	Market Square Arena	16,530	1974
Los Angeles Clippers	Los Angeles Memorial Sports Arena	16,005	1984
Los Angeles Lakers	The Great Western Forum	17,505	1967
Miami Heat	Miami Arena	15,200	1988
Milwaukee Bucks	Bradley Center	18,633	1988
Minnesota Timberwolves	Target Center	19,006	1990
New Jersey Nets	Meadowlands Arena	20,029	1981
New York Knicks	Madison Square Garden	19,763	1968
Orlando Magic	Orlando Arena	16,010	1989
Philadelphia 76ers	CoreStates Center	21,000	1996
Phoenix Suns	America West Arena	19,023	1992
Portland Trail Blazers	The Rose Garden	21,500	1995
Sacramento Kings	ARCO Arena	17,317	1988
San Antonio Spurs	Alamodome	20,662	1993
Seattle SuperSonics	Key Arena	17,100	1995
Toronto Raptors	SkyDome	22,911	1995
Utah Jazz	Delta Center	19,911	1991
Vancouver Grizzlies	General Motors Place	20,004	1995
Washington Bullets	USAir Arena	18,756	1973

A LITTLE BIT OF TEXAS *San Antonio's 20,662-seat Alamodome is located in Mr. Robinson's neighborhood in the upscale NBA*

HOME IN THE DOME *Toronto's spacious SkyDome, the NBA's biggest arena, provides a festive atmosphere for the Raptors, a 1995–96 expansion newcomer*

THE BUSINESS OF THE NBA

Don't blame the Dream Team. The NBA's globalization ball had started dribbling well before the 1992 Olympic Games and it probably would have penetrated the international consciousness without a marketing assist from Michael Jordan, Charles Barkley, Magic Johnson, Larry Bird et al.

But give the Dream Team credit for speeding delivery of the basketball message. With an impact that startled even the public relations-savvy NBA community and its spotlight-conscious top guns, that message was delivered before, during and after the Barcelona Games like a no-look, above-the-rim pass that set up an easy marketing slam.

Never mind the Barcelona score sheets—suffice to say the U.S. romped to eight victories, averaged a winning margin of 44 points per game and captured the gold medal. The Dream Team was more about presence, hype, fan appeal, glamour and mystique. It was the greatest collection of stars ever assembled on one roster in the history of sports and the first international team made up primarily of professional players.

The "professional look" was made possible by a landmark 1989 ruling by the Federation de Basketball International (FIBA), the amateur game's governing body. Before 1989, FIBA had insisted on a strict separation of amateurs and professionals while trying to maintain "the sanctity of the sport." But the 1989 ruling

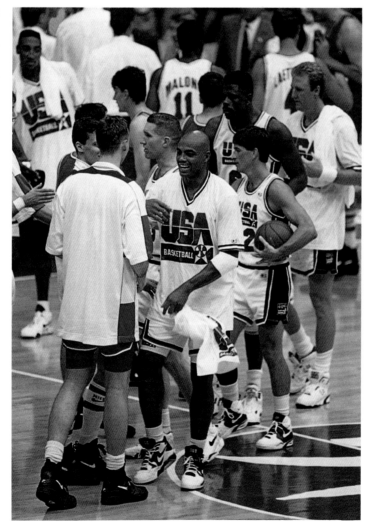

opened the door for professionals to compete internationally, allowed the NBA to join the American federation—USA Basketball— and gave rise to the idea for a team of NBA superstars that could demonstrate basketball played at its highest level.

NBA players embraced the idea and a roster was constructed with Jordan, Bird, Johnson, Barkley, Karl Malone, David Robinson, Patrick Ewing, Scottie Pippen, Clyde Drexler, Chris Mullin, John Stockton and Christian Laettner, the lone representative from the collegiate ranks. The individual players already were international icons whose basketball feats had reached legendary status. Now the world would get to see their artistry, charm and charisma first hand.

And so the plot played out. The world, given the opportunity to see the best basketball had to offer, embraced the Dream Team,

NO SWEAT *Dream Teamers (left) mauled opponents, then shook hands*

MAGIC MOMENT *Johnson (right) and friends brought gold to the U.S.*

INTERNATIONAL FLAVOR *The 1995 McDonald's Championship featured champions from England, Spain and other countries*

oohed and aahed with every Jordan slam and Johnson no-look pass and became mesmerized by the game they were playing. The Dream Team touched off an international uproar on its gold-medal journey. Mobs of delirious fans packed airports, hotel lobbies, streets and other sites the players might appear, hoping to get a glimpse. The team traveled everywhere by motorcade and was smothered by heavy security. Instead of enjoying the pageantry of the Opening Ceremonies, the Dream Teamers spent most of the evening signing autographs for other athletes.

By the time the Dream Team had posted its 117–85 gold medal-securing victory over Croatia, its status was beyond celebrity and the NBA's world had expanded to previously unthinkable horizons. Perhaps the real power of the Dream Team was the grip basketball took on the international community as it moved into a position to challenge soccer (football) as the world's most popular team sport.

The aftermath of the Dream Team's Olympic victory was nothing short of incredible. The NBA was swamped with international requests for exhibition games; foreign television markets wanted NBA games and other NBA-related programming, and NBA merchandise became a big international seller; FIBA asked for the NBA's help in sponsoring grass-roots programs and events to promote the sport internationally; and basketball-hungry fans deluged the league for information and features about its teams, coaches and players. In short, anything associated with the NBA or bearing its logo became a hot ticket.

That Magic Touch

From not to hot, the NBA has become a marketing bonanza with an increasingly blurry line separating its sports and business personalities. When the 1980s dawned, the NBA was a star-depleted, uninteresting entity groping for direction. But after

LONDON CALLING *Dominique Wilkins led the Hawks in a 1993 weekend exhibition series against Orlando in England*

eral—toward global acceptance and recognition.

Youngsters in every corner of the world wanted to "Be Like Mike." They also wanted to soar in their Air Jordans, rebound like Sir Charles and pass like the Magic man. And as its individual players became international figures with spectacular athletic skills and deep pockets, the NBA's prominence began to grow by leaps and bounds.

Jordan at his peak was reported to be pulling in $35 million annually in endorsements alone. Other players such as Barkley, Shaquille O'Neal and Hakeem Olajuwon have ridden the NBA's popularity wave to fame and fortune beyond the basketball court and that's fine with Stern, who knows that player success rubs off on the league he is trying to energize.

Before the 1992 Olympic Games in Barcelona, the NBA's international efforts were handled as part-time projects by a handful of employees. Now the league has regional offices with full-time staffers in Geneva, Hong Kong, Tokyo, Toronto, Sydney, Mexico City, Barcelona and Miami (serving the Latin American countries). One of their primary duties is assisting global sponsors like Coca-Cola, McDonald's, Reebok and Nike in formulating NBA-theme promotions and projects.

But what Jordan and the Dream Team provided more than anything else was a lust for everything that carried an NBA logo, team logos and colors or player likenesses. Since Stern's first year as commissioner, the NBA's gross from the sale of team merchandise has increased from $10 million to about $3 billion.

Nothing, it seems, is sacred. Everything from T-shirts to coffee mugs, from trash cans (with nets) to license plates, from caps to posters bear the NBA touch. Sponsors like Reebok and Nike vie for the licensing rights to the NBA's clothing and apparel business, which has become enormous both in the U.S. and abroad.

the arrival of Larry Bird and Magic Johnson and the 1984 selection of David Stern as the league's fourth commissioner, the league literally vaulted into world prominence.

Stern's first order of business was to market the league's assets and he did so with a vengeance. He began lining up sponsors who accepted his pitch on the marketability of players like Bird, Magic, Kareem Abdul-Jabbar, Dominique Wilkins, Charles

Barkley and, of course, Michael Jordan. With creativity and purpose, the players were promoted, merchandised and packaged into international heroes and Stern used their prominence to propel the NBA—and basketball in gen-

Michael Jordan—a walking, talking business empire

The numbers are only estimates and the economic effects are intangible, but everybody agrees on one thing: Michael Jordan, the Chicago Bulls' high-flying, charismatic scoring machine, is a walking, talking gold mine.

In 1995, Jordan pulled in about $4 million as a basketball player and an estimated $35 million from product endorsements. That put him at the top of the annual "Ten Most Wanted List" compiled by the Sports Marketing Letter, far ahead of second-place Shaquille O 'Neal, the Orlando Magic center who pulled in an estimated $14.5 million from endorsements. The only other NBA star on the list was Houston center Hakeem Olajuwon, who ranked No. 9 at about $3.8 million.

But Jordan's real economic impact transcends his personal bank account. According to Chicago television news accounts after his 1995 return from a year-plus retirement, Jordan is worth as much as $1 billion to the NBA and the local economies of the cities where he plays. Consider these facts and estimates, as cited by various media sources after his comeback:

● When Jordan began practicing with the Bulls near the end of the 1994–95 season, the stock in five companies that had him signed to endorsement contracts (McDonald's, Sara Lee, Quaker Oats, Nike and General Mills) rose, incredibly, by $2.3 billion on Wall Street.

● Chicago's cable station, SportsChannel, broadcast 24 consecutive hours of Jordan programming entitled "Scrapbook of a Champion."

● When Jordan scored 55 points in a game against the New York Knicks at Madison Square Garden—his fifth game back—the effort was viewed by almost 350 reporters from 12 countries. Some New York fans paid scalpers $1,000 for tickets and

TNT drew a cable audience estimated at 12 million.

● NBC, the television network that carried the first game after Jordan's comeback, recorded a 10.9 rating and a 30 share—the most-watched regular-season game in NBA history at the time.

● Some sources claim Jordan generates $16 million per game to the local economy where he plays; $20 million per playoff game.

● The North Carolina plant that is licensed to produce Jordan jerseys added a third shift when he came out of retirement to fulfill 240,000 orders. At Chicago's United Center, fans snapped up almost 2,000 Jordan jerseys in a four-game span—paying $50 for each one.

POWERFUL PRESENCE *When it comes to winning MVP awards and making money, Michael Jordan is all business*

Have Team, Will Travel

Stern's global vision began taking form when he negotiated the long-overdue peace agreement with FIBA. The first cooperative venture was the 1987 McDonald's Open, a three-team tournament in Milwaukee that matched the Soviet National Team, Tracer Milan of Italy and the NBA's Milwaukee Bucks. The 1988 McDonald's Open was held in Madrid and featured four teams—the Boston Celtics, Real Madrid, Scavolini Pesaro of Italy and the Yugoslavian National Team. By 1995, the tournament, now called the McDonald's Championship, featured the two-time NBA-champion Houston Rockets competing against champions from five other world basketball leagues.

And the success of the McDonald's venture spawned the Dream Team and a growing series of NBA preseason exhibition tours. Teams traveled to England, Mexico and Canada in 1995 after trips to France, Spain and Puerto Rico in 1994. In 1990, pre-Dream Team, the Phoenix Suns and Utah Jazz opened regular-season play with two games in Tokyo, Japan.

But the real proof of the NBA's permeating global presence can be found in the league's ever-growing television package. The 1995 NBA Finals were carried by satellite to fans in 164 countries on six continents and coverage was presented in 40 different languages. The 1996 All-Star Game was seen in more than 170 countries and 200 million homes worldwide.

And the league's popularity continues to grow almost daily. Special publications are devoted entirely to the NBA and the league recently became an active member of the Internet's World Wide Web. The league even has its own production house that offers services to Hollywood studios in development of basketball-theme movies. NBA Entertainment, which also is active in NBA-related television programming for children, provides players, uniforms and arenas for filmmakers in addition to developing projects

of its own.

But nothing is more visible than the constant barrage of endorsement ads that promote products and turn NBA stars into entertainment celebrities. The McDonald's Corp. has paired stars like Jordan and Barkley with Warner Brothers cartoon characters like Bugs Bunny, the Tazmanian Devil and the Roadrunner in a creative attention-grabbing campaign of television ads. In another commercial blitz aimed at the youthful audience, the NBA has launched several rounds of "I Love This Stuff" spots featuring young stars like Grant Hill, Jason Kidd and Glenn Robinson.

Among the NBA's current and planned television ventures are a Saturday afternoon sitcom about a high school basketball team called "Hang Time" and an animated series about a fictional group of professionals who travel the galaxy taking on all alien challengers.

Wanna Play Some Ball?

While Stern has turned the NBA into a marketing machine, he also has joined hands with FIBA in the grass-roots expansion of basketball into world markets. The premise is simple: The game is entrancing, it's easy to learn and there's a whole generation of potential new fans just looking for a reason to care.

The NBA is trying to provide that reason through a series of entry-level programs aimed at teaching, promoting and delivering the basketball message to the masses.

The Converse/3-on-3 World Tour, the cornerstone of the grass-roots campaign, was created in 1993 and has met with instant world-wide success. The first tour visited 13 foreign cities and attracted 3-player teams of all ages to compete in a street-side basketball tournament in the downtown area. The event takes on a festival atmosphere and promotes itself by drawing spectators from participants and their friends as well as curious passers-by. The

Surfin' the Net

The NBA's ever-extending tentacles now are reaching through cyberspace, feeding news and information to millions of fans on the Internet's World Wide Web.

The NBA, never missing an opportunity to market its product to the global community, reinforced its already powerful world presence in November 1995, when the league opened its web site at NBA.com and began offering a package of basketball information designed to satiate the appetite of its hungriest fans.

Among the offerings: Home pages (or Home Courts) for all 29 teams with basic information like player biographies, rosters, arena charts and transactions; player features and regular chat

sessions with players, coaches and general managers; photos, video clips and audio clips of great players and plays; All-Star ballots that allow fans around the world to cast votes for their favorite players; and information designed for the international fan who wants to learn more about the game.

Not surprisingly, the NBA site was an immediate winner, generating more than a million file requests over its first weekend and attracting more than 200,000 fans in its first week. Quick contact was made with fans in Mexico, Colombia, Costa Rica, Greece, Indonesia, Korea, Singapore, Taiwan, Brazil, Argentina, Canada, Australia, New Zealand and numerous other countries.

1993 tournament in Paris drew more than 2,000 players and 180,000 spectators jammed the Trocadero plaza to see what all the commotion was about. The 1994 3-on-3 tour visited 25 cities in 11 countries and the 1995 tour expanded even more.

The NBA's Fleer-sponsored Jam Session, a hands-on NBA exhibit that offers activity centers, competition activities, photo opportunities and other multimedia high-tech elements, was introduced at the 1993 All-Star Game in Salt Lake City and has since been staged in Australia, Canada, Japan, Europe and Mexico. The NBA also offers a Stay in School Program targeted for young fans and regularly sends players and coaches on offseason world tours, where they conduct clinics, provide encouragement and generally spread the message of basketball—and the NBA.

The Big-Money Game

Business or pleasure? The answer, of course, is both. The NBA still is about competition and entertainment, but now it has a bottom

line—an impressive and ever-growing bottom line.

Players still soar above the rim, dribble behind their back and drop long-range bombs on opponents. But now they do it while modeling their sponsor-labeled shoes, wristbands and other paraphernalia. Players and coaches sign autographs and appear away from the court in designer clothing. Sponsors are everywhere—signing players to hefty endorsement contracts, buying name association with NBA awards and products, getting involved with special NBA promotions and paying high prices for licensing rights.

It all adds up to big money and big questions that filter through the very fibers of the game. Can sport retain its competitive purity in a big-money atmosphere? Can its players perform with hunger and intensity with long-term, multi-million-dollar contracts and endorsement deals?

The answers are not easy and the money-versus-sport questions are only going to get more complicated. Business or pleasure? Just keep your eye on the bouncing ball.

THE RULES OF BASKETBALL

When Dr. James Naismith drew up a list of 13 rules to govern his new game of "basket ball" in 1891, he provided the framework for an athletic phenomenon that would explode into worldwide prominence. Not only was the good professor uncanny in his assessment of the American sports psyche, he also was visionary in the fundamental guidelines that would survive the test of time.

Dr. Naismith simply provided the game's concepts and tools, letting the natural evolutionary process take care of details. It's fascinating, more than a century later, to examine Naismith's basic premises: a (peach) basket positioned at each end of a gymnasium, attached to a balcony 10 feet above the playing surface; players from competing teams trying to throw a round soccer ball into their respective baskets; a passing game (no running or moving with the ball) that promoted teamwork; limited contact between opposing players with "fouls" and penalties discouraging transgressions; a referee to call violations and fouls; two 15-minute halves, with a five-minute rest between.

Sound familiar? The rules have been fine-tuned, the players have become increasingly athletic and the game has risen from the floor to the stratosphere, but the basic tenets have remained remarkably entrenched. So entrenched that if Dr. Naismith could see a 1990s-style basketball game, he still would

recognize the 1890s-era sport he invented—with some degree of open-mouthed amazement.

While the college and professional games have followed slightly different evolutionary trails, the basic focus of one has never strayed far from the other. Today's college and pro games differ only in customized playing rules, not in fundamentals, equipment or concepts. The basics are simple:

● The baskets, still 10-feet high, no longer are baskets. They are steel rims, attached to a rectangular backboard, with a net that hangs down and makes it easy to tell if a shot passes through. A field goal counts two points, a free throw (a 15-foot shot given to a player who has been fouled) counts one and a long field goal (23-feet, 9-inches from the top of the key in the NBA; 19-feet, 9-inches in college) counts three. The team that scores the most points in the specified time wins.

● The professional game is played in four 12-minute quarters with a

15-minute halftime. The college game is played in 20-minute halves. Any game that is tied after regulation is decided by one or more 5-minute overtime periods.

● The professional and college courts are a regulation 94 feet in length and 50 feet in width. After experimenting in the early years

SHOT-BLOCKER *Dikembo Mutombo*

with court size and number of players, it was determined that five players to a team provided a comfortable fit with optimal strategic potential. Today's rules allow free substitution and professional rosters are allowed to contain 12 players.

The following sections will describe and analyze the positions, mechanics and strategies of basketball—professional and college.

The Positions

Most teams employ a lineup consisting of two guards, two forwards and a center. The non-center positions are broken down as point guard and shooting guard, small forward and power forward.

Because the center usually is the tallest player on the team, he mans the middle on both offense and defense and scores most of his points close to the basket. He can be a big scorer, but his most important functions are grabbing rebounds, defending the basket and discouraging would-be lane

INSTANT OFFENSE *Steve Kerr (25) comes off Chicago's bench as one of the NBA's top 3-point threats*

penetrators with his shot-blocking skills. The best NBA centers are intimidating: Wilt Chamberlain, Bill Russell and Kareem Abdul-Jabbar from the past; David Robinson, Shaquille O'Neal, Hakeem Olajuwon and Alonzo Mourning in today's NBA.

The guards provide ballhandling and structure for the offense. The point guard primarily is a playmaker who handles the ball with error-free consistency and runs the offense. The shooting guard is more offensive, especially from long range. John Stockton is the NBA's premier point man; Michael Jordan and Clyde Drexler are classic shooting guards.

The forwards perform a variety of frontcourt duties. The power forward, big and physical, will spend much of the game close to the basket, battling for rebounds and defending key big men. The small forward is a shooter or slasher who usually can post big scoring numbers. He is not necessarily small, but he is usually mobile with outstanding athleticism. Former NBA greats Elgin Baylor and Adrian Dantley were small forwards. Utah's Karl Malone is one of today's best power forwards.

The Shot

Of all the game's mechanics, the methods for delivering ball to basket have evolved most dramatically. For years, basketball was played with feet glued firmly to the ground and those who showed upward mobility were chastised as showboats. Layups and hook shots were the primary scoring methods inside; two-handed set shots were the long-range weapon.

That all changed in the mid 1930s when Stanford University star Hank Luisetti introduced a one-hand shot that he got off with shocking quickness and accuracy. Other players were quick to copy and Luisetti's innovation evolved into the running one-hander, the jump shot (delivered with a flick of the wrist, hands extending ball above the head at the top of a jump) and a variety of moving

MAGIC SHOTMAKER *Anfernee Hardaway always knows his way to the basket*

jumpers from unusual angles, complete with mid-air adjustments and hang time.

As players grew taller and more athletic, the dunk shot became a powerful weapon. Players would simply leap high enough to slam the ball through the hoop—a high-percentage shot that pleases coaches and excites fans.

Today's creative players are masterful at finding new ways of getting the ball into the basket. And high-flying stars such as Anfernee Hardaway, Grant Hill and Michael Jordan are constantly updating their arsenals with never-before-seen maneuvers that sometimes defy imagination.

The Dribble

This may be the least appreciated of the basketball player's tools. And its evolution was probably more painful than that of any other rule.

Early players were not permitted to dribble the ball—it was strictly a passing game. And the early ball, a crude leather cover over an inflatable bladder with an inflation tube sticking out, did not permit dribbling control anyway.

At various times and depending on whether you were watching the college or professional game, players were allowed one bounce;

one bounce with no shot; two-handed, starting and stopping dribbles, and multiple dribbles with no progress toward the basket. The rule was not refined until the late 1930s, when the modern molded ball (without protruding stem) was introduced. Since then, the dribble has become more than a tool—it's a weapon that can break down defenses.

Nobody demonstrated that weapon better than former Boston Celtics guard Bob Cousy, who dribbled the ball with amazing control, took it behind his back in traffic and either shot or passed without breaking stride. Today's NBA players, most of whom have grown up with a basketball in their hands, are proficient off the dribble—shooting, passing or leaping for a dunk. They go behind the back or between the legs with little thought and don't hesitate to put the ball on the floor in traffic.

Today's dribble rules are simple: one hand, no stopping and re-starting. The bouncing ball can be switched from one hand to the other without breaking dribble, but a player is never allowed to dribble with both hands. Once a player stops his dribble, he must either pass or shoot. Palming (bringing hand under ball in a semi-circular motion) is not allowed.

The NBA's best dribblers normally will be found at the point guard position.

The Rebound

While scorers win fan affection, rebounders win and lose games. The concept is simple: Rebounders position themselves near the basket and fight for missed shots. It's physical, it's intense and it's survival of the fittest.

Rebounding on the defensive end of the court favors the defender, who has natural position between his man and the

basket and needs only to block out for basket control. Offensive rebounding is more difficult for opposite reasons. Because the defender has superior position, it is necessary for the offensive player to fight his way around blocks and through traffic. Offensive rebounding often is a

matter of intensity—wanting the ball more than an opponent—and it pays off with put-back chances and a lot of easy points.

Teams that win the rebounding wars often can win games even when they don't shoot well. Good teams usually will dominate the boards.

MASTER AT WORK
In the great tradition of Bob Cousy, Portland's Kenny Anderson is one of the game's most proficient ballhandlers and creative passers

BEWARE OF THE SHAQ *The area close to the basket belongs to intimidating center Shaquille O'Neal*

The Pass

Dr. Naismith wanted teamwork to be the strategic focus of his new game and his vision was fulfilled. NBA championships are won by teams built around unselfish players, and the heart and soul of every offense is crisp passing.

There's nothing complicated about the concept. The player with the ball looks for an open man and "passes" to him, hopefully advancing his team's strategic position. Good NBA offenses are built around quick passing by players who are constantly moving and setting screens to help each other get away from defenders.

There are four basic passes. The bounce pass limits the reach of defenders who cannot bend quickly enough to pick it off. Bounce passes are most effective in heavy traffic. The chest pass is delivered on a line to a man in an open area. The baseball pass is thrown long distance on a line, usually to someone on a fast break. And the lob pass is a high-arcing toss, usually over a defender to a center with his back to the basket.

There are variations. A lob pass can go deep over two or three defenders. Or it can be thrown as an "alley-oop" to a player who times his jump, catches the ball above the rim and slams it through the basket before returning to the floor.

The modern players will use creative behind-the-back and no-look passes to confound defenders, primarily on the fast break. Among the modern-day passing fancies are Isiah Thomas, John Stockton and Magic Johnson.

The Free Throw

The free throw is a penalty assessed by the referee against those players who become too physical and use excessive contact, either accidentally or intentionally, to gain advantage over an opponent. The "free" or uncontested shot is taken by the "fouled" player from behind a line 15 feet from the basket.

Free throws are awarded in

FREE ADVICE

Any team that hopes to beat the Indiana Pacers must keep sharp-shooting Reggie Miller off the free-throw line.

different ways. When a player makes illegal contact against a player in the act of shooting, two free throws are awarded if the shot does not go through the basket. If the player's shot does go in, the team is awarded the 2 points and the player gets one free throw. Players fouled in the act of shooting from 3-point range are awarded three free throws. Fouls committed against a player not in the act of shooting will result in an out-of-bounds throw in or free throws, depending on the number of fouls the team already has committed.

Free-throw shooting has evolved into an important element of the game. Teams that make a high percentage of free throws can score a lot of uncontested points and thus increase their chances for victory. Teams that miss a lot of free throws can lose games they probably should win. The most successful free-throw shooters (former players like Rick Barry and Larry Bird; such current stars as Reggie Miller and Mark Price) will make about 90 percent (9 of every 10) of their free throws. Poor free-throw shooters (for instance, Wilt Chamberlain and Shaquille O'Neal) might be in the 50 percent (5 of every 10) range.

Teams build game plans around free-throw shooting. It makes sense to force O'Neal to score his points from the line rather than get easy 2-point shots under the basket. Conversely, it's better to keep teams that make 75 percent of their free throws away from the line.

Free throws have always been an important part of basketball's end game. Teams trailing by two or three points in the final minute will commit fouls with the hope that the opposition will miss important free throws and give them a chance to catch up with 2 or 3-point baskets. Teams that cannot make their free throws have been known to lose good leads going into the final minutes of games because of it.

BULL'S EYE *Rebounding is intensity, and Dennis Rodman has plenty of that*

Defense

In simplest terms, defense means guarding your basket against opponents intent on scoring points. Those teams that limit scoring opportunities greatly increase their chance of winning.

College teams play two kinds of defense: the man-to-man, in which each player guards an opponent face to face, and the zone, in which players guard assigned areas of the court. Zones are outlawed in the NBA, a move that promotes more one-on-one moves and inside play.

While the basic principles of good defense are obvious—move your feet, keep your body between your man and the basket, force him to attempt difficult shots, deny him the ball, take away passing lanes, don't foul—the intricacies of the man-to-man are more complicated. Forty-eight minutes of fighting through screens, diving for loose balls, expending energy chasing a quick opponent and banging bodies for position can take its toll. While basketball might be a non-contact sport in theory, it's a brutal physical game in practice.

Winning teams usually are the ones that protect the ball on offense and force turnovers and other mental mistakes on defense.

The following definitions provide an insight into the rules and strategies that govern the game of basketball:

Assist: A player is credited with an "assist" when his pass leads directly to a basket by a teammate.

Backcourt: The court is divided in half by a center line. The backcourt area is where the opponent's basket is located when a team is on offense. If a team can't advance the ball out of its backcourt within 10 seconds after a throw-in, a violation is called and the ball goes to the opponent. Once across the center line, the offensive team cannot return to the backcourt area on that possession. "Backcourt" also can refer to a team's guard tandem.

Charge: A foul called against an offensive player for "charging" into a stationary defender who has established position.

Fast Break: A scoring strategy by a team that pushes the ball upcourt quickly before the defensive team can get set. A good fast break gives the offensive team an advantage in numbers.

Foul Lane: The area under the basket and extending from the base line to the free throw line. It is 16 feet wide and always painted a different color for contrast. An offensive player is allowed only 3 consecutive seconds in the lane on any possession—a rule designed to keep big men from camping under the basket.

Frontcourt: The area of the court where an offensive team's basket is located. A team has 10 seconds to advance the ball into its frontcourt after a backcourt throw in. "Frontcourt" also can refer to a team's front line—two forwards and a center.

Held Ball: When two players gain possession of the ball at the same time, the referee calls a held ball and possession is determined by a jump ball.

Jump Ball: Every game begins with a center jump—the two tallest players from each team contesting a

Naismith's Original 13 Rules of "Basket Ball"

The following rules, drafted by Dr. James Naismith for his new game of basket ball, were first published in January 1892 in *The Triangle*—the Springfield College newspaper.

1. The ball may be thrown in any direction with one or both hands.

2. The ball may be batted in any direction with one or both hands, never with the fist.

3. A player cannot run with the ball; the player must throw it from the spot where he catches it, allowance being made for a man who catches the ball when running at a good speed.

4. The ball must be held in or between the hands; the arms or body must not be used for holding it.

5. No shouldering, holding, pushing, tripping or striking in any way the person of an opponent is to be allowed. The first infringement of this rule by any person shall count as a foul; the second shall disqualify him until the next goal is made, or if there was evident intent to injure the person, for the whole game; no substitute allowed.

6. A foul is striking the ball with the fist, violation of Rules 3 and 4, and such as described in Rule 5.

7. If either side makes three consecutive fouls it shall count for a goal for the opponents. (Consecutive means without the opponents making a foul.)

8. A goal shall be made when the ball is thrown or batted from the grounds into the basket and stays there, providing those defending the goal do not touch or disturb the goal. If the ball rests on the edge and the opponent moves the basket, it shall count as a goal.

9. When the ball goes out of bounds it shall be thrown into the field, and played by the person first touching it. In case of a dispute, the Umpire shall throw it straight into the field. The thrower is allowed five seconds; if he holds it longer, it shall go to the opponent. If any side persists in delaying the game, the Umpire shall call a foul on them.

10. The Umpire shall be the judge of the men, and shall note the fouls, and notify the Referee when three consecutive fouls have been made. He shall have power to disqualify men according to Rule 5.

11. The Referee shall be judge of the ball, and shall decide when the ball is in play, in bounds, and to which side it belongs, and shall keep time. He shall decide when a goal has been made, and keep account of the goals, with any other duties that are usually performed by a Referee.

12. The time shall be two 15-minute halves, five minutes between.

13. The side making the most goals shall be the winner. In case of a draw, the game may, by agreement of captains, be continued until another goal is made.

ball tossed into the air between them by a referee. The players try to tap the ball to a teammate positioned around the center-court circle. Jump balls also occur when the referee calls a held ball, at the beginning of overtime, after a double foul, after a double free throw violation (players stepping into the foul lane before the ball is released), after an inadvertent whistle and other unusual instances specified in the NBA rules book.

Pivot Foot: When a player has possession of the ball but is not dribbling, passing or shooting, he must maintain contact with one foot on the floor. He can step with the opposite foot while "pivoting" around in a circular fashion to

keep the ball away from defenders.

Referees: Each game is governed by a crew chief, a referee and an umpire. They call fouls, maintain order and make sure the games run smoothly and fairly.

Screen: The act of one player blocking the path of a defensive player so his teammate can get open to receive a pass. The screen, also called a pick, is legal as long as the screening player is stationary on contact.

Shot Clock: In the NBA, when a team gains possession, it has 24 seconds to get off a shot that touches the rim or goes into the basket. Failure to beat the clock

results in a turnover. College clocks are set at 35 seconds.

Timeouts: Each NBA team can call seven regular timeouts and two 20-second timeouts during a regulation game. Timeouts are used to plan strategy, to regroup or to stop another team's momentum.

Turnover: A misplay by the offensive team that results in change of possession.

Walking: If a player takes excessive steps without dribbling or shuffles his pivot foot without passing or shooting, a violation is called and the other team gains possession. This violation also is called traveling.

EQUIPMENT

It's simple.

Basketball, for all of its complex strategies and nuances at the high school, college and professional levels, is a simple game with simple rules and simple equipment needs. A goal or basket, a ball and a pair of sneakers will get any aspiring player all the air time he can handle. Unlike football and hockey, sports that require more costly equipment, basketball has challenged baseball as the sport of the masses.

At the organized level, the game is played on a precisely defined wood-surfaced court with a molded ball that bounces true and never loses shape like its early century predecessor. The orange-rimmed basket cylinder with lace net is supported by a rectangular backboard, and uniforms consist of numbered jersey tops and short pants, varying only in style from generation to generation. Sneakers have evolved from the plain high-top tennis shoes of yesteryear to the sophisticated "Air" this and "Air" that athletic footwear we know today. Just lace up the shoes, follow the bouncing ball—and shoot.

It's simple.

(ABOVE) READY, SET, JUMP

Until 1937, many games were decided in the center-jump area, which served as the starting point of every game and the re-starting point after every made basket. Not surprisingly, teams with a tall center thrived. Today's center-jump area is artistic, if not a strategic factor, although 7-footers like Houston's Hakeem Olajuwon (left) and Orlando's Shaquille O'Neal do make appearances there.

(LEFT) A BASKET CASE

From the boxes and peach baskets of Dr. James Naismith's early game, the goal has evolved into a round metal rim, painted orange to aid shooter efficiency. At one point in the game's development, iron hoops with closed bottoms were used, necessitating retrieval of every made field goal. Today's hoops support a funnel shaped nylon net that hangs down about 18 inches and checks the ball as it goes through, making it easy to see that a goal has been scored.

(ABOVE) OH, SHOOT!
An overhead view shows Phoenix star Charles Barkley shooting a free throw on one of the multi-colored NBA courts of the 1990s.

(LEFT) THE BOUNCING BALL
Today's basketball, a perfectly round, precisely inflated work of art, is the ancestor of the early leather ball with rubber bladder and protruding inflation tube. The early ball was hard to dribble and lost its shape after extended use. Its tube created awkward bounces. Today's durable ball is molded with an inset tube, a worthy successor to the stitched balls of the pre-1940s college and professional games. The ball, like the rim, usually has an orange coloring.

(ABOVE) UP AND OVER
The 10-foot basket height has withstood the test of time, if not the athletic advancements of modern players who perform their artistry above the rim. But the backboard has undergone a steady stream of changes. The first backboards were strips of screen that kept over-enthusiastic spectators from interfering with shots. The screens were followed by wooden, rectangular and fan-shaped backboards and today's glass, rectangular boards. A rectangle painted above the rim still provides a target for bank shots.

AWESOME SNEAKERS AND WICKED SHORTS

During its incredible leap from secondary status to major phenomenon, the NBA became computer literate, a world traveler and a fashion trendsetter. A whole new generation of young basketball fans, from the streets of London, Paris and Rome to the inner cities and suburbs of New York, Los Angeles and Chicago, not only wanted to play basketball like Mike, they wanted to dress like him, too.

As the NBA went baggy in the early 1990s, so did the youth of America and beyond. The league displayed its vast marketing muscle by changing the course of casual sportswear. And as the opportunistic fashion designers rushed to meet demands for baggy shorts, pants and T-shirts, the tennis shoe, once an unnoticed tool of the basketball trade, became even more of a fashion statement with competing brand names, endorsed by star players, defining status and prestige.

The much-quoted adage that clothes make the man certainly applies to today's NBA liberated athlete.

DRESSED TO KILL

Something old and something new. In the case of basketball uniforms, it's easy to tell the difference. The Original Celtics of 1923 (left to right: Johnny Beckman, Johnny Witte, Nat Holman, Pete Barry and Chris Leonard) were natty in their tight-fitting jerseys, shorts, kneepads, long socks and high-top shoes. But today's players are hip, literally swimming in their baggy shorts and loose-fitting jerseys and brimming in their designer shoes. Not only are Chicago's Michael Jordan (23) and Milwaukee's Glenn Robinson (13) outstanding players, they're also walking, talking fashion statements.

SHOE-INS

Whether you're talking about the size 22s of Lakers center Shaquille O'Neal or the more moderate-sized, state-of-the-art footwear sported by other NBA stars, one thing's for sure: There's plenty of "Air" for everyone. As Nike fights its battle against commercial rival Reebok and both shoe manufacturers hear the footsteps of other would-be sneaker czars, shoe designers continue to add performance-enhancing features to their products. The "Air More Uptempo" models (above) are described by Nike as having maximum basketball impact protection, full-grain leather and the most Air cushioning in the history of the game.

BASKETBALL UNITES AMERICA

From the playgrounds of the inner city to the glitzy arenas of the NBA, basketball fever has reached epidemic proportions. Drive anywhere, through any neighborhood in any section of any city in the United States and you see its effects. Basketball goals—everywhere. Worn-out, netless rims protruding from a single post cemented into a blacktop surface; NBA-regulation backboards bolted on to garages with driveway surfaces; adjustable and movable poles with rims to accommodate players of all ages and sizes; baskets hanging from trees, buildings, utility poles, fences and every other backstop imaginable. And, of course, the players—children, teenagers and adults competing in three and four-man games, or individuals simply honing their shooting skills, alone, without an audience or anyone to impress but themselves.

(LEFT) TIME OUT

The game must go on. At the Maricopa County Jail in Phoenix, basketball hoops offer a chance for exercise and a needed diversion from the gloom and darkness of life behind bars.

(ABOVE) LOFTY GOALS

Wanna play some ball? This Los Angeles high school playground can accommodate everybody who wants to play—and then some. If basketball is indeed the game for the masses, then this is the place to be.

(BELOW) GARAGE BALL

No self-respecting American garage is complete without a basketball goal hanging over the driveway. Likewise, no driveway basket is complete without a would-be NBA star, young or old, to take his best shot at fame and glory.

(ABOVE) RESERVATION NEEDED

Basketball is not a city phenomenon. It also has found its way to rural America and even some of the more isolated areas of the country. The weather-beaten, pole-supported basket and abandoned ball are signs of the time on the Salt River Indian Reservation in Arizona.

(BELOW) PLAYGROUND BALL

The New York playgrounds are famous for the quality of basketball they inspire, and the hope for life away from the mean streets of the inner city. Playground baskets often are the hub of activity for neighborhoods with few other recreational options.

(ABOVE) BEACH BALL

Palm trees form a scenic background for a street game at Venice Beach, Calif. No matter where young players get together for a little friendly competition, the result is always the same: good health, good friends and lots of fun.

THE HALL OF FAME

The Naismith Memorial Hall of Fame has evolved, much like the sport it honors, in the city where the first ball was tossed into a peach basket more than a century ago. The idea for a basketball memorial took root in the 1940s, spread slowly with nourishment from dedicated coaches and officials and eventually blossomed into a state-of-the-art, high-tech, crowd-pleasing testimonial to the elegant athletes, past and present, who perform for the modern fan.

From Dr. James Naismith's 1891 invention of basketball to his death in 1939, he could never have imagined a game that has soared into the stratosphere of worldwide popularity, much less the Springfield, Mass., shrine that bears his name and helps visitors form a lasting bond with its greatest players and most memorable moments.

The first Hall of Fame class was elected in 1959, and the first Hall of Fame museum was dedicated February 18, 1968—an unpretentious two-story, red-brick building on the Springfield College campus. That humble abode stood in stark contrast to the expanded $11.5 million, three-story, 54,000-square-foot structure that replaced it in 1985, sitting majestically off Interstate 91, on the banks of the Connecticut River near downtown Springfield.

Where Legends Live Forever

The Hall of Fame visitor gets a large dose of basketball history and nostalgia, but the primary attractions are interactive videos, shooting and jumping arcades and three movie theaters that highlight such memorable moments as NBA All-Star Weekends, NBA Finals, NCAA Final Fours and Olympic Games. The museum is a wide-ranging tribute to the game on every level—men and women, professional and amateur, American and foreign—and more than 150,000 visitors pass through its turnstiles annually.

The first class of 18 inductees featured Naismith, George Mikan and two teams—Naismith's "first" 1891 team and the Original Celtics of the 1920s and '30s. By the 1968 building dedication, the Hall already had a 66-member roster that has since grown to 217 men and women and four teams.

Anybody is eligible, but potential inductees have to be nominated on special ballots, pass through a screening committee and receive 18 votes from the 24-member Honors Committee. Players and referees are eligible five years after retirement; coaches become eligible after 25 years in the game, or five years of retirement; and contributors can be elected any time after retirement. Induction ceremonies are held every May.

The following Hall of Fame players, coaches and contributors have been associated with the NBA.

Hall of Fame Enshrinees
NBA-Associated Personnel

Kareem Abdul-Jabbar: 7–2, 267-pound center. Born April 16, 1947, at New York. Attended UCLA. Played 20 seasons with Bucks, Lakers. Member of Bucks' 1971 and Lakers' 1980, 1982, 1985, 1987, 1988 championship teams. Scoring champion 1971 (31.7), 1972 (34.8). Rebounding champion 1976 (16.9). Rookie of the Year 1970. Regular-season MVP 1971, 1972, 1974, 1976, 1977, 1980. NBA Finals MVP 1971, 1985. Career totals: 38,387 points, 17,440 rebounds, 5,660 assists. Member of 35th Anniversary All-Time Team. Elected 1995.

Nate (Tiny) Archibald: 6–1, 160-pound point guard. Born September 2, 1948, at New York. Attended Arizona Western, Texas-El Paso. Played 13 seasons with Royals/Kings, Nets, Celtics, Bucks. Member of Celtics' 1981 championship team. Scoring champion 1973 (34.0). Assist champion 1973 (11.4). All-Star Game MVP 1981. Career totals: 16,481 points, 6,476 assists. Elected 1991.

Paul Arizin: 6–4, 200-pound guard/forward. Born April 9, 1928, at Philadelphia. Attended Villanova. Played 10 seasons with Warriors. Member of Warriors' 1956 championship team. Scoring champion 1952 (25.4), 1957 (25.6). All-Star Game MVP 1952. Career totals: 16,266 points, 6,129 rebounds. Member of the 25th Anniversary All-Time Team. Elected 1977.

Rick Barry: 6–7, 220-pound forward. Born March 28, 1944, at Elizabeth, N.J. Attended Miami (Fla.). Played 14 seasons with Warriors, Oaks/Capitols/Squires (ABA), Nets (ABA), Rockets. Member of Oaks' 1969 and Warriors' 1975 championship teams. Scoring champion 1967 (35.6), 1969 (34.0, ABA). Rookie of the Year 1966. NBA Finals MVP 1975. All-Star Game MVP 1967. Career totals ABA/NBA:

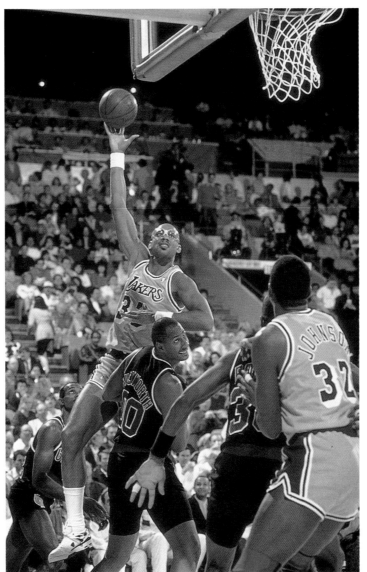

UP AND OVER *The sky hook carried Kareem Abdul-Jabbar to six MVP awards*

25,279 points, 6,863 rebounds, 4,952 assists. Elected 1987.

Elgin Baylor: 6–5, 225-pound forward. Born September 16, 1934, at Washington, D.C. Attended College of Idaho, Seattle. Played 14 seasons with Lakers. Rookie of the Year 1959. All-Star Game co-MVP 1959. Career totals: 23,149 points, 11,463 rebounds, 3,650 assists. Member of the 35th Anniversary All-Time Team. Coached 4 NBA seasons (86–135). Elected 1976.

Walt Bellamy: 6–11, 245-pound center. Born July 24, 1939, at New Bern, N.C. Attended Indiana. Played 14 seasons with Packers/Zephyrs/Bullets, Knicks,

Pistons, Hawks, Jazz. Rookie of the Year 1962. Career totals: 20,941 points, 14,241 rebounds. Elected 1993.

Dave Bing: 6–3, 185-pound guard. Born November 24, 1943, at Washington, D.C. Attended Syracuse. Played 12 seasons with Pistons, Bullets, Celtics. Scoring champion 1968 (27.1). Rookie of the Year 1967. All-Star Game MVP 1976. Career totals: 18,327 points, 5,397 assists. Elected 1990.

Bill Bradley: 6–5, 205-pound forward. Born July 28, 1943, at Crystal City, Mo. Attended Princeton. Played 10 seasons with Knicks. Member of Knicks' 1970, 1973 championship teams. Career

totals: 9,217 points, 2,533 assists. Elected 1982.

Al (Digger) Cervi: 5–11, 185-pound guard. Born February 12, 1917, at Buffalo, N.Y. Played 5 NBL seasons with Buffalo, Rochester, Syracuse; 4 NBA seasons with Nationals. Career NBA totals: 1,591 points. Coached 9 NBA seasons (326–241). Elected 1984.

Wilt (the Stilt) Chamberlain: 7–1, 275-pound center. Born August 21, 1936, at Philadelphia. Attended Kansas. Played 14 seasons with Warriors, 76ers, Lakers. Member of 76ers' 1967 and Lakers' 1972 championship teams. Scoring champion 1960 (37.6), 1961 (38.4), 1962 (50.4), 1963 (44.8), 1964 (36.9), 1965 (34.7), 1966 (33.5). Rebounding champion 1960 (27.0), 1961 (27.2), 1962 (25.7), 1963 (24.3), 1966 (24.6), 1967 (24.2), 1968 (23.8), 1969 (21.1), 1971 (18.2), 1972 (19.2), 1973 (18.6). Rookie of the Year 1960. Regular-season MVP 1960, 1966, 1967, 1968. NBA Finals MVP 1972. All-Star Game MVP 1960. Career totals: 31,419 points, 23,924 rebounds, 4,643 assists. Member of 35th Anniversary All-Time Team. Elected 1978.

Bob Cousy: 6–1, 175-pound point guard. Born August 9, 1928, at New York. Attended Holy Cross. Played 14 seasons with Celtics, Royals. Member of Celtics' 1957, 1959, 1960, 1961, 1962, 1963 championship teams. Assist champion 1953 (7.7), 1954 (7.2), 1955 (7.8), 1956 (8.9), 1957 (7.5), 1958 (7.1), 1959 (8.6), 1960 (9.5). Regular-season MVP 1957. All-Star Game MVP 1954, 1957. Career totals: 16,960 points, 4,786 rebounds, 6,955 assists. Member of 25th and 35th Anniversary All-Time Teams. Coached 5 NBA seasons (141–209). Elected 1970.

Dave Cowens: 6–9, 230-pound center. Born October 25, 1948, at Newport, Ky. Attended Florida State. Played 11 seasons with Celtics, Bucks. Member of Celtics' 1974, 1976 championship teams.

Co-Rookie of the Year 1971. Regular-season MVP 1973. All-Star Game MVP 1973. Career totals: 13,516 points, 10,444 rebounds. Coached 1 NBA season (27–41). Elected 1991.

Billy Cunningham: 6–7, 210-pound forward. Born June 3, 1943, at Brooklyn, N.Y. Attended North Carolina. Played 11 seasons with 76ers, Cougars (ABA). Member of 76ers' 1967 championship team. Regular-season MVP 1973 (ABA). Career totals ABA/NBA: 16,310 points, 7,981 rebounds, 3,305 assists. Coached 8 NBA seasons (454–196). Elected 1986.

Bob Davies: 6–1, 175-pound guard. Born January 15, 1920, at Harrisburg, Pa. Attended Franklin & Marshall, Seton Hall. Played 3 NBL seasons with Rochester; 7 BAA/NBA seasons with Royals. Member of Royals' 1951 championship team. Assist champion 1949 (5.4). Career NBA totals:

6,594 points. Member of 25th Anniversary All-Time Team. Elected 1969.

Dave DeBusschere: 6–6, 235-pound forward. Born October 16, 1940, at Detroit. Attended Detroit. Played 12 seasons with Pistons, Knicks. Member of Knicks' 1970, 1973 championship teams. Career totals: 14,053 points, 9,618 rebounds. Coached 3 NBA seasons (79–143). Elected 1982.

Julius (Dr. J) Erving: 6–7, 210-pound forward. Born February 22, 1950, at Roosevelt, N.Y. Attended Massachusetts. Played 16 seasons with Squires (ABA), Nets (ABA), 76ers. Member of Nets' 1974 (ABA), 1976 (ABA) and 76ers' 1983 championship teams. Scoring champion 1973 (31.9, ABA), 1974 (27.4, ABA), 1976 (29.3, ABA). Regular-season MVP 1974 (ABA), 1975 (ABA), 1976 (ABA), 1981. Playoff MVP

1974 (ABA), 1976 (ABA). All-Star Game MVP 1977, 1983. Career totals ABA/NBA: 30,026 points, 10,525 rebounds, 5,176 assists. Elected 1993.

Walt (Clyde) Frazier: 6–4, 205-pound point guard. Born March 29, 1945, at Atlanta, Ga. Attended Southern Illinois. Played 13 seasons with Knicks, Cavaliers. Member of Knicks' 1970, 1973 championship teams. All-Star Game MVP 1975. Career totals: 15,581 points, 4,830 rebounds, 5,040 assists. Elected 1987.

Joe Fulks: 6–5, 190-pound forward/center. Born October 26, 1921, at Birmingham, Ky. Attended Murray State. Played 8 seasons with Warriors. Member of Warriors' 1947 championship team. Scoring champion 1947 (23.2), 1948 (22.1). Career totals: 8,003 points. Member of 25th Anniversary All-Time Team. Elected 1977.

Harry Gallatin: 6–6, 215-pound forward/center. Born April 26, 1927, at Roxana, Ill. Attended Northeast Missouri State. Played 10 seasons with Knicks, Pistons. Rebounding champion 1954 (15.3). Career totals: 8,843 points. Coached 4 NBA seasons (136–120). Elected 1991.

George Gervin: 6–7, 185-pound guard. Born April 27, 1952, at Detroit. Attended Long Beach State, Eastern Michigan. Played 14 seasons for Virginia Squires (ABA), Spurs (ABA, NBA), Bulls. Scoring champion 1978 (27.2), 1979 (29.6), 1980 (33.1), 1982 (32.3). All-Star Game MVP 1980. Career totals ABA/NBA: 26,595 points, 5,602 rebounds, 2,798 assists. Elected 1996.

Tom Gola: 6–6, 205-pound guard/forward. Born January 13, 1933, at Philadelphia. Attended La Salle. Played 10 seasons with Warriors, Knicks. Member of Warriors' 1956 championship team. Career totals: 7,871 points, 5,605 rebounds. Elected 1975.

Gail Goodrich: 6–1, 175-pound guard. Born April 23, 1943, at Los Angeles. Attended UCLA. Played 14 seasons for Lakers, Suns, Jazz. Member of Lakers' 1972 championship team. Career totals: 19,181 points, 4,805 assists. Elected 1996.

Hal Greer: 6–2, 175-pound guard. Born June 26, 1936, at Huntington, W. Va. Attended Marshall. Played 15 seasons with Nationals/76ers. Member of 76ers' 1967 championship team. All-Star Game MVP 1968. Career totals: 21,586 points, 5,665 rebounds, 4,540 assists. Elected 1981.

Cliff Hagan: 6–4, 215-pound forward. Born December 9, 1931, at Owensboro, Ky. Attended Kentucky. Played 13 seasons with Hawks, Chaparrals (ABA). Member of Hawks' 1958 championship team. Career totals ABA/NBA: 14,870 points, 5,555 rebounds. Elected 1977.

John (Hondo) Havlicek: 6–5, 205-pound guard/forward. Born April 8, 1940, at Martins Ferry, O. Attended Ohio State. Played 16 seasons with Celtics. Member of Celtics' 1963, 1964, 1965, 1966, 1968, 1969, 1974, 1976 championship teams. NBA Finals MVP 1974. Career totals: 26,395 points, 8,007 rebounds, 6,114 assists. Member of 35th Anniversary All-Time Team. Elected 1983.

Connie Hawkins: 6–8, 215-pound forward/center. Born July 17, 1942, at Brooklyn, N.Y. Attended Iowa. Played 9 seasons with Pipers (ABA), Suns, Lakers, Hawks. Member of Pipers' 1968 championship team. Scoring champion 1968 (26.8, ABA). Regular-season MVP 1968 (ABA). Career totals ABA/NBA: 11,528 points, 5,450 rebounds, 2,556 assists. Elected 1992.

Elvin Hayes: 6–9, 235-pound forward/center. Born November 17, 1945, at Rayville, La. Attended Houston. Played 16 seasons with Rockets, Bullets. Member of Bullets' 1978 championship team.

FAST FORWARD *Undersized Boston forward Dave Cowens was big in the clutch*

Scoring champion 1969 (28.4). Rebounding champion 1970 (16.9), 1974 (18.1). Career totals: 27,313 points, 16,279 rebounds. Elected 1990.

Tom Heinsohn: 6–7, 218-pound forward. Born August 26, 1934, at Jersey City, N.J. Attended Holy Cross. Played 9 seasons with Celtics. Member of Celtics' 1957, 1959, 1960, 1961, 1962, 1963, 1964, 1965 championship teams. Rookie of the Year 1957. Career totals: 12,194 points, 5,749 rebounds. Coached 9 NBA seasons (427–263). Elected 1986.

Dan Issel: 6–9, 240-pound forward. Born October 25, 1948, at Batavia, Ill. Attended Kentucky. Played 15 seasons with Colonels (ABA), Nuggets (ABA, NBA). Member of Colonels' 1975 championship team. Scoring champion 1971 (29.9, ABA). Co-Rookie of the Year 1971 (ABA). All-Star Game MVP 1972 (ABA). Career totals ABA/NBA: 27,482 points, 11,133 rebounds. Coached 3 NBA seasons (96–102). Elected 1993.

Buddy Jeannette: 5–11, 175-pound point guard. Born September 15, 1917, at New Kensington, Pa. Attended Washington & Jefferson. Played 7 NBL seasons with Warren, Cleveland, Detroit, Sheboygan, and Fort Wayne; 3 BAA/NBA seasons with Bullets. Member of Bullets' 1948 championship team. Career NBA totals: 997 points. Coached 6 NBA seasons (136–173). Elected 1994.

Neil Johnston: 6–8, 210-pound center. Born February 4, 1929, at Chillicothe, O. Attended Ohio State. Played 8 seasons with Warriors. Member of Warriors' 1956 championship team. Scoring champion 1953 (22.3), 1954 (24.4), 1955 (22.7). Rebounding champion 1955 (15.1). Career totals: 10,023 points, 5,856 rebounds. Coached 2 NBA seasons (95–59). Elected 1990.

K.C. Jones: 6–1, 200-pound point guard. Born May 25, 1932, at

SHOOTING STAR *Gail Goodrich was equal parts shooting guard and point guard*

Taylor, Tex. Attended San Francisco. Played 9 seasons with Celtics. Member of Celtics' 1959, 1960, 1961, 1962, 1963, 1964, 1965, 1966 championship teams. Career totals: 5,011 points, 2,908 assists. Coached 10 NBA seasons (522–252). Elected 1989.

Sam Jones: 6–4, 205-pound guard. Born June 24, 1933, at Wilmington, N.C. Attended North Carolina Central. Played 12 seasons with Celtics. Member of Celtics' 1959, 1960, 1961, 1962, 1963, 1964, 1965, 1966, 1968, 1969 championship teams. Career totals: 15,411 points, 4,305 rebounds, 2,209 assists. Member of 25th Anniversary All-Time Team. Elected 1983.

Bob Lanier: 6–11, 265-pound center. Born September 10, 1948,

at Buffalo, N.Y. Attended St. Bonaventure. Played 14 seasons with Pistons, Bucks. All-Star Game MVP 1974. Career totals: 19,248 points, 9,698 rebounds, 3,007 assists. Coached 1 NBA season (12–25). Elected 1992.

Joe Lapchick: 6–5, 185-pound center. Born April 12, 1900, at Yonkers, N.Y. Playing career was pre-BAA/NBA. Coached 9 NBA seasons (326–247). Elected 1966.

Clyde Lovellette: 6–9, 235-pound forward/center. Born September 7, 1929, at Petersburg, Ind. Attended Kansas. Played 11 seasons with Lakers, Royals, Hawks, Celtics. Member of Lakers' 1954 and Celtics' 1963, 1964 championship teams. Career totals: 11,947 points, 6,663 rebounds. Elected 1988.

Jerry Lucas: 6–8, 235-pound forward/center. Born March 30, 1940, at Middletown, Ohio. Attended Ohio State. Played 11 seasons with Royals, Warriors, Knicks. Member of Knicks' 1973 championship team. Rookie of the Year 1964. All-Star Game MVP 1965. Career totals: 14,053 points, 12,942 rebounds. Elected 1979.

(Easy) Ed Macauley: 6–8, 190-pound forward/center. Born March 22, 1928, at St. Louis. Attended St. Louis University. Played 10 seasons with Bombers, Celtics, Hawks. Member of Hawks' 1958 championship team. All-Star Game MVP 1951. Career totals: 11,234 points. Coached 2 NBA seasons (89–48). Elected 1960.

(Pistol) Pete Maravich: 6–5, 200-pound guard. Born June 22, 1947, at Aliquippa, Pa. Attended Louisiana State. Played 10 seasons with Hawks, Jazz, Celtics. Scoring champion 1977 (31.1). Career totals: 15,948 points, 3,563 assists. Elected 1987.

Slater Martin: 5–10, 170-pound point guard. Born October 22, 1925, at Houston. Attended Texas. Played 11 seasons with Lakers, Knicks, Hawks. Member of Lakers' 1950, 1952, 1953, 1954 and Hawks' 1958 championship teams. Career totals: 7,337 points, 3,160 assists. Coached 1 NBA season (5–3). Elected 1981.

Dick McGuire: 6–0, 180-pound point guard. Born January 25, 1926, at Huntington, N.Y. Attended St. John's, Dartmouth. Played 11 seasons with Knicks, Pistons. Assist co-champion 1951 (6.3). Career totals: 5,921 points, 4,205 assists. Coached 7 NBA seasons (197–260). Elected 1993.

George Mikan: 6–10, 245-pound center. Born June 18, 1924, at Joliet, Ill. Attended DePaul. Played 2 NBL seasons with Chicago, Minneapolis; 7 BAA/NBA seasons with Lakers. Member of Lakers' 1949, 1950, 1952, 1953, 1954 championship teams. Scoring champion

1949 (28.3), 1950 (27.4), 1951 (28.4), 1952 (23.8). Rebounding champion 1952 (13.5), 1953 (14.4). All-Star Game MVP 1953. Career totals: 10,156 points, 4,167 rebounds. Coached 1 NBA season (9–30). Member of 25th and 35th Anniversary All-Time Teams. Elected 1959.

Vern Mikkelsen: 6–7, 230-pound forward/center. Born October 21, 1928, at Fresno, Calif. Attended Hamline. Played 10 seasons with Lakers. Member of Lakers' 1950, 1952, 1953, 1954 championship teams. Career totals: 10,063 points. Elected 1995.

Earl (the Pearl) Monroe: 6–3, 190-pound guard. Born November 21, 1944, at Philadelphia. Attended Winston-Salem State. Played 13 seasons with Bullets, Knicks. Member of Knicks' 1973 championship team. Rookie of the Year 1968. Career totals: 17,454 points, 3,594 assists. Elected 1990.

Calvin Murphy: 5–9, 165-pound guard. Born May 9, 1948, at Norwalk, Conn. Attended Niagara. Played 13 seasons with Rockets. Career totals: 17,949 points, 4,402 assists. Elected 1993.

Bob Pettit: 6–9, 215-pound forward. Born December 12, 1932, at Baton Rouge, La. Attended Louisiana State. Played 11 seasons with Hawks. Member of Hawks' 1958 championship team. Scoring champion 1956 (25.7), 1959 (29.2). Rookie of the Year 1955. Regular-season MVP 1956, 1959. All-Star Game MVP 1956, 1958, 1962. Career totals: 20,880 points, 12,849 rebounds. Coached 1 NBA season (4–2). Member of 25th and 35th Anniversary All-Time Teams. Elected 1970.

Andy Phillip: 6–2, 195-pound point guard. Born March 7, 1922, at Granite City, Ill. Attended Illinois. Played 11 seasons with Stags, Warriors, Pistons, Celtics. Member of Celtics' 1957 championship team. Assist champion 1950 (5.8), 1951 (6.3), 1952 (8.2).

Career totals: 6,384 points, 3,759 assists. Elected 1961.

Jim Pollard: 6–5, 185-pound forward. Born July 9, 1922, at Oakland, Calif. Attended Stanford. Played 1 NBL season with Minneapolis; 7 BAA/NBA seasons with Lakers. Member of Lakers' 1949, 1950, 1952, 1953, 1954 championship teams. Career totals: 5,762 points. Coached 2 NBA seasons (32–87). Elected 1977.

Frank Ramsey: 6–3, 190-pound guard. Born July 13, 1931, at Corydon, Ky. Attended Kentucky. Played 9 seasons with Celtics. Member of Celtics' 1957, 1959, 1960, 1961, 1962, 1963, 1964 championship teams. Career totals: 8,378 points, 3,410 rebounds. Elected 1981.

Willis Reed: 6–10, 240-pound center. Born June 25, 1942, at Hico, La. Attended Grambling State. Played 10 seasons with Knicks. Member of Knicks' 1970 and 1973 championship teams. Rookie of the Year 1965. Regular-season MVP 1970. NBA Finals MVP 1970, 1973. All-Star Game MVP 1970. Career totals: 12,183 points, 8,414 rebounds. Coached 4 NBA seasons (82–124). Elected 1981.

Oscar (Big O) Robertson: 6–5, 220-pound guard. Born November 24, 1938, at Charlotte, Tenn. Attended Cincinnati. Played 14 seasons with Royals, Bucks. Member of Bucks' 1971 championship team. Scoring champion 1968 (29.2). Assist champion 1961 (9.7), 1962 (11.4), 1964 (11.0), 1965 (11.5), 1966 (11.1), 1967 (10.7), 1968 (9.7), 1969 (9.8). Rookie of the Year 1961. Regular-season MVP 1964. All-Star Game MVP 1961, 1964, 1969. Career totals: 26,710 points, 7,804 rebounds, 9,887 assists. Member of 35th Anniversary All-Time Team. Elected 1979.

John (Honey) Russell: 6–1, 195-pound guard. Born May 31, 1902, at Brooklyn, N.Y. Attended Seton

Hall. Playing career was pre-BAA/NBA. Coached 2 NBA seasons (42–66). Elected 1964.

Bill Russell: 6–10, 220-pound center. Born February 12, 1934, at Monroe, La. Attended San Francisco. Played 13 seasons with Celtics. Member of Celtics' 1957, 1959, 1960, 1961, 1962, 1963, 1964, 1965, 1966, 1968, 1969 championship teams. Rebounding champion 1957 (19.6), 1958 (22.7), 1959 (23.0), 1964 (24.7), 1965 (24.1). Regular-season MVP 1958, 1961, 1962, 1963, 1965. All-Star Game MVP 1963. Career totals: 14,522 points, 21,620 rebounds, 4,100 assists. Coached 8 NBA seasons (341–290). Member of 25th and 35th Anniversary All-Time Teams. Elected 1974.

Dolph Schayes: 6–8, 220-pound forward/center. Born May 19, 1928, at New York. Attended New York University. Played 1 NBL season with Syracuse; 15 seasons with Nationals/76ers. Member of Nationals' 1955 championship team. Rebounding champion 1951 (16.4). Career totals: 18,438 points, 11,256 rebounds. Coached 5 NBA seasons (151–172). Member of 25th Anniversary All-Time Team. Elected 1972.

Bill Sharman: 6–1, 190-pound guard. Born May 25, 1926, at Abilene, Tex. Attended Southern California. Played 11 seasons with Capitols, Celtics. Member of Celtics' 1957, 1959, 1960, 1961 championship teams. All-Star Game MVP 1955. Career totals: 12,665 points, 2,779 rebounds. Coached 7 NBA seasons (333–240). Member of 25th Anniversary All-Time Team. Elected 1975.

David Thompson: 6–5, 195-pound guard/forward. Born July 13, 1954, at Shelby, N.C. Attended North Carolina State. Played 9 seasons with Nuggets (ABA, NBA), SuperSonics. Career totals ABA/NBA: 13,422 points, 2,446 rebounds, 1,939 assists. Elected 1996.

Nate Thurmond: 6–11, 235-pound center. Born July 25, 1941, at Akron, Ohio. Attended Bowling Green State. Played 14 seasons with Warriors, Bulls, Cavaliers. Career totals: 14,437 points, 14,464 rebounds. Elected 1984.

Jack Twyman: 6–6, 210-pound guard/ forward. Born May 11, 1934, at Pittsburgh, Pa. Attended Cincinnati. Played 11 seasons with Royals. Career totals: 15,840 points, 5,424 rebounds. Elected 1982.

Wes Unseld: 6–7, 245-pound center. Born March 14, 1946, at Louisville, Ky. Attended Louisville. Played 13 seasons with Bullets. Member of Bullets' 1978 championship team. Rebounding champion 1975 (14.8). Rookie of the Year 1969. Regular-season MVP 1969. NBA Finals MVP (1978). Career totals: 10,624 points, 13,769 rebounds, 3,822 assists. Coached 7 NBA seasons (202–345). Elected 1988.

Bill Walton: 6–11, 235-pound center. Born November 5, 1952, at La Mesa, Calif. Attended UCLA. Played 10 seasons with Trail Blazers, Clippers, Celtics. Member of Trail Blazers' 1977 and Celtics' 1986 championship teams. Rebounding champion 1977 (14.4). Regular-season MVP 1978. NBA Finals MVP 1977. Career totals: 6,215 points, 4,923 rebounds. Elected 1993.

Bobby Wanzer: 6–0, 170-pound guard. Born June 4, 1921, at New York. Attended Seton Hall. Played 1 NBL season with Rochester; 9 seasons with Royals. Member of Royals' 1951 championship team. Career totals: 6,924 points. Coached 4 NBA seasons (98–136). Elected 1987.

Jerry West: 6–2, 185-pound guard. Born May 28, 1938, at Cheylan, W. Va. Attended West Virginia. Played 14 seasons with Lakers. Member of Lakers' 1972 championship team. Scoring champion 1970 (31.2). Assist champion 1972 (9.7). NBA Finals MVP 1969.

FINGER ROLL *Point guard Andy Phillip (17) helped the Boston Celtics capture their first championship in 1957*

All-Star Game MVP 1972. Career totals: 25,192 points, 5,376 rebounds, 6,238 assists. Coached 3 NBA seasons (145–101). Member of the NBA 35th Anniversary All-Time Team. Elected 1979.

Lenny Wilkens: 6–1, 180-pound guard. Born October 28, 1937, at Brooklyn, N.Y. Attended Providence. Played 15 seasons with Hawks, SuperSonics, Cavaliers, Trail Blazers. All-Star Game MVP 1971. Career totals: 17,772 points, 5,030 rebounds, 7,211 assists. Has coached 23 NBA seasons (1,014-–850). Elected 1989.

George Yardley: 6–5, 195-pound forward. Born November 23, 1928, at Hollywood, Calif. Attended Stanford. Played 7 seasons with Pistons, Nationals. Scoring champion 1958 (27.8). Career totals: 9,063 points, 4,220 rebounds. Elected 1996.

NBA-Associated Coaches

Red Auerbach: Born September 20, 1917, at Brooklyn, N.Y. Coached 20 BAA/NBA seasons (938–479) with Capitols, Blackhawks, Celtics. Coached Celtics' 1957, 1959, 1960, 1961, 1962, 1963, 1964, 1965, 1966 championship teams. NBA Coach of the Year 1965. Coach of 25th Anniversary All-Time Team. Elected 1968.

Chuck Daly: Born July 20, 1930, at St. Mary's, Pa. Coached 12 NBA seasons (564–379) with Cavaliers, Pistons, Nets. Coached Pistons' 1989, 1990 championship teams. Coached U.S. Dream Team to Olympic gold medal in 1992. Coached 8 college seasons (151–62) at Boston College, Pennsylvania. Elected 1994.

Red Holzman: Born August 10, 1920, at Brooklyn, N.Y. Coached 18 NBA seasons (696–604) with Hawks, Knicks. Coached Knicks' 1970, 1973 championship teams. NBA Coach of the Year 1970. Elected 1986.

Alvin (Doggie) Julian: Born April 5, 1901, at Reading, Pa. Coached 2 NBA seasons (47–81) with Celtics. Coached Holy Cross to 1947 NCAA Tournament championship. Also coached at Albright, Muhlenberg, Dartmouth. Elected 1967.

Ken Loeffler: Born April 14, 1902, at Beaver Falls, Pa. Coached 3 BAA seasons (79–90) with Bombers, Steamrollers. Coached La Stelle to 1954 NCAA Tournament championship and 1952 NIT title. Coached Geneva, Yale, La Salle and Texas A&M to 310 victories. Elected 1964.

Frank McGuire: Born November 8, 1916, at New York. Coached 1 NBA season (49–31) with Warriors. Coached North Carolina to 1957 NCAA Tournament championship. Coached St. John's, North Carolina and South Carolina to 550–235 record. NCAA Coach of the Year three times. Elected 1976.

Jack Ramsay: Born February 21, 1925, at Philadelphia. Coached 21 NBA seasons (864–783) with 76ers, Braves, Trail Blazers, Pacers. Coached Trail Blazers' 1977 championship team. Coached 11 college seasons (234–72) with St. Joseph's. Elected 1992.

Other NBA Contributors

Clair Bee: Former NBA coach and innovator. Instrumental in development of 3-second rule and 24-second clock. Elected 1967.

Walter Brown: One of NBA's founding fathers and organizer of Boston Celtics franchise. Elected 1965.

Larry Fleisher: General counsel of NBA Players Association for more than 25 years. Elected 1990.

Eddie Gottlieb: One of NBA's founding fathers and coach of the league's first champion, the Philadelphia Warriors, in 1947. Elected 1971.

Lester Harrison: Long-time owner and coach of Rochester Royals; led team to 1951 NBA championship. Elected 1979.

Ned Irish: One of NBA's founding fathers and organizer of New York Knickerbockers franchise. Long-time basketball director of New York's Madison Square Garden. Elected 1964.

J. Walter Kennedy: Commissioner of NBA, 1963–75. Elected 1980.

Larry O'Brien: Commissioner of NBA, 1975–84. Elected 1991.

Maurice Podoloff: President of BAA/NBA from its founding in 1946 until 1963. Elected 1973.

NBA RECORDS

NBA Career Leaders

Regular Season
Scoring

Player	Pts.
1. Kareem Abdul-Jabbar	38,387
2. Wilt Chamberlain	31,419
3. Moses Malone	27,409
4. Elvin Hayes	27,313
5. Oscar Robertson	26,710
6. John Havlicek	26,395
7. Alex English	25,613
8. Dominique Wilkins	25,389
9. Jerry West	25,192
10. Michael Jordan	24,489

Per Game Scoring Average
(minimum 14,000 points)

Player	Avg.
1. Michael Jordan	32.0
2. Wilt Chamberlain	30.1
3. Elgin Baylor	27.4
4. Jerry West	27.0
5. Bob Pettit	26.4
6. George Gervin	26.2
7. Karl Malone	26.0
8. Dominique Wilkins	25.8
9. Oscar Robertson	25.7
10. David Robinson	25.6

Field Goals Made

Player	No.
1. Kareem Abdul-Jabbar	15,837
2. Wilt Chamberlain	12,681
3. Elvin Hayes	10,976
4. Alex English	10,659
5. John Havlicek	10,513
6. Robert Parish	9,544
7. Dominique Wilkins	9,516
8. Oscar Robertson	9,508
9. Moses Malone	9,435
10. Michael Jordan	9,161

Free Throws Made

Player	No.
1. Moses Malone	8,531
2. Oscar Robertson	7,694
3. Jerry West	7,160
4. Dolph Schayes	6,979
5. Adrian Dantley	6,832
6. Kareem Abdul-Jabbar	6,712
7. Bob Pettit	6,182
8. Wilt Chamberlain	6,057
9. Karl Malone	5,984
10. Elgin Baylor	5,763

CAPTAIN HOOK *Kareem Abdul-Jabbar piled up 38,387 career points*

Games

Player	No.
1. Robert Parish	1,568
2. Kareem Abdul-Jabbar	1,560
3. Moses Malone	1,329
4. Elvin Hayes	1,303
5. John Havlicek	1,270
6. Paul Silas	1,254
7. Alex English	1,193
8. Buck Williams	1,192
9. James Edwards	1,168
10. Tree Rollins	1,156

Minutes

Player	No.
1. Kareem Abdul-Jabbar	57,446
2. Elvin Hayes	50,000
3. Wilt Chamberlain	47,859
4. John Havlicek	46,471
5. Robert Parish	45,298
6. Moses Malone	45,071
7. Oscar Robertson	43,866
8. Bill Russell	40,726
9. Buck Williams	40,260
10. Hal Greer	39,788

Rebounds

Player	No.
1. Wilt Chamberlain	23,924
2. Bill Russell	21,620
3. Kareem Abdul-Jabbar	17,440
4. Elvin Hayes	16,279
5. Moses Malone	16,212
6. Robert Parish	14,626
7. Nate Thurmond	14,464
8. Walt Bellamy	14,241
9. Wes Unseld	13,769
10. Jerry Lucas	12,942

Assists

Player	No.
1. John Stockton	11,310
2. Magic Johnson	10,141
3. Oscar Robertson	9,887
4. Isiah Thomas	9,061
5. Maurice Cheeks	7,392
6. Lenny Wilkens	7,211
7. Bob Cousy	6,955
8. Guy Rodgers	6,917
9. Nate Archibald	6,476
10. John Lucas	6,454

Steals

Player	No.
1. John Stockton	2,365
2. Maurice Cheeks	2,310
3. Alvin Robertson	2,112
4. Michael Jordan	2,025
5. Clyde Drexler	1,962
6. Isiah Thomas	1,861
7. Derek Harper	1,749
8. Magic Johnson	1,724
9. Fat Lever	1,666
10. Gus Williams	1,638

Blocked Shots

Player	No.
1. Hakeem Olajuwon	3,190
2. Kareem Abdul-Jabbar	3,189
3. Mark Eaton	3,064
4. Tree Rollins	2,542
5. Robert Parish	2,342
6. Patrick Ewing	2,327
7. Manute Bol	2,086
8. George Johnson	2,082
9. Larry Nance	2,027
10. David Robinson	2,006

NBA Career Leaders

Playoffs

Scoring

Player	Pts.
1. Kareem Abdul-Jabbar	5,762
2. Michael Jordan	4,717
3. Jerry West	4,457
4. Larry Bird	3,897
5. John Havlicek	3,776
6. Magic Johnson	3,701
7. Elgin Baylor	3,623
8. Wilt Chamberlain	3,607
9. Hakeem Olajuwon	3,202
10. Kevin McHale	3,182

Per Game Scoring Average (minimum 1,000 points)

Player	Avg.
1. Michael Jordan	33.9
2. Jerry West	29.1
3. Hakeem Olajuwon	27.8
4. Karl Malone	27.3
5. Elgin Baylor	27.0
6. George Gervin	27.0
7. Dominique Wilkins	25.8
8. Bob Pettit	25.5
9. Rick Barry	24.8
10. Reggie Miller	24.7

Field Goals Made

Player	No.
1. Kareem Abdul-Jabbar	2,356
2. Michael Jordan	1,718
3. Jerry West	1,622
4. Larry Bird	1,458
5. John Havlicek	1,451
6. Wilt Chamberlain	1,425
7. Elgin Baylor	1,388
8. Magic Johnson	1,291
9. Hakeem Olajuwon	1,283
10. James Worthy	1,267

Free Throws Made

Player	No.
1. Jerry West	1,213
2. Michael Jordan	1,159
3. Magic Johnson	1,068
4. Kareem Abdul-Jabbar	1,050
5. Larry Bird	901
6. John Havlicek	874
7. Elgin Baylor	847
8. Kevin McHale	766
9. Wilt Chamberlain	757
10. Dennis Johnson	756

Games

Player	No.
1. Kareem Abdul-Jabbar	237
2. Danny Ainge	193
3. Magic Johnson	190
4. Robert Parish	182
5. Dennis Johnson	180
6. Byron Scott	175
7. John Havlicek	172
8. Kevin McHale	169
9. Michael Cooper	168
10. Bill Russell	165

Minutes

Player	No.
1. Kareem Abdul-Jabbar	8,851
2. Wilt Chamberlain	7,559
3. Magic Johnson	7,538
4. Bill Russell	7,497
5. Dennis Johnson	6,994
6. Larry Bird	6,886
7. John Havlicek	6,860
8. Jerry West	6,321
9. Robert Parish	6,159
10. Michael Jordan	5,798

Rebounds

Player	No.
1. Bill Russell	4,104
2. Wilt Chamberlain	3,913
3. Kareem Abdul-Jabbar	2,481
4. Wes Unseld	1,777
5. Robert Parish	1,761
6. Elgin Baylor	1,724
7. Larry Bird	1,683
8. Paul Silas	1,527
9. Magic Johnson	1,465
10. Hakeem Olajuwon	1,345

Assists

Player	No.
1. Magic Johnson	2,346
2. John Stockton	1,175
3. Larry Bird	1,062
4. Dennis Johnson	1,006
5. Isiah Thomas	987
6. Jerry West	970
7. Bob Cousy	937
8. Maurice Cheeks	922
9. Kevin Johnson	863
10. John Havlicek	825

Steals

Player	No.
1. Magic Johnson	358
2. Michael Jordan	314
3. Larry Bird	296
4. Maurice Cheeks	295
5. Scottie Pippen	271
6. Dennis Johnson	247
7. Clyde Drexler	244
8. Julius Erving	235
9. Isiah Thomas	234
10. Byron Scott	225

Blocked Shots

Player	No.
1. Kareem Abdul-Jabbar	476
2. Hakeem Olajuwon	408
3. Robert Parish	306
4. Kevin McHale	281
5. Patrick Ewing	244
6. Julius Erving	239
7. Caldwell Jones	223
8. Elvin Hayes	222
9. Mark Eaton	210
10. Darryl Dawkins	165
David Robinson	165

NBA Finals

Scoring

Player	Pts.
1. Jerry West	1,679
2. Kareem Abdul-Jabbar	1,317
3. Elgin Baylor	1,161
4. Bill Russell	1,151
5. Sam Jones	1,143
6. Tom Heinsohn	1,035
7. John Havlicek	1,020
8. Magic Johnson	971
9. Michael Jordan	781
10. James Worthy	754

Per Game Scoring Average (Minimum 225 points)

Player	Avg.
1. Rick Barry	36.3
2. Michael Jordan	34.0
3. Jerry West	30.5
4. Bob Pettit	28.4
5. Hakeem Olajuwon	27.5
6. Elgin Baylor	26.4
7. Julius Erving	25.5
8. Clyde Drexler	25.5
9. Joe Fulks	24.7
10. Andrew Toney	24.4

Field Goals Made

Player	No.
1. Jerry West	612
2. Kareem Abdul-Jabbar	544
3. Sam Jones	458
4. Elgin Baylor	442
5. Bill Russell	415
6. Tom Heinsohn	407
7. John Havlicek	390
8. Magic Johnson	339
9. James Worthy	314
10. Michael Jordan	296

Free Throws Made

Player	No.
1. Jerry West	455
2. Bill Russell	321
3. Magic Johnson	284
4. Elgin Baylor	277
5. George Mikan	259
6. John Havlicek	240
7. Kareem Abdul-Jabbar	229
8. Sam Jones	227
9. Bob Pettit	227
10. Tom Heinsohn	221

Games

Player	No.
1. Bill Russell	70
2. Sam Jones	64
3. Kareem Abdul-Jabbar	56
4. Jerry West	55
5. Tom Heinsohn	52
6. Magic Johnson	50
7. John Havlicek	47
8. Frank Ramsey	47
9. Michael Cooper	46
10. Elgin Baylor/K.C. Jones (tie)	44

Minutes

Player	No.
1. Bill Russell	3,185
2. Jerry West	2,375
3. Kareem Abdul-Jabbar	2,082
4. Magic Johnson	2,044
5. John Havlicek	1,872
6. Sam Jones	1,871
7. Elgin Baylor	1,850
8. Wilt Chamberlain	1,657
9. Bob Cousy	1,639
10. Tom Heinsohn	1,602

Rebounds

Player	No.
1. Bill Russell	1,718
2. Wilt Chamberlain	862
3. Elgin Baylor	593
4. Kareem Abdul-Jabbar	507
5. Tom Heinsohn	473
6. Bob Pettit	416
7. Magic Johnson	397
8. Larry Bird	361
9. John Havlicek	350
10. Sam Jones	313

Assists

Player	No.
1. Magic Johnson	584
2. Bob Cousy	400
3. Bill Russell	315
4. Jerry West	306
5. Dennis Johnson	228
6. John Havlicek	195
7. Larry Bird	187
8. Kareem Abdul-Jabbar	181
9. Michael Cooper	178
10. Elgin Baylor	167

Steals

Player	No.
1. Magic Johnson	102
2. Larry Bird	63
3. Michael Cooper	59
4. Dennis Johnson	48
5. Danny Ainge	46
6. Kareem Abdul-Jabbar	45
7. Julius Erving	44
8. Maurice Cheeks	38
9. Byron Scott	35
10. Michael Jordan	10

Blocked Shots

Player	No.
1. Kareem Abdul-Jabbar	116
2. Hakeem Olajuwon	54
3. Robert Parish	54
4. Kevin McHale	44
5. Caldwell Jones	42
6. Julius Erving	40
7. Dennis Johnson	39
8. Darryl Dawkins	35
9. Elvin Hayes	35
10. John Salley	32

NBA Career Leaders

Regular Season (ABA/NBA)
Scoring

Player	Pts.
1. Kareem Abdul-Jabbar	38,387
2. Wilt Chamberlain	31,419
3. Julius Erving	30,026
4. Moses Malone	29,580
5. Dan Issel	27,482
6. Elvin Hayes	27,313
7. Oscar Robertson	26,710
8. George Gervin	26,595
9. John Havlicek	26,395
10. Alex English	25,613

Per Game Scoring Average
(Minimum 14,000 points)

Player	Avg.
1. Michael Jordan	32.0
2. Wilt Chamberlain	30.1
3. Elgin Baylor	27.4
4. Jerry West	27.0
5. Bob Pettit	26.4
6. Karl Malone	26.0
7. Dominique Wilkins	25.8
8. Oscar Robertson	25.7
9. David Robinson	25.6
10. George Gervin	25.1

Field Goals Made

Player	No.
1. Kareem Abdul-Jabbar	15,837
2. Wilt Chamberlain	12,681
3. Julius Erving	11,818
4. Elvin Hayes	10,976
5. Alex English	10,659
6. John Havlicek	10,513
7. Dan Issel	10,431
8. George Gervin	10,368
9. Moses Malone	10,277
10. Rick Barry	9,695

Free Throws Made

Player	No.
1. Moses Malone	9,018
2. Oscar Robertson	7,694
3. Jerry West	7,160
4. Dolph Schayes	6,979
5. Adrian Dantley	6,832
6. Kareem Abdul-Jabbar	6,712
7. Dan Issel	6,591
8. Julius Erving	6,256
9. Bob Pettit	6,182
10. Artis Gilmore	6,132

Games

Player	No.
1. Robert Parish	1,568
2. Kareem Abdul-Jabbar	1,560
3. Moses Malone	1,455
4. Artis Gilmore	1,329
5. Elvin Hayes	1,303
6. Caldwell Jones	1,299
7. John Havlicek	1,270
8. Paul Silas	1,254
9. Julius Erving	1,243
10. Dan Issel	1,218

Minutes

Player	No.
1. Kareem Abdul-Jabbar	57,446
2. Elvin Hayes	50,000
3. Moses Malone	49,444
4. Wilt Chamberlain	47,859
5. Artis Gilmore	47,134
6. John Havlicek	46,471
7. Robert Parish	45,298
8. Julius Erving	45,227
9. Oscar Robertson	43,866
10. Dan Issel	41,786

Rebounds

Player	No.
1. Wilt Chamberlain	23,924
2. Bill Russell	21,620
3. Moses Malone	17,834
4. Kareem Abdul-Jabbar	17,440
5. Artis Gilmore	16,330
6. Elvin Hayes	16,279
7. Robert Parish	14,626
8. Nate Thurmond	14,464
9. Walt Bellamy	14,241
10. Wes Unseld	13,769

Assists

Player	No.
1. John Stockton	11,310
2. Magic Johnson	10,141
3. Oscar Robertson	9,887
4. Isiah Thomas	9,061
5. Maurice Cheeks	7,392
6. Lenny Wilkens	7,211
7. Bob Cousy	6,955
8. Guy Rodgers	6,917
9. Nate Archibald	6,476
10. John Lucas	6,454

Steals

Player	No.
1. John Stockton	2,365
2. Maurice Cheeks	2,310
3. Julius Erving	2,272
4. Alvin Robertson	2,112
5. Michael Jordan	2,025
6. Clyde Drexler	1,962
7. Isiah Thomas	1,861
8. Don Buse	1,818
9. Derek Harper	1,749
10. Magic Johnson	1,724

Blocked Shots

Player	No.
1. Hakeem Olajuwon	3,190
2. Kareem Abdul-Jabbar	3,189
3. Artis Gilmore	3,178
4. Mark Eaton	3,064
5. Tree Rollins	2,542
6. Robert Parish	2,342
7. Patrick Ewing	2,327
8. Caldwell Jones	2,297
9. Manute Bol	2,086
10. George Johnson	2,082

NBA All-Star Game
Scoring

Player	Pts.
1. Kareem Abdul-Jabbar	251
2. Oscar Robertson	246
3. Bob Pettit	224
4. Julius Erving	221
5. Elgin Baylor	218
6. Michael Jordan	197
7. Wilt Chamberlain	191
8. Isiah Thomas	185
9. John Havlicek	179
10. Magic Johnson	176

Field Goals Made

Player	No.
1. Kareem Abdul-Jabbar	105
2. Oscar Robertson	88
3. Julius Erving	85
4. Michael Jordan	82
5. Bob Pettit	81
6. Isiah Thomas	76
7. John Havlicek	74
8. Wilt Chamberlain	72
9. Elgin Baylor	70
10. Magic Johnson	64

Free Throws Made

Player	No.
1. Elgin Baylor	78
2. Oscar Robertson	70
3. Bob Pettit	62
4. Julius Erving	50
5. Wilt Chamberlain	47
6. Bob Cousy	43
7. Dolph Schayes	42
8. Kareem Abdul-Jabbar	41
9. Moses Malone	40
10. Magic Johnson	38

Games

Player	No.
1. Kareem Abdul-Jabbar	18
2. Wilt Chamberlain	13
Bob Cousy	13
John Havlicek	13
5. Elvin Hayes	12
Oscar Robertson	12
Bill Russell	12
Jerry West	12
9. Many players tied with 11	

OVER TIME *Wilt Chamberlain (right) scores two of his 31,419 career points*

NBA Career Leaders

Minutes

Player	No.
1. Kareem Abdul-Jabbar	449
2. Wilt Chamberlain	388
3. Oscar Robertson	380
4. Bob Cousy	368
5. Bob Pettit	360
6. Bill Russell	343
7. Jerry West	341
8. Magic Johnson	331
9. Elgin Baylor	321
10. Isiah Thomas	318

Rebounds

Player	No.
1. Wilt Chamberlain	197
2. Bob Pettit	178
3. Kareem Abdul-Jabbar	149
4. Bill Russell	139
5. Moses Malone	108
6. Dolph Schayes	105
7. Elgin Baylor	99
8. Elvin Hayes	92
9. Hakeem Olajuwon	91
10. Dave Cowens	81

Assists

Player	No.
1. Magic Johnson	127
2. Isiah Thomas	97
3. Bob Cousy	86
4. Oscar Robertson	81
5. John Stockton	64
6. Jerry West	55
7. Kareem Abdul-Jabbar	51
8. Larry Bird	41
9. Nate Archibald	40
10. Bill Russell	39

Steals

Player	No.
1. Isiah Thomas	31
2. Michael Jordan	28
3. Larry Bird	23
4. Magic Johnson	21
5. Julius Erving	18
6. Scottie Pippen	17
7. Rick Barry	16
George Gervin	16
9. Hakeem Olajuwon	15
10. John Stockton	14

Blocked Shots

Player	No.
1. Kareem Abdul-Jabbar	31
2. Hakeem Olajuwon	22
3. Patrick Ewing	16
4. Kevin McHale	12
5. Julius Erving	11
David Robinson	11
7. George Gervin	9
8. Robert Parish	8
Shaquille O'Neal	8
10. Magic Johnson/Jack Sikma	7

STAR GAZING *Michael Jordan is climbing the All-Star scoring ladder*

NBA Single-Game Highs

Regular Season

Points

Player/Team	Date	Pts.
1. Wilt Chamberlain, Phil.	3–2–62	100
2. Wilt Chamberlain, Phil.	12–8–61	78 (3 OT)
3. Wilt Chamberlain, Phil.	1–13–62	73
Wilt Chamberlain, S.F.	11–16–62	73
David Thompson, Den.	4–9–78	73
6. Wilt Chamberlain, S.F.	11–3–62	72
7. Elgin Baylor, L.A.	11–15–60	71
David Robinson, S.A.	4–24–94	71
9. Wilt Chamberlain, S.F.	3–10–63	70
10. Michael Jordan, Chi.	3–28–90	69 (OT)

Field Goals Made

Player/Team	Date	No.
1. Wilt Chamberlain, Phil.	3–2–62	36
2. Wilt Chamberlain, Phil.	12–8–61	31 (3 OT)
3. Wilt Chamberlain, Phil.	12–16–67	30
Rick Barry, G.S.	3–26–74	30
5. Wilt Chamberlain, Phil.	1–13–62	29
Wilt Chamberlain, S.F.	11–3–62	29
Wilt Chamberlain, S.F.	11–16–62	29
Wilt Chamberlain, L.A.	2–9–69	29
9. Elgin Baylor, L.A.	11–15–60	28
Wilt Chamberlain, Phil.	12–9–61	28
Wilt Chamberlain, S.F.	1–11–63	28
Wilt Chamberlain, Phil.	2–7–66	28
David Thompson, Den.	4–9–78	28

Free Throws Made

Player/Team	Date	No.
1. Wilt Chamberlain, Phil.	3–2–62	28
Adrian Dantley, Utah	1–4–84	28
3. Adrian Dantley, Utah	11–25–83	27
4. Adrian Dantley, Utah	10–31–80	26
Michael Jordan, Chi.	2–26–87	26
6. Frank Selvy, Mil.	12–2–54	24
Willie Burton, Phil.	12–13–94	24
8. Dolph Schayes, Syr.	1–17–52	23 (3 OT)
Nate Archibald, Cin.	2–5–72	23
Nate Archibald, K.C./Oma.	1–21–75	23
Pete Maravich, N.O.	10–26–75	23 (2 OT)
Kevin Johnson, Phoe.	4–9–90	23
Dominique Wilkins, Atl.	12–8–92	23

Rebounds

Player/Team	Date	No.
1. Wilt Chamberlain, Phil.	11–24–60	55
2. Bill Russell, Bos.	2–5–60	51
3. Bill Russell, Bos.	11–16–57	49
Bill Russell, Bos.	3–11–65	49
5. Wilt Chamberlain, Phil.	2–6–60	45
Wilt Chamberlain, Phil.	1–21–61	45
7. Wilt Chamberlain, Phil.	11–10–59	43
Wilt Chamberlain, Phil.	12–8–61	43 (3 OT)
Bill Russell, Bos.	1–20–63	43
Wilt Chamberlain, Phil.	3–6–65	43

Assists

Player/Team	Date	No.
1. Scott Skiles, Orl.	12–30–90	30
2. Kevin Porter, N.J.	2–24–78	29
3. Bob Cousy, Bos.	2–27–59	28
Guy Rodgers, S.F.	3–14–63	28
John Stockton, Utah	1–15–91	28
6. Geoff Huston, Cle.	1–27–82	27
John Stockton, Utah	12–19–89	27
8. John Stockton, Utah	4–14–88	26

Steals

Player/Team	Date	No.
1. Larry Kenon, S.A.	12–26–76	11
2. Jerry West, L.A.	12–7–73	10
Larry Steele, Port.	11–16–74	10
Fred Brown, Sea.	12–3–76	10
Gus Williams, Sea.	2–22–78	10
Eddie Jordan, N.J.	3–23–79	10
Johnny Moore, S.A.	3–6–85	10
Fat Lever, Den.	3–9–85	10
Clyde Drexler, Port.	1–10–86	10
Alvin Robertson, S.A.	2–18–86	10
Alvin Robertson, S.A.	11–22–86	10
Ron Harper, Cle.	3–10–87	10
Michael Jordan, Chi.	1–29–88	10
Alvin Robertson, S.A.	1–11–89	10 (OT)
Alvin Robertson, Mil.	11–19–90	10
Kevin Johnson, Phoe.	12–9–93	10

NBA Single-Game Highs

Blocked Shots

Player/Team	Date	No.
1. Elmore Smith, L.A.	10–28–73	17
2. Manute Bol, Wash.	1–25–86	15
Manute Bol, Wash.	2–26–87	15
Shaquille O'Neal, Orl.	11–20–93	15
5. Elmore Smith, L.A.	10–26–73	14
Elmore Smith, L.A.	11–4–73	14
Mark Eaton, Utah	1–18–85	14
Mark Eaton, Utah	2–18–89	14
9. George Johnson, S.A.	2–24–81	13
Mark Eaton, Utah	2–18–83	13
Darryl Dawkins, N.J.	11–5–83	13
Ralph Sampson, Hou.	12–9–83	13 (OT)
Manute Bol, G.S.	2–2–90	13

Playoffs

Scoring

Player/Team	Date	Pts.
1. Michael Jordan, Chi.	4–20–86	63 (2 OT)
2. Elgin Baylor, L.A.	4–14–62	61
3. Wilt Chamberlain, Phil.	3–22–62	56
Michael Jordan, Chi.	4–29–92	56
Charles Barkley, Phoe.	5–4–94	56
6. Rick Barry, S.F.	4–18–67	55
Michael Jordan, Chi.	5–1–88	55
Michael Jordan, Chi.	6–16–93	55
9. John Havlicek, Bos.	4–1–73	54
Michael Jordan, Chi.	5–31–93	54

Field Goals Made

Player/Team	Date	No.
1. Wilt Chamberlain, Phil.	3–14–60	24
John Havlicek, Bos.	4–1–73	24
Michael Jordan, Chi.	5–1–88	24
4. Charles Barkley, Phoe.	5–4–94	23
5. Wilt Chamberlain, Phil.	3–22–60	22
Wilt Chamberlain, Phil.	3–22–62	22
Elgin Baylor, L.A.	4–14–62	22
Wilt Chamberlain, S.F.	4–10–64	22
Rick Barry, S.F.	4–18–67	22
Billy Cunningham, Phil.	4–1–70	22
Michael Jordan, Chi.	4–20–86	22 (2 OT)

Free Throws Made

Player/Team	Date	No.
1. Bob Cousy, Bos.	3–21–53	30 (4 OT)
2. Michael Jordan, Chi.	5–14–89	23
3. Michael Jordan, Chi.	5–5–89	22 (OT)
Karl Malone, Utah	5–3–92	22
5. Oscar Robertson, Cin.	4–10–63	21
Derrick Coleman, N.J.	5–6–94	21
Kevin Johnson, Phoe.	5–20–95	21
8. Bob Cousy, Bos.	3–17–54	20 (OT)
Jerry West, L.A.	4–3–62	20
Jerry West, L.A.	4–5–65	20
Magic Johnson, L.A.	5–8–91	20
Karl Malone, Utah	5–9–91	20

Rebounds

Player/Team	Date	No.
1. Wilt Chamberlain, Phil.	4–5–67	41
2. Bill Russell, Bos.	3–23–58	40
Bill Russell, Bos.	3–29–60	40
Bill Russell, Bos.	4–18–62	40 (OT)
5. Bill Russell, Bos.	3–19–60	39
Bill Russell, Bos.	3–23–61	39
Wilt Chamberlain, Phil.	4–6–65	39
8. Bill Russell, Bos.	4–11–61	38
Bill Russell, Bos.	4–16–63	38
Wilt Chamberlain, S.F.	4–24–64	38
Wilt Chamberlain, Phil.	4–16–67	38

Assists

Player/Team	Date	No.
1. Magic Johnson, L.A.	5–15–84	24
John Stockton, Utah	5–17–88	24
3. Magic Johnson, L.A.	5–3–85	23
John Stockton, Utah	4–25–96	23
5. Doc Rivers, Atl.	5–16–88	22
6. Magic Johnson, L.A.	6–3–84	21
Magic Johnson, L.A.	4–27–91	21
Magic Johnson, L.A.	5–18–91	21
John Stockton, Utah	4–24–92	21
10. Many players tied with 20		

Steals

Player/Team	Date	No.
1. Rick Barry, G.S.	4–14–75	8
Lionel Hollins, Port.	5–8–77	8
Maurice Cheeks, Phil.	4–11–79	8
Craig Hodges, Mil.	5–9–86	8
Tim Hardaway, G.S.	5–8–91	8
Tim Hardaway, G.S.	4–30–92	8
Mookie Blaylock, Atl.	4–29–96	8
8. Many players tied with 7		

Blocked Shots

Player/Team	Date	No.
1. Mark Eaton, Utah	4–26–85	10
1. Hakeem Olajuwon, Hou.	4–29–90	10
3. Kareem Abdul-Jabbar, L.A.	4–22–77	9
Manute Bol, Wash.	4–18–86	9
Hakeem Olajuwon, Hou.	4–29–93	9
Derrick Coleman, N.J.	5–7–93	9
7. Many players tied with 8; Last:		
Patrick Ewing, N.Y.	6–17–94	8

ASSIST MAN *Lakers star Magic Johnson*

NBA Finals

Scoring

Player/Team	Date	Pts.
1. Elgin Baylor, L.A.	4–14–62	61
2. Rick Barry, S.F.	4–18–67	55
Michael Jordan, Chi.	6–16–93	55
4. Jerry West, L.A.	4–23–69	53
5. Bob Pettit, St.L.	4–12–58	50
6. Michael Jordan, Chi.	6–12–92	46
7. Jerry West, L.A.	4–19–65	45
Jerry West, L.A.	4–22–66	45
Wilt Chamberlain, L.A.	5–6–70	45
10. Rick Barry, S.F.	4–24–67	44
Michael Jordan, Chi.	6–13–93	44 (3 OT)

Field Goals Made

Player/Team	Date	No.
1. Elgin Baylor, L.A.	4–14–62	22
Rick Barry, S.F.	4–18–67	22
3. Jerry West, L.A.	4–23–69	21
Michael Jordan, Chi.	6–16–93	21
5. Wilt Chamberlain, L.A.	5–6–70	20
6. Bob Pettit, St.L.	4–12–58	19
Jerry West, L.A.	4–22–66	19
Kareem Abdul-Jabbar, L.A.	5–7–80	19
Michael Jordan, Chi.	6–13–93	19 (3 OT)
10. Isiah Thomas, Det.	6–19–88	18
Michael Jordan, Chi.	6–11–93	18

Free Throws Made

Player/Team	Date	No.
1. Bob Pettit, St.L.	4–9–58	19
2. Cliff Hagan, St.L.	3–30–58	17
Elgin Baylor, L.A.	4–14–62	17
Jerry West, L.A.	4–21–65	17
Jerry West, L.A.	4–25–69	17
6. Bob Pettit, St.L.	4–11–57	16
Michael Jordan, Chi.	6–12–92	16
8. Bob Pettit, St.L.	3–30–57	15 (2 OT)
Frank Ramsey, Bos.	4–18–62	15 (OT)
Elgin Baylor, L.A.	4–18–62	15 (OT)
Elgin Baylor, L.A.	4–24–66	15
Jerry West, L.A.	4–24–70	15
Terry Porter, Port.	6–7–90	15 (OT)

Rebounds

Player/Team	Date	No.
1. Bill Russell, Bos.	3–29–60	40
Bill Russell, Bos.	4–18–62	40 (OT)
3. Bill Russell, Bos.	4–11–61	38
Bill Russell, Bos.	4–16–63	38
Wilt Chamberlain, S.F.	4–24–64	38
Wilt Chamberlain, Phil.	4–16–67	38
7. Bill Russell, Bos.	4–9–60	35
8. Wilt Chamberlain, Phil.	4–14–67	33 (OT)
9. Bill Russell, Bos.	4–13–57	32 (2 OT)
Bill Russell, Bos.	4–22–64	32
Bill Russell, Bos.	4–28–66	32

NBA Single-Game Highs

Assists

Player/Team	Date	No.
1. Magic Johnson, L.A.	6–3–84	21
2. Magic Johnson, L.A.	6–4–87	20
Magic Johnson, L.A.	6–12–91	20
4. Bob Cousy, Bos.	4–9–57	19
Bob Cousy, Bos.	4–7–59	19
Walt Frazier, N.Y.	5–8–70	19
Magic Johnson, L.A.	6–14–87	19
Magic Johnson, L.A.	6–19–88	19
9. Jerry West, L.A.	5–1–70	18 (OT)
10. Many players tied with 17; Last:		
Magic Johnson, L.A.	6–16–88	17

Steals

Player/Team	Date	No.
1. Robert Horry, Hou.	6–9–95	7
2. John Havlicek, Bos.	5–3–74	6
Steve Mix, Phil.	5–22–77	6
Maurice Cheeks, Phil.	5–7–80	6
Isiah Thomas, Det.	6–19–88	6
6. Many players tied with 5; Last:		
Michael Jordan, Chi.	6–9–93	5

Blocked Shots

Player/Team	Date	No.
1. Bill Walton, Port.	6–5–77	8
Hakeem Olajuwon, Hous.	6–5–86	8
Patrick Ewing, N.Y.	6–17–94	8
4. Dennis Johnson, Sea.	5–28–78	7
Patrick Ewing, N.Y.	6–12–94	7
Hakeem Olajuwon, Hou.	6–12–94	7
7. Kareem Abdul-Jabbar, L.A.	5–4–80	6
Patrick Ewing, N.Y.	6–10–94	6
9. Many players tied with 5; Last:		
Robert Horry, Hou.	6–7–95	5 (OT)

NBA Regular Season Leaders

Most Times Leading League

Scoring	Michael Jordan, 8
Field Goal Percentage	Wilt Chamberlain, 9
Field Goals	Michael Jordan, 8
Free Throw Percentage	Bill Sharman, 7
Free Throws	Adrian Dantley, 5
	Karl Malone, 5
Rebounds	Wilt Chamberlain, 11
Assists	John Stockton, 9
Steals	Micheal Ray Richardson, 3
	Alvin Robertson, 3
	Michael Jordan, 3
Blocked Shots	Kareem Abdul-Jabbar, 4
	Mark Eaton, 4

Career Coaching Leaders

Regular Season

Victories

Coach	No.
1. Lenny Wilkens	1,014
2. Red Auerbach	938
3. Dick Motta	918
4. Bill Fitch	891
5. Jack Ramsay	864
6. Don Nelson	851
7. Cotton Fitzsimmons	832
8. Pat Riley	798
9. Gene Shue	784
10. John MacLeod	707

Games

Coach	No.
1. Bill Fitch	1,886
2. Dick Motta	1,883
3. Lenny Wilkens	1,864
4. Jack Ramsay	1,647
5. Gene Shue	1,645
6. Cotton Fitzsimmons	1,599
7. Don Nelson	1,480
8. Red Auerbach	1,417
9. John MacLeod	1,364
10. Red Holzman	1,300

Winning Percentage (Minimum 450 games)

Coach	Pct.
1. Phil Jackson	.721
2. Pat Riley	.702
3. Billy Cunningham	.698
4. K.C. Jones	.674
5. Red Auerbach	.662
6. Lester Harrison	.620
7. Tom Heinsohn	.619
8. Jerry Sloan	.601
9. Chuck Daly	.598
10. Larry Costello	.589

Playoffs

Victories

Coach	No.
1. Pat Riley	137
2. Red Auerbach	99
3. K.C. Jones	81
Phil Jackson	81
5. Chuck Daly	74
6. Billy Cunningham	66
7. Lenny Wilkens	64
8. John Kundla	60
9. Red Holzman	58
10. Dick Motta	56

Games

Coach	No.
1. Pat Riley	215
2. Red Auerbach	168
3. K.C. Jones	138
4. Lenny Wilkens	134
5. Dick Motta	126
6. Chuck Daly	122
7. Phil Jackson	112
Don Nelson	112
9. Bill Fitch	106
10. B Cunningham/R. Holzman	105

Winning Percentage (Minimum 50 games)

Coach	Pct.
1. Phil Jackson	.723
2. Pat Riley	.637
3. John Kundla	.632
4. Billy Cunningham	.629
5. Larry Costello	.617
6. Chuck Daly	.607
7. Rudy Tomjanovich	.600
8. Red Auerbach	.589
9. Tom Heinsohn	.588
10. K.C. Jones	.587

All-Time Team Victories

Regular Season

Team	No.
1. Boston Celtics	2,422
2. Los Angeles Lakers	2,292
3. Philadelphia 76ers	2,035
4. New York Knicks	1,979
6. Atlanta Hawks	1,884
5. Golden State Warriors	1,878
7. Detroit Pistons	1,783
8. Sacramento Kings	1,731
9. Washington Bullets	1,334
10. Chicago Bulls	1,316
4. New York Knicks	146
5. Chicago Bulls	117
6. Detroit Pistons	111
7. Atlanta Hawks	109
8. Golden State Warriors	99
9. Houston Rockets	88
10. Phoenix Suns	87

Playoffs

Team	No.
1. Los Angeles Lakers	301
2. Boston Celtics	272
3. Philadelphia 76ers	175

NBA Finals

Team	No.
1. Boston Celtics	70
2. Los Angeles Lakers	66
3. Philadelphia 76ers	23
4. New York Knicks	19
5. Golden State Warriors	17
6. Chicago Bulls	16
7. Detroit Pistons	15
8. Houston Rockets	12
9. Atlanta Hawks	11
10. Seattle SuperSonics	9

NBA Championships

Team	No.
1. Boston Celtics	16
2. Los Angeles Lakers	11
3. Chicago Bulls	4
4. Golden State Warriors	3
Philadelphia 76ers	3
6. Detroit Pistons	2
Houston Rockets	2
New York Knicks	2

SIX IS A CHARM *Boston celebrate in 1964*

CHRONOLOGY
OF PROFESSIONAL BASKETBALL

1891 (December) Dr. James Naismith introduces his new game of "basket ball" to a physical education class at the Springfield Men's Christian Association Training School at Springfield, Mass.

1892 (March 11) The first public basketball game is played between students and teachers at the Springfield Christian Association Training School. Football coaching great Amos Alonzo Stagg scores the teachers' only goal in a 5–1 loss.

1893 Backboards are introduced to protect the ball from spectator interference.

1894 Free throws are introduced and the free-throw line is moved from 20 to 15 feet.

1895 The point value of field goals is changed from three to two and free throws from three to one.

1896 The first known professional basketball game is played in Trenton, N.J., by teams trying to pay rent for the local armory.

1897 Five players to a team – the game gains structure.

1898 The six-team National Basketball League is introduced as the game's first professional circuit.

1925 The American Basketball League, the first attempt at a national professional circuit, is organized with teams ranging from New York to Chicago.

1927 (January 7) Abe Saperstein organizes the Harlem Globetrotters, a barnstorming team that will gain international acclaim and popularity.

1929 The professional cage, a court surrounded by rope or chicken wire, is eliminated.

1932 Basketball courts are divided into frontcourt and backcourt and the new three-second rule limits time in the lane.

1936 (August) Basketball is played for the first time as an official Olympic sport.

1936 (December 30) During a college contest at New York's Madison Square Garden, Stanford star Hank Luisetti introduces his one-handed shot, an innovation that would speed the evolution of the game.

1937 (March 17) The center jump after each basket is eliminated, a far-reaching decision that speeds up the game at all levels of play. The 10-second rule also is introduced.

1937 The National Basketball League, with 13 teams stretching from Buffalo and Pittsburgh in the East to Kankakee, Ill., and Oshkosh, Wis., in the Midwest, begins play.

1939 (November 28) Dr. James Naismith, basketball's inventor, dies in Lawrence, Kan., triggering a drive that eventually leads to creation of a basketball Hall of Fame in his honor.

1946 (June 6) The Basketball Association of America, the forerunner to the National Basketball Association, is organized with Maurice Podoloff as its president.

1946 (November 1) The New York Knickerbockers defeat the Toronto Huskies 68–66 in the first BAA game. The contest, ironically, is played on Canadian soil in Toronto.

1947 (January 11) The BAA outlaws zone defenses.

1947 (April 22) Joe Fulks scores 34 points and the Philadelphia Warriors clinch the BAA's first championship series with an 83–80 Game 5 victory over the Chicago Stags.

1949 (August 3) When six National Basketball League teams and the newly formed Indianapolis Olympians merge into the BAA, the new 17-team circuit is renamed "National Basketball Association".

1950 (April 23) George Mikan scores 40 points and the Minneapolis Lakers become the NBA's first back-to-back champions with a 110–95 Game 6 triumph over the Syracuse Nationals.

1950 (October 31) Washington's Earl Lloyd becomes the first black player in NBA history when he plays in a game against Rochester.

1950 (November 22) Fort Wayne defeats Minneapolis 19–18 in the lowest-scoring game in NBA history.

1951 (January 6) Indianapolis defeats Rochester 75–73 in six overtimes – the longest game in NBA history.

1951 (March 2) East 111, West 94 in the NBA's first All-Star Game at Boston Garden.

1952 The NBA foul lane is widened from 6 to 12 feet, a move designed to neutralize the dominance of Minneapolis big man George Mikan.

1954 (April 12) Jim Pollard scores 22 points and the Minneapolis Lakers defeat the Syracuse Nationals 87–80 in Game 7 of the NBA Finals, becoming the first team to win three straight championships.

1954 (October 30) Rochester defeats Boston 98–95 in the first NBA game played with a 24-second shot clock.

1957 (April 13) Boston defeats St. Louis 125–123 in a double-overtime Game 7 classic, winning the first of 11 championships the Celtics would capture in a 13-year period.

1959 The first Hall of Fame class is enshrined – 15 individuals and two teams.

1959 (April 9) The Boston Celtics overpower the Minneapolis Lakers 118–113, completing the first NBA Finals sweep in history and winning the first of eight straight championships.

1960 (October 19) The "Los Angeles Lakers" open their first West Coast season with a 140–123 loss at Cincinnati.

1960 (November 15) Lakers forward Elgin Baylor erupts for an NBA-record 71 points in a 123–108 victory over the New York Knicks in a game at Madison Square Garden.

1960 (November 24) Philadelphia center Wilt Chamberlain sets a single-game rebounding record when he grabs 55 in a 132–129 loss to Boston.

1961 The NBA expands to nine with the addition of the Chicago Packers – a team that would move to Baltimore after two seasons.

1962 (March 2) Chamberlain scores an incredible 100 points in the Warriors' 169–147 victory over New York.

1962 (April 14) Lakers star Baylor scores a still-standing NBA Finals record 61 points in a 126–121 Game 5 victory over Boston.

1963 (September 1) Walter Kennedy becomes the NBA's second president – a title that would be changed to commissioner four years later.

1964 The NBA widens its foul lane from 12 to 16 feet.

1964 (November 13) St. Louis Hawks forward Bob Pettit becomes the NBA's first 20,000-point scorer in a 123–106 loss to Cincinnati.

1965 (January 15) San Francisco trades Chamberlain to the Philadelphia 76ers for $150,000 and three players.

1966 (February 14) Chamberlain passes Pettit as the NBA's all-time leading scorer when he notches his 20,881st point in a game against Detroit.

1966 (April 28) The Boston Celtics win their eighth straight championship. The seventh-game 95–93 victory over the Lakers marks Red Auerbach's last game as Boston coach and sets the stage for center Bill Russell to become the NBA's first black coach.

1966 The NBA expands to 10 with the addition of the Chicago Bulls.

1967 Two more expansion teams – the San Diego Rockets and Seattle SuperSonics bring the NBA field to 12.

1967 (February 2) The rival American Basketball Association begins operation with former NBA great George Mikan as its commissioner.

1967 (April 24) The Philadelphia 76ers complete an amazing 79–17 season with a six-game victory over San Francisco in the NBA Finals, officially ending Boston's eight-year title reign.

1967 (October 13) The ABA begins play with the Oakland Oaks recording a 134–129 victory over the Anaheim Amigos.

1967 (November 19) Indiana's Jerry Harkness connects on a 92-foot shot in an ABA game against Dallas – the longest basket in professional history.

1968 The Milwaukee Bucks and Phoenix Suns expansion teams bring the NBA roster to 14.

1968 (February 17) The Naismith Memorial Basketball Hall of Fame opens in Springfield, Mass. – the site where Dr. James Naismith invented the game more than three-quarters of a century earlier.

1968 (May 4) The Pittsburgh Pipers record a 122–113 Game 7 victory over the New Orleans Buccaneers and win the ABA's first championship.

1968 (April 2) UCLA star Lew Alcindor spurns the ABA and signs a five-year contract with the NBA's Milwaukee Bucks.

1968 (July 5) The Philadelphia 76ers trade Chamberlain to the Los Angeles Lakers for three players and cash.

1969 (May 5) The Celtics earn their 11th championship in 13 years and officially close out the "Bill Russell Era" with a 108-106 Game 7 victory over Los Angeles.

1970 The NBA expands to 17 with the addition of teams in Buffalo, Cleveland and Portland and realigns into four divisions – the Atlantic, Central, Midwest and Pacific.

1971 (March 9) The Bulls end Milwaukee's record 20-game winning streak with a 110–103 victory at Chicago.

1972 (January 9) The Los Angeles Lakers, winners of a professional-sports record 33 straight games, drop a 120-104 streak-ending decision at Milwaukee.

1972 (February 16) Lakers center Wilt Chamberlain becomes the first NBA player to reach 30,000 points during a 110-109 victory at Phoenix.

1972 (March 26) The Los Angeles Lakers complete the NBA's most successful regular season (69–13) with a 124-98 victory over the Seattle SuperSonics.

1974 (March 7) The New Orleans Jazz begins operation as the NBA's 18th franchise.

1974 (August 29) The ABA's Utah Stars sign Moses Malone, the first high school player to jump directly to the professional level.

1975 (February 14) The ABA's San Diego Conquistadors defeat New York in the highest scoring game in professional history, 176–166.

1975 (June 1) Larry O'Brien succeeds Walter Kennedy as NBA commissioner.

1975 (June 16) The Milwaukee Bucks change the NBA's balance of power when they send 7-foot-2 center Kareem Abdul-Jabbar to Los Angeles in a blockbuster six-player trade.

1976 (June 17) The 9-year-old ABA goes out of business and the NBA absorbs four teams – the Denver Nuggets, Indiana Pacers, San Antonio Spurs and New York Nets – raising membership to 22.

1976 (October 21) The Philadelphia 76ers purchase the rights to forward Julius Erving from the cash-depleted New York Nets for $3 million.

1978 (April 9) In a season-closing scoring title duel, Denver's David Thompson scores 73 points in one game and San Antonio's George Gervin notches 63 in another. Gervin wins the title, 27.22 to 27.15.

1978 (July 7) An NBA franchise swap: John Y. Brown and Harry Mangurian trade their Buffalo Braves team to Irv Levin for the Boston Celtics.

1978 The NBA adds a third referee.

1979 The NBA adopts the 3-point field goal and eliminates the third referee.

1979 (October 12) The first 3-point field gold: Chris Ford connects for Boston in a game against Houston.

1980 (May 1) The Dallas Mavericks organize as the NBA's 23rd franchise.

1983 (December 13) The highest scoring game in NBA history lasts three overtimes and ends Detroit 186, Denver 184.

1984 (February 1) David Stern succeeds Larry O'Brien as NBA commissioner.

1984 (April 5) Lakers center Kareem Abdul-Jabbar becomes the NBA's all-time leading scorer when he surpasses Chamberlain's career total of 31,419 points in a game against Utah.

1985 (June 18) The New York Knicks, winner of the NBA's first Draft Lottery, select Georgetown center Patrick Ewing with their first pick.

1985 (June 30) The new $11.4-million Naismith Hall of Fame is dedicated in Springfield, Mass.

1986 (April 20) Chicago's Michael Jordan scores a playoff-record 63 points in a 135-131 double-overtime loss to Boston in a first-round game.

1987 (March 1) The Boston Celtics become the first team to reach 2,000 regular-season victories.

1987 (April 22) An NBA record crowd of 61,983 watches the Pistons beat the Celtics at Detroit's Pontiac Silverdome.

1988 (June 21) The Los Angeles Lakers become the first repeat champions in 19 years with a 108-105 Game 7 victory over the Detroit Pistons – their fifth title of the 1980s.

1988 (June 28) The annual draft is reduced from seven to three rounds.

1988 The NBA returns to its once abandoned three-referee plan. More expansion sees the arrival of the Charlotte Hornets and Miami Heat.

1989 (June 27) The draft is reduced from three rounds to two.

1989 League membership expands to 27 as the Minnesota Timberwolves and Orlando Magic begin play.

1990 (November 3) Phoenix defeats Utah 119–96 in a game at Japan's Tokyo Metropolitan Gymnasium – the first regular-season NBA game played outside North America.

1991 (November 7) Magic Johnson, one of the NBA's greatest stars, announces his retirement from the Los Angeles Lakers because he has tested positive for HIV.

1992 (August 8) The NBA-powered Dream Team, representing the U.S. in the Olympic Games at Barcelona, Spain, defeats Croatia 117–85 and captures the gold medal.

1993 (June 20) John Paxson's 3-point basket gives Chicago a 99–98 victory over Phoenix and the Bulls become the first team in 27 years to win three consecutive championships.

1993 The NBA expands to 28 with the addition of the Canadian city of Toronto.

1993 (October 6) Michael Jordan, saying he has no more basketball worlds to conquer after leading the Chicago Bulls to three straight NBA championships, retires. He will return in 1995.

1994 (April 27) The NBA awards its 29th franchise to Vancouver. The Grizzlies and Toronto Raptors will start playing in the 1995–96 season.

1995 (February 1) Utah guard John Stockton records career assist 9,922 in a game against Denver, replacing Magic Johnson as the NBA's all-time leader.

1996 (January 30) Magic Johnson begins his comeback attempt at age 36 in a game against Golden State. He would retire again after the season.

1996 (February 21) Stockton breaks another all-time NBA record when he intercepts a Boston pass for career steal No. 2,311, passing former star Maurice Cheeks.

1996 (March 1) When the Atlanta Hawks defeat the Cleveland Cavaliers, 74–68, Lenny Wilkens becomes the first NBA coach to reach 1,000 victories.

1996 (April 21)The Chicago Bulls complete the greatest regular season in NBA history when they defeat Washington 103–93 on the final day, lifting their record to an unprecedented 72–10. They would go on to defeat Seattle and claim their fourth championship of the decade.

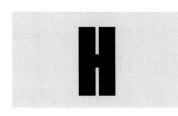

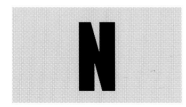

Quadruple-double 7

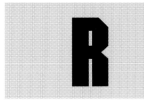

The publishers would like to thank the following sources for their permission to reproduce the photographs in this book:

Allsport/Brian Bahr, Al Bello, Andrew Bernstein, Shaun Botterill, Clive Brunskill, Simon Bruty, Vince Bucci, Mike Cooper, Glenn Cratty, J.D Cuban, Scott Cunningham, Jonathan Daniel, Tim Defrisco, Steve Dipaola, Stephen Dunn, Brian Drake, Otto Greule, Jim Gund, Jed Jacobsen, Bruce Kluckhorn, David Leah, Gary Newkirk, Doug Pensinger, Mike Powell, Todd Rosenberg, Harry Scull, Tom Smart, B Spurlock, Rick Stewart, Damian Strohmeyer;   **Corbis/Bettmann/UPI; Rob Gallagher; NIKE UK Limited.**